THE
PSYCHO-ANALYTIC
READER

An Anthology of Essential Papers with
Critical Introductions

EDITED BY

ROBERT FLIESS, M.D.

INTERNATIONAL UNIVERSITIES PRESS, Inc.

NEW YORK   NEW YORK

TO THE STUDENT OF PSYCHO-ANALYSIS

CONTENTS

PART III

MISCELLANEOUS

PART IV

UNCOLLECTED PAPERS BY KARL ABRAHAM

PART V

REFERENCES BY FREUD

FOREWORD

The *Psycho-analytic Reader* is a compilation of representative papers in psycho-analysis, hitherto uncollected. The contributions united here have been gathered by scanning the complete literature of the field, from the oldest Viennese *Jahrbuch für Psychoanalyse*, founded in 1909, to the British and American psycho-analytic periodicals of today. In these journals important work has remained scattered amongst much ephemeral material, and much that, valid at the date of publication, has in the meantime become obsolete. In addition, certain papers which one would not want to miss, have remained untranslated into English; and the periodicals carrying them are, naturally, long out of print. Thus a good deal of the literature has become difficult of access.

The hitherto uncollected or untranslated papers of Freud himself belong, of course, in a complete English edition of his work, and therefore do not appear in this collection. The contributions by others, such as Abraham, Ferenczi, Jones, Sachs, and Nunberg, already gathered in book form, shall likewise not be found in the *Reader*, which therefore lays claim to third place in a library where Freud's collected works and those of his earliest pupils stand first and second. (Certain monographs by authors working close to Freud fall without doubt somewhere in between.)

As far as the choice of material is concerned, an anthologist must always expect criticism for having included what he should have left out and excluded what he should have included. In view of this he can do no more than state the principles which have determined his selection:

(1) The most general principle is implied in the title of the collection. "Psycho-analysis" is a term introduced by Freud to denote his particular method of psychiatric investigation and treatment. It pertains to the clinical findings obtained by this method as well as to their theoretical formulation. At the time when his first pupils began working under him, Freud encouraged them to publish their findings in the same journals, devoted to the new science, in which

ix

he published his own. It is from these periodicals and their successors [1] that the *Reader* draws its material.

(2) In attempting to extract from the journals devoted to psychoanalysis a maximum of valuable addenda to Freud's work, it was natural to exclude the majority of those papers which serve no other purpose than to confirm Freud's original observations; for the mere duplication of Freud's basic findings, necessary though it may have been in the initial period of psycho-analysis, is now out of date.

(3) However, some papers acknowledged as addenda to psychoanalysis by Freud himself, who incorporated quotations from them in his own work, have likewise been excluded from this collection for the reason that the passage quoted by Freud, or the abstract given by him, contains all that is still worth preserving.

(4) The next category of contributions to be considered is that of the "spurious" addenda. Freud's work is disparate; he has stated precisely what he felt able to state, and has left much unsaid, which, although it may have appeared dialectically called for, could not be abstracted from clinical observation. This has sometimes proven a pitfall for the unwary. An author, misjudging the true nature of such an apparent opportunity to emend the theory of a subject, is apt to expend much labour in creating little more than an inflation of thought. Such work, naturally, has likewise been omitted.

(5) Another category, sometimes—but not always—to be rejected is that of the "premature" contribution. In such instances, an author has occasionally attempted to atttack a problem before Freud had arrived at the basic discoveries requisite to its solution. [2] In so doing the writer has become a victim, so to speak, of the historical situation. Yet the result is, nevertheless, sometimes worthy of preservation; and the decision as to whether or not a given article of this kind should be included, depends ultimately on the relative indispensability of the later discovery for a proper, if incomplete, earlier treatment of the subject.

(6) In general, it has always been the particular article—not the

[1] They are, in the order of their appearance: *Jahrbuch für Psychoanalyse, Centralblatt für Psychoanalyse, Internationale Zeitschrift für Psychoanalyse, Imago, Zeitschrift für Psychoanalytische Pädagogik, Die Psychoanalytische Bewegung, Psychoanalytischer Almanach, The International Journal for Psycho-Analysis, The Psychoanalytic Review,* and *The Psychoanalytic Quarterly.*

[2] Such as, for instance, the discovery of the preœdipal phase, the establishment of some particular metapsychological concept, the second topography (ego, superego, and id), etc.

author—that has been kept under consideration. The latter may have, for example, subsequent to the publication of such an article, entered the ranks of those who, starting with the rejection of any one of the fundamentals of psycho-analysis, finished by forming a new "school of thought". To such a "school", regardless of the name given it, the term "psycho-analysis", as defined previously, does not apply. Yet it may still apply to the author's earlier communications.

These principles, incomplete as they are, must be supplemented by judgment. Its exercise is assisted by the historical fact that the initial phase of analytic discovery lies behind us, and is therefore reviewable with a modicum of detachment. A residual personal factor can be eliminated by consultation.

The articles have been arranged according to topics, rather than chronologically. This appeared the most expedient method for the presentation of scientific material, accumulated over a long period of time. The different contributions contained in a section will therefore frequently show a wide spread in the dates of first publication. It is the object of the introductory notes to adjust this discrepancy by "placing" the papers historically, and by intimating their common denominator, while adding, wherever required, a reference to Freud's writings pertinent to the subject. In a few instances the insertion of a critical remark promised to facilitate the study of the particular contribution; in one a historical survey of the development of the subject seemed necessary. A considerable number of the papers in the present volume have not previously appeared in English; certain of the papers have notes or emendations added to them by the authors themselves.

The particular articles contained in *Volume One* represent, naturally, a more or less arbitrary selection from those to be chosen, since the subsequent volumes are intended to carry in part the same, in part new headings, until the material collected under these headings is exhausted.

Permission for the reprinting of all articles contained in this book has been obtained from the respective authors or their representatives, and from the copyright owners. In this connection the editor wishes to thank all those persons and firms who have so readily co-operated with him, and to acknowledge his obligation to them. The first page of each article carries the source of the article in question, in the first footnote.

The translation of Reich's "The Genital and the Neurotic Character" is the work of Mrs. Marga Franck, to whom thanks are due as the then librarian of the New York Psycho-analytic Institute, for her bibliographic assistance. The translations of Abraham's "Shall We Have the Patients Write Down their Dreams?", "Two Communications on Symbolism", and "Observations on Ferenczi's 'Sunday Neurosis' " were made by Mrs. Franck under the supervision of Dr. Henry A. Bunker. The latter translated Reich's "On Character Analysis", the short reprints in Section Five, and condensed and translated Federn's "Dreams of Flying".

The list of those to whom I am indebted is incomplete as long as it does not include my wife, Elenore Stratton Fliess. Without her competent and devoted co-operation—in capacities ranging from proof reader to assistant in editorial matters—the present volume would not have come into existence.

*

In view of the interest that an anthology of this kind may find on the part of psychiatrists, psychologists, and perhaps even some men of science or letters, it might be opportune to state here, in answer as it were, to an unspoken question, why this collection limits itself to the "Freudian school".

It is the fashion to call this school "orthodox" although the use of this term, applicable to faith alone, negates the scientific character of psycho-analysis, and transforms as by sleight of hand, the description of, and the abstractions derived from ascertainable facts, into dogma. Yet the method by which these facts are observed is no more difficult of access, and the abstractions based upon them no more hypothetical than are method and theory of all modern science.[3] Neither the intricacies of the means of obtaining data nor

[3] Those disinclined to recognize psycho-analysis as a science because it fails to comply with certain accepted standards of method (experiment) or result (expressibility in mathematical symbols) might be reminded that in the last analysis, standards derive from science, not science from standards. The latter reflect the exigencies of scientific investigation and are therefore conditioned by the nature of the object of this investigation. As far as the

the hypothetical character of the ordering principles for their integration reflects, however, in any of the other sciences, upon the authenticity of their tenets. In the case of these sciences it is also generally acknowledged that the appreciation of their results is ultimately contingent upon that of their methods, and that the mastery of a method is prerequisite to its evaluation. Modern man, aware of his lack of conversance with the complicated arrangements upon which science has to rely in order to gain valid data, has relinquished the exercise of his function of judgment in scientific questions to a small number of highly specialized experts. He would, consequently, not think of challenging the validity of a chemical formula, the existence of a physiological process, nor the aptness of a hypothetical concept in physics on the grounds that they failed to appeal to his imagination or interfered with his personal preconceptions. To put it briefly: in an age when neither imaginability nor compliance with general prejudice are any longer criteria for the validity of a scientific conclusion, the "naïve"

object proper of psycho-analysis is concerned, it must be recognized as fundamentally different from any other. It is an object conceived as composed of elements whose perceptory sources are those of internal perception. To be sure, the verbalizations of an analysand, the text of a myth, an historical document, or the content of a work of art are subject to external perception; and as such are no different from the point of a needle over a scale, a change in colour, or an ultramicroscopic alteration in shape. But their observation is analytic only in so far as the data elicited by it are indicative of certain products of internal perception, in the patient, the author (individual or collective), the historical personage, or the artist. These perceptory products are elements of the "inner" world; and their observation is scientific inasmuch as it allows for the establishment of ordering principles whose adaptation to the observable data is comparable to that of hypothesis to experience in the sciences studying the "external" world. The obvious differences in method of observation as well as description employed by analysis as compared with the rest of the natural sciences reflect merely the dissimilarities of their objects.

The predicament of the theoretician in psycho-analysis—and it is here that he will ask forbearance—stems from the potency, not the deficiency, of his method. While the latter enables him to make new observations he has, in abstracting from these, to rely upon old metaphor, handed down to him from the sciences that have outgrown it. He must posit nonspatial "loci", describe processes as "dynamic", ignorant of the forms of energy sustaining them, and even postulate "economic" relations between quantities which he is altogether unable to measure. Yet, at present at least, he can do no better than work for a closer adaptation of these concepts to his particular subject; in other words, for the improvement, made possible by the collection of further empirical data, of their definition.

observer has become obsolete, and the "trained" observer has taken his place.

Not so in psychological matters. Here an anachronism prevails. While the discovery—that is, the scientific description—of the unconscious has actually deprived the naïve observer of his last province, he is as yet unaware of his deposition. Unacquainted with his incompetence, he believes himself, on the strength of possessing a psyche, capable of evaluating a psychological statement. He persists, consequently, in calling his soul his own, looks upon the hypothesis of the unconscious as a product of pure fiction, and conceives of the writings of Freud as an aphoristic collection of psychological observations, which he is free to find true or fantastic, penetrating or absurd, as he pleases.

This is really to be expected. Psycho-analysis is only half a century old. History, contrary to opinion held today, is not unlikely to record that but little of Freudian thought had to date penetrated the resistant medium of general erudition; that most of it had dissolved in the volatile vehicle of belles-lettres; and that, perhaps, even psychiatry had remained unaware of the true nature of the proposition confronting it at this time, which is that of becoming a field within analysis, rather than the reverse. The somewhat phrenetic interest in psychology shown today in the urban sections of the Western world, will be explained as, in part at least, merely the initial reaction to a disturbance. And it may be noted that, after the violence of this reaction had subsided and the sensation of yesterday had become the commonplace of tomorrow, the recognition of psycho-analysis, as a science, and the penetration by it of biology, most of medicine, epistomology, and the humanities, was yet to come.

But a historical orientation in this matter is incomplete if it fails to account for the situation of those who, by becoming analysts, have attempted the transformation of naïve into trained observer, mentioned above. In an established science this transformation is effected by the student's passage through the curriculum, and the academic degree is, for all practical purposes, indicative of its completion. In applying this precedent to the learning of psycho-analysis, one is apt to transfer the standards of an old discipline to a new one, without regard to the benefits of tradition, and the particularities of educational method. Amongst these latter is one which, peculiar to psycho-analysis, demands explanation.

The apprehension of intra-psychic occurrences in someone else is, in analysis as it is elsewhere, dependent upon the empathic employment of introspection. Psychological observation, in other words, is—in part at least—applied self-observation. While the faculty for this is a native endowment, its development to the extent to which the analyst has to rely upon it, and the training in its correct exercise must be acquired.[5] This cannot, however, be done anywhere but in a thorough psycho-analysis of the student. Even if his psychic health is satisfactory, his personality suitable, and his characterological peculiarities compatible with, or even propitious for, the mastery of any other scientific subject (not excluding the numerous psychotherapies), the future analyst, in order to comprehend his particular subject, has to submit to the same radical alteration of certain parts of his personality as does the patient in order to cure his disturbance.

This requirement, rigorous as it is, must be met, since the accessibility of unconscious psychic content to conscious apperception is, in both analyst and patient alike, dependent upon the same intrapsychic constellation. It is thus a singular fact, and specific for psycho-analytic education, that the better part of the metamorphosis of the naïve into the trained analytic observer is identical with the transformation of neurotic or characterological affliction into normality.

Both undertakings are, of course, more often begun than completed. For both require, although in the interest of a different goal, an uncommon combination of intelligence, perseverance, and self-abnegation in the face of opposing tendencies of the most powerful nature. Under the influence of these tendencies, every analysand, whether student or patient, will occasionally contend that this or that psychological finding must be erroneous, because—as can always be verified clinically—he is not prepared to apply it to his own person. As a patient he has, by entering the analysis, consented to being the variable in the equation between the truth and his person. He has committed himself to an alteration of his personality that will ultimately preclude the maintaining of his negation and will enable him to verify introspectively the hitherto unacceptable statement about himself. And the reward for the overcoming of his "resistances" is, eventually, the liberation from his affliction. If, however, the analysand is a future analyst, he may feel free to choose the other alternative; that is, he may consider himself the

[5] Compare e.g. the development of an individual's "musicality" into musicianship, through professional training.

constant, and vary the truth, instead of confirming it through im-
proved introspection. In other words, his resistance may acquire
the form of "dissension". He may, of course, do so in any phase of
his education. He may, for instance, already working as an analyst,
be confronted with equally unacceptable data by his patient, and
be compelled by the consequent imminence of an empathic disturbance to gravitate, in the interest of his own psychic equilibrium,
in the direction of an attenuated version of the theory of the unconscious. Or he may, in planning his training, unwittingly sidestep
an as yet merely potential conflict of the same nature, by selecting a
school of dissension, whose very existence derives from the same
predicament in its founder. For it is here that the origin of dissension must be sought. The impact of psychic forces activated within
an investigator in the course of his work may cause them to be
reflected upon the collective object of his investigation and to direct
his theoretical thinking. And if the personality of the individual thus
imposed upon is a strong one, he is apt to break the ties of an
inadequate education, and effect the foundation of a new school of
psychological thought.

There are, naturally, concurring motives for establishment of
these "schools". The historical closeness to Freud, the consequent
"personalization" of learning, and the demand to accept a whole
discipline practically from the hands of one man of genius, are a
challenge to anyone's independence of mind. It is this intellectual
independence which has indeed not infrequently led the dissenter-
to-be, before he yielded to the public demand for the expurgation
of psycho-analysis, to notable contribution to psycho-analysis in the
sense in which it is here discussed. Yet it has never done so thereafter. For the denial of any one of the basic and interdependent facts
found by Freud cannot but cause a defective crystallization of
thought around the hollow necleus of negation.

It is not amongst the purposes of the *Reader* to demonstrate the
correctness of this statement. Neither the general disorientation
promoted by the existence and steady multiplication of the "dissent-
ing" schools, nor the rôle undoubtedly played by them in the
dissemination of certain elements of Freudian thought amongst the
public, are the concern of its editor, whose responsibility to the
reader is confined to the presentation of scientific material.

If, at a future time, the extravagant growth of contemporary
psychological teaching should be pruned back to the live stem of
observation and theory of the first, the Freudian, period of its

existence, psycho-analysis will regain its original independence of the preconceptions of the general as well as the learned public. It will then acquire the status of a scientific discipline comparable to others. Scholars from various fields will be given the opportunity to become competent in it, and, putting an old Jesuitic practice to secular purpose, will school themselves in both disciplines, psychoanalysis and their own. And an elaborate post-graduate education will be preventive of wasteful effort by including in its requirements that dissension be generally subjected to clearance in an analysis supplementary to the training analysis of the dissenter.

Authors publishing under such circumstances will continue the work recorded, in part, in the pages of this collection.

R. F.

New York,
  March, 1948.

I
CLINICAL

NEUROSES

TRANSVESTISM AND FETISHISM

Transvestism and fetishism, the subjects of the two papers united in this section, are closely related. The two perversions not only occur occasionally in the same individual, but they are sometimes convertible into each other. The transvestist may employ his costume sexually as a fetish, and the fetishist may wear his fetish in the exercise of his perversion. (It is more than coincidental that the initial enjoyment of feminine clothing by the transvestist of Fenichel's observation was an olfactory one, and that the mackintosh fetish investigated by Payne was, occasionally, put on by one of her patients for the purpose of masturbation.)

However, the mutually complementary nature of the two studies reprinted here is not so confined. In the first of them the accent, if the ad hoc *adoption of an old terminology be permissible, is placed upon the "instincts"; in the second it lies upon the "ego". Both authors study the unconscious conflicts underlying a clinical manifestation. The first of them lays emphasis upon the vicissitudes of the instinct involved, the second upon the malformations of the ego, with the result that their presentation of a perversion and a pervert, respectively, amount thus, jointly, to the monographic treatment of a subject that has held the interest of sexologists for a long period of time. Both conditions, transvestism as well as fetishism, had to await their elucidation until Freud was able to add, in 1927, his brief paper on "Fetishism" to his* Three Contributions, *in which the perversion, as such, had been recognized as a survival of, or a return to, the originally perverse sexuality of the child.*

In combination the two articles are representative of the rare instances where psycho-analysis can accept the challenge of nosology by clearing up all the essential features of a familiar clinical picture. Yet the analyst's paramount interest in the perversion is a different one. It is the interest in perhaps the most powerful and most intrapsychic constellation conditioning human behaviour: the castration-complex.

Dr. Fenichel, with whom we corresponded before his death, felt that his aricle should be reprinted unchanged. Dr. Payne has been kind enough to contribute an Author's Comment (*page 30*) *and an* Author's

3

Note (*page 26*) *and to inform us that she considers her paper as "suffering from over-condensation and lack of elaboration in many places" because of the limitation to twenty minutes for its original reading.*

ON TRANSVESTISM* (1930)

By Otto Fenichel

All authors who have dealt with the subject of transvestism are agreed that the mysterious behaviour of the victims of this perversion has points of contact with various other perverse practices. It was not until 1910 that this manifestation of *psychopathia sexualis* was, rightly, described by Hirschfeld as a specific form of perversion.[1] Earlier authors had classified cases of the sort on the basis of their points of contact with other perversions. This affinity leads us to hope that the psycho-analytical elucidation of transvestism may contribute something of importance to the explanation of the psychology of perversions in general. Again, in so far as the allied perversions have already been exhaustively studied by analytical methods, the fact that it is akin to them will enable us to understand the phenomenon of transvestism.

The behaviour of many transvestists gives an entirely masochistic impression: we call to mind, for instance, the figure which is the ideal of many such perverts—Hercules clothed in woman's garments and serving his mistress, Omphale. We know, too, that many who practise this perversion obtain gratification only when they are seen in the clothes of the opposite sex, i.e. strictly speaking, they are exhibitionists. But there are other, far more obvious, points in which transvestism is related to fetishism and homosexuality, and these points have already been the subject of scientific controversy. I refer to the over-estimation of clothing and body-linen, and to many fetishistic traits in cases of the sort, e.g. a particular preference for shoes or ear-rings. These characteristics have led writers on the subject to conceive of transvestism as a specific type of fetishism. Hirschfeld [2] and Ellis,[3] on the contrary, rightly emphasize the fact that the transvestist has one characteristic which is foreign to fetishism proper. To him the fetish becomes a fetish only when brought into relation with the person of the patient, not (or

* Reprinted from *The International Journal of Psycho-Analysis*, XI, 1930, p. 211. (Original Title: The Psychology of Transvestism.)

[1] M. Hirschfeld, *Die Transvestiten*, Berlin, 1910.

[2] *Loc. cit.*

[3] Eonism. *Studies in the Psychology of Sex*, Vol. VII, Philadelphia, 1928.

at any rate only in a very modified degree) as an object in itself. But transvestists want not only to wear women's clothes but to live altogether like women; that is to say, they are effeminate. This fact afforded sufficient reason for their being frequently grouped with passive homosexuals, a view energetically controverted by Hirschfeld, who demonstrated that transvestists in general are erotically attracted exclusively to persons of the opposite sex. Later, he [4] and Näcke [5] classified transvestists according to their sexual aim as the heterosexual, homosexual, narcissistic and asexual types. To psychoanalysts there is no meaning in such a classification, because it is based solely on the manifest expressions of instinct and completely disregards the unconscious instinctual processes. In this connection Stekel [6] is of opinion that transvestism should be construed simply as a mask for homosexuality. But the problem which then confronts us is to find out under what conditions this mask in particular is selected.

To sum up: the point which the transvestist has in common with the fetishist is the over-estimation of feminine clothes and bodylinen, while he shares with the passive homosexual (and the feminine masochist) the feminine psychic attitude. The point of difference between him and both these other types of perverts lies in his specific sexual wish to assume the dress of the opposite sex. Psychoanalysts will suspect that where there is this manifest agreement, there will be a corresponding resemblance in the fundamental unconscious mechanisms. And the analysis of transvestists entirely confirms this suspicion.

Fetishism and passive homosexuality in men have been so exhaustively studied analytically that the results of the investigation can be reduced to certain short formulæ. According to Freud [7] castration-anxiety prevents the fetishist from accepting the fact of the lack of the penis in women, and he can love only when he has supplied his female love-object with an illusory penis. The cause of the feminine homosexual's abnormality is, likewise, castration-anxiety. He is incapable of loving a being who lacks the penis; castration-anxiety (and, of course, also constitutional factors) have

[4] *Jahrbuch für sexuelle Zwischenstufen*, 1923.

[5] Zum Kapitel der Transvestiten, *Archiv für Kriminalanthropologie*, Bd. XVII.

[6] Cf. Der Fetischismus and Onanie und Homosexualität.

[7] Freud: Fetishism, *The International Journal of Psycho-Analysis*, IX, p. 161.

led him to solve his œdipus complex by substituting identification with his mother for his love of her. He is now himself the mother, the woman, and in this rôle he seeks for new objects, whether it be the father or a representative of his own self.[8] The transvestist, who is akin to both these types of pervert, seems to be the one to whom both formulæ simultaneously apply: he has not been able to give up his belief in the phallic nature of women and, in addition, he has identified himself with the woman with the penis. Identification with the woman, as a substitute, for, or side by side with, love for her, is so plain in the manifest clinical picture that Ellis, as we shall hear presently, regarded it as the essence of transvestism.[9] But the woman with whom the transvestist identifies himself is conceived of by him as phallic, and *this* is the essential feature in the situation— a feature which, since it is unconscious, could not have been discovered but for psycho-analysis.

In the act of transvestism both object-love and identification are present, the forms in which each manifests itself being modified by the castration-complex and the patient's obstinate retention of his belief in the woman's possession of the phallus. The act has a twofold significance: (1) object-erotic (fetishistic), and (2) narcissistic (homo-sexual). (1) Instead of coitus with the mother or her substitute the patient enters into fetishistic relations with her clothes, which he brings into as close contact as he can with his own person, and particularly with his genital organs. This is the explanation of the "condition of love" frequently met with, that the garments or body-linen in question should have been used and, if possible, should still retain something of the warmth and odour of the woman's body. This intercourse is conceived of in typically sadistic terms. (2) The patient himself represents a woman with a penis. A woman: he shouts that abroad. A woman *with a penis*: that is revealed by analysis. Here we have a twofold representation of the penis: (*a*) in the patient's genital, actually present under the woman's clothes (one transvestist had recurrent fantasies of the amazement of a lover who, approaching him under the impression that he was a woman, discovered the penis when the woman's clothes were removed); (*b*) in the garment, which is a symbolic substitute for the penis and which the transvestist (even if he indulges his passion only secretly and onanistically) always wants to display—a form of dis-

[8] Cf., for instance, Drei Abhandlungen zur Sexualtheorie, *Ges. Sch.*, Bd. V, S. 18, footnote.
[9] *Loc. cit.*

placed exhibitionism which, like true exhibitionism, is designed to
refute the idea of castration. In order to make the clinical picture of
transvestism intelligible in terms of psycho-analysis we must expand
these formulæ by a description of the way in which the transvestist,
like the homosexual, proceeds to fresh object-choices, having completed his identification with the woman. In these choices we shall
again find an element both of narcissism and of object-erotism.
With regard to the former we must note that only in a subject of a
peculiarly narcissistic disposition is it possible for object-love to be
so extensively replaced by identification. It is a fact that the narcissistic regression manifested in this identification goes far beyond that
which we are accustomed to observe in homosexuals. Love for the
subject's own self—fantasies that the masculine element in his
nature can have intercourse with the feminine (i.e. with himself) are
not uncommon. Love for the phallic mother is often transformed
into love for the ego in which a change has been wrought by identification with her. This is a feature in the psychic picture which has
struck even non-analytical writers, who have described a narcissistic
type of transvestist besides the heterosexual and homosexual types.

On the other hand, patients are influenced by their feminine
identification in their choice even of real objects; they want to be
looked upon and loved as women or, alternatively, where the primal
sadism has been turned against the ego, to suffer masochistic tortures. (Here again we note in the passive sexual aim, which, in spite
of the phallic character of the illusory woman, dominates the picture,
the introduction of the narcissistic factor.) Analysis demonstrates
that this object-tendency of the transvestist is directed (1) in the
deeper mental strata towards the *father*. In this point the transvestist
resembles the passive homosexual, but the former is seldom conscious of the homosexual character of this object-choice. He says in
effect to the father: "Love me, I am just as beautiful (in the phallic
sense) as my mother." Or, more correctly: "Love me as you love my
mother; it is not true that this wish of mine places my penis in
jeopardy!" But the tendency of which we are speaking is also directed
(2) towards the mother. This is the more superficial and obvious
relation, and it was this which justified Hirschfeld, who did not
include the unconscious in his purview, in denying the homosexuality of the transvestist. Perverts of this type consciously take
a special interest in feminine homosexuality; they want to be loved
as women by women, to be in the relation of the slave to her mistress.
The analytical explanation is to be found in the most important

accidental factor in transvestism, namely, that, as a rule, contemporaneously with the identification with the mother, there exists in another, more superficial psychic stratum, a similar identification with *a little girl*. This is designed to secure for the subject all the advantages of a regression into early childhood. (For example, a patient of this type who had handled a female infant during the day, dreamt the following night that he put on women's clothes and during the dream he wetted his bed.) This second process of identification may occur when, as seems often to be the case, a sister has at an early period to a great extent become a mother-substitute. Then the transvestist not only addresses the father as we have already described, but at the same time to the mother: "Love me, I am just as beautiful (in the phallic sense) as my sister." Or, more correctly: "Love me as you love my sister! It is not true that this wish of mine places my penis in jeopardy."

II

I think it now behooves me to cite some analytical material in proof of these propositions. I will confine myself to putting before you the most important points in a case which was subjected to a thorough analysis, and I hope that they will illustrate the meaning of transvestism as I have tried to present it to you.

The patient was a married man forty years old, who, in spite of his neurosis, was successful in his professional life and was the father of several children. He suffered from obsessional neurosis and hypochondria with certain paranoid symptoms. He loved his wife deeply and was very considerate and affectionate to her, but sexual intercourse with her left him unsatisfied. He could obtain gratification only in onanism; this he practised with the accompaniment either of transvestist fantasies, or, more often, of actual transvestist behaviour—dressing himself in his wife' sclothes. The content of the accompanying fantasy was simply: "I am a woman." Of the details which he communicated in analysis I may mention the following: he indulged in an additional important fantasy, whose content was: "And I am seen to be a woman," and, further, gratification was conditional upon the wearing of women's clothes being a matter of everyday occurrence, i.e. he experienced the most lively excitation when he imagined that he was putting on women's clothes not for the purpose of stimulation but because it was natural for him to be dressed so. He had, in addition, various masochistic fantasies of the type in which the female slave serves her mistress, and he entertained the desire to be a woman, quite apart from any actual sexual situation.

From the history of the patient's childhood I may communicate the following facts. His mother died early and his father soon married again. His father was a man of a petty, fault-finding, anal character, while the step-mother was domineering, quarrelsome and very strict with the children. Evidently there must have existed a very strong sensual (probably passive-anal) bond between the father and the step-mother, but at the same time the former kept up a kind of cult of the memory of his first wife. In everything the step-mother ruled the house (here we have the type of "the feeble father"), so that the patient had plenty of opportunity to believe in her phallic nature. His attitude to her was ambivalent throughout, but both in his hatred (fear) and his love he remained entirely passive. There emanated from her a strong atmosphere of prohibition; the castrating figures in his dreams proved to be screen-figures standing for her. When the patient was a little boy, she had forced him to wear gloves and had bound his hands to prevent his practising masturbation (or possibly to prevent his scratching himself at a time when he was being treated for worms). (This binding gave rise later to masochistic fantasies.) Moreover, as a little boy he suffered from prolapse of the rectum and, every time he defecated, she pressed back the rectum with her finger. In analysis the patient could still recall the tremendously pleasurable feeling which this gave him.

His principal sexual object in childhood was a sister three years older than himself, with whom he indulged in all manner of sexual games, mutual masturbation, and the like. Probably this elder sister originally played the part of seducer, and this seduction caused a similar disturbance in his sexual development as is recorded in that of the Wolf-man.[10] There certainly was a period in which he assumed the active rôle in their mutual relations; for example, he remembered that on one occasion he had purposely wetted her with urine. This relation, like his relation with his step-mother, was highly ambivalent. He not only loved his sister, but hated her as a rival. This hatred combined with the sensual element to produce a markedly sadistic attitude (possibly to cancel the seduction). One day this attitude vanished, and the patient became purely passive in his relation to his sister. We shall return to the question of this later passive attitude, and discuss when it developed and why. During analysis it was still recognizable in a certain apprehensiveness of an obsessional nature and, further, in an important screen-memory in which the patient professed to have pulled one of his sister's arms from its socket. Otherwise, the passive attitude was repressed, and

[10] Freud, The History of an Infantile Neurosis, *Collected Papers*, Vol. III.

the underlying tendency, having been diverted towards the subject's ego, had been converted into masochism.

It was from his relation to his sister that the patient developed his transvestism. His sister used to play at "dressing dolls", and she would dress up the living doll—her little brother—putting clothes of her own on him. This used to happen when the patient was about four years old, and at first he disliked it, because it degraded him into a doll. After some repetitions, however, he began to enjoy the game, because he derived sexual pleasure from the smell of his sister, which clung to things she wore, especially to her hair-ribbon and pinafore. In his eighth and tenth years the children used to act little plays, in which they changed clothes with one another. They went on doing this in their games, and the patient, when he imagined he was a girl and especially that others regarded him as a girl, experienced pleasure which was unquestionably sexual, and was accompanied by sensations resembling orgasm. Presently his sister became bored with the game, and he had to be more and more artful in persuading her to play it. Finally he took to putting on her clothes in secret, when he was alone, and the pleasure this gave him roused a lively sense of guilt. At the age of about thirteen he forgot this game, but in his seventeenth year he recollected it and began it again with unmistakable sexual excitation. From that time on, dressing-up in women's clothes became associated with manual masturbation, and the beginning of the perversion dates from this. It is noteworthy that for a long time the patient made use of his *sister's* clothes and, later, those of sister-substitutes. The idea of putting on garments belonging to his step-mother or to women resembling her did not stimulate his imagination in the least.

What then is the meaning of this perversion? The object-erotic factor is the easier and simpler to understand from the case-history. The pleasure which the patient derived proceeded in the first instance from the smell of the clothes: a hair-ribbon and, above all, a pinafore, represented parts of the body of his sister, with whom he was in the habit of masturbating. This practice sometimes took the form of his sister's sitting on his knee and sliding backwards and forwards. When he wore her pinafore he used to move it about in a similar way. The pinafore represented his sister's body. Later, when he made use of her clothes instead of her person, he had the advantage of ceasing to be dependent, for his sexual enjoyment, on the caprices of his sister, who was not always inclined to gratify him. Another circumstance was that, originally, using the same bed or the same bathwater as she had the same significance as wearing her clothes. How came it about that the sister herself gradually lost her sexual significance for him, whilst "symbols" (her clothes) were substituted for her? Analysis revealed the answer unmistakably. It was because the brother discovered that she had no penis. We mentioned the remarkable screen-memory of his pulling his sister's arm from its socket. This memory "screened" their mutual onanism and especially the patient's sadism. Once, when he and his sister were having a bath together in the bathroom, he caught sight of her genitals, and this reactivated a still earlier, repressed recollection of his step-mother's genitals. It happened that at the same period his sister was having electric treatment for enuresis (the patient himself used for a time to wet his bed) and used to scream dreadfully when the treatment was in process. There could then, he reasoned, be only two possibilities: either the electric treatment was the punishment by castration for sexual naughtiness; in that case he was threatened with it, after his sister. Or it was a medical remedy for the lack of the penis, which had fallen a victim to his own sadism. In that case it was but just that the talion punishment of castration should await him. In this anxiety he desisted altogether from his sadistic behaviour and turned the tendency against himself. He wanted to have nothing more to do with his sister, who reminded him of the mischief he had done, and he substituted for her her clothes, which did away with the dreadful nakedness. The bath (and, later, water in general) remained a situation of terror. We shall have to discuss the fact that his anxiety took the form that the water in running out might carry off one of his fingers or his whole body and that the dread became displaced to the water-closet, where the flush might wash away the whole child as well as his motion. So far, the patient's mental processes followed the scheme which Freud has worked out for fetishism.

The patient, however, became a transvestist because his retention of the idea of the female penis was reinforced by his identification with the woman. In later years it became transparently clear that he himself was enacting the rôle of the sister, whom he desired to *be*. In imagination he lived her life, and in the same way, after his marriage, he would feel unwell during his wife's period of menstruation. This has a significance in connection with the question of punishment. It meant: I harboured the wish to do my sister an injury, so now I am forced to become like her, so as to submit to suffering. From the point of view of his instinctual life he had sufficient reason to envy his sister. She was the elder, and both parents evidently made a favourite of her. He was especially jealous of her relation to their step-mother, who talked "feminine secrets" with her. Later he developed a neurosis, when his parents were about to arrange a marriage for his sister. Analysis revealed the jealous thought: "Why do they arrange for her to marry and not for me?" The patient had also a recollection, important in connection with the deeper mental strata, of a fit of envy which overtook him one Christmas, when his mother with much ceremony presented his sister with a particularly beautiful doll. Such ambivalent feelings indicated that, in obedience to the inner prohibition by which his castration-anxiety prevented his entering into an object-relation with his sister, he had regressed to identification.

Now this identification with the girl was bound to come into direct opposition to the most intense castration-anxiety. The influence of this made itself felt in the aim which the patient set before him: "I want to be my sister and yet to retain my penis." When indulging in his perverse practices, it was his custom, as soon as ejaculation had taken place, to tear the borrowed clothes off as quickly as possible. In connection with this he had the association that he had been warned that, if one made faces and the clock struck, one's face would stay so. Thus he was afraid that he might actually "remain stuck" in his feminine rôle, and this would involve his forfeiting his penis. His transvestist behaviour was designed to counter his castration-anxiety. We have evidence of this in a recollection that, when on one occasion he caught sight of a crippled boy, he felt an impulse to change clothes with him. The implication was a denial that the boy really was a cripple. The patient combined his femininity with a naïve, narcissistic love for his own penis, upon which he bestowed a number of pet names, as though it were a child. Moreover, the girl's name, which he chose to be known by when enacting the rôle of a girl, had a striking resemblance to one pet name for the penis. The first time he had sexual intercourse with a woman, he did not know where to find the vagina and looked for it on the upper part of her thigh. Even at the time when I knew him, he always had a feeling during coitus that he must look for something which he could not find. At one of the dramatic performances, in which he acted the part of a girl, he represented an Easter Hare. He recollected being troubled because he thought the hare's ears and tail were not stiff enough. Here we have a proof of the phallic nature of the woman whose rôle he assumed—a matter which becomes more intelligible to us when we picture the overwhelming castration-anxiety under which the patient laboured. We have mentioned that his step-mother represented to his mind the person who castrates. From the innumerable screen-memories connected with the idea of castration I will quote a single example. An obsessive action of the patient's was that of clutching at his penis (analytically interpreted: to see if it was still there) and of counting his toes (to see that none was missing). Analysis revealed that he had dreaded that his mother, in pressing back the prolapsed rectum, might rob him of the intestine, and at that time he was haunted by the fear that it might fall into the lavatory-pan. The uncanny thing about the water-closet and the bath was that the fæces and the water simply disappeared—were no longer there—just so, he feared, had his sister's penis vanished. Further, this idea of being "gone" was his conception of death. And in his mind the whole terrifying mystery of castration was intertwined with the terrifying mystery of his mother's death. The content of his unconscious anxiety was not simply: "My sister's penis vanished because of some sexual act," but also, "My own mother died because of some sexual act." Accordingly, particularly during the period of his subsequent hypochondria, the patient suffered from the most intense dread of death (and especially the dread of infection, as I will show later). Detailed analysis of this anxiety led us first of all to ideas about the colour " black" and of "hair". (As a child he himself had long hair and dreaded its being cut. He treasured up the locks which were cut off. His step-mother wore false hair, i.e. hair which could be taken off. The hair of the head stood for pubic hair.) These ideas led back to dreams of the primal scene and to occasions, long before his experiences with his sister, when, with anxiety and a feeling of protest, he became aware of the nature of his mother's genitals.[11]

Thus, the patient's transvestism was evidently an attempt to allay these various anxieties. The content of the perversion was: "Phallic girls do exist; I myself am one."

Let us now examine his search for new love-objects, when once the identification had been completed and let us consider the relation to the mother which underlay that to the sister.

The factor of narcissism was transparently clear. Not only did he love himself in the rôle of a girl (acting a woman in plays, posturing before the looking-glass, a preference for a girl's long hair), but this love took an *active* form, such as he longed for from his sister. Thus he dreamt that he was embracing a little boy, saying to him tenderly: "My little brother!" In passing on to consider his actual choice of new love-objects, we will again begin with a dream. This was as follows: "My wife had a disease of the lungs. A stout woman stabbed her in the back from behind. Thereupon I found myself in a theatre, with the upper part of my body naked." The exhibition-situation at the end prepares us for the fact that the dream relates to transvestism. Actually the patient, who was a hypochondriac, suffered from a dread of lung affections. In the dream, he is the woman whom another woman stabs from the rear. His associations to this stab were as follows: the uvula, fantasies of poisoning by way of the anus

---

[11] The female genital, when thus caught sight of, becomes an object of fear not simply because of the lack of the penis but because it is regarded as a menacing weapon. (The waste-pipes of the water-closet and the bath are thought of as devouring mouths.) Cf. my article: Zur Angst vor dem Gefressenwerden, *Internationale Zeitschrift für Psychoanalyse*, Bd. XIV, 1928, p. 404.

and, finally, enemas which his step-mother had given him as a child. Before going to sleep on the night of this dream, the patient had indulged in his perverse practices. Hence we arrive at the interpretation: "When I am in women's clothes I should like my step-mother to stick something into my 'behind', but at the same time I dread it." The passive-anal desires implied in the patient's femininity had become abundantly clear: the recollections of enemas and the prolapsed rectum showed that these wishes had reference to the mother whom he conceived of as phallic. This is where the fantasies of the female slaves come in, the meaning being: "I want my step-mother to treat me like a little girl, but there is no need for me to fear castration." In correspondence with this wish the patient cherished in his mind two types of female imagos between which he strictly differentiated: the "little girl" and the "Amazon", i.e. the sister and the step-mother. The woman whose clothes he desired to put on belonged to the first type only; on the other hand, he wished to enter into masochistic relations only with women of the second, masculine type.

Having discovered this anal dependence on women it seemed obvious to reason as follows: the patient's œdipus complex was normal in so far as he, like other males, wished to take his father's place with his mother. Only, the real father's attitude to his second wife was of a passive-anal nature; similarly, the patient wished to enter into a passive-anal relation to the phallic mother. In actual fact the step-mother tended the father in connection with his anal functions and this did really rouse in the patient the wish that his father would die.

But the child had not always seen his father in such a helpless and passive guise. Once he too had been strong and active, and it was to him that in the deepest mental strata the patient's feminine attitude had reference.

Analysis of his social inhibitions revealed that his passivity and anxiety related, fundamentally, not to women but to men. Again, his exhibitionist tendency—the craving to be admired as a woman by people in general—had reference to men. When we were investigating this subject of the father of his infantile days, the first thing that emerged in his memory was a long-forgotten figure which was a "screen-figure" for his father: a carpenter, who had done some work in the patient's home and whose admiration he had solicited. Next, he felt an urgent impulse to change into the women's clothes in front of his father's portrait. Finally, there came recollections of excitation, obviously sexual and accompanied by anxiety, which he experienced when lying in bed with his father. But the most striking thing about this part of the analysis was the way in which the patient suddenly grasped the meaning of many inhibitions from which he suffered in his real relations with men! The picture was then blurred once more by a recollection of his later childhood: "I wanted to thrust something into my father's 'behind'." We found that this implied: "I want to love you, father, in just the same way as my step-mother does." But we were obliged to conjecture that, before he felt the desire to stick something into his father, he must have wished his father to stick something into *him*. Quite in accordance with this interpretation was the fact that he had *not* identified himself with his step-mother; on the contrary, behind the identification with his sister lay the first identification of all—that with his own mother. His heart cried out to his father: "Do not put away the memory of your first wife. Remember her; she lives still, in me. Love me, your first wife, more than my step-mother!" And the content of the fearful anxiety which came into conflict with these wishes was this: "Did not death overtake my mother because she let my father love her? Then I, too, shall have to die." It now becomes clear that the overwhelming castration-anxiety, which the transvestism was designed to eliminate, was at bottom a dread of impregnation by the father. This was the meaning of the dread of infection, poison and water and also of a number of screen-memories in which the patient envied the act of parturition. As a child he must have fantasied that his mother perished through pregnancy and must have evolved the theory that having children meant losing the penis. In his transvestism he was trying to repudiate this dread also, saying to himself: "I may wish to be a woman and capable of bearing children—and yet keep my penis!"[12]

III

We have adduced analytical material in proof of all the hypotheses we put forward in Section I. If, now, we are in search of a pathognomonic ætiology of the patient's transvestism, we are obliged to admit that we have not discovered one. We must in any case assume that he had a special bisexual disposition, for otherwise the desire to bear children, for example, could never have acquired such importance. But we do not know whether, if life had brought him different experiences, his strong sadism might not have enabled his masculine

[12] Deeper analysis of the narcissitic mental strata finally revealed that the identification with his dead mother (her "spirit") was performed by means of introjection (inhaling) and that in the unconscious the introjected mother was equated with his own penis. Thus we arrived at the following symbolic equation: patient in women's clothes = the mother with a penis = the penis in general. We recollect the similarity between the girl's name by which he so much wished to be called and his pet name for the penis.

side to develop satisfactorily. But this mental make-up is common to homosexual and transvestist alike. Again, the series of experiences: the primal scene—castration-anxiety—flight into femininity, based on narcissism, occurs in other clinical pictures, and we do not know what circumstances cause the belief in the phallic woman to be retained with the specific perversion of transvestism, since the above series is present in other forms of nervous disease as well. It is true that we frequently find transvestism combined with precisely these diseases: narcissistic neuroses, hypochondria (cf. the case quoted by Alexander [13]) and other perversions. Over and above all this, the case we are examining seems to have been determined by specific environmental factors: the characters of his father, mother and sister, and their interplay, seem to have thrust the patient's rôle upon him. But, again, similar specific environmental conditions appear by no means rare, for all writers on the subject tell us of transvestists whose mothers had a very great desire for a daughter! Ellis goes so far as to cite this circumstance as a proof of the purely hereditary ætiology of transvestism, but in this he is in error.

Such communications about this perversion as are to be found in analytical literature bear a remarkable resemblance to our own conclusions. It is only thanks to the writings of Freud which have appeared since Sadger [14] and Boehm [15] discussed the question that it has been possible for me to give a greater coherence to my account. Sadger evolved the following formula as summing up the transvestist's train of thought: "As a female I should be loved more by my mother and, indeed, by everyone. When I put on my mother's dress I feel as if I were she herself and so could arouse sexual feeling in my father and possibly supplant her with him. And, finally, a third person derives as much pleasure from a woman's clothes as from herself and looks on the putting-on of her frock as a sexual act." This formula is correct, but in my opinion it leaves out the phallic factor, which is so important and which Sadger does mention accidentally elsewhere, though there are yet other passages in which he contradicts this by asserting that it is the vulva which is the fetish. Boehm, again, lays stress in isolated instances on precisely this phallic character of the transvestist's perversion ("In the clothes

[13] Alexander, *Psycho-analyse der Gesamtpersönlichkeit*, VII. Vorlesung.
[14] Sadger, *Die Lehre von Geschlechtsverirrungen*, Vienna, 1921.
[15] Boehm, Bermerkungen zum Transvestitismus, *Internationale Zeitschrift für Psychoanalyse*, IX, p. 497.

which they put on they represent the mother with the penis"),[16] and on the sadistic nature of the wishes which originally related to the mother. Stekel contents himself with the incomplete statement that transvestism is based on homosexuality and mother-fixation. Pre-analytic literature gives but a meagre account of the matter to analysts, nevertheless, even the manifest material of such cases as are described in it contains all sorts of data which go to prove our hypothesis. We note, side by side with the transvestism, fetishistic, masochistic and exhibitionistic tendencies, fantasies of the mistress and the female slave, identification with the mother, histories of seduction by elder sisters, aversion from physical sexuality and especially from nakedness, the naked female body and from homosexuality, the *retour à l'enfance* (Ellis), but also a passion for women of a masculine type (Hirschfeld). One of Hirschfeld's cases gave rein to his transvestist tendencies by joining in a display of trick-shooting in the guise of a woman, thus publicly courting admiration as an "armed woman".[17] Ellis quotes one case which seems to contradict our view, because the patient's sexual aim was quite obviously castration, but this same man used to put on women's shoes and ear-rings, which indicates that, although he wished for castration, he was always impelled to cancel it again.[18] Cases of actual self-castration by transvestists or of disgust felt by them for the male genital and longing for that of the female would have to be examined analytically before we could make any pronouncement about them. Ellis's theory is as follows: All normal love contains an element of identification; in the perversion of transvestism this element is hypertrophied: "He has put too much of 'me' into the 'you' that attracts him." [19] This theory is, in our view, correct but incomplete. We think that we have been able to predicate something about the nature and causes of this identification. Just as correct and just as incomplete is Ellis's formula about the relation of transvestism to homosexuality; they are, he says, "two allotropic modifications of bisexuality". But it is possible to differentiate the characteristics of these modifications.

---

[16] Dr. Boehm has been kind enough to tell me that further analyses of transvestists have confirmed this view. He had one patient who used to turn a bottle upside down on his penis and then to put on women's clothes and dance in front of a looking-glass and so, finally, to masturbate.

[17] *Die Transvestiten*, Case V.

[18] *Loc. cit.*, pp. 63 ff.

[19] *Loc. cit.*, p. 108.

IV

We have recognized that the specific factor in the perversion of transvestism is its relation to the castration-complex. It remains for us to ask whether this conclusion contributes anything to our understanding of the psychology of the perversions in general. Sachs, in an article in which he examines the latter question, demonstrates that what characterizes the pervert is his capacity to transfer part of his infantile sexuality over to the ego, to permit himself to indulge it and by this very means to hold in repression those infantile sexual impulses which still remain (i.e. the œdipus complex).[20] The riddle we have to solve is how this process is possible, under what conditions can perverse component instincts retain or acquire the capacity to produce orgasm. As we now know that *all* perversions, including transvestism, are so intimately connected with the castration-complex, we can at least reply with the following hypothesis: normally, what conditions the disappearance of infantile sexuality (the passing of the œdipus complex) is the dread of castration.[21] Now the homosexual has no regard for any human being who lacks the penis, the fetishist denies that such beings exist, while the exhibitionist, the scoptophiliac and the transvestist try incessantly to refute the fact. Thus we see that these perverts are endeavouring to master their anxiety by denying its cause. In so far as they succeed in maintaining the illusion that there is no such thing as a lack of the penis, they save themselves anxiety and can indulge in infantile sexual practices *because*, just in proportion as they can effectively deny the grounds for it, their castration-anxiety, which otherwise would act as a check on such sexual behaviour, is diminished. We must, however, qualify this statement by saying that this process succeeds only up to a certain point. That is to say, such infantile activities are bound up with a simultaneous, incessantly renewed denial of the reason for anxiety, and it is this denial which is represented in the perverse practice. The behaviour of the pervert implies: "You have no need to be afraid" and, so long as he believes himself, his infantile sexual activities can produce orgasm, which signifies the gratification of his œdipus wishes.

It is true that this hypothesis makes the feminine perversion and

[20] Zur Genese der Perversionen, *Internationale Zeitschrift für Psychoanalyse*, Bd. IX, p. 172.

[21] Freud, The Passing of the Œdipus Complex, *Collected Papers*, Vol. II.

the whole subject of the castration-complex in women all the more problematic. Indeed, one does receive the impression that they are to some extent different in character from, though akin to, perversions in men. This strikes us, for instance, when we think of female exhibitionists and recall Hárnik's work on the differences between masculine and feminine narcissism.[22] Female fetishists are extremely rare, and female transvestists seem to be simply women who covet the penis and, out of desire to possess it, have identified themselves with men.

[22] Hárnik, The Various Developments Undergone by Narcissism in Men and in Women, *The International Journal of Psycho-Analysis*, V, p. 66.

THE FETISHIST AND HIS EGO * (1939)

By S. M. Payne

Freud first described the significance of the fetish in his classical work entitled *Three Contributions to the Theory of Sex*. He showed that the fetish was a substitute for an infantile sexual object, and that the selection of the fetish object was influenced by a coprophilic smell attraction. In later works he emphasized the fact that the fetish symbolized the penis and its presence relieved the castration fear of the male which was aroused by the sight of the female genital.

In an account of a case of shoe and corset fetishism Abraham laid stress on the part played by coprophilic and scoptophilic impulses in the psychical development of the fetishist. Bálint recorded in a recent article his recognition of the fact that the fetish not only symbolizes a genital, male or female, but also has a fæcal significance.

I had made a similar observation independently while working on the cases which I shall refer to in this paper.

Freud's recognition that the presence of the fetish not only stimulated the man's sexual desires but also allayed his castration anxiety introduced a new approach, namely that of the relation of the fetish to ego defence mechanisms and ego development.

In this contribution I hope to show (*a*) that the necessity to make a defence against an archaic sexual aim is one of the determinants of fetishism—the aim being to kill the love object; (*b*) to describe the type of situation in which the fixation of this sexual aim occurs; (*c*) to make some observations on the form of ego development which accompanies the adoption of this abnormal sexual behaviour.

I have had the opportunity of analysing two cases of fetishism and of observing work done on another case. I shall illustrate my paper from the analysis of a patient whose fetish was a mackintosh. I have been struck by the fact that the special type of sexual behaviour which demands the presence of a fetish is only one manifestation of a pathological mental state, which includes acute attacks of depression and anxiety, the presence of fears and fantasies of a

* Reprinted from *The International Journal of Psycho-Analysis*, X, 1939, p. 161. (Original title: Some Observations on the Ego Development of the Fetishist.)

paranoid type, suicidal tendencies which in one case were manifested first in childhood, and serious inhibitions. For this reason I shall state briefly certain facts concerning the general psychological state of my patient as far as it is necessary for the understanding of the problem of the fetish.

In spite of the severe symptoms there was good intellectual ability and an attainment of success in life up to a certain point. Bodily activities, especially in the form of games and dancing were inhibited; occasionally hypomanic outbursts of activity in walking, riding and swimming occurred, but on the whole the only sustained form of activity involving contact with other people was in the form of conversation. My patient loved talking and obtained his chief pleasure in conversation. His attitude to the parents was characteristic. He was not financially dependent on the parents owing to his own successful exertions, but he retained an unusually strong sense of guilt and obligation in connection with them, which was not dictated by an immediate actual reality situation, as the parents were in a position to look after themselves. He manifested a dependence which made him regard the ageing parents with horror and anxiety; the signs of old age seemed peculiarly intolerable. On the whole, the parents and especially the mother seemed frightful to him, and the redeeming features only appeared when the analysis had proceeded a considerable way. The decay of the parents was as menacing as if they were actually part of the child and as if the child was responsible. He had an oral type of relationship to objects reminiscent of the neurotic woman who seems to be occupied in defending herself from the necessity to internalize every external situation which arouses anxiety.

It had been recognized for a long time by psycho-analysts that the incorporation of an anxiety situation is a common mechanism of defence in childhood.

Recently Melanie Klein's work on ego mechanisms in the early phases of the œdipus complex has thrown light on the complicated relationships between internal and external situations which arise as a result of the interaction of the mechanisms of introjection and projection, and the tendency to internalize the anxiety situations.

Anna Freud draws attention to a special form of this reaction under the title of "Identification with the Aggressor" in her book *The Ego and the Mechanisms of Defence*.

When the mackintosh fetishist (whom I shall call Mr. A.) was confronted with an anxiety situation, which might be a rivalry in his work or the fear of the loss of an external good object, he invariably reacted in the same way, and combated depression by eating to excess, usually sausages and eggs, and sometimes by drinking to excess; his behaviour had a hypomanic character. At the same time he tended to isolate himself and become an "onlooker".

Mr. A. was a sleep-walker and had been so from early childhood. His sleep-walking was accompanied by an anxiety dream in which he was in danger of swallowing and he must either vomit it up or prevent it going down. Usually there were two objects which he was in danger of swallowing. In childhood he went to the lavatory when sleep-walking, and in adult life an alternative to vomiting was urinating or putting on the light. Sleep-walking occurred as a result of the same stresses as the excessive eating.

It was clear that he invariably employed the same method of ego defence in a situation in which he was in danger of losing a good object, and that was to internalize the experience which stimulated the anxiety and introject the lost object. A simple illustration occurred during the course of the analysis; he was attracted by a ballet dancer and made sexual advances to her, but she did not respond readily and he retreated in anger. A close friend of his also approached the girl and was successful. He was quite open with his unsuccessful rival who manifested no jealousy and discussed freely all the intimate details of the affair. Some time later my patient saw the dancer unexpectedly and to his surprise he was overcome with embarrassment. He said he felt that he was experiencing the guilt reactions of the guilty couple, identifying especially with the girl.

It was possible in this patient's case to recognize different forms which the necessity to incorporate and have control over the parents could take, and to show how the infantile sadism was bound up with the necessity to have control over the parents and their imagos, and in this way to take part in their sexual relationship. My patient had slept in his parents' room until the age of five years. The analysis showed that the sexual wishes were not separate from the fulfilment of death wishes, and while it was clear that there was a strong libidinal attachment to the parents it was equally clear that the aggressive component had come to dominate the unconscious situation, and that the inhibitions and restrictions of the ego were bound up with the persistence of an unconscious sadistic aim which involved the destruction of the love objects or his own castration.

Klein's work on children has enlarged our knowledge of the infantile sadistic aims, which include the wish to eat, to burn, drown, or soil with excreta and to penetrate destructively. The degree of aggression is partly proportionate to the helplessness of the ego.

The ego activities and functions which must be mobilized if the aims are burning, drowning, soiling with excreta or penetrating are to be realized were inhibited in these cases.

Mr. A. could not urinate or defæcate in any place where he might be seen or heard, and his fear of penetration was shown by anxiety associated with intercourse and the symptom of *ejaculatio præcox*. He had not had satisfactory intercourse when he came for treatment.

In childhood there were fantasies acted out in which the boy aimed at obtaining control over his parents by urinating and defæcating and by eating the parent's fæces. These fantasies were not confined to infancy but were manifested at the age of four or five, and later in a setting appropriate to his age. For example, he flooded the garden with a hose pipe and walked about naked in it. At four he had an hallucination which he kept secret of seeing a man and woman kissing in a hedge where he and his brother used to urinate. The picture was in a flood of light.

Then he was given a magic lantern and was thrilled by the power it gave him to throw a picture anywhere he liked and move it about. In adult life he dared not use a camera partly because it had the unconscious significance of a sadistic magical penis which could devour and do what it liked with its victims.

Abundance of material showed that sexuality was bound up with his sadistic fantasies concerning the parental sexual relationship and that the introjection of a sadistic primal scene and the experiences in the parents' room formed the core of his neurosis. The relationship between his parents was very bad, and separation took place when he was eleven years old.

He had been told many times by his mother that he nearly killed her at birth.

The infantile sadism aroused by jealousy and fear in connection with the parents' relationship is first discharged in excretory acts, urination and defæcation, and at the same time (as Melanie Klein has shown) the parents' excreta and their excretory acts stand for their sexuality and are the objects of the child's sexual interest. In this situation the control of the parents becomes synonymous with the control of the sadistic id-impulses, which have been projected into the parents, and internalized again when the parents are introjected.

The relationship to the introjected parents in my patient was such that sometimes an identification with the mother and sometimes with the father dominated the picture, and it was easy to recognize which was prevailing.

He had entered the phallic phase and had partially regressed after puberty. The inability to establish adult genitality was due to regression to a fixation in the oral and anal phases, and the persistence of an unconscious primitive sexual aim, which involved the death of the love object or castration of himself. The weakness of ego development is one aspect of the weakness of genitality, and denotes interference with the libidinization, formation and integration of the body ego, especially of the *penis imago*. This brings about an exaggeration of the first mechanisms of defence which are employed, namely the projection and introjection mechanisms and an exaggerated dependence on the introjected objects, but no sustained identification with any.

It was possible in the case of Mr. A. to uncover a number of infantile situations which were concerned in causing the ego weakness and strengthened the dependence on the parents. I wish to mention these shortly because I think they demonstrate the kind of situation which helps to make infantile sadism unmanageable and therefore provoke neurotic defence mechanisms. The patient was bottle-fed, and there was no actual history of difficulty in feeding; if anything I should think his mother tried to overfeed him. He was circumcised at six months and nearly died of bronchitis shortly afterwards. He was rather fat and the doctor did not allow him to stand or walk until he was two years old. The fact was not remembered and was discovered in the analysis and confirmed by his mother, who said that he made the most distressing scenes and had to be tied down, and that he used to try to get up at night. The interference with the development of normal muscular activity, together with the circumcision and serious illness during the first year held up the integration and development of the body ego. Aggression is more easily discharged through the muscular system than in any other way, and the energy expended in learning to walk is probably greater than on any other function. This castration significance of the prohibition of this ego activity was stupendous and in my opinion played an overwhelming part in encouraging the relatively passive orientation which the defence by internalization shows, and increased the tendency to a feminine identification. The aggression normally discharged through the muscular system had to be focussed on excretory discharges which are also the main erotic outlet, hence the sadistic element of these pregenital activities increased. An exaggerated fear of aggression, which represents the death instinct, is undoubtedly fostered by serious physical illness either of the child itself or of one of the parents. This situation was present in all the cases of fetishism which I have observed closely.

It has been recognized that libidinization of the *penis imago* is the basis of ego development, and at this phase it represents the ego.[1] I think the erect position attained in standing in infancy and erection of the penis have comparable narcissistic values, and that castration fears are associated with a threat to either. The ego which cannot increase its strength by proving its own capacity actively is driven to reinforce itself by reliance on objects and continues to employ primitive methods of control, and is forced to submit to the parents and their internal representatives.

An attempt to deal with the helplessness is an adoption of magical means such as I have described in connection with Mr. A.'s eating activities and his use of the camera and magic-lantern. The presence of the fetish as a necessary accompaniment of sexuality after puberty is a further manifestation of the same phase of physical development.

A study of what the fetish means to the fetishist reveals that it is possible to demonstrate that every component of the infantile sexual instinct has some connection with the fetish object, so that this object is associated with all the repressed infantile sexual experiences.

In the case of the mackintosh fetish the smell was connected with scoptophilic and coprophilic interests and activities, and with oral sadistic and oral erotic desires demonstrated in memories of chewing rubber teats, and eating fæces, sucking bull's-eyes and in innumerable dreams and fantasies. The texture of the smooth or rough mackintosh was connected with the stimulation of skin erotism, dating from a memory of his nurse's lap and of the examination of a little girl's smooth white genitals.

A vivid memory from the third year of life when he was forced to wear mackintosh padding drawers was connected with exhibitionism, viewing and fear of castration.

Sadistic and masochistic impulses were manifested in anal or

---

[1] *Author's Note.—Penis imago* refers to Freud's organ representation of the penis. The significance of the penis as a psychical part object standing for the father and introjected as such, can be connected here with the phase of ego development referred to.

urethral activities in which a mackintosh or rubber object always found a place.

The prominence of the sadistic component was undoubted, and the necessity to control this component could be regarded as the factor which determined the distinctive mode of defence. The mackintosh is more obviously a protection than the shoe or corset.

The relationship of a man to his fetish is the same as his relationship to his internalized parents. Sometimes Mr. A. identified with the father, then he put on the mackintosh and would masturbate with a fantasy of intercourse with a woman.

At other times he put on the mackintosh and had a passive anal fantasy.

On other occasions the mackintosh must be present in the room when he masturbated. Sometimes he placed it over his genitals as if to protect them. He preferred a mackintosh which was stolen. In his relations with women he had no desire to penetrate if she had a mackintosh, and he regarded its presence as certain to produce the symptom of *ejaculatio præcox*. The general explanation of this was that the fetish reanimates the pregenital substitutes for genital sexuality, and also provides special defences against the aggression of pregenital sexuality. The aggression of genital sexuality, although in reality of much less significance than that of the anal and oral levels, may take on the aggression associated with pregenital sexuality if genital masturbation is precociously developed, as it is likely to have been in this case owing to enforced passivity and the resulting limitation of external interests.

The mackintosh fetish itself stood for the father's penis or the woman's genital, nipple, body, and tract, or the parents' fæces.

In other words, it was symbolic of part objects and also of a combined parent imago. These imagos, as we all know, have special significance in connection with the earliest phase of ego development before relationships to whole or real objects are firmly established. Klein has pointed out that the introjected part objects are identified with fæces, and this identification is brought out in the choice of the fetish.

The fetish therefore stands for part objects which have been eaten, and also preserved. The internalized objects may have the significance of pregenital superego formations and as we all know can be feared or loved by the ego. In the latter case the ego seeks protection and support from the superego and it may be said that the superego and loved object are identical.

When this internalized object is projected into the fetish, the latter represents the loved object and the superego.

In the case of the mackintosh its defensive and protective function rests on its capacity to defend against sadistic attacks, especially those connected with excretory activities. It is interesting to note that the mackintosh will allow the child to excrete, that is to say to have a libidinal pleasure without injuring other objects. In other words, the defensive function refers to the destructive impulse, while the stimulating function refers to the libido.

The fact that the mackintosh, the chosen substitute object, is an object which actually functions in childhood as a protection against the disasters of that period suggests a measure of development of the sense of reality not present perhaps in the choice of other fetishes. In common with other fetishes it is a real external object and as a substitute for a love object denotes an effort to find contact with an external object and externalize an internal conflict. In this connection I had the opportunity to observe a tendency to develop a mackintosh fetish during the analysis of an obsessional neurosis. This patient, a man of twenty-seven, professed complete ignorance of the sexual act and of the anatomy of the female genitals in animals and human beings. His actions and thoughts were dominated by compulsive mechanisms of all kinds. After some months' analysis his repressed interest in both male and female sexuality and the genitals began to appear, and with this he started to dream of mackintoshes. It was as if the mackintosh heralded his approach to sexual activity and the genital which is the organ through which activity is experienced. I think that the fetish defence denotes that libidinal development has attempted to pass the anal phases, and that the phallic phase is partially reached. Repression falls on experiences connected with the phallic and anal phases. Actually memories of seeing the female genital at an early age were retained in my cases, but the knowledge of menstruation in childhood was repressed, and the evidence suggested that it was linked with repressed material connected with excretory activities. The identification of fæces and menstruation is commonly present. The prominence of oral mechanisms was due not only to an oral fixation but also to displacement from the genital and anal positions.

The attraction of the oral zone is due to the possibility of egosyntonic activities and to the fact that ego development was partially fixated on an oral and early anal level, and had never satisfactorily passed the phase in which the helpless infantile ego is dependent on a good introjected object. The fetish representing as it does a combination of part objects, the combined parents represented by their fæces, and also in many situations the father's penis, stands for a good introjected object.

Any sexual potency which these patients could lay claim to depended on their unconscious belief in an introjected father's or brother's penis.

Actually from whatever point the problems connected with these cases are approached we are confronted with the weakness and dependence of the ego bound up with interference with genital potency, and I have been impressed by the importance of ego development in the first two years of life in this connection.

Klein's work on depressed states and their connection with an early phase of ego development is supported by the analysis of the psychical background of the individual who has the necessity for a fetish.

A real comprehension of the causes of this sexual anomaly can only be obtained by considering the fetish in its relation to the individual's whole psychical development and by taking into account the other morbid symptoms which are invariably present.

The relation of fetishism to a perversion and to neurosis is not a simple problem. Although fetishism is not actually classed as a perversion a study of the literature reveals a tendency to treat the two forms of abnormal sexual behaviour as if they had much in common. In my opinion the fetish saves the individual from a perverse form of sexuality. The component impulse which would prevail if not placed under special control is the sadistic impulse.

The fetishist has much more conscious anxiety and guilt than an individual with an established perversion, and in this respect resembles the psycho-neurotic.

The over-determination of the fetish both from the point of view of sexuality and ego defence can be compared to that of a neurotic symptom.

In common with phobia the mechanism of projection and displacement is used and a substitute object is selected, but there is a reversal of affect, as the object is to attract not to repel. The projection is for purposes of reassurance and to provide a good external object. It provides a reassurance that the sadistic wishes have not destroyed the objects.

The importance of the pregenital fixations is shown by a recognition of the sublimations which are capable of replacing the fetish.

In two patients it was literary work. One patient said repeatedly that he really loved books not the mackintosh. He collected books, and always wanted to defæcate when he entered a book-shop.

His literary work was inhibited when his sexual anomaly was active, and when he came for treatment he was in danger of losing his power to produce books.

In an unpublished paper read to the British Psycho-analytical Society some time ago Ella Sharpe described the unconscious connections between a shoe fetish and the production of a picture.

The unconscious connection with artistic products is further evidence of the association of the fetish with the introjected imagos of the early phases of ego development. In conclusion it is abundantly shown in this contribution that the psychology of the fetishist is dominated by castration fear, and I have traced this fear in these cases to infantile situations connected with unusual tension of the aggressive impulses inseparably bound up with sexuality.

AUTHOR'S COMMENT

Comments on this article make it obvious that the reason why more references were not made to the patient's defences against homosexuality should have been stated. It should have been made clear also that no attempt has been made to estimate the relative importance of genital and pre-genital factors in the etiology of fetishism in this work.

PSYCHOSES

ON THE ORIGIN OF THE "INFLUENCING MACHINE" IN SCHIZOPHRENIA* (1919)

By Victor Tausk

It is infrequent that a single contribution to a problem causes the reader to reflect upon the direction in which that problem might have developed had the author not left it so early in his life. The memorial on Victor Tausk's sudden death at the age of forty-two is contained in the same volume of the Internationale Zeitschrift of 1919 as the article reprinted here. Yet this first, and at the same time, last major contribution of Dr. Tausk has, for more than a quarter of a century, never ceased to inspire subsequent authors, and in rereading it one is again struck by the still-untapped wealth of ideas, touching upon so many of the analyst's daily clinical problems.

Tausk, originally a lawyer, joined Freud's first pupils in 1909, studied medicine, became a practising psychiatrist, and absorbed analysis the while into a mind perhaps exceeding most of his contemporaries in its capaciousness. The acuity of observation, and ingenuity of conception evinced in the article here to follow, remind one of Abraham's work.

Yet the paper violates almost all pedestrian standards for publication. Much of the text is contained in footnotes, no section can be given an adequate heading, and the paper cannot be abstracted without being practically rewritten. This is so because, while dealing with the interpretation of but a single symbolic element in a psychotic delusion, the author discourses at varying length, but with unvarying acumen upon all manner of disparate subjects. Many of these are, of course, attacked prematurely, and the reader today has the task of transferring much of the article's

---

* First published under the title: Über den Beeinflussungsapparat in der Schizophrenie, *Internationale Zeitschrift für Psychoanalyse*, V, 1919, p. 1.

Reprinted from *The Psychoanalytic Quarterly*, II, 1933, p. 519. Translated by Dorian Feigenbaum.

*terminology into that of today. Yet no part of it is without value;
and the impulse at first experienced by this editor, to omit as
obsolete certain sections has, upon second reading, been rejected.
The most prematurely theoretical passage, comprising several
pages, appears on pages 47–53, and a number of brief subheadings have been provided in order to point the way, as it
were, through a difficult paper.*

I

METHODOLOGICAL OBSERVATIONS. The following considerations
are based upon a single example of the "influencing machine" complained of by a certain type of schizophrenic patient. Although in
this particular case the structure of the machine differs materially,
to the best of my knowledge, from all other varieties of apparatus of
this sort, it is hoped that the present example will nevertheless
facilitate psycho-ananalytic insight into the genesis and purpose of
this delusional instrument.

My example is a variant—a very rare variant—of the typical
influencing machine. The objection can of course be made that it is
rash to draw general conclusions from the study of a single case,
and that generalizations, to be regarded as scientifically valid, should
be based on a larger mass of material. My justification is that I have
simply not encountered any further case material in support of my
conclusions, and that to the best of my knowledge psychiatric literature contains no descriptions of individual cases of the influencing
machine phenomenon, such as would make my paper superfluous.
There exist only general descriptions of the apparatus, and its
regular features and functions are given only as perfunctory clinical
illustrations. Clinical psychiatry, interested only in general descriptions, lays no stress upon the significance of individual symptoms
for the study of the dynamics of psychoses. Psychiatry has not
hitherto sufficiently investigated the origin, the meaning, and the
purpose of a symptom, because, not employing the psycho-analytical
method, it does not even postulate such problems. Yet, in principle,
it is permissible to derive general conclusions from exceptional
types. Variants and mixed forms stimulate inquiry into general
types. The conformity of typical cases may have the ultimate effect
of an impenetrable barrier, while a deviation from type, on the other
hand, may be a window in the wall through which a clear view is to
be obtained.

Deviations from the rule and ambiguous types compel the assumption that a given phenomenon may be of diverse origin. It is only when an unexpected departure from the accustomed occurs that one feels the necessity of investigating the uniformity which had previously characterized the phenomenon or at least had seemed to do so. Inquiry into extraordinary causative factors has often stimulated inquiry into those ordinarily encountered.

It is to be hoped only that the example taken as a basis for the following conclusions will prove to justify them, and that the origin and significance of this variant example have been correctly conceived and formulated.

II

The schizophrenic influencing machine is a machine of mystical nature. The patients are able to give only vague hints of its construction. It consists of boxes, cranks, levers, wheels, buttons, wires, batteries, and the like. Patients endeavour to discover the construction of the apparatus by means of their technical knowledge, and it appears that with the progressive popularization of the sciences, all the forces known to technology are utilized to explain the functioning of the apparatus. All the discoveries of mankind, however, are regarded as inadequate to explain the marvellous powers of this machine, by which the patients feel themselves persecuted.

THE PATIENTS' COMPLAINTS UNDERSTOOD AS "EFFECTS" OF THE "INFLUENCING MACHINE". The main effects of the influencing machine are the following:

(1) It makes the patients see pictures. When this is the case, the machine is generally a magic-lantern or cinematograph. The pictures are seen on a single plane, on walls or window-panes, and unlike typical visual hallucinations are not three-dimensional.

(2) It produces, as well as removes, thoughts and feelings by means of waves or rays or mysterious forces which the patient's knowledge of physics is inadequate to explain. In such cases, the machine is often called a "suggestion-apparatus". Its construction cannot be explained, but its function consists in the transmission or "draining off" of thoughts and feelings by one or several persecutors.

(3) It produces motor phenomena in the body, erections and seminal emissions, that are intended to deprive the patient of his male potency and weaken him. This is accomplished either by means of suggestion or by air-currents, electricity, magnetism, or X-rays.

(4) It creates sensations that in part cannot be described, because they are strange to the patient himself, and that in part are sensed as electrical, magnetic, or due to air-currents.

(5) It is also responsible for other occurrences in the patient's body, such as cutaneous eruptions, abscesses, and other pathological processes.

The machine serves to persecute the patient and is operated by enemies. To the best of my knowledge, the latter are exclusively of the male sex. They are predominantly physicians by whom the patient has been treated. The manipulation of the apparatus is likewise obscure, the patient rarely having a clear idea of its operation. Buttons are pushed, levers set in motion, cranks turned. The connection with the patient is often established by means of invisible wires leading into his bed, in which case the patient is influenced by the machine only when he is in bed.

THE SAME COMPLAINTS WITHOUT INFLUENCING MACHINE. However, it is noteworthy that a large number of patients complain of all these ailments without ascribing them to the influence of a machine. Many patients consider the cause of all these alien or hostile sensations of physical or psychic change to be simply an external mental influence, suggestion or telepathic power, emanating from enemies. My own observations and those of other authors leave no room for doubt that these complaints precede the symptom of the influencing apparatus, and that the latter is a subsequent pathological development. Its appearance, as many observers state, serves the purpose of an explanation for the pathologic changes that are felt as alien and painful and dominate the patient's emotional life and sensations.

According to this view, the idea of the influencing machine originates in the need for causality that is inherent in man; and the same need for causality will probably also account for the persecutors who act not through the medium of an apparatus but merely by suggestion or by telepathy. Clinical psychiatry explains the symptom of an influencing machine as analogous to the ideas of persecution in paranoia (which, it is known, the patient invents in order to justify his delusions of grandeur), and calls it *"paranoia somatica"*.

However, there is a group of patients that dispenses completely with any gratification of the need for causality, and complains simply of emotional changes and strange apparitions within the physical and psychic personality, without the intervention of a foreign or hostile power. It is particularly declared by some patients that their visions are not foisted upon them in any way but that, to their great astonishment, they simply see them. There also occur other strange sensations for which there is no evidence of an originator, especially, for instance, the complaint of a loss or change of thoughts and feelings, without the thoughts or feelings being "drained" from them or "foisted" upon them; and of a similar nature are complaints of a change of sensations in the skin, face, and extremities. This group of patients does not complain of influences originating from a foreign, hostile force, but of a feeling of inner estrangement. They become strange to themselves, no longer understand themselves: limbs, face, facial expression, thoughts, and feelings, have become estranged. These symptoms clearly are part of an early stage of dementia præcox, although they may also be observed in advanced stages.

"INFLUENCING MACHINE" TERMINAL IN A SYMPTOMATOLOGY, BEGINNING WITH FEELINGS OF ALIENATION. In some cases it may be stated with certainty, and in others with strong probability, that the sense of persecution originates from the sensations of change accompanied by a sense of estrangement. These feelings of persecution are ascribed to a foreign, personal interference, "suggestion", or "telepathic influence". In other cases, the ideas of persecution or influence may be seen entering into the construction of an influencing apparatus. It is necessary to assume, therefore, that the influencing apparatus represents the terminal stage in the evolution of the symptom, which started with simple sensations of change. I do not believe that heretofore the entire sequence in the development of the symptom could have been studied completely from a single case. But I have observed the connection between at least two stages (of which I shall present an example later), and I have no hesitation in maintaining that under especially favourable circumstances it may be possible to observe the entire series of developmental stages in a single patient. Meanwhile, I am in the position of the observer of plasmodia who notes various pathological forms in the blood cells as developmental stages of a continuous cycle of growth, although he is never able to observe in any one blood corpuscle more than a single phase.

Recognition of the various symptoms as stages of a unified developmental process is rendered difficult not merely by inaccurate observation but by other factors as well. Patients conceal single stages behind secondary and correlative symptoms—each patient in accordance with his morbid disposition. Changes of feeling are covered up by a simultaneously or consecutively produced psychosis or neurosis belonging to another clinical group, such as depression, mania, paranoia, compulsion neurosis, anxiety hysteria, or amentia; and these clinical pictures, advancing to the foreground, conceal from the observer the more subtle elements in the development of the delusion of reference. It is, besides, very likely that in many cases not every stage of development reaches consciousness, and that one stage or another runs its course in the unconscious and thus leaves gaps in the conscious psyche. Finally, depending upon the rapidity of the pathological process and upon the individual disposition, some of the stages may be missing altogether.

Ideas of reference in schizophrenia develop equally with or without the influencing apparatus. In but one case [1] have I been able to observe electrical currents in the absence of the influencing apparatus to which those are usually ascribed—in the absence, in fact, of any hostile powers whatsoever.

DISCUSSION OF CASES. This observation was made in the case of a thirty-four year old man, Josef H., an inmate of insane asylums at frequent intervals throughout his life. He felt electrical currents streaming through him, which entered the earth through his legs; he produced the current within himself, declaring with pride that that was his power! How and for what purpose he did this he refused to disclose. Upon discovering these currents in himself for the first time, he was (he admitted) somewhat astonished, but he soon came to the conclusion that this manifestation had a special significance— that the currents served a mysterious end, regarding which he refused any information.

I shall now cite another instance, a singular case of "*paranoia somatica*", having, as will later be seen, a significance of its own in substantiating the developmental process which I have assumed. The same example has already been cited by Freud in another connection. Miss Emma A. felt herself influenced by her lover in a singular manner; she maintained that her eyes were no longer properly placed in her head but were entirely twisted out of position, and this she attributed to the fact that her lover was an evil, deceitful person who twisted eyes. At church one day she suddenly felt a

---

[1] At the Belgrade Neuropsychiatric Division.

thrust, as if she were being moved from her place, which had its cause in the fact that her lover disguised himself,[2] and that he had already ruined her and made her as evil as himself.

This patient did not merely feel herself persecuted and influenced; hers was a case of being influenced by identification with the persecutor. If we take into consideration the view held by Freud and myself that in object-choice the mechanism of identification precedes the cathexis proper by projection, we may regard the case of Miss Emma A. as representing the stage in the development of the delusion of reference preceding the projection (namely, on to a distant persecutor in the outer world). The identification is obviously an attempt to project the feelings of the inner change on to the outer world. It constitutes a bridge between the feelings of an inner change without external cause and the attribution of these changes to the power of an external person, a kind of intermediary position between the feeling of self-estrangement and the delusion of reference. This rounds out especially well, and substantiates psycho-analytically, the concept of the development of the symptom, up to its crystallization in the influencing machine. We are here concerned with the discovery, or rather the invention, of a hostile object; but for the intellectual process it is unimportant whether the objects observed are hostile or friendly, and the psycho-analyst, at least, will certainly have no objection to the equating of love and hate in this instance. Among the illustrations that may be given of the various forms or stages of the delusion of reference, the case of Staudenmayer (whose autobiography was presented before the Vienna Psycho-analytic Society some years ago) may be mentioned.

Staudenmayer—who, if I am not mistaken, was declared to be a paranoiac and is at any rate considered to be one by me—described his sensations during his bowel movements from the beginning of the movement to its conclusion, and attributed every single peristaltic motion coming to his awareness to the activity of special demons allegedly located in the intestines and entrusted with the performance of each separate motion.

THE COMPLETE SYMPTOMATOLOGY. We may now summarize and describe schematically the phenomena that in some cases appear to be produced by the influencing machine and that in other cases occur without it.

---

[2] This patient's words, "Sich verstellt"—taken literally, mean "moves himself from one place to another ".—*Translator*.

(1) We note, first, simple sensations of inner change, in the beginning devoid of, and later accompanied by, a sense of estrangement, without awareness of an originator. The sensations are of changes in the psychical and physical functions within various parts of one's own body. In many cases this stage of the illness probably occurs at a very early age, before puberty. Since at this age no exact reports can be obtained on inner conditions, and since, in addition, pathological changes are not infrequently compensated by infantile peculiarities of character, such as naughtiness, aggressiveness, concealed fantasies, masturbation, seclusiveness, dullness and so forth, this stage either remains unrecognized or else is misnamed. It is only at puberty, when special adjustments to the environment are required of the individual, who is compelled to relinquish all crude expressions of his abnormality, that the illness comes to the surface; it is at this time, too, that further development of symptoms is stimulated.

(2) Feelings of inner change in the form of abnormal sensations, with awareness of an originator,—in this instance the patient himself (case Josef H.).

(3) Feelings of inner change accompanied by awareness of an originator, who, although existing within the patient, is nevertheless not the patient himself (case Staudenmayer).

(4) Feelings of inner change accompanied by hallucinatory projection of the inner occurrence to the external world, without awareness of an originator; at first, feelings of estrangement are not present, but later on they appear (seeing pictures).

(5) Feelings of inner change accompanied by awareness of an external originator as a result of identification (case Emma A.).

(6) Feelings of inner change accompanied by projection of the inner occurrence to the outer world and belief in an originator produced by the paranoid mechanism (causing pictures to appear, influencing by suggestion, hypnotism, electricity, producing or draining off thoughts and feelings, effecting bodily motions, weakening potency, producing erection, seminal emissions, and so forth).

(7) Feelings of inner change attributed to the workings of the influencing machine manipulated by enemies. At first, the enemies are usually unknown to the patient and only vaguely discerned by him; later on he is able to make them out, knows who they are, and enlarges their circle after the pattern of the paranoid conspiracy. Similarly, the patient is at first completely unable to explain the

construction of the influencing apparatus, but familiarizes himself with it gradually.

Having solved the relation between ideas of reference and the influencing apparatus, we may proceed to an examination of the latter without reference to its effects.

THE CONSTRUCTION OF THE "INFLUENCING MACHINE". It is not necessary to discuss the magic-lantern which produces pictures or images, because its structure harmonizes perfectly with the function attributed to it, and because it does not reveal any error of judgment beyond the fact of its non existence. This rational superstructure is absolutely impenetrable. We must, at the start, use structures less solidly built, the walls of which reveal gaps through which it is possible to look inside.

(a) The ordinary influencing machine has a very obscure construction; large parts of it are completely unimaginable. In cases where the patient believes he understands the construction of the apparatus well, it is obvious that this feeling is, at best, analogous to that of a dreamer who has a feeling of understanding, but has not the understanding itself. This characteristic may be discovered whenever an accurate description of the apparatus is demanded of the patient.

(b) The apparatus is, as far as I know, always a machine; and a very complicated one.

THE "MACHINE"—A SYMBOL OF INDIVIDUAL'S GENITALS (cf. DREAMS OF MACHINES). The psycho-analyst cannot for a moment doubt that this machine must be a symbol—a view recently emphasized by Freud in one of his lectures, in which he stated that the complicated machines appearing in dreams always represent the genitalia. Having studied machine dreams analytically over a long period of time, I can fully confirm Freud's statement; I may add, moreover, that the machines always stand for the dreamer's own genitalia and that the dreams are of a masturbatory character. I can state further that these dreams are dreams of escape, of the type described in my paper on alcoholic delirium.[3] In this paper it is shown that whenever an urge to masturbate, or rather a readiness to ejaculate semen, leads to a dream fantasy which is favourable to discharge, another fantasy is hastily substituted, by means of which a new state of inhibition is induced momentarily, and the ejaculation

[3] Tausk, Victor: Zur Psychologie des alkohol. Beschäftigungsdelir., *Internationale Zeitschrift für Psychoanalyse*, III, 1915.

of semen is made difficult if not impossible. The dream reacts to the repudiated wish for discharge with a successive alteration of symbols.

The machine dream possesses an analogous mechanism, except that the introduction of single components of the machine is not accompanied by the simultaneous disappearance of the other components for which they are substituted, the new components being simply added to the old ones. This is how the hopelessly complex machine originates. In order to strengthen the inhibition, the symbol has been made complex, instead of being displaced by another one; but the result is the same. Each complexity draws the attention of the dreamer to himself, rouses his intellectual interest, reciprocally weakens his libidinal interest, and effects in this manner inhibition of instinct.

In machine dreams the dreamer awakens, more often than not, with his hand on his genitalia, after having dreamed of manipulating the machine. It may, therefore, be assumed that the influencing apparatus is a representation of the patient's genitalia projected to the outer world, analogous in origin to the machine in dreams. The frequent complaint of the schizophrenic that the apparatus causes erection, drains off semen, and weakens potency only confirms this view. At any rate, the analogy of the symptom to a dream production, as well as the accessibility of the symptom to psycho-analytic dream interpretation is a step beyond the rationalizations and the demand for causal connections that underlie the usual clinical interpretation of the influencing machine in schizophrenia. I can now present my example, which will not only strengthen our hypothesis, but will enlarge it materially.

THE CASE OF NATALIJA A.: REPORT. The patient is Miss Natalija A., thirty-one years old, formerly a student of philosophy. She has been completely deaf for a great number of years, due to an ulcer of the ear, and can make herself understood only by means of writing. She declares that for six and a half years she has been under the influence of an electrical machine made in Berlin, though this machine's use is prohibited by the police. It has the form of a human body, indeed, the patient's own form, though not in all details. Her mother, likewise the patient's male and female friends, are also under the influence of this machine or of similar machines. Of the latter she gives no explanation, describing only the apparatus to which she herself is subjected. She is certain that for men there is a masculine machine representing the masculine form and for women a female one. The trunk (torso) has the shape of a lid, resembling the lid of a coffin and is lined with silk or velvet. Regarding the limbs two significant explanations are given. At the first interview she described them as entirely natural parts of the body. A few weeks later these limbs were not placed on the coffin lid in their natural form, but were merely drawn on it in two dimensions, in the position they would occupy in the natural state of the body. She cannot see the head—she says that she is not sure about it and she does not know whether the machine bears her own head. She has practically nothing to report about the head. The patient does not know definitely how this machine is to be handled, neither does she know how it is connected with her; but she vaguely thinks that it is by means of telepathy. The outstanding fact about the machine is that it is being manipulated by someone in a certain manner, and everything that occurs to it happens also to her. When someone strikes this machine, she feels the blow in the corresponding part of her body. The ulcer (lupus) now present on her nose was first produced on the nose of the machine, and some time later the patient herself became afflicted with it. The inner parts of the machine consist of electric batteries, which are supposed to represent the internal organs of the human body. Those who handle the machine produce a slimy substance in her nose, disgusting smells, dreams, thoughts, feelings, and disturb her while she is thinking, reading or writing. At an earlier stage, sexual sensations were produced in her through manipulation of the genitalia of the machine; but now the machine no longer possesses any genitalia, though why or how they disappeared she cannot tell. Ever since the machine lost its genitalia, the patient has ceased to experience sexual sensations.

She became familiar with the apparatus, about which she had previously heard, through all kinds of occurrences, especially through conversations among people, that is, through auditory hallucinations. The man who utilizes the apparatus to persecute her, her rejected suitor, a college professor, is prompted by jealousy. Very soon after she had refused his courtship she felt that he was trying by means of suggestion to bring about a friendship between his sister-in-law, her mother, and herself, his obvious purpose being to use this influence to make her accept him. When, however, suggestion failed, he subjected her to the influence of the machine; not only she herself but also her mother, her physicians, her friends, all those who had her welfare at heart, came under the influence of this diabolic apparatus, with the result that the physicians submitted a mistaken diagnosis to her, the apparatus deluding them into diagnosing other ailments than those with which she was afflicted. She could no longer get along with her friends and relatives, arousing everyone's animosity, and feeling compelled to run away. It was impossible to obtain any further details from the patient. On her third visit she became inaccessible and only stated that the analyst, too, was under the influence of the apparatus, that he had become hostile to her, and that they could no longer understand each other.

THE CASE OF NATALIJA A.: INTERPRETATION. This case provides a definite reason for believing that the influencing machine represents a stage in the development of a symptom which can also appear without this stage, as a delusion of reference. The patient clearly stated that her persecutor had recourse to the apparatus only when his attempt to influence her by suggestion failed. The fact that she seems to have previously heard about the machine is also enlightening. This vague recognition obviously awakened in the patient old familiar sensations that she had experienced before she was subjected to the apparatus; this is analogous to the well-known fact that persons in a state of infatuation have the feeling of having always known the beloved one—in reality they are merely rediscovering one of their old libidinal imagos. We shall hear later in how remote a past she had first experienced sensations similar to those caused by the influencing apparatus.

The peculiar construction of the machine substantiates our assumptions to a great extent, especially with regard to the significance of the machine as a projected symbol of the genitalia. We may add that the apparatus represents not only the patient's genitalia but obviously, her whole person. It represents the projection of the patient's body on to the outer world. At least, the following results are unquestionably obtained from the patient's report: the apparatus is distinguished above all by its human form, easily recognized despite many non-human characteristics. In form it resembles the patient herself, and she senses all manipulations performed on the apparatus in the corresponding part of her own body and in the same manner. All effects and changes undergone by the apparatus take place simultaneously in the patient's body, and *vice versa*. Thus, the apparatus loses its genitalia following the patient's loss of her genital sensations; it had possessed genitalia for as long a period as her genital sensations had lasted.

Applying the technique of dream interpretation to this case, it may be said that the patient's inability to provide any detailed description of the head of the apparatus, and especially her inability to decide whether it was her own head or not, proves conclusively that it is her own head. We know from analytic observations that the person not recognized in a dream is actually the dreamer himself. In my analysis of the *Dream of the Clinic*,[4] it was clear that the dreamer meant herself when she dreamt of a person whose head she could not see.

A further detail in the description of the apparatus—namely, that the lid is lined with silk or velvet—may substantiate this opinion. Women very frequently describe in such terms the feelings evoked by caressing their own skin. That the intestines appear in the form of batteries is only of slight significance here, although it will assume a profounder meaning later on. This superficial interpretation may be associated with the information given directly or indirectly to school children to the effect that the viscera resemble a very complicated machine. In our case the tendency seems to be towards a verbal interpretation of this infantile conception. This conclusion regarding its ontogeny is arrived at with the help of the description given by the patient of her influencing apparatus.

At the very beginning the patient reported that the limbs of the apparatus appeared in their natural form and position. Several weeks later, she declared that the limbs were drawn on the lid. This

[4] Published in *Internationale Zeitschrift für Psychoanalyse*, II, 1914, p. 466. Miss N. dreams: "I am seated on an upper bench in the surgical amphitheatre. Below a woman is being operated on. She lies with her head towards me, but I cannot see the head, as it seems to be concealed by the lower benches. I see the woman only from her chest down. I see both thighs and a heap of white towels and linens. I see nothing else clearly."

Analysis of the dream reveals that the dreamer sees herself as the woman operated on. A few days before the night of the dream, the dreamer called on a young physician who made advances to her. On this occasion she was reclining on a couch. The physician raised her skirts and while he operated "below", she perceived the heap of white underclothes overhead. Just as much as she saw of herself in this situation, she sees of the woman in the dream, and the woman's head remains invisible to her in the same way as she could not see her own head in the actual situation. According to Freud, the "woman without a head" in a dream represents the mother. The basic reason for this interpretation will not be discussed here, but will be treated in another section of this paper.

is obviously a manifestation of the progressive distortion undergone by the apparatus, which, consequently, eventually loses all human characteristics and becomes a typical, unintelligible, influencing machine. First the genitalia, then the limbs are eliminated in this process. The patient, to be sure, is unable to report how the genitalia are removed. She states, however, that the limbs are removed in the following manner: they lose their three-dimensional human form and flatten to a two-dimensional plane. It would not have been surprising if after a lapse of several weeks, the patient had declared that the apparatus did not possess any limbs at all. Nor would it have been astonishing had she stated that the apparatus had never had any limbs. A failure to recall the developmental stages of the apparatus has obviously the same significance as that of forgetting the origin of dream pictures. It is not too bold a conclusion to draw that the coffin lid of the machine is a product of such successive distortions and that originally it had represented a human being— namely, the patient herself.

Psycho-analytic experience brings to light the causative factors in such distortion. Underlying every distortion of a psychic phenomenon there is a defence mechanism which has as its aim the protection of the conscious ego against the appearance or reappearance of undisguised fantasies. The patient obviously seeks not to recognize herself in the influencing machine and therfore in self protection she divests it of all human features; in a word, the less human the appearance of the delusion, the less does she recognize herself in it. The origin of this rejection will be examined later.

When the influencing machine of Miss Natalija A. first came to my attention, it was in a special stage of development; I was fortunate, moreover, in observing the machine in the process of development as concerned the limbs, and also in obtaining specific information from the patient herself regarding the genitalia. I assume that this process will end with the production of the typical influencing apparatus known to clinical observation, but I cannot affirm that this apparatus will pass through all the stages of development to the very end. It is very possible that it will stop at a middle point, without proceeding further.

III

In the meantime, we may consider a second hypothesis that may have suggested itself to the reader. It must be taken into considera-

tion that, notwithstanding all that has been said above, the influencing machine of Miss Natalija A. may be merely an inexplicable
exception to the general rule. The complex, unintelligible machine
as fantastically described and interpreted by other patients would
perhaps first have to be studied and defined before an explanation
of Miss N.'s influencing machine could be undertaken. For want of
other material at hand to substantiate our hypothesis, except the
machine dream, we shall start with the assumption that the influencing apparatus is a projection of the patient's genitalia. In
presenting this second hypothesis together with, or in lieu of, the
first, I realize how much indulgence is exacted of the reader, and I
should not be surprised if I were reproached with levity or leger-
demain. I myself was unpleasantly surprised to discover that this
second hypothesis was probably as valid as the first, and that in
consequence both became improbable or worthless, since their
content differs and each leads to quite a different theory. Fortunately, another theory suggests itself which brings into immediate
harmony both interpretations of the influencing apparatus. This
problem will be touched upon again towards the end of this
paper.

REGRESSIVE LOSS OF EGO BOUNDARIES. Attention may be called
now to a symptom in schizophrenia, which I have named "loss of
ego boundaries". This symptom is a complaint that "everyone"
knows the patient's thoughts, that his thoughts are not enclosed in
his own head, but are spread throughout the world and occur simultaneously in the heads of all persons. The patient seems no longer
to realize that he is a separate psychical entity, an ego with individual
boundaries. A sixteen-year-old patient in the Wagner-Jauregg Clinic
indulged in gay laughter whenever she was asked for her thoughts.
Catamnesis revealed that for a long while when being questioned,
she had believed I had been jesting; she knew that I must be familiar
with her thoughts, since they occurred at the same time in my own
head.

We are familiar with this infantile stage of thinking, in which a
strong belief exists that others know of the child's thoughts. Until
the child has been successful in its first lie, the parents are supposed
to know everything, even its most secret thoughts. Later on, in the
event that the child has been caught lying, this conception may be
formed again, now caused by the feeling of guilt. The striving for
the right to have secrets from which the parents are excluded is one

of the most powerful factors in the formation of the ego, especially in establishing and carrying out one's own will. The developmental stage observed in the above-mentioned case falls into this period, in which the child does not yet sense this right to privacy and does not yet doubt that the parents and educators know everything.[5]

The symptom with the content that "thoughts are given to them", the patients deduce subsequently from their thoughts. This must be attributed to the infantile impression originating in an earlier period in life, when the child knows nothing through its own efforts but obtains all its knowledge from others: how to make use of its limbs, its language, its thoughts. At that period all is "given to" the child, all joy and all sorrow, and it is difficult to evaluate what share the child itself has in its accomplishments.[6] The sudden discovery that it is able to accomplish a task without the help of others is greeted by the child with a great deal of surprise and excitement. It is probable, therefore, that this symptom represents a

[5] This would fall into the period before the first successful lie, which occurs very early in infancy. Lies fabricated in the first year of life are nothing unusual; they can be observed especially in children who resist the regular elimination of bodily wastes when, by means of grimaces, gestures and inarticulated words, they mislead the training person into believing that they have had satisfactory evacuation. The educator who allows herself to be deceived by the child must ultimately look to divine guidance in order to keep the child within the truth, when the latter, to gain forbidden pleasure, begins to enjoy the practice of lying. Very soon the time arrives when recourse to the highest authority of omniscience becomes necessary. The introduction of the omniscient God in the educational system becomes, indeed, a necessity, since, *de facto*, children learn to lie from parents and upbringers, who by misrepresentations and unkept promises make the child obey and teach him to disguise his true purposes. In order to safeguard the success of education, teachers cannot but transfer the power of omniscience to God—an authority which they themselves have abandoned. The incomprehensible nature of this deity precludes the possibility of practising deception on him. Nevertheless, many children do not submit even to this authority, continually test their God with regard to his omniscience, and not infrequently actually succeed in unmasking him as a phantom of the dethroned parental, specifically paternal, power.

[6] In the discussion of this paper at the Vienna Psycho-analytic Society, Freud emphasized that the infant's conception that others knew its thoughts has its source in the process of learning to speak. Having obtained its language from others, the infant has also received thoughts from them; and the child's feeling that others know his thoughts as well as that others have "made" him the language and, along with it, his thoughts, has therefore some basis in reality.

regression to this particular stage of infancy. But this special period of infancy presents a problem: How far back does it go? What causes the formation of the ego and, as a reaction to the outer world, the ego boundaries, and what arouses the realization of individuality, of self, as a distinct psychical unit?

Theoretically we cannot assume that the ego begins to take form earlier than the time of object finding. The latter comes with gratification and renunciation of instinctual drives, whereas an awareness of the outer world, independent of the infant's drives and desires, is established only gradually. It is hardly possible that the sex instincts should have a greater influence upon the development of this awareness than the drive to be nourished. To be sure, the sex instincts will soon take on a special significance which must not be underestimated. But for the time being, it should be stated that there is a stage when no objects of the outer world exist, and therefore there is no realization that one has an ego.

At that period there nevertheless exist desires and drives, and a specific urge to obtain mastery over whatever stimulates the sex organs is observable.

SOME THEORETICAL SPECULATIONS. The developmental stage that precedes the stage of object finding has been recognized as that of *identification*. This became evident from the analysis of neurotics, in whom the inability to obtain possession of objects of gratification, or to reach goals of pleasure, was seen to be due to their identification with the objects. The neurotic himself simply stands for what attracts him in the outer world; he has not found his way to the outer world and, therefore, is unable to develop an adequate ego in his stunted, exclusively libidinal relationships. This peculiar organization of libido has been termed narcissistic. The libido in such cases has been directed towards the neurotic's own personality; it is attached to his own ego and not the objects of the outer world. Observations and theoretical considerations, especially those of Freud, have led to the assumption that this libido organization characterizes the beginning of psychical development, the "objectless" period, and that, at any rate, this libido organization must be considered a correlate, if not a cause, of the "objectlessness". This organization of libido corresponds also to the stage of intellectual development in which the person considers all the sensory stimuli he receives as endogenous and immanent. At this stage of development the psyche does not yet perceive that intervals of time and space exist between the object from which the stimulus emanates and the sensory response.

The next stage of development is then that of an outward projection of the stimulus and the attributing of this stimulus to a distant object, hence a stage of distancing and objectivation of the intellect, and along with this a transfer of libido to the discovered, or rather, self-created, outer world. As a safeguard to this psychical achievement, and as a kind of critical authority for objectivation, there is evolved at the same time the faculty of distinguishing between objectivity and subjectivity, an awareness of reality, which enables the individual to recognize his inner experiences as distinct from the outer stimuli—in other words, to regard inner experiences as internal and not to confuse them with the objects of sensory response.

This correlative developmental process, however, is apt to meet with inhibitions. There are inhibitions from the intellectual side, or as we say, from the ego—the chief weapon of which is the intellect—and there are inhibitions that arise from the transference of libido in various stages of development, and with various results depending upon the relation of the ego to the libido. These points of inhibition are called, after Freud, fixation-points. In most cases the factor that causes ego disturbances, seems to lie in lesions of the libido. Thus, it is clear from Freud's interpretation that paranoia is a reaction to repressed homosexuality. The prohibition against finding an object for the homosexual drive, which results in an inhibition of the transference of homosexual libido organization, should be recognized as originating from within and remaining within. This projection is a defensive measure of the ego against the renounced homosexual libido that emerges with onrushing force out of repression. Libidinal inhibition leads to intellectual inhibition, which may be manifested in impaired judgment, or in insanity. An internal psychical process due to displacement and projection is mistaken for an external one, which leads to more or less marked "effective weakness of judgment", with the accompanying reactions of the psyche quantitatively and qualitatively determined by the morbid process.

We may say that in the case of an impaired libido organization, the ego finds itself facing the task of mastering an insane outer world, and hence behaves insanely.[7]

In the neuropsychoses that usually appear in later life, with a

[7] The cases in which inhibition endangers the intellect primarily are to be attributed to dementia.

history of previous relative psychic health, it is not difficult to observe that the impairment of the ego is caused by an impairment of the libido. However, in cases of psychosis that develop gradually and insidiously, beginning with earliest infancy, we may assume not so much a successive impairment of libido and ego as a correlative inhibition, primarily, of the entire development of the individual. The one group of instinctual drives does not develop normally, and this is paralleled by an arrest of the functions of the other group of drives and by a simultaneous development of secondary relations, which are to be regarded as attempts at self-cure and at adaptation to the functional disturbance by means of compensations and over-compensations. Furthermore, there occur regressions on the part of functions which have developed normally but which, whenever there is a marked discordance between the diseased and the normal portions of the psyche, abandon their normal level and retreat, for the purpose of adaptation, to the lower level of the impaired functions. During this retreat, there may arise various temporary or permanent symptom formations of different clinical types; and from these develop all mixed psychotic formations. The existence of these partial processes and their great variety with regard to levels of regression at a given moment requires careful consideration. In considering inhibitions of instinctual drives we must constantly keep in mind that all inhibited drives are capable of being transformed into, or being discharged as, anxiety. To quote Freud, "It may be said that, in a certain theoretical sense, symptoms are formed only in order to forestall an otherwise inevitable development of anxiety".

IV

We have learned from Freud that the projection of the homosexual libido in paranoia is to be regarded as a defensive measure of the ego against an inopportune and socially reprehensible sexual urge pressing from the unconscious. Is it possible to regard the projection of the patient's own body in the case of Miss Natalija as an analogous situation? Naturally, the projection would have to subserve the defence of that libido which belongs to the patient's own body, and which has become either too extensive or too inopportune in its demands for the patient to be able to tolerate it as her own. It is also necessary to assume that this projection pertains only to the libido of the body and not to the libido of the psychic ego

as well, that, moreover, the libido of the psychic ego [8] has facilitated
the defence against the bodily libido because it was, so to speak,

[8] The projection of the libido position of the psychic ego produces the
symptoms of simple paranoia, the mechanism of which was discovered by
Freud. In what follows we shall omit from consideration the fact that ego-
libido is necessarily homosexual in its strivings, that is, attracted by the sex
which the ego itself represents. We shall describe briefly only one mechanism, which appears to be out of harmony with object-libido and which is
exemplified by the symptomatology of our patient, Miss Natalija.

The patient reports: After she had rejected her suitor, she felt that he
suggested that her mother and she strike up a friendship with his sister-in-
law, so that the patient might be more amenable to a later proposal on his
part. What appears here as suggestion on the suitor's part is nothing more
than the projection of the patient's own unconscious inclination to accept
the proposal of marriage. She had rejected the proposal not without inner
conflict and had vacillated between accepting and rejecting her suitor. She
gave realization in action to the rejection, while she projected her inclination
to accept the proposal on to the object of her conflicting desires and made
it appear as the sensory effect of an influence on the part of the object, or
in other words as her symptom.

The patient was ambivalent towards her suitor, and projected one side
of the conflict, the positive libidinal one, while manifesting in action the
negative side, the rejection, because this procedure was in conformity with
her ego. The choice, which in this instance has projection as its outcome,
may in other cases be the reverse one. Here I am merely calling attention
to the mechanism of partial projection of ambivalent tendencies.

A special contribution to the subject of the projection mechanism, which
also made me aware of this principle, was made by Dr. Helene Deutsch
in her discussion of this paper at the Vienna Psycho-analytic Society. A
schizophrenic patient had the feeling that her friends always laid down
their work when she herself began to work and that they sat down whenever
she stood up; in brief, that others were always performing the opposite of
what she herself was doing. The patient merely felt this; she could not
possibly see it, since she was blind. Dr. Deutsch regarded the symptom as
a projection of one of two tendencies present in every one of her patient's
actions—namely, the tendency to do and the tendency not to do. This
interpretation was confirmed by cases presented by other discussers. On
this occasion Freud proposed the formulation that it is ambivalence that
makes the projection mechanism possible. Once expressed, this thesis
appears self-evident. It has corollary in another contention of Freud's,
to the effect that ambivalence produces repression. This has as its natural
consequence the formulation mentioned above, since only what is repressed
is projected, in so far as boundaries between the unconscious and the conscious still obtain. The entire problem furnishes special justification for
Bleuler's term "schizophrenia", and at the same time corroborates Pötzl's
views discussed in footnote 14.

The present paper shows how, albeit unconsciously, I had been demon-
strating Freud's formulation.

ashamed of it. That a projection mechanism has been chosen for the purpose of defence—a mechanism belonging to the primary functioning of the ego in the process of object finding—gives us reason to believe that we are here dealing with a libido position which is coëval with the beginnings of intellectual object finding and which is achieved either by regression or by the persistence of a vestigial phenomenon (*Resterscheinung*—Freud), which has been for years and up to the onset of the illness effectively compensated or concealed. In regressions, however, there is always an effort to reach the formerly uninhibited libido positions. In paranoia, regression reaches a stage when homosexual object choice has not yet come under the prohibition of the ego and there is free homosexual libida which is only later subjected to repression at the behest of the cultural demands of the ego.

The libido directed towards a person's own self, which the ego tries to get rid of by projecting its own body, naturally, is characteristic of a period when it was still free from conflict with the demands of other love-objects. This period must coincide with the developmental stage of the psyche in which object finding still occurs within the individual's own body, and when the latter is still regarded as part of the outer world.

I am intentionally differentiating between object choice and object finding. By the former, I mean only libidinal cathexis; by the latter, the intellectual awareness of this cathexis. An object is *found* by the intellect, and *chosen* by the libido. These processes may occur either simultaneously or in sequence, but for my purpose they are to be regarded as distinct.

The projection of one's body may, then, be traced back to the developmental stage in which one's own body is the goal of the object finding. This must be the time when the infant is discovering his body, part by part, as the outer world, and is still groping for his hands and feet as though they were foreign objects. At this time, everything that "happens" to him emanates from his own body; his psyche is the object of stimuli arising in his own body but acting upon it as if produced by outer objects. These disjecta membra are later on pieced together and systematized into a unified whole under the supervision of a psychic unity that receives all sensations of pleasure and pain from these separate parts. This process takes place by means of identification with one's own body. The ego, thus discovered, is cathected with the available libido; in accordance with the psychic nature of the ego, narcissism develops;

and, in accordance with the function of individual organs as sources of pleasure, autoeroticism results.

But if the psycho-analytic theories previously employed are correct, this object finding within one's own organs, which can be regarded as parts of the outer world only by projection, must be preceded by a stage of identification with a narcissistic libido position,[9] and it is necessary to assume two successive stages of identification and projection.

The projection which participated in the object finding within one's own organs would, then, be the second phase of the preceding stage, although the part that depends upon the postulated identification has still to be discovered.

I am, then, assuming the existence of these two successive phases of identification and projection in object finding and object choice within one's own body.

I do not run counter to psycho-analytic conceptions in contending that the individual comes into the world as an organic unity in which libido and ego are not yet separated, and all available libido is related to that organic unity, which does not deserve the name "ego" (i.e., a psychical self-protective organization) any more than does the cell. In this situation the individual is equally a sexual and an individual being, simultaneously performing ego and reproductive functions, like the cell that takes nourishment up to the time when it divides. This stage of the newly born child is biological up to the time of conception, but must be regarded as psychological from the time when—at an indeterminable stage of fœtal life—cerebral development takes place. From the point of view of libido, we may say that the newly born child is a sexual being. I am in accord with Freud's assumption that the individual's first renunciation is the renunciation of the protection of the mother's body imposed upon the libido and accompanied by that expression of anxiety, the birth-cry. However, once this first trauma is over and no discontent arises to bring the infant into a clash with himself and with the environment, he is in complete possession of his own libido and knows nothing of the outer world, not even that part of the world which he will soon discover within himself. It is this stage of

[9] Freud has already indicated in his paper on the Schreber biography, that the libido in schizophrenia is located at a stage even earlier than autoeroticism. I arrive at the same conclusion by a different route, and I take the liberty of presenting this fact as proof of the correctness of Freud's contentions.

identity that precedes the first projection for the purpose of object finding within one's own body. This stage did not come about because of that psychic activity which may be called identification, but is present from the beginning. Nevertheless the result is the same as in actively established identity—absolute self-satisfaction, no outer world, no objects. Let us designate this stage as the innate narcissistic one. In this situation the libido is directed outward, first cathects the subject's own body by the indirect way of projection, and returns by way of self-discovery to the ego. In the meantime, the ego has undergone a decided alteration under the influence of these first psychic stirrings, which one may call experience, and is now again cathected by libido. Let us call this stage: acquired narcissism. The latter finds a considerable quantity of innate narcissism already present and is superimposed on it. The condition of innate narcissism normally remains attached for all time to the organs and their functions, and is in constant conflict with the various further stages of ego development which, with the assistance of anxiety and judgment, take place under the ægis of all the faculties that have been gradually acquired in the meantime. The struggle is carried on, at first, chiefly in the sphere of excretory functions and of the autoerotic sources of pleasure, since these are the spheres that give rise to the greatest difficulties in the individual's relation to the environment. Nevertheless, we must definitely understand that throughout life the ego develops with constant shiftings in the narcissistic libido position, that man in his struggle for existence is constantly compelled to find and recognize himself anew, and that the acquisition of narcissism is immanent in culture and is conceivable only on the basis of intact inborn narcissism that serves as a source of nourishment and regeneration. This constant struggle centring about the self occurs in various degrees in relation to various instinctual drives; it concerns homo- and hetero-sexuality and every libido component in different degrees at different times, and provokes various reactions, compensations, superstructures and eliminations. These secondary psychical formations then enter again into combination and produce insoluble dynamic, qualitative, relative and modal relations, resulting in a great variety of character types and symptoms. The development both of the ego and of the libido—so far as concerns either alone or in their relation to each other—may become arrested and may set up goals of regression at as many points as there are primary, secondary, tertiary (etc.) factors of relationship and development.

PATHOLOGICAL PROJECTION AS A DEFENCE AGAINST NARCISSISTIC REGRESSION OF LIBIDO. The entire problem is further complicated by the elements of time and space and so made insoluble. Let us suppose that the projection of one's own body is a pathological repetition of that psychical stage when the individual was endeavouring to discover his body by means of projection. It would not be too much to say that just as the projection in normal primary development has been successful because the innate narcissistic libido position had to be renounced under the attack of outer stimuli, so also pathological projection takes place because there has developed an accumulation of narcissistic libido analogous to the primary narcissism, though here anachronistic, regressive or fixated, but resembling it in character in so far as it isolates the individual from the outer world. Hence, projection of one's own body may be regarded as a defence against a libido position corresponding to the end of fœtal existence and the beginning of extrauterine development. Freud, indeed, has not hesitated to declare, in his *Introductory Lectures*, that psychological problems are to be traced back to intrauterine existence.

EXPLANATION OF SEVERAL PSYCHOTIC PHENOMENA ON THIS BASIS. These considerations may be used as a starting point for the explanation of various schizophrenic symptoms. Is it not possible that catalepsy, *flexibilitas cerea*, corresponds to the stage when man senses his own organs as foreign, as not belonging to himself, and as being dominated by an outside force? A similar instance is the symptom of having one's limbs moved by someone. This symptom reproduces especially well the situation in which one's own body becomes strange and, so to speak, part of an outer world dominated by outer forces. May we not say that catatonic stupor, which represents a complete rejection of the outer world, is a return to the uterus? May not these severest catatonic symptoms be the ultimate refuge of a psyche that has given up even the most primitive ego functions and has retreated *in toto* to the fœtal and nursing stages, because it cannot use in the present state of its libido even the simplest ego functions that maintain the relation to the outer world? The catatonic symptom, the negativistic stare of the schizophrenic, is nothing else than a renunciation of the outer world expressed in "organ language". Does not also the "nursing reflex" in the terminal stages of general paralysis indicate such a regression to infancy? [10]

[10] Many patients are actually aware of this regression to infancy and to the embryonic stage—the latter, though, only as a threat of further illness.

The psychic correlate of *flexibilitas cerea* and that stage in which man regards himself as a part of the outer world, lacks consciousness of his own volition and of his own ego boundaries, is the feeling that everyone knows and is in possession of the thoughts of the patient. In the period here duplicated pathologically there are indeed no thoughts, but even thoughts are subjected, as already stated above, to the same process of being regarded at first as coming from the outer world before they are accounted among the functions of the ego. Thoughts must first be assimilated into the consciousness of ego-unity before they can be an automatic ego-function; and this cannot occur before the intellect has advanced to the stage of memory perceptions. Freud has taught that this, too, is a later process, and that it is preceded by the stage of hallucinations of memory pictures, that is, a stage when the perceptions actually appear in the outer world and are not regarded as internal occurrences. Moreover, this stage of hallucinatory perceptions, in itself representing a kind of objectivation, object finding and object choice, also belongs to the first period of life. The regression, of course, does not occur equally in all psychical faculties and relationships. The capacity for thinking with memory perceptions is still intact, but the libido is already degraded to the nursing stage and sets up a relation with the thinking faculty as it exists. The consciousness of personality has been lost, and this loss is shown in the patient's inability to locate his intact psychical inventory. The

A patient said to me: "I feel that I am constantly becoming younger and smaller. Now I am four years old. Shortly, I shall get into diapers and then back into mother."

Dr. Helene Deutsch, during the discussion of this paper, reported the case of a thirty-one year old female schizophrenic who wet and soiled her bed and stated as her justification that "they were making a baby of her".

On the same occasion Freud, referring especially to the influencing machine of Miss Natalija, and to the interchangeability of sexuality and death, called attention to the significance of the mode of burial of Egyptian mummies. To place the mummy in a case resembling the human body suggests the idea of the return to "mother earth", the return to the mother's body in death. Freud's reference shows how as a compensation for the bitterness of death, men take for granted the bliss of existence in the uterus. The fantasy of return to the uterus is, then, an atavistic one, a preformed fantasy; and as such it may be added to the "primal fantasies" postulated by Freud. This fantasy appears symptomatically in schizophrenia as the pathological reality of the regressing, disintegrating psyche. The mummy returns to the mother's body by physical, and the schizophrenic by psychical death. ("*Mutterleibsphantasie*"—an expression, as far as I know, first used by Gustav Grüner.)

patient who declares that his thoughts and feelings are in all people's minds merely declares, in words and concepts derived from the memory-reserve of a later developmental stage that his libido finds itself at the stage when it is still identical with the outer world, still has no ego-boundaries set up against the outer world, and his libido is now compelled therefore to renounce the normal intellectual object relations in so far as these depend upon the degraded libido position.

These feelings and this mode of expression depend upon the intactness of the psyche's ability to operate with memory perceptions. This faculty, too, may undergo regression.[11] In this case the patient hallucinates. The libido has retreated behind the stage of identification, the intellect no longer knows how to establish a relation to the outer world, even by means of identification. The psyche is approaching closer and closer to the mother's womb.

Furthermore, may not perhaps "picture-seeing in planes" represent a stage of the development of the visual sense still earlier than the hallucinatory stage?

V

I have stated that narcissistic self-discovery and self-choice repeat themselves with every new acquistion of the ego, to this effect, that, under the guidance of conscience and judgment, each new acquisition is either rejected, or cathected with libido and attributed to the ego. Let us call this narcissism, psychic narcissism, and let us contrast it with the organic narcissism that guarantees in the unconscious the unity and functioning of the organism. There is nothing new in calling attention to the great dependence of physical health, and even of life itself, upon what is called love of life, or in the reminder that one can actually die of a "broken heart", and that, as Ostwald mentions in his book on *Great Men*, university professors emeritus often die soon after they have been absolved of their duties, even when they have previously been in the best of health. They die, not of old age, but because they lose the love of life when they

[11] For further discussion of this subject, see Freud: Metapsychologische Ergänzung zur Traumlehre. *Internationale Zeitschrift für Psychoanalyse*, VI, 1916/17. This work appeared while the present paper was in proofs. I am pleased to be able to refer to the many points of agreement between my contentions and Freud's in his paper, of which I had no knowledge at the time. (Translated under the title "Metapsychological Supplement to the Theory of Dreams: *Collected Papers*, IV, 137–152.—Ed.)

can no longer perform the duties they have loved. Freud tells of a famous musician who succumbed to his illness because of the discontinuance of his creative work.

THE DISTRIBUTION OF NARCISSISTIC LIBIDO AND ITS SIGNIFICANCE FOR: HYPOCHRONDRIASIS, "ENTFREMDUNG", AND PROJECTION. We must assume that the libido flows through the entire body, perhaps like a substance (Freud's view), and that the integration of the organism is effected by a libido tonus, the oscillations of which correspond to the oscillations of psychic narcissism and object libido.[12] Upon this tonus depends the resistance to illness and death. Love of life has saved many a man who was given up by physicians as incurable.

Whenever there occurs an influx of organic narcissism to a given organ as a site of predilection,[13] there may also occur a consciousness of organ relations and organic functions which in normal life are relegated to an unconscious and vegetative rôle. Analogously, objects cathected by psychic narcissism and object love come to consciousness wherever the cathexis has reached a sufficient degree of strength. This influx of libido directs attention to the organ and

[12] Melancholia is the illness, the mechanism of which consists in the disintegration of psychic narcissism, in the renunciation of love for the psychic ego. Melanchola, in pure culture, is the paradigm of the dependence of the organic upon the psychic narcissism. The separation of libido from the psychic ego, i.e., the rejection and condemnation of the *raison d'être* of the psychic person, brings with it the rejection of the physical person, the tendency to physical self-destruction. There occurs a consecutive separation of the libido from those organs which guarantee the functioning and the value of the physical individuality, a separation by means of which the organs' function is impaired or given up. Hence appetite is lost, constipation occurs, menstruation ceases, and potency is lost—all as a result of unconscious mechanisms. This failure of function is to be traced to the destruction of the respective organic libido positions which are essentially vegetative, i.e., unconscious; it is thus to be strictly differentiated from the conscious, deliberate suicidal tendency expressed in refusal of nourishment or in activities inimical to life.

Melancholia is the persecution psychosis without projection; its structure is due to a specific mechanism of identification. (Further discussion on this point in my paper Diagnostische Erörterungen auf Grund der Zustandsbilder der sogen. Kriegspsychosen, *Wiener med. Wochenschrift*, XXXVII–XXXVIII, 1916. While this paper was in proof, Freud's article Trauer und Melancholie [translated in *Collected Papers* IV, 152–173] appeared, to which I refer in this connection.)

[13] This involves the Freudian principle of the erotogenicity of organs, that is, of the erotogenic zones.

provides the consciousness of a transformation of the organ or its functions, i.e., the feeling of estrangement. This is the mechanism described by Freud as hypochondria. This influx of libido is followed by the turning away of the ego from the organ pathologically over-charged with libido, or from its functions; that is, by estrange-ment.[14] This is to be considered a defensive measure against the anxiety associated with hypochondria. The feeling of strangeness is a defence against libidinal cathexis, no matter whether it concerns

[14] Dr. Otto Pötzl suggested on a certain occasion (I do not remember whether it was in connection with a thesis of his own or as an addendum to theories of others) that the catatonic stare is an expression of the patient's inability to apportion his motor impulses disintegrated by the split of his volition into agonistic and antagonistic elements, so that a purposeful action may again be performed. (In Meyrinck's story, *Der Fluch der Kröte* ["The Curse of the Toad"], the milliped is unable to move a limb the moment he focuses his attention upon the activity of any one of his thousand legs.)

THEORY OF CATATONIA. Pötzl's conception is in harmony with the psycho-analytic theory that the regressive narcissistic libido undergoes a pathological division with the cathexis of the individual functions of the psyche and the organs so that the agonistic and antagonistic portions of the purposefully directed antithetical pair of forces are brought into the reach of awareness by the disturbance of the equilibrium between their respective libido quantities and are deprived of automatic functioning. This would be a special case of hypochondria and estrangement related to the anti-thetical pairs of forces with their respective specific consequences.

Pötzl's view does not contradict the assumption that the outer world may be eliminated as a result of regressive narcissistic libido, and it actually allows the application of the theory of hypochondria to further special points in the psycho-physical make-up of men. Pötzl's concept even sug-gests the hypothesis that there was in the life of man a period—a not definitely determinable one, it is true, and perhaps only potential—in which the activity of the antagonistic pair of forces was still automatic and had to be discovered and learned by the person himself as if from an alien outer world. This period may well be present in ontogenesis only as an "engram" of phylogenetic stages which comprised the origin of the now complex motor organs from the simplest single-tracked active formations. Regression in schizophrenia would then be traceable to those "engrams" of the oldest era of the race, and the theory would demand that these phylogenetic traces of function retain their capacity for being reactivated. We must not shrink from this hypothesis. It provides us with another idea to use in investigating problems in schizophrenia: perhaps this remarkable disease consists in just this—that the phylogenetic vestiges of function retain in many indivi-duals an extraordinary capacity for being reactivated. Psycho-analysis would have to make room for this conception, since psycho-analysis has already in many instances uncovered the roots of symptoms in the history of the species. From this it may perhaps be possible, via ontogenesis, to proceed

objects of the outer world, one's own body, or its parts. Of course, the estrangement does not cause the giving up of the unconscious libido position. The estrangement is not a destructive force but merely a denial of the pathological cathexis; it is an instance of the ostrich tactics of the ego, which may be very easily reduced *ad absurdum*, and which must ultimately be supplanted by other or more effective measures of defence.

When, in paranoia, the feeling of estrangement no longer affords protection, the libidinal drive towards the homosexual object is projected on to the latter and appears, by a reversal of direction, as aggression towards the loving one (the patient himself) in the form of a sense of persecution. Strangers become enemies. The enmity is a new and more energetic attempt at protection against the rejected unconscious libido.

The narcissistic organ libido in schizophrenia may undergo a similar transformation. The estranged organ—in our case, the entire body—appears as an outer enemy, as a machine used to afflict the patient.

THREE STAGES IN THE HISTORY OF THE DEVELOPMENT OF THE "INFLUENCING MACHINE". We are, then, compelled to distinguish three principal stages in the history of the "influencing machine":

(1) The sense of internal alteration produced by the influx of libido into a given organ (hypochondria).

(2) The feeling of estrangement produced by rejection, whereby the pathologically altered organs or their functions are so to speak denied and eliminated as something alien to the wholly or partially sound organs and functions accepted by the ego.

(3) The sense of persecution (*paranoia somatica*) arising from projection of the pathological alteration on to the outer world, (*a*) by attribution of the alteration to a foreign hostile power, (*b*) by the construction of the influencing machine as a summation of some or all of the pathologically altered organs (the whole body) projected outward. It is to be noted that among these organs the genitals take precedence in the projection.

to an explanation of the mysterious "electrical currents" complained of by patients. This paræsthesia may once have been a sensation that accompanied the first nerve and muscle functions. It is perhaps reminiscence of the sensation of the newly born being who enters the strange air of the external world out of the comfortable covering of the mother's womb, or for whom the latter is replaced by its first garments. The bed he first lay in, is perhaps that one which comes to the patient's consciousness when he feels himself, while lying in bed, electrified by invisible wires.

The assumption of an influx of libido into specific organs in the physiological sense of the word should receive proper consideration. On the basis of this assumption transient swellings of organs often observed in schizophrenia without inflammation and without an actual œdema may be interpreted as equivalents of erection, produced like erections of the penis and clitoris by an overflow of secretion resulting from libidinal charges of organs.[15]

VI

DIFFERENTIATION OF TWO TYPES OF PROJECTED OBJECTS IN THEIR RELATION TO THE "MACHINE". It is not at all surprising that the hostile apparatus is handled by persons who to an objective observer cannot but appear as love objects—suitors, lovers, physicians. All these persons are associated with sensuousness, deal with the body, and demand a transfer of libido to themselves. This is what actually occurs in normal situations. But the narcissistic libido, whenever too strongly fixated, cannot but regard this demand made by love objects as inimical, and looks upon the object as an enemy. It is to be noted, however, that another group of love objects— mother, the patient's present physician, close friends of the family— are not counted among the patient's persecutors but among the persecuted, compelled to share his fate in being subjected to the influencing machine. In contrast to paranoia, the persecuted and not the persecutors are organized into a passive conspiracy, and this conspiracy is of passive nature. Of this phenomenon the following explanation may be offered:

[15] These psychological assumptions are strongly supported from the organological standpoint by a report made some years ago by Fauser at Stuttgart on the presence of sexual secretion in the blood of dementia præcox patients, as demonstrated by Abderhalden's dialytic method. New and important findings in this connection are to be expected from Steinach's experiments. When the present paper was completed, there appeared in the *Münchner mediz. Wochenschrift*, No. 6, 1918, under the title: Umstimmungen der Homosexualität durch Austausch der Pubertätsdrüsen ("Transformations of Homosexuality by Exchange of Puberty Glands"), a very interesting and significant article by Steinach and Lichtenstern, which realized these expectations. After the completion of this paper there also appeared in the *Internationale Zeitschrift f. ärztl. Psa.*, Volume IV, 1917, an article by S. Ferenczi, Von Krankheits- und Pathoneurosen ("Disease- or Patho-Neuroses", in *Further Contributions to the Theory and Technique of Psychoanalysis*, p. 78–79, London, 1926) in which the assumption of the libidinal cathexis of individual organs in the sense above described appears to be applied with notable success.

It is noteworthy that the persecutors are all persons who live at some distance from the patient, whereas the persecuted belong to the closest circle of acquaintanceship and—including the physicians who are imagos of the father and hence also family members—represent a kind of constantly present family. Now, the family members are those love objects who because of their presence from the beginning of the patient's life are subjected to the narcissistic object choice by identification. To these persons our patient still applies this form of object choice in so far as she subjects them to her own fate, identifying herself with them. Normally, the demand for transfer of libido with respect to members of the family is not felt either as requiring the overcoming of any great distance or any substantial sacrifice of narcissism. In establishing an identification with these persons the patient follows a well-trodden path, which does not appear sufficiently inimical to the patient to force her to revolt against the cathexis of these objects and to regard them as hostile. It is different with lovers and suitors. These threaten a narcissistic position with their substantial demands for object libido and are, therefore, repulsed as enemies. The fact that these persons are spatially distant evokes a feeling of distance on the part of the libido. The transfer of libido *par distance* is felt as an extraordinary strong demand for the acknowledgement of an object position, as a demand for self-denial. This also holds for normal conditions. Spatial distance separating the beloved threatens the object libido; it even leads people ultimately to withdraw themselves and give up the object. To have to love at a distance is a difficult task, only unwillingly performed. Our patient, however, cannot simply give up her love objects in a normal way, because she has not cathected them normally. To those demanding much from her she can only react with the paranoid mechanism; to those demanding less, only with identification. I do not know why the persons who work the influencing machine are in my observation exclusively male. This may be due to faulty observation or to chance. Further investigations must clarify this point. However, that heterosexual objects can appear as persecutors in contradiction to Freud's theory of the exclusively homosexual genesis of paranoia, may be explained by the fact that the influencing machine corresponds to a regressive psychic stage in which the important distinction is not between the sexes but between narcissistic and object libido, and every object demanding a transfer of libido is regarded as hostile irrespective of its sex.

VII

After this long digression—which, I hope, will not be regarded as superfluous—we may return to the question of how even the ordinary, clinically familiar, influencing machine in its typical form can be a projection of the patient's body, as was true in the case of Miss Natalija. The answer should not be difficult to discover. If we do not want to assume that the machine has been established by successive substitutions of the parts of the patient's idea of his own body picture (*"wie Fuchs aus alopex"*),[16] and if we make use, instead of the genetality of the machine, as previously established, to explain the typical influencing machine, we may avail ourselves of the following considerations:

The regression of libido to the early infantile stage determines the re-transformation of the meanwhile genitally centralized libido into the pregenital stage, in which the entire body is a libidinal zone —in which the entire body is a genital. Such fantasies are also found in cases of narcissistically strongly cathected, sexually extremely infantile, neurosis. I have myself observed such cases. The fantasy originates in the intrauterine (mother's body) complex and usually has the content of the man's desire to creep completely into the genital from which he came, refusing to content himself with any lesser satisfaction. The entire individual is in this case a penis. Further, the road of identification with the father (the penis of the father) is overdetermined in the symptom formation of male patients. The symptom is also to be conceived as regression to a stage of diffuse narcissistic organ libido and is in most cases associated with genital impotence. The genital, too, is renounced.[17] The

[16] "Like fox from alopex"—a student parody on etymological derivations consisting of the stringing together of rhyming and nearly rhyming words. —*Translator.*

[17] This renunciation of the genitalia is felt by the male schizophrenic as a loss of virility, which is "drained off" from him, or else as a direct transformation into a woman, corresponding to the infantile notion of boys that there is only one kind of genital, namely their own, and that those of women are the result of castration and really represent a loss of the genital. The castration complex is often combined with the infantile identification of semen with urine resulting from urethral eroticism. I have observed an attack of castration anxiety while catheterizing a schizophrenic who refused to empty his bladder. He maintained that I was practising coitus with him by means of the catheter and that I had emptied him of all his semen. Thus his retention of urine appears as a refusal to yield semen representing his virility. The patient's playing with excrement is explicable by the

same situation is revealed by the lack of genitalia in the influencing machine of Miss N. The intrauterine fantasy and the identification [18] with mother probably find expression in the dome-like lid of the trunk which perhaps represented the patient's mother during pregnancy. The enclosed batteries are perhaps the child, which is the patient herself. The fact that the child is equated with the batteries, that is, with a machine, lends further support to the supposition that the person feels himself to be a genital, and this all the more because the machine's lack of genitalia stands for the pregenital—in a certain sense, non-genital stage.

The construction of the influencing apparatus in the form of a machine therefore represents a projection of the entire body, now wholly a genital.

The fact that the machine in dreams is nothing but a representation of the genital raised to primacy in no way contradicts the possibility that it is in schizophrenia a symbol of the entire body conceived as a penis, and hence a representative of the pregenital epoch. The patient has indeed not lost the ideational content of his past life. The picture of the genital as a representation of sexuality has been retained in the psychical apparatus. It is therefore used as a means of representation, a mode of expression, a language in which phenomena existing prior to this means of expression are communicated. Here the genital is merely a symbol of a sexuality older than the symbolism and than any means of social expression. The picture, then, is in the language of the later genital period nothing but: "I am sexuality." But the context is, "I am wholly a genital". This test has of course to be translated into the language suited to the actual libido conditions.

It is possible that the ordinary influencing apparatus in the form of the machine owes its existence simply to the fact that its early stages were not formed gradually, because the pathological process seized too precipitately upon remote phases of existence. It is also possible that the early stages were not noticed by observers and not reported by the patient, or not recognized and evaluated as early stages. Thus the connection between the influencing apparatus of Miss N. and the ordinary influencing machine has been lost to science.

narcissistically rooted conception that fæces and urine are parts of the body. Coprophagia is not inhibited by the thought that the excreta are nothing else than the body from which they come.

[18] The proof of this identification derived from symbolic language has already been given in the dream of "the woman without a head", footnote 4.

But the contradiction between the two concepts—on the one hand, that the machine form of the influencing apparatus originated through successive distortions of the influencing apparatus that represents the projection of the body, and, on the other hand, that the machine form of the influencing apparatus represents, like the machine in a dream, a projection of the genitalia, is now abolished. The evolution by distortion of the human apparatus into a machine is a projection that corresponds to the development of the pathological process which converts the ego into a diffuse sexual being, or —expressed in the language of the genital period—into a genital, a machine independent of the aims of the ego and subordinated to a foreign will.[19] It is no longer subordinated to the will of the ego, but dominates it. Here, too, we are reminded of the astonishment of boys when they become aware for the first time of erection. And the fact that the erection is shortly conceived as an exceptional and mysterious feat, supports the assumption that erection is felt to be a thing independent of the ego, a part of the outer world not completely mastered.

[19] Indeed, the machines produced by man's ingenuity and created in the image of man are unconscious projections of man's bodily structure. Man's ingenuity seems to be unable to free itself from its relation to the unconscious. [See Hanns Sachs' The Delay of the Machine Age in *The Psychoanalytic Quarterly*, vol. II, 1933.]

A SUPPLEMENT TO FREUD'S
"HISTORY OF AN INFANTILE NEUROSIS" *
(1928)

By Ruth Mack Brunswick

This article—best explained by its title—was brought up to date by the author in the following note to the editor of the Reader: "The analysis of the Wolf-man *reported here occupied the five months from October 1926 to February 1927. Thereafter the* Wolf-Man *was well and relatively productive in a small bureaucratic capacity.*

"It was after about two years that he returned for the resumption of an analysis as rewarding to me as to him. There was no trace of psychosis or of patanoid trends. Potency disturbances of a strictly neurotic character had occurred in the course of a sudden, violent and repetitive love-relation. This time the analysis, extending somewhat irregularly over a period of several years, revealed new material and important, hitherto forgotten memories, all relating to the complicated attachment to the pre-schizophrenic girl and her small brother. The therapeutic results were excellent and remained so, according to my last information in 1940, despite major personal crises resulting in only a small measure from world events. . . ."

New York,   R. M. B.
September, 1945.

I. Description of the Present Illness

In October, 1926, the patient whom we have learned to know as the Wolf-Man of Freud's "History of an Infantile Neurosis" consulted Professor Freud, whom he had seen from time to time since the completion of his analysis in 1920. Circumstances which I shall relate shortly had wrought great changes in the Wolf-Man's way of living. The former millionaire was now earning barely enough to feed his ailing wife and himself. Nevertheless, things went smoothly

* Reprinted from *The International Journal of Psycho-Analysis*, IX, 1928, p. 439.

with him until the summer of 1926, when certain symptoms appeared which caused him to consult Freud. At this time it was suggested that if he felt in need of analysis he should come to me. He presented himself in my office at the beginning of October, 1926.

He was suffering from a hypochondriacal *idée fixe*. He complained that he was the victim of a nasal injury caused by electrolysis, which had been used in the treatment of obstructed sebaceous glands of the nose. According to him, the injury consisted varyingly of a scar, a hole, or a groove in the scar tissue. The contour of the nose was ruined. Let me state at once that nothing whatsoever was visible on the small, snub, typically Russian nose of the patient. And the patient himself, while insisting that the injury was all too noticeable, nevertheless realized that his reaction to it was abnormal. For this reason, having exhausted all dermatological resources, he consulted Freud. If nothing could be done for his nose, then something must be done for his state of mind, whether the cause was real or imagined. At first sight, this sensible and logical point of view seemed due to the insight won from the earlier analysis. But only in part did this prove to be the motive for the present analysis. On the other hand, the insight was undoubtedly responsible for the one atypical characteristic of the case: its ultimate accessibility to analysis, which otherwise would certainly not have been present.

He was in a state of despair. Having been told that nothing could be done for his nose because nothing was wrong with it, he felt unable to go on living in what he considered his irreparably mutilated state. He expressed the complaint voiced in all his earlier illnesses: as a child when he soiled his drawers and thought he had dysentery; as a young man, when he acquired gonorrhœa; and finally in so many of the later situations of his analysis with Freud. This complaint, containing the nucleus of his pathogenic mother-identification, was: "I can't go on living like this any more" ("So kann ich nicht mehr leben"). The "veil" of his earlier illness completely enveloped him. He neglected his daily life and work because he was engrossed, to the exclusion of all else, in the state of his nose. On the street he looked at himself in every shop-window; he carried a pocket mirror which he took out to look at every few minutes. First he would powder his nose; a moment later he would inspect it and remove the powder. He would then examine the pores, to see if they were enlarging, to catch the hole, as it were, in its moment of growth and development. Then he would again powder his nose, put away the mirror, and a moment later begin the process anew.

His life was centred on the little mirror in his pocket, and his fate depended on what it revealed or was about to reveal.

The maid who opened the door in my apartment was afraid of him, because, as she said, he always rushed past her like a lunatic to the long mirror in the poorly-lighted reception hall. He would not sit down and wait, like the other patients, to be admitted to my office; he walked incessantly up and down the small hall, taking out his mirror and examining his nose in this light and that. It was in this condition that he began his analysis with me.

I would at this point ask the reader to refresh his memory by re-reading the fragment of this patient's story published by Freud under the title "From the History of an Infantile Neurosis". All the childhood material appears there; nothing new whatsoever made its appearance in the analysis with me. The source of the new illness was an unresolved remnant of the transference, which after fourteen years, under the stress of peculiar circumstances, became the basis for a new form of an old illness.

II. 1920–1923

Before giving a detailed description of the present illness and its treatment, it is necessary to recount in some detail the life and circumstances of the patient during and following his analysis with Freud.

It will be remembered that the Wolf-Man was very rich, and that he had inherited his money from his father, who died in the patient's twenty-first year—two years after the patient's gonorrhœal infection and two years before he came to Freud. It will also be recalled that the patient was exceedingly neurotic in his attitude towards money. He frequently, and on his own admission without any justification, accused his mother of appropriating his inheritance. He was boastful, and ascribed to money an undue importance and power. Even his sister's death proved a welcome event, because by it he became the sole heir of his father. He was excessively extravagant in his personal habits, especially in regard to clothes.

The Russian revolution and Bolshevist *régime* changed all this. The Wolf-Man and his family lost literally all their money and all their property as well. After a distressing period, during which the patient had neither money nor work, he finally secured a small position in Vienna.

At the end of 1919 he had come out of Russia and returned to

Freud for a few months of analysis, with the purpose, successfully accomplished, of clearing up his hysterical constipation. He apparently believed that he would be able to pay for these months of analysis although with what basis is hard to say. In any case, he was unable to do so. Moreover, at the end of this time, the Wolf-Man had no work and nothing to live on; his wife was ill, and he was in desperate straits. Freud then collected a sum of money for this former patient, who had served the theoretical ends of analysis so well, and repeated this collection every spring for six years. This money enabled the patient to pay his wife's hospital bills, to send her to the country, and occasionally to take a short holiday himself.

At the beginning of 1922 an acquaintance of the patient came to Vienna from Russia, bringing what was left of the patient's family jewels. They were supposedly worth thousands of dollars, but later attempts to sell them disclosed the fact that their value did not exceed a few hundred dollars. The patient told no one except his wife about the jewels; and she, womanlike, immediately advised him not to tell Freud, because, she said, he would surely over-estimate their value and refuse to give any more aid. The necklace and earrings were his entire capital; if he were forced to sell them to live on the money he would have nothing to fall back on. He therefore told no one that the jewels were in his possession. In his fear of losing Freud's help, it evidently did not occur to him that Freud would never have considered permitting the patient to use up his little capital. He took his wife's advice because, as he admitted, it coincided with some inner feeling of his own. And from this time on his greed for money from Freud increased: he was always wondering how large the next present would be—it varied from year to year with the amount collected; how it should be expended, etc. The patient now acquired a lack of candour remarkable in a hitherto compulsively honest individual. He began concealing financial facts from his wife, and in the period of inflation, he who had always been unduly cautious, speculated and lost considerable amounts of money. In all his financial affairs there now appeared a certain dishonesty which, despite his formerly neurotic attitude, had never before been present.

Nevertheless, to all intents and purposes, the patient was well. The man who had come with his own physician and orderly, who had been unable even to dress himself, was now working hard at any task obtainable and supporting to the best of his ability a sick and disappointed wife. His interests and ambitions, in comparison with those of his youth, were limited. Apparently he was paying this price for his former illness and its cure. However, he continued to paint, and in the summer of 1922 he did a portrait of himself which required him to spend considerable time looking at himself in the mirror.

In April, 1923, Professor Freud had his first minor operation on his mouth. When the Wolf-Man went to see him before the summer to receive his money he was shocked at Freud's appearance. He thought little about it, however, and went on his vacation. While in the country he began to masturbate with obscene pictures. He was not excessive, and was not particularly troubled by the appearance of this symptom. His wife was often ill and disinclined towards coitus. When he returned to Vienna in the autumn, Freud was again operated on, and this time the serious nature of his illness was known to all of us, including the Wolf-Man.

III. History of the Present Illness

I shall now attempt to relate as closely as possible in the patient's own words the story of his present illness, written down for me by him immediately after the close of our analysis in February, 1927.

In November, 1923, the patient's mother arrived from Russia. When he met her at the station, he observed a black wart on her nose. In reply to his question, she told him that she had been to various doctors, most of whom told her to have the wart removed. However, the doctors were themselves uncertain of its nature, because of its curious way of coming and going. At times it was present and at times it was not. Therefore she had refused to have it operated on, and was now very glad of her decision. But the patient noticed that she had become somewhat hypochondriacal; she was afraid of draughts and dust and infection of all kinds.

At the beginning of 1924 the patient began to have trouble with his teeth, which until 1921 had been particularly good. At that time it had been necessary to extract two teeth, the first he had ever lost. The dentist who performed this extraction and who prophesied that the patient would soon lose all his teeth because of the violence of his bite, was named—Dr. Wolf! Because of his prophecy the patient did not return to this dentist, but went instead to various others, with none of whom he was entirely satisfied. Once, while having an infected root-canal treated, he fainted. From time to time small pustules were present on his gums.

At this time certain changes went into effect in the office where the patient was employed, which resulted in the loss of his hitherto independent position and his transfer to another, this time exceedingly gruff and inconsiderate, superior.

The chief symptom of the present illness appeared in February, 1924, when the patient began to have queer thoughts about his nose. Always dissatisfied with his small snub nose, he had been teased about it in school, and called Mops (pug dog). At the age of puberty a nasal catarrh had caused sores on his nose and upper lip, requiring salves for their treatment. These were prescribed by the same doctor who later treated him for another catarrh, namely, the gonorrhœal. During the analysis with Freud, the patient had been treated by a leading Viennese dermatologist, Professor X., for obstructed sebaceous glands. Thus it is evident that the patient's nose had always been the object of a certain amount of thought and dissatisfaction on his part.

In the years following the war, the exigencies of life had kept him too busy to permit of much thought or worry about his appearance; he had even become rather proud (I suspect because of his many Jewish contacts) of his own nose. It now occurred to him that he was really exceptionally lucky to have a nose without a blemish! Some people had warts—his wife had had a wart on her nose for years—others had moles or pimples. But, his thoughts continued, how terrible it would be if *he*, for instance, had a wart on his nose!

He now began to examine his nose for obstructed sebaceous glands, and about a month later managed to find certain nasal pores that stood out "like black points" (presumably blackheads). These caused him to become slightly uneasy and, remembering the success of X.'s earlier treatment, he thought of returning to him. This seems, however, to have been more an idea than a real plan, for the patient made no attempt to put it into execution.

In May the patient's mother returned to Russia. A fortnight later he noticed a small pimple in the middle of his nose, which, to use his own words, had a very odd appearance and refused to disappear. The pimple then became hard, and the patient remembered that an aunt of his had had a similar affection, which had never cleared up.

The constipation, which, it will be remembered, represented the hysterical attachment behind the compulsion neurosis, now reappeared. This symptom had been the subject of the four months of analysis with Freud from November, 1919, to February, 1920. Except for rare attacks during illnesses, the patient had been free of his constipation for six years. With its reappearance he became aware of a marked fatigue. He went to the *Krankenkasse* [1] and asked to be given a series of invigorating baths. He was obliged to be examined by the physician in charge, who ordered pine baths and cold compresses to the abdomen. The latter were disapproved of by the patient, who, like his mother, was afraid of catching cold. As usual, his fears were realized; on Whitsuntide he went to bed with influenza. (It will be observed throughout that this patient, born on Christmas Day, always chose the important holidays for the production of symptoms or for other significant acts. I once remarked that, surprisingly enough in one of his violent nature, he had never indulged excessively in masturbation. He replied: "Oh no, of course I only masturbated regularly on the big holidays.")

The patient had had a slight cough all winter; he was now convinced that, as a result of the physician's prescriptions, his influenza would develop into pneumonia. This development, however, failed to take place, and when, shortly afterwards, he again consulted this doctor (he always returned for a time to the physician or dentist with whom he was already dissatisfied), a curious incident occurred. The patient remembered that on the occasion of his last visit the doctor had complained to him of a kidney malady of his own. As he now sat talking to the physician, whom he liked very much, he thought to himself: "How agreeable it is that I, the patient, am really healthy, whereas he, the doctor, has a serious illness!"

His pleasure in this situation seemed to him to deserve punishment. He went home, lay down to rest a little, and involuntarily ran his hand over his nose. Feeling the hard pimple under the skin, he scratched it out. Then he went to a mirror and looked at his nose. Where the pimple had been there was now a deep hole. From this moment on, his chief preoccupation was with the thought, will the hole heal? And when? He was now compelled to look at his pocket mirror every few minutes, presumably to observe the progress of healing. However, the hole did not entirely close, and its failure to do so embittered his life. Nevertheless, he continued to look in his mirror, hoping against hope that within a few months everything would be all right again. For now he could find no pleasure in anything, and he began to feel that everybody was looking at the hole in his nose.

Finally, just before the summer holidays, the patient consulted

[1] The Austrian system of *Krankenkassen* represented an obligatory health insurance.

Professor X., oddly enough, not for the hole in his nose, but for the enlarged sebaceous glands which he had at last succeeded in finding. X., who had not seen the patient since the war and the reversal of his fortunes, was very friendly. He warned the patient that, while the glands could easily be remedied, the nose would for a time be red. He then took an instrument and opened several of the glands. For those remaining he prescribed various medicines, a liquid and a salve. (At the age of twelve the patient had also been given a salve for a similar condition.)

X.'s warning was fulfilled; the patient's nose remained so red for several days that he almost regretted his visit to X. His wife disapproved of the medicines and, perhaps only apparently against the will of the patient, threw them away.

Suddenly, on the day before his departure for the country, for no obvious reason, the patient became fearful that the tooth which had troubled him some months previously might spoil his vacation. He therefore went to the dentist and allowed him to pull what afterwards turned out to be the wrong tooth. On the following day the patient deeply regretted this visit, feeling sure that another tooth was at fault. Some bronchial symptoms caused him additional worry.

However, the holiday in the country was a success. The patient painted industriously and thought less and less about his nose and teeth. As a matter of fact, in the absence of a real cause he rarely became hypochondriacal about his teeth. Once the cause was present, however, his distrust of the dentist in charge became pronounced. (Professor Freud has told me that the patient's attitude toward tailors precisely duplicated this later dissatisfaction with and distrust of dentists. So, too, in his first analysis, he went about from tailor to tailor, bribing, begging, raging, making scenes, always finding something wrong, and always staying for a time with the tailor who displeased him.)

The autumn and winter of 1924–25 were uneventful. When the patient, who had almost forgotten his nasal symptoms, again examined his nose in a mirror, he was unable even to find the place where the hole had been. With a sense of relief he regarded the incident as a thing of the past.

During this time certain changes occurred in his sexual life. He resorted to his former habit of following women in the street. The reader of the "History of an Infantile Neurosis" will recall the fact that the patient had had a variety of sexual experiences with women of the lower classes. He now frequently accompanied prostitutes to their lodging where, on account of his fear of venereal disease, his relations with them were limited to masturbation in their presence. The masturbation which had begun in the summer of 1923 had been performed while the patient gazed at obscene pictures. His relations with prostitutes were thus a further step in this direction.

The patient's preoccupation with his nose had lasted from February, 1924, until approximately the end of the ensuing summer—that is, some six months.

It was on Easter Day, 1925, that the nose symptoms reappeared. While the patient was sitting with his wife in a park he became aware of a painful sensation in his nose. He borrowed his wife's pocket-mirror and, looking into it, discovered a large, painful pimple on the right side of his nose. Despite its size and painfulness it seemed an ordinary pimple, and as such caused the patient no worry. Expecting it soon to disappear, he waited several weeks, during which time it would occasionally improve and then again show pus. (His mother's wart had come and gone.) As Whitsuntide approached the Wolf-Man began to lose patience. On Whit-Sunday he went with his wife to see the cinema film "The White Sister". Hereupon he was reminded of his own sister, dead so many years, who shortly before her suicide had voiced his own complaint that she was not beautiful enough. He remembered how often she too had worried about the pimples on her face. Much depressed he went home. Next day he consulted the dermatologist of the *Krankenkasse* (one wonders why he changed dermatologists at this point), who said that the pimple on the patient's nose was an ordinary one, which would in course of time disappear. But when the patient, unimproved, returned to him two weeks later, the physician said that the pimple must in reality be an infected sebaceous gland. To the patient's questions as whether it would disappear by itself, or whether something should be done for it, the doctor answered negatively.

And now the utmost despair seized the patient. He asked how it was possible that there was no treatment for such a disease, and whether he was condemned to go his whole life with such a thing on his nose. The doctor glanced at him indifferently and again replied that nothing could be done. And now, as the patient states, the whole world turned on its axis. The structure of his life collapsed. This was the end for him; thus mutilated he could not go on living.

From the *Krankenkasse* doctor he rushed to Professor X., who received him cordially and quieted him, saying that the matter was easily remedied. He would at once take out the gland. With the aid of an instrument he pressed the infected spot on the patient's nose; the patient cried out, and blood flowed from the place where the gland had been. As his analysis later revealed, he experienced at the sight of his own blood flowing under the doctor's hand an acute ecstasy. He drew a deep breath, hardly able to contain his joy. Two hours before he had stood on the verge of suicide, and now a miracle had rescued him from disaster.

But a few days later, when the dried blood had fallen away with the scab from the wound, the patient observed to his horror a slightly reddened elevation where the wound had been. The whole area looked a little swollen. The question now presented itself; would the swelling disappear, or had the *Krankenkasse* doctor been right in saying that nothing could be done for a thing of this kind?

Simultaneously small pustules on the patient's gums caused him to go to the dentist. On hearing from him that the gum-boils were of no importance, he decided that he must have an additional opinion. For some time he had had little faith in his dentist. He now went to one recommended by an acquaintance in his office. The new dentist declared that, whatever the condition of the tooth which had been extracted, a really dangerous tooth had remained in the patient's mouth. This tooth he considered responsible for all the patient's troubles, including the pimple on his nose. It was so badly infected that unless it was pulled immediately the pus could extend to any organ in the body and cause a generalized sepsis. Had this tooth been pulled in the beginning the patient would have had no further trouble with his teeth or with the pimple or the purulent sebaceous gland. Inasmuch as this opinion tallied with the patient's own, he allowed the tooth to be drawn at once.

He now blamed this last dentist for all his troubles. But with the extraction of the tooth, his interest was once more directed to his nose, which seemed to be swelling to such an extent that it no longer resembled its original self. All day long now the patient gazed at the swollen area, tormented by the fact that his nose was "not as it had been". He went again to Professor X., who assured him that nothing was wrong with his nose. Not in the least impressed or reassured by these words, the patient became exceedingly frightened. His nose had increased so rapidly in size that one half of it seemed entirely out of harmony with the other half. Moreover, it was still swelling. Terrified at the possibility of further extension, he went again to Professor X. His frequent visits no longer interested the dermatologist, who, standing with his back to the room and looking out of the window, left the patient to the care of his assistant. "Persecuted by fate and abandoned by medicine", the patient now conceived a new plan to attract X.'s attention. He decided to have his wife, who, it will be remembered, had a wart on the tip of her nose, accompany him to Professor X., whom he was afraid to visit alone. X., extremely cordial, immediately removed the wart. When, however, the patient approached him with his familiar query as to the future of his own nose, X. became irritated. He finally stated that the patient was suffering from vascular distension, and that this, like the wart, was best treated with electrolysis. He added that the patient could return in a few days for treatment.

On the one hand, the patient was unhappy at having a new illness —vascular distension; on the other hand, this gave him the renewed hope of cure. But he was doubtful of the diagnosis. An habitual abstainer from alcohol, he did not see how he could have acquired an enlargement of the calibre of the blood vessels, essentially a disease of drinkers. Moreover, he was young for it. His wife advised him not to go back to X. before the summer holidays. "He is angry with you now," she said, "and will perhaps do something to you that you will be sorry for the rest of your life." Both felt that Professor X. was treating the poor Russian refugee differently from the rich Russian patient of Freud.

At the beginning of August the patient visited the acquaintance who had recommended the new dentist. Asked if he could observe anything in particular on the patient's nose, his friend looked at him carefully and said that he could not see the place where the gland had been removed, but that he did notice that one side of the nose seemed a little swollen. This remark threw the patient into great excitement. He felt that his disease was not improving, and that it was useless to postpone the electrolysis until the autumn. He lost what patience remained to him and made up his mind to have the treatment suggested by Professor X, but as usual he wanted a control opinion. He therefore went to another dermatologist, who, it is worthy to note, had his office at the corner of the street in which Freud lived.

The new consultant confirmed X.'s diagnosis and added that the infected sebaceous glands had been skilfully removed. He considered electrolysis harmless but inappropriate for this malady, and recommended diathermy. He was extremely pleasant, and, unaware of the financial situation of the patient, who had chosen him by looking up dermatologists in the telephone book and apparently allowing himself to be influenced by their location, he charged him the usual sum for one visit. The patient, who paid X. nothing whatsoever, felt elated at once more "paying like a gentleman".

He was now completely reassured about the judgment of Professor X., who had thus far evidently done the right thing, and who was therefore probably also to be trusted in his preference for electrolysis over diathermy. Moreover, the advocate of diathermy was leaving Vienna on the very day of this visit, therefore his treatment was out of the question. The patient wanted the entire matter disposed of before his own vacation. He therefore went at once to Professor X., who, he learned, was leaving town the next day for the summer. In a spirit of exceeding confidence and trust, the patient allowed himself to be treated with electrolysis by X., who, it seemed to him, was unusually friendly. When he went home, his wife cried out: "For heaven's sake, what have you done to your nose?" The treatment had left certain marks, which, however, did not disquiet the patient. The other dermatologist's opinion of X. and his words in general had so restored the patient's equilibrium that he felt himself once more master of the situation. He also had a curious feeling of having been reconciled to the first dermatologist by the second.

Three days later the patient and his wife went away to the country. The holiday proved pleasant. Although the patient was still somewhat occupied with thoughts of his nose, and although the scars due to the electrolysis were a matter of concern to him, he managed to enjoy his holiday. He painted, went on excursions, and felt well in general. When in the autumn he returned to the city he was apparently normal, except for the fact that he looked for or at the scars on his nose more than was necessary.

His interest now returned to his teeth. His last dentist had put in five fillings and had wanted to make a new crown, which, he said, was badly needed. But the patient, not certain of the dentist's judgment, had refused to have the crown made before receiving advice from another dentist, who in his turn stated that a new crown was entirely superfluous, but that six new fillings were required. Inasmuch as five new fillings had been made only two months previously, the patient now became distrustful of this dentist, and went to still another. The latest of these recruits said that the crown was indeed adequate, but that two fillings, not six, were needed! However, since, according to the third dentist, the second had been right about the crown, the patient decided to go back to him, although doing so meant acquiring six new fillings. But now the *Krankenkasse* doctor refused the patient permission for so much dental work, adding that it was a pity to spoil such beautiful teeth with so many fillings. He then asked the patient not to mention his having made this remark, which struck thè patient as being so odd (apparently because of the implied homosexual admiration) that he repeated it to the friend who had examined his nose. This friend now recommended a dentist who was supposed to be a man of great judgment and experience, capable of passing judgment on the works of all the others. This man, apparently a dean among dentists, was named—Dr. Wolf!

The second Dr. Wolf approved the work of the latest dentist, to whom, therefore, the patient, despite his own dissatisfaction, returned. This dentist now told him, like an earlier one of the long series, that he had a "hard bite" and would soon probably lose not only the fillings, but all his teeth as well.

Until Christmas, 1925, despite a certain amount of concern as to when the nasal scars would disappear, the patient, who was now having difficulties at his office, felt fairly well. But with the beginning of the year 1926, the nasal symptoms again became prominent, occupying more and more of his attention. By the time Easter came, the mirror was again playing an important rôle, and the patient was doubtful whether the scars, now present for almost a year, would ever disappear.

The summer of 1926 brought the full development of his symptoms. On June 16 he called on Freud and received the annual sum of collected money. He, of course, said nothing about his symptoms. Two days before he had been to see the *Krankenkasse* physician, whom he had called on frequently of late because of increasingly violent palpitations of the heart. He had read a newspaper article in which the statement was made that cod-liver oil caused heart trouble; and inasmuch as he had, for some unknown reason, been taking cod-liver oil for two years, he became afraid that he had injured himself. The doctor made a diagnosis of "heart neurosis".

Suddenly, on the next day, June 17, the patient made up his mind to go to the dermatologist whose words had so consoled him once before. He immediately put his decision in execution. The dermatologist entirely failed to see any scar left by the infected sebaceous gland; on the other hand, he stated that the area treated by electrolysis (he had recommended diathermy) was scarred and evident. To the patient's remark that such scarring must disappear with time, he replied that scars never disappeared and were not amenable to any sort of treatment. How was it possible that such a thing had been treated with electrolysis? Had the patient really gone to a full-fledged dermatologist? This certainly did not seem to be the work of a specialist.

At the words "scars never disappear" a terrible sensation took possession of the patient. He was in the grip of a bottomless despair such as he had never, in all his earlier illness, been the victim of. There was no way out then, no possibility of escape. The words of the dermatologist rang incessantly in his ears: scars never disappear. There remained for him only one activity, comfortless though it was, and that was to look constantly in his pocket mirror, attempting to establish the degree of his mutilation. Not for a moment was he separated from his little mirror. In the course of time he went again to the dermatologist, imploring his aid, and insisting that there must be some mitigating treatment, if no cure. The physician replied that there was no treatment and that none was necessary: only the finest white line, he declared, was visible on a nose that even a prima donna could be proud of. He attempted to quiet the patient, whom he advised to distract his mind from the thought of his nose, which, he added, had evidently become an *idée fixe*.

But now his words were without effect on the patient. Indeed, he felt that they were but alms thrown to a crippled beggar. (See Freud's "Infantile Neurosis," where the attitude towards beggars, and especially toward the deaf-and-dumb servant, is shown to be derived from the pitying narcissistic concern with the castrated father.) He went to a third dermatologist, who found nothing whatever wrong with the patient's nose. In his utter hopelessness the patient was pursued by the following thoughts: how could Professor X., the foremost dermatologist in Vienna, have been guilty of such irreparable injury to the patient? Was it by some sheer and terrible accident, or out of negligence, or perhaps even unconscious intention? And where, continues the thought of this singularly schooled and keen-minded patient, does the unconscious end and the conscious begin? With all his heart the patient hated Professor X. as his mortal enemy.

IV. THE COURSE OF THE PRESENT ANALYSIS

This, then, is the story of the illness which brought the patient into my care. I must confess that at first it was difficult for me to believe that this was indeed the Wolf-Man of the "History of an Infantile Neurosis", and of Professor Freud's later descriptions:

a reputable, compulsively honest and conscientious individual, absolutely reliable from every point of view. The man who presented himself to me was guilty of innumerable minor dishonesties: he was concealing the possession of money from a benefactor with whom he had every reason to be candid. Most striking of all was his total unawareness of his own dishonesty. It seemed to him a matter of no moment that he was actually accepting money under false pretences (given the fact that the jewels were worth, as he then thought, thousands of dollars).

In the analysis his attitude was one of hypocrisy. He refused to discuss his nose or his dealings with dermatologists. Any mention of Freud was passed over with an odd, indulgent little laugh. He talked at great length about the marvels of analysis as a science, the accuracy of my technique, which he professed to be able to judge at once, his feeling of safety at being in my hands, my kindness in treating him without payment, and other kindred topics. When I passed through the waiting-room before his hour, I saw him pacing up and down, looking first in the large mirror and then in his pocket one. But when I mentioned his conduct to him I was met with the utmost firmness: there were other matters than his nose to be discussed, and until they were disposed of—a matter of some weeks—the patient would give his attention to nothing else. When it finally came to dealing with the subject of the nose itself, I became acquainted with the patient's firmness in all its ramifications. But even now his walled-off quality became apparent. At all times unusually closed to suggestion, probably by reason of his narcissism, he now proceeded to entrench himself behind his impermeability; and a trait ordinarily of great value to the accuracy of an analysis became its chief resistance.

His first dream was a version of the famous wolf dream; many others were mere restatements. One amusing change had occurred: the wolves, formerly white, were now invariably grey. When visiting Freud, the patient had on more than one occasion seen his large grey police dog, which looked like a domesticated wolf. The fact that the first dream was again a wolf dream was considered by the patient a corroboration of his statement that all his difficulties came from his relation to the father; for this reason, he added, he was glad to be in analysis with a woman. This statement revealed his attempt to evade his father, although it also contained a kernel of justification. It was indeed safer now for him to be analysed by a woman, because he hereby avoided the homosexual transference which at this point was evidently so strong that it would have become a danger to the cure, rather than an instrument of it. The later course of treatment seemed to confirm this point of view.

It is perhaps unnecessary to recall the fact that the wolf dream at four years of age contained the nucleus of the patient's passive attitude to his father, which had its origin in his identification with his mother during his coitus observation at one-and-a-half years.

Following the patient's repeated comments on my kindness in treating him without payment, he brought this dream, betraying his possession of the jewels:

He is standing at the prow of a ship, carrying a bag containing jewellery—his wife's earrings and her silver mirror. He leans against the rail, breaks the mirror, and realizes that, as a result, he will have seven years of bad luck.

In Russian the ship's prow is called its "nose", and this was the place where the patient's bad luck began. The mirror, which played such a large rôle in his symptomatology, was also present; and the fact that it belonged to his wife had the same significance as the fact that the patient borrowed first his wife's mirror, in order to examine his nose, and then, as it were, her feminine habit of frequently looking at herself in it. Moreover, when one breaks a mirror one simultaneously breaks one's own reflection. Thus the patient's own face was damaged along with the mirror.

The purpose of the dream is the disclosure of the patient's possession of the jewels, amongst which were actually the earrings of the dream. The seven years are the years since the analysis with Freud, during a part of which time the jewels were concealed. But beyond the spontaneous interpretation of the number of years, the patient refused to discuss in this connection any possible dishonesty. He admitted that it would have been better to have told about the jewels at once, because, he said, he would then have been easier in his mind. But women—meaning his wife—were always like that: distrustful and suspicious and afraid of losing something. And it was his wife who had suggested this concealment.

I was again brought up against a point on which the patient proved absolutely inaccessible; and it took me a short time to realize that his unscrupulousness as well as his failure to acknowledge it as such were signs of a profound character-change. Beyond his intellectual acuity and analytic perception, my patient had little in common with the original Wolf-Man, who, for instance, was domineering with women, especially his wife and mother. My patient, on the other hand, was completely under the control of his wife; she bought his clothing, criticized his doctors, and managed his finances. The passivity formerly directed entirely toward the father and even here masked as activity, had now broken its bounds and included in its sweep both homosexual and heterosexual relations. A number of petty deceptions resulted; for instance, the patient, now grown negligent of his work, left the office whenever he pleased. In the event of being apprehended, he made up any excuse.

These symptoms, perhaps not striking in themselves, were at such variance with the former character of the patient that one was forced to accept them as indications of a change of character as profound as that which had occurred in him at three-and-a-half years.

An attack of diarrhœa at the beginning of the analysis heralded the important subject of money. But the patient, apparently satisfied by the symptom itself, gave no other evidence of repaying his debt. To the contrary, it became clear that the gifts of money from Freud were accepted as the patient's due, and as the token of a father's love for his son. In this manner the patient recompensed himself for the old humiliation of his father's preference for his sister. But with this attitude went certain ideas of grandeur. The patient began to tell me of the unusual intimacy of his relation with Freud. It was, he stated, far more friendly than professional. Indeed, Freud had felt so keen a personal interest in him that he had been led to give what later turned out to be unsound advice. During the months of analysis in 1919 and 1920 the patient had wanted to go back to Russia to save his fortune. It is true that his mother and lawyer were in Russia at this time, and were presumably competent to look after matters there; nevertheless the patient felt that only he could save the family fortune. Freud, however—and here the patient, in various subtle ways, indicated that Freud's advice was motivated not by the facts but by his concern for the patient's safety—stated that the patient's desire to go home was merely a resistance; and by his persuasion (sic!) kept the patient in Vienna. While the patient obviously was flattered by what he considered Freud's motivation, he nevertheless blamed him severely for the loss of his fortune. On the other hand, he at no time suspected Freud of intentional injury. Probably his blame of Freud justified him in accepting financial aid from him. As a matter of actual fact, it would at that time have been impossible for the patient to return to Russia. His father had been a famous Liberal leader there, and the patient himself would undoubtedly have been shot.

For a time, despite the patient's invulnerability on important topics, or because of it, my relations with him were most sunny. He brought the clearest dreams in order that I might show my skill at interpreting them, thus confirming his statement that he was better off in my hands than in Freud's; the dreams in his previous analysis, he said, had been confused and difficult to understand. There had also been interminable periods of resistance, during which no material at all was forthcoming. Now and then he would hint that he was safer with me because I was more objective in my attitude toward him than Freud had been; I, for instance, would certainly not have made that mistake about the patient's returning to Russia. And then, too, Freud's personal influence had been so strong: the whole atmosphere of the present analysis was clearer than that of the previous one. Each day brought some new light on his relations to Freud, to his wife, or to me. Only he refused to discuss his nose or his attitude to Professor X. Beyond the statement that he had been to X. during his first analysis, that X. had been recommended by Freud and was a friend of Freud's, and about of an age with Freud, and obviously, as the patient said at once, a substitute for Freud, no advance was possible.

And then fate played into my hands. A few weeks after the Wolf-Man began his analysis with me, Professor X. died suddenly on a Sunday night. In Vienna there is no good morning newspaper on Monday; the Wolf-Man was due at my office at about the time of the appearance of the afternoon edition. Thus my first question was: "Have you seen today's paper?" As I expected, he answered in the negative. I then said: "Professor X. died last night." He sprang from the couch, clenching his fists and raising his arms with a truly Russian air of melodrama. "My God", he said, "now I can't kill him any more!"

Thus the wedge was entered. I encouraged him to talk about X. He had had no definite plans for killing him, but he had had ideas of suing him, of suddenly appearing in his office and exposing him, of litigating with the purpose of obtaining financial recompense for his mutilation, etc. (I call attention to the querulent-paranoic trend shown here). He had wanted to kill him, had wished him dead a thousand times, and had tried to think of ways of injuring X., as he himself had been injured by X. But for that injury, he stated, only death was an equivalent.

I now remarked that the patient himself had admitted that X. was an obvious substitute for Freud, and that therefore these feelings of enmity toward X. must have their counterpart in hostility to Freud. This he denied emphatically. There was no possible reason for hostility to Freud, who had always shown him the most tremendous partiality and affection. Again he stressed the non-professional quality of their relation. I now asked why, if such were the case, he was never seen socially at the Freuds'. He was obliged to admit that he had never met Freud's family, thereby badly damaging his entire case. His replies were vague and unsatisfactory, perhaps even to himself. His arguments had an extraordinary tone: they were not exactly specious, but they contained an astounding mixture of fantasy and fact. Granted the tenets, he could, with his logical, obsessional intelligence, make the most improbable notions plausible. Thus he maintained his point of view.

So long as he combined his two techniques of satisfaction, on the one hand blaming Freud for the loss of his fortune and therefore accepting all possible financial aid from him, and, on the other hand, maintaining, on this basis, his position as the favourite son, it was impossible to make progress in treatment. Through this impenetrable wall one could not attack the chief symptom of the patient's illness. My technique therefore consisted in a concentrated attempt to undermine the patient's idea of himself as the favourite son, since it was obvious that by means of it he was protecting himself from feelings of a very different nature. I drove home to him his actual position with Freud, the total absence (as I knew from Freud to be the fact) of any social or personal relationship between them. I remarked that his was not the only published case—this being a source of enormous pride to the patient. He countered with the statement that no other patient had been analysed for so long a period: this too I was able to contradict. From a state of war we now reached a state of siege.

As a result of my attack, his dreams at last began to change. The first of this period reveals a woman wearing trousers and high boots, standing in a sleigh which she drives in a masterful manner, and declaiming verse in excellent Russian. The patient remarked that the trousers were a little humorous, and not, like a man's, entirely practical. The Russian declamation even he was obliged to recognize as the height of mockery: I had never been able to understand a single word of the Russian phrases which he occasionally interjected into his German sentences. The next dream was even more direct: in the street, in the front of the house of Professor X., who is analysing him, stands an old gypsy woman. While selling newspapers (I had performed the office of a newspaper in telling him of X.'s death), she chatters away and talks at random *to herself* (no one listens to her!). Gypsies, of course, are notorious liars.

Two factors are evident here: first, the contempt for me, and secondly, the wish to be back in analysis with Freud (Professor X.). I remarked that the patient was, after all, despite his many compliments, apparently regretting his choice of analyst and wishing to be back with Freud. This he denied. He added that through me he was really getting all the benefit of Freud's knowledge and experience, without coming directly under his influence. When I asked how this was possible, he said that he was sure that I discussed all the details of his case with Freud, so as to be advised by him! I remarked that this was not the case, that I had, at the beginning of his analysis, asked Professor Freud for an account of his former illness, and that since that time I had barely mentioned him nor had Freud inquired for him. This statement enraged and shocked the patient. He could not believe that Freud could show so little interest in his (famous) case. He had always thought Freud sincerely interested in him. Freud, in sending him to me, had even said—but here his recollection of what had been said became hazy. He left my office in a rage at Freud, which led to a dream in which his father is obviously castrated:

The patient's father, in the dream a professor, resembling, however, a begging musician known to the patient, sits at a table and warns the others present not to talk about financial matters before the patient, because of his tendency to speculate. His father's nose is long and hooked, causing the patient to wonder at its change.

The musician has in reality tried to sell old music to the patient, who, after his refusal to buy it, feels very guilty. (His old attitude to beggars is here recalled.) The musician is bearded and looks like Christ. An association recalls an incident in which the patient's father was termed a "sale juif"—which of course he was not!

The begging musician who looks like Christ and the patient's father, and is at the same time a professor, is obviously according to his nose a Jew. Since the nose is throughout the symbol for the genital, the change in the father's nose making it Jewish denotes circumcision—castration. Also a beggar is for the patient a castrated person. Thus from the anger against the father, due to unrequited love, we come to a castration of that father, and, in the associations immediately following this interpretation of the dream, to the subject of Freud's operations and the patient's reaction to them—in other words, the death-wish against the father. I would emphasize the point that here the death-wish is due not to any masculine rivalry, but to the passive, unsatisfied, rejected love of the son.

It will be remembered that the patient's first glimpse of Freud at this time had shocked him. As he went away, he wondered whether Freud would die, and if so, what his own fate would be. He hoped for a small legacy, but feared it might amount to less than the collected sums of several years. Thus it would be more profitable for him if Freud recovered. The patient had profited so enormously by the death of his own father that it is not surprising that his expectation of inheritance should triumph over his rational calculations. As he said, despite them he expected Freud's death to bring him something.

But if the patient's nasal injury can only be avenged by death, that is a sign that castration is the equivalent of death. In that case the castrated father is the dead father, killed, presumably, by his son. The abuse of money also enters the dream, in the father's remark about his son's speculating. It is true that the patient speculated with whatever funds were at his disposal; and of course an inheritance from the father could also have been used for this purpose. In other words, the father in the dream is afraid of being killed for his money. From the Christ-like (castrated) appearance of the father, it is obvious that the patient identifies himself with this castrated father.

With the expression of the patient's death-wish against Freud, we gathered the results of my attack on the patient's over-compensating megalomania. From now on, the analysis proceeded; and the death-wish reappeared in all its manifestations. The father has castrated the son, and is for this reason to be killed by him. In the many dreams of the castrated father, the death-wish is always present. So much the patient could admit; but the further mechanism by means of which his own hostility was projected on to the father and then perceived by the son as persecution, required far more effort.

A dream out of the high-school period of the patient's life brought out an incident which, occurring in his thirteenth year, served as the model for his future illness. At that time he had a nasal catarrh which proved very resistant to treatment. Coming at puberty, it was probably psychogenic. It was treated with salves and ointments, which caused a general acne; at least the acne, so common at puberty, was attributed to the medication. Thus the patient's attention was

drawn to his nose and skin, which became so covered with pimples
that he was forced to stay away from school. He was also troubled
by blushing and by an enlarged sebaceous gland. A cold-water treatment proved of little value. On his return to school, he was mercilessly teased and nicknamed Mops (pug dog). As a rich and sensitive
boy, he had always provided an excellent target for the school. But
now he had become so over-sensitive about his nose that he could
not bear the teasing which formerly had merely annoyed him. He
became more and more seclusive, read Byron, and took great care of
his body and clothing. Just at this time another school-boy was
known to have acquired gonorrhœa. This boy was an object of horror
to our patient, who was especially terrified by any illness of a chronic
nature. He resolved never to acquire such a disease. Yet at the age
of seventeen-and-a-half he too had gonorrhœa; and the words of the
doctor, "It is a chronic form", caused his first break-down. So long
as the disease was acute, he was unhappy but not hopeless. The
chronic discharge, however, discouraged him, and afforded him an
opportunity for compulsive thoughts about the presence or absence
of gonococci: were they present, he was lost. Thus the cause of an
early period of seclusiveness and misery was an actual nasal affection.
The second trauma, the gonorrhœa, was also real, and was, in the
sense of directly affecting the genital, a true castration. But the third
illness, the scar on the patient's nose, was purely imaginary. The
fact that on the occasion of his first visit to Professor X. he made no
mention of the hole, asking only about the sebaceous glands, seems
to indicate that the patient himself must have perceived the fictitious
nature of his complaint.

The patient's identification of himself with the castrated father
(partly, of course, out of guilt because of the death-wish) is continued by a further dream in which he shows Freud a long scratch
on his hand. Freud answers something, repeating the word "whole"
several times. This comforting dream contains Freud's reassurance
that the patient is not castrated. The theme of castration is further
developed in the following dream:

The patient is lying on a couch in my office. Suddenly there
appears near the ceiling a brilliant half-moon and star. The patient
knows that this is a hallucination, and in despair, because he feels
he is going mad, he throws himself at my feet.

The moon and star, he says, mean Turkey, the land of the eunuch.
His gesture of throwing himself at my feet indicates his passivity.

His insanity is due, therefore, to a *hallucinated* castration—i.e the hole in his nose.

From the castration of the father, the patient's identification with him, and finally his own independent castration and consequent complete passivity, we now approach the actual persecutory material:

In a broad street is a wall containing a closed door. To the left of the door is a large, empty wardrobe with straight and crooked drawers. The patient stands before the wardrobe; his wife, a shadowy figure, is behind him. Close to the other end of the wall stands a large, heavy woman, looking as if she wanted to go round and behind the wall. But behind the wall is a pack of grey wolves, crowding toward the door and rushing up and down. Their eyes gleam, and it is evident that they want to rush at the patient, his wife, and the other woman. The patient is terrified, fearing that they will succeed in breaking through the wall.

The large woman is a combination of me and another woman, in reality very tall, whom the patient has seen, and whom he knows to have a tiny scar on her nose, which, to his surprise, does not in the least trouble her. She is, therefore, a courageous person who fears neither wolves nor scars—the juxtaposition indicating a connection between the two.

His wife, a shadowy figure behind him, is his own feminine self. The door is the window of the original wolf-dream. The empty wardrobe is one which the Bolsheviki emptied: the patient's mother related that when it was broken open, the cross was found in it with which the patient had been baptized, and which to his sorrow he had lost at the age of ten. Also the wardrobe reminds the patient of his fantasies about the Czarevitch, in which the latter is shut up in a room (the wardrobe) and beaten. In this connection Professor X. occurs to him: during the patient's first visit, X. had spoken of Alexander III with great sympathy, and then made some scornful remark about his weak successor, Nicolas II. This recalls in turn the stories of Peter the Great and his son Alexi, whom he killed. So, too, God allowed his son to die. Both these sons, Christ and Alexi, were tormented and persecuted by their fathers. At the word *persecuted*, the wolves in the dream occur to the patient, with the further association of Rome (Romulus and Remus), and the persecution of the early Christians. He then connects this dream, through the wolves, with his wolf-dream at the age of four, in which the wolves sat motionless on the tree, staring fixedly at the child. The interpretation revealed a contradiction: the child staring at its parents, not the parents at the child. The shining eyes of the wolves now remind the patient that for some time following the dream at four years he could not bear to be looked at fixedly. He would fly into a temper and cry: "Why do you stare at me like that?" An observant glance would recall the dream to him, with all its nightmare quality. The recollection of this early symptom, directly dependent upon the childish wolf-dream, completely refutes Rank's attempt to displace the dream from the patient's fourth year to the time of his analysis with Freud. To my question, as to whether the wolf-dream really had occurred at four years, the patient scarcely deigned to reply!

Of course the dream derives its chief significance from its persecutory content: for him the wolf has always been the father; and here the wolves—all the fathers, or doctors!—are trying to get at him to destroy him. If the door opens (the original window, permitting the view of the coitus), the wolves will devour him.

And now, with the destruction of the patient's ideas of grandeur, his full persecution mania made its appearance. It was more diffuse than the one hypochrondriacal symptom had led one to expect. X. had intentionally disfigured him; and now that he was dead, there remained no means of retribution. All the dentists had treated him badly, and since he was again mentally ill, Freud too had treated him poorly. Indeed, the whole medical profession was against him: since his earliest youth he had suffered abuse and mistreatment at the hands of his doctors. He constantly compared the story of his sufferings to that of Christ, whom a cruel God, intensely feared by the patient in his childhood, had permitted to go a similar way. The Christ and Czarevitch identifications combine a comparison of misery and a compensation for it; for Christ and the heir to the throne are exalted figures. The same combination resulted in the patient's believing himself to be the favourite of Freud.

During this trying period the patient conducted himself in the most abnormal manner. He looked slovenly and harassed, and as if devils were at his heels, as he rushed from one shop window to another to inspect his nose. During the analytic hours he talked wildly in terms of his fantasies, completely cut off from reality. He threatened to shoot both Freud and me—now that X. was dead!— and somehow these threats sounded less empty than those which one is accustomed to hear. One felt him capable of anything because he was in such complete desperation. I realized how necessary and protective his megalomania had been: he now seemed plunged into a situation which neither he nor the analysis could cope with. When the following dream occurred, with its good portent, I was relieved and surprised, and entirely at a loss to account for the change by any fact save the obvious one that the patient had finally worked his way through the unconscious material behind his delusions of persecution.

The patient and his mother are together in a room, one corner of whose walls is covered with holy pictures. His mother takes the pictures down and throws them to the floor. The pictures break and fall into bits. The patient wonders at this act on the part of his pious mother.

It was the patient's mother who, in despair at the child's irritability and anxiety, taught him, at four-and-a-half years, the story of Christ. The result was that the little boy who had been unable to fall asleep because of his fear of bad dreams now exchanged these for a ceremonial which permitted him to fall asleep at once. It consisted in his going about the room at bedtime, crossing himself and praying, and kissing the holy pictures one after another. This ceremonial was the beginning of his obsessional neurosis.

In the dream I am the mother, but in a rôle contrary to the historical one; instead of giving the patient religion, I destroy it for him. What I actually destroy is the Christ fantasy, with all that it implies.

The dream of the next day was in substance a clarified wolf-dream.

The patient stands looking out of his window at a meadow, beyond which is a wood. The sun shines through the trees, dappling the grass; the stones in the meadow are of a curious mauve shade. The patient regards particularly the branches of a certain tree, admiring the way in which they are intertwined. He cannot understand why he has not yet painted this landscape.

The landscape of this dream is to be compared to that of the wolf-dream at four years. Now the sun is shining: then it was night, always a frightening time. The branches of the tree where the terrifying wolves sat are now empty, and are intertwined in a beautiful pattern. (The parents in the sexual embrace.) What was fearful and ominous has become beautiful and reassuring. The patient wonders at his never having painted this scene before; that is, his failure until now to admire it.

This reconciliation to what formerly terrified him can only mean that he has overcome the fear of his own castration, and can now admire what others find beautiful—a love scene between a man and woman. So long as he identified himself with the woman, he was incapable of such admiration; his entire narcissism reacted against the acceptance of the implied castration. If, however, he has abandoned his identification with the woman, he need no longer fear castration.

As was to be expected, the patient had not made quite the progress present in the dream. The next day he brought a dream in which he is lying at my feet: a return to his passivity. He is in a sky-scraper with me, whose only means of exit is a window (see the original wolf-dream as well as the dream just cited), from which a ladder extends dangerously to the ground. To get out he must go through the window. That is to say, he cannot remain inside, looking out, as in the other dreams, but must overcome his fear and go out. He awakens in great anxiety, looking desperately for another way of escape.

But the only way out was through the acceptance of his own castration: either this, or the actual retracing of his childish steps to the scene which was pathogenic for his feminine attitude to the father. He now realized that all his ideas of grandeur and fear of the father and, above all, his feeling of irreparable injury by the father were but cloaks for his passivity. And once these disguises were revealed, the passivity itself, whose unacceptability has necessitated the delusion, became intolerable. What appeared to be a choice between acceptance or refusal of the feminine rôle was in reality no choice at all: had the patient been capable of assuming the feminine rôle and admitting his passivity to the full, he could have spared himself this illness, which was based on the mechanisms of defence against such a rôle.

A second dream of the same night revealed the cause of the restriction of the patient's sublimations. Freud, to whom he is telling his ambition to study criminal law, advises against this course and recommends political economy.

The patient, whose father was a Russian Liberal, active in politics and economics, had always been especially interested in criminal law (he was a lawyer). But throughout his analysis he insisted that Freud always discouraged him in these ambitions, telling him to devote himself to political economy, in which he (evidently in reaction against his father) had no interest. Now I knew his idea about Freud to be incorrect, yet until this dream I had been unable to convince the patient of this fact.

His inability to be the father in his sublimations had made him project the restricting influence on to Freud. He was not to be allowed to make his own choice, but was instead obediently to follow in the footsteps of his father.

He now talked at some length about his need to sublimate his homosexuality, and the difficulty of finding a means. He was aware of having been hampered by circumstance and inner incapacity. It is true that in Austria today the opportunity for the type of work that interests him is limited, but he might have used his free time, of which there was a great deal, for study. Here his work inhibition prevented his development. Indeed, this man, who once studied with industry and intelligence, and read voluminously, had now for years been unable to read a novel.

The next series of dreams, immediately following, illuminates the father-son relation and demonstrates the beginning of freedom for the son. The submissive son stands in apposition to the patient, who shows the beginnings of a father-identification.

A young Austrian who has lived many years in Russia and lost all his money there visits the patient. This young Austrian now has a minor position in a bank in Vienna. He complains of a headache, and the patient asks his wife for a powder, not telling her that he requires it for his friend, out of fear of her refusing to give it to him. To the patient's surprise, she gives him also a piece of cake, which, however, is not big enough for both him and his friend.

Obviously the young Austrian is the patient himself. During his illness (the headache), he is treated with a powder, whereas the (healthy) patient receives, as an obvious reward, a piece of cake— the sublimation he so desires. But there is not enough for both of them; that is to say, there is only enough for the (healthy) patient.

The next dream reverted to the castrated father:

The patient is in the office of a doctor with a full, round face (like Professor X.). He is afraid that he has not enough money in his purse to pay the doctor. However, the latter says that his bill is very small, that he will be satisfied with 100,000 *Kronen*. As the patient leaves, the doctor tries to persuade him to take some old music, which, however, the patient refuses, saying he has no use for it. But at the door the doctor presses on him some coloured postcards, which he has not the courage to refuse. Suddenly the patient's (woman) analyst appears, dressed like a page in a blue velvet knickerbocker suit and three-cornered hat. Despite her attire, which is boyish rather than masculine, she looks entirely feminine. The patient embraces her and takes her on his knee.

The patient's fear of being unable to pay the doctor's bill is both actual and satirical. He was in fact unable to pay Freud for his last analysis; on the other hand, he had formerly as a rich patient paid enough to feel somewhat justified in accepting gratis treatment now. In the earlier analysis 100,000 *Kronen* would have meant nothing to him. But at the beginning of the year 1927, when this dream occurred, 100,000 (gold) *Kronen* would have meant a fortune to the impoverished Russian. He still spoke in terms of Kronen, perhaps because the sums sounded so much larger, although Austria now had shillings. He did not know whether the 100,000 *Kronen* in the dream represented 100,000 gold crowns or ten shillings. Thus he was either so rich that 100,000 gold crowns meant nothing to him, or else the doctor's bill of ten shillings was laughably small—presumably on the basis of his worth. In either case, the patient is able to pay his debt, though possibly through the depreciation of both the currency and the doctor's value.

The round, full face of the doctor is opposed to Freud's, which had looked so thin and ill to the patient. This detail apparently represents an attempt to discount the illness of the father, although everything else in the dream tends to emphasize the fact of his castration and the depreciation of his worth. He is in reality the begging musician (see the dream on p. 84), but instead of trying to *sell* the music, he wants to give it to the patient. But it is really too worthless: the patient refuses it, only to be presented with the coloured (i.e. cheap) postcards. Certainly these are symbols of the gifts of Freud, now grown valueless to the patient. The meaning is clear: no gift is now sufficient to compensate the patient for the passivity involved in its acceptance. Thus at last gifts, which at the time of the patient's fourth birthday on Christmas Day, had precipitated the wolf-dream and, indeed, the entire infantile neurosis, and had played a leading rôle in all his later life and analytic treatment, were now robbed of their libidinal value.

The doctor in the dream is a particularly harmless individual; that is to say, he is castrated, or as good as dead.

The nature of the heterosexuality in this dream is historically correct. It will be remembered that the patient was seduced at an early age by his elder and always precocious and aggressive sister. This seduction activated his latent passivity, directing it toward the woman. Thus my boyish costume has several meanings: first, the historic one of the sister's aggression; secondly, my rôle, as analyst, of a father-substitute; and thirdly, an attempt on the part of the patient to deny the castration of the woman, and attribute a phallus to her. In the dream I resemble those pages on the stage whose parts are usually and obviously taken by women. Thus I am neither man nor woman, a creature of neuter gender. However, the attribution of the phallus to the woman turned into a conquest for the patient who immediately discovers her femininity and proceeds to make love to her. Thus an additional purpose of her masculinity is disclosed: the patient has granted her the phallus in order to take it away from her, in other words, to castrate her in his father-identification as he has in the past wished to be castrated by that father.

It will be observed that this is the first dream where the heterosexuality of the patient, as well as a positive erotic transference, is clearly present. An element of identification with the woman is undoubtedly present, but the patient's leading rôle is a masculine one. Apparently only now has his father-identification become strong enough to enable him to develop a normal, heterosexual transference to me.

In the final dream of this analysis the patient is walking in the street with the second dermatologist, who with great interest is discoursing about venereal disease. The patient mentions the name of the doctor who treated his gonorrhœa with too severe a medication. On hearing his name, the dermatologist says no, no, not he— another.

Here the final link was established between the patient's present illness and the gonorrhœa which caused his first breakdown. It will be recalled that the patient's mother had some pelvic disease with bleeding and pain, and that the patient as a child held his father, perhaps not wrongly, responsible for this condition. When, then, in the dream the patient mentions the doctor who treated him so radically, in contrast to his own conservative family physician, who had treated him all his life, he means Professor X., whose radical electrolysis supposedly worked much the same damage as that of the earlier radical treatment. When the dermatologist says it is not this man but another, he can mean only the father (or Freud), the unnamed one responsible for all treatment as well as all disease. That disease represents castration is obvious.

Only after this dream did the patient actually and completely relinquish his delusion. He was now able to realize that his nasal symptom was not a fact but an idea, based on his unconscious wish and the defence against it which together had proved stronger than his sense of reality.

His final restoration took place suddenly and in an apparently trivial manner. All at once he found that he could read and enjoy novels. He stated that up to now two factors had held him back from what once had been his chief source of pleasure; on the one hand, he had refused to identify himself with the hero of a book, because that hero, created by the author, was wholly in the power of his creator; on the other hand, his sense of creative inhibition had made it impossible for him to identify himself with the author. Thus he fell between two stools—as in his psychosis.

From this moment on he was well. He could paint, and plan work and study in his chosen field, and again take the general intelligent interest in life and the arts and literature which naturally was his.

Again his character changed, this time reverting to the normal in a manner as striking as that in which his delusion disappeared. He was once more the man one had learned to know in Freud's story— a keen, scrupulous and attractive personality, with a variety of interests and attainments, and a depth of analytic understanding and accuracy which was a constant source of pleasure.

He was at a loss to understand his own conduct. The concealment of the jewels, the casual acceptance of the yearly money, the petty dishonesties, were all a mystery to him. And yet their secret lay in his remark about his wife: "Women are always like that—distrustful and suspicious and afraid of losing something."

V. Diagnosis

The diagnosis of paranoia seems to me to require little more evidence than that supplied by the history of the case itself. The picture is typical for those cases known as the hypochondriacal type of paranoia. True hypochondria is not a neurosis; it belongs more nearly to the psychoses. The term in this sense is not used to cover those cases where anxiety concerning the general health is the chief symptom, as in the anxiety neuroses; nor does it coincide with neurasthenia. It presents a characteristic picture, in which there is an exclusive preoccupation with one organ (or sometimes several organs), in the belief that that organ is injured or diseased. The head symptoms so common in early schizophrenia are an example of this type of hypochondria. Occasionally a slight illness affords the apparent basis for the idea of illness, which, however, is ordinarily present without any foundation whatsoever in reality. It thus comes under the heading of a delusion. (In the non-hypochondriacal forms of paranoia any one idea may form the leading symptom. Indeed, paranoia is typically a monosymptomatic, delusional disease, classified according to the nature of the delusion—persecutory, jealous, or hypochondriacal. In its earliest forms it may frequently appear as the so-called *überwertige Idee;* this "idea" being of any nature whatsoever.)

Bleuler states that although text-books mention the hypochondriacal form of paranoia, he personally has never seen it. It will be observed that while the present case undoubtedly belongs to this category, nevertheless the hypochondriacal idea merely serves to cloak those of a persecutory nature behind it. Thus though the form is hypochondriacal, the entire content of the psychosis is persecutory. The patient maintained that his nose had been intentionally ruined by an individual who bore him a grudge. The possibility of unintentional injury was cleverly taken care of by this analytically-schooled patient, who remarked: "Who can tell where unconscious activity ends, and conscious begins?" And he added that surely the leading man in his specialty could not be so poor a therapist. He then went on to blame himself for Professor X.'s anger at him: he had by his frequent visits and persistent questioning exhausted X.'s patience. If one regards the latent rather than the manifest content of this idea, one sees in it (1) the patient's construction of the persecutory situation, and (2) his awareness of his own responsibility for it. We know that the persecution is in reality the hostility of the patient himself projected upon his object. Indeed, the Wolf-Man had a particular talent for creating situations which lent themselves well to his feelings of distrust. At the age of twelve he had used so much of the medicine prescribed for his nasal catarrh that he had ruined his complexion; and the doctor was blamed for giving him "too strong" a salve. In the course of his gonorrhœa he became dissatisfied with the mild treatment of his own physician, and went to another, who gave him "too sharp" an irrigation. The judgment of one dentist had always to be checked by that of another, until it became inevitable that somewhere an error would be made. Indeed, when the patient finally made up his mind to have a tooth pulled, apparently under a compulsion to lose a tooth at this time, the extraction was performed on a healthy tooth, necessitating a second extraction later. Professor Freud told me that the patient's behaviour with dentists at this time was a replica of his earlier one with tailors, whom he begged, bribed and implored to work well for him, and with whom he was never satisfied. Here, too, he always remained for a time the customer of the particular tailor with whom he was dissatisfied. I would remark that not only is the tailor (*Schneider*) a common figure for the castrator, but that in addition the patient's early history had predisposed him to this choice. It will be remembered that the childish wolf-dream was based largely on his grandfather's story of the tailor who pulled off the wolf's tail.

The patient's statement that no doctor or dentist ever seemed to treat him properly is superficially to some extent justified. But when one examines the circumstances surrounding the long line of the patient's medical and dental experiences, one is forced to the conclusion that he himself demanded and facilitated bad treatment on the part of his attendants. Distrust was a prime condition of treatment. The normal individual breaks off treatment when he becomes dissatisfied with his physician; he certainly does not permit himself to be operated upon by some one whom he regards as his enemy. The passive nature of our patient makes every breach with a father-substitute difficult: his first attempt is to placate the assumed enemy. This attitude will be recalled from the earlier analysis, where his gesture of turning toward the analyst meant: Be good to me. This same gesture, with the identical content, occurred in the course of the analysis with me.

Professor X. was, of course, the chief persecutor; the patient had at once remarked that X. was an obvious substitute for Freud. In regard to Freud himself, the persecution was less evident. The patient blamed Freud for the loss of his fortune in Russia, but laughed at the idea that Freud's advice could have been intentionally malicious. It was necessary for him to seek out an indifferent but equally symbolic persecutor, to whom he could consciously and wholeheartedly ascribe the most vicious motives. There were, in addition, various minor persons by whom the patient considered himself imposed on, badly treated, and sometimes cheated. It is worthy of note that in just those relations where he probably really was imposed on, he was entirely unsuspecting.

The leading diagnostic points are, briefly:

(1.) The hypochondriacal delusion.
(2.) The delusion of persecution.

(3.) The regression to narcissism as shown in the delusion of grandeur.

(4.) The absence of hallucinations in the presence of delusions.

(5.) Mild ideas of reference.

(6.) The absence of mental deterioration.

(7.) The character change.

(8.) The monosymptomatic nature of the psychosis. The patient, when talking about anything except his nose, was entirely sane. The mention of that organ made him act like the classic lunatic.

(9.) The ecstasy experienced by the patient when X. removed the gland from his nose is not indeed typically psychotic, but is essentially non-neurotic. A neurotic may desire and fear castration, but he does not welcome it.

The hypochondriacal delusion cloaks the ideas of persecution, providing a convenient form for the content of the entire illness. The mechanism of condensation employed here reminds one of that in dreams.

VI. MECHANISMS

A word as to the mechanisms and symbolism of the psychosis. The nose is, of course, the genital; and it is a fact that the patient has always considered both his nose and his penis undersized. The wound is inflicted on his nose first by himself and then by X. The patient's failure to be satisfied by his self-castration reveals a motive beyond the usual masochistic one of guilt, which, regardless of the perpetrator, would be satisfied by the act itself. The further motive is, of course, the libidinal one, the desire for castration at the hands of the father as an expression in anal-sadistic language of that father's love. In addition, there is the wish to be made into a woman for the sake of sexual satisfaction from the father. I call attention here to the patient's hallucinatory experience in early childhood, when he thought he had cut off his finger.

Throughout the psychosis the "veil" of the earlier illness enveloped the patient. Nothing penetrated it. A somewhat obscure remark to the effect that sometimes the analytic hour with me seemed the equivalent of this veiled state corroborated its earlier interpretation as a womb-fantasy. In this connection, the patient's idea that he occupied a kind of mid-position between Professor Freud and me is interesting; it will be recalled (p. 84) that he had many fantasies about the discussions which Freud and I were supposed to have had about him. He himself remarked that he was our "child"; and one of his dreams revealed him lying next to me, with Freud sitting at his back. (The importance of *coitus a tergo* is again shown here.) In the language of the womb-fantasy, he is indeed partaking of the parental intercourse.

It is interesting to note the difference between the present psychotic mother-identification and the past hysterical one. Formerly the patient's feminine rôle seemed at odds with his personality; it was evident that he was playing a part. At times he was a man—as in his relation to women—although at other times, toward the analyst and other father-figures, he was obviously the woman. But now there was no dissociation: the feminine rôle had flooded his personality, and he was entirely at one with it. He was a bad, a petty personality, but he was not a dissociated one. A remark of Dr. Wulff, formerly of Moscow and now of Berlin, to whom I described the case, and who knew and attended the patient and both his parents, best illustrates this point. He said: "He no longer plays the mother, he *is* the mother, down to the least detail."

The elements of the mother-identification were striking. The patient began thinking about his nose after the arrival of his mother with a wart on hers. Fate played into his hands by permitting his wife to have the same blemish in the same place. His sister had had trouble with her skin and was, like the patient, troubled about her appearance. Worry about the complexion is in itself rather a feminine trait. The stereotype complaint of the patient is directly taken over from his mother: "I can't go on living like this any more." The mother's hysterical anxiety about her health was reflected in the patient during childhood and later life, as for instance in the present illness in his fear of catching cold. Moreover, the patient's dishonesty about money was in part an identification with the mother whom he had so often and so unjustly accused of cheating him out of his inheritance.

Perhaps the height of the mother-identification was attained in the patient's ecstasy at the sight of his own blood flowing under X.'s hand. We remember his childish fear of dysentery and blood in his stool, following the complaint of his mother to the doctor about "bleeding" (presumably vaginal). The child thought his mother's pelvic disease the result of coitus with the father. Thus it was a passive coitus fantasy which caused the ecstasy when Professor X. took his instrument and removed the little gland. Obviously the element of giving birth, of being delivered, is also present.

The patient's most feminine trait was his trick of taking out a pocket mirror and looking at himself and powdering his nose. On the first occasion he borrowed his wife's mirror; later he purchased one, complete with face powder, behaving exactly like a woman in these days of mirrored compact powder cases.

If the nasal symptoms were a mother-identification, the dental symptoms were a father-identification, but an identification with the castrated father. Freud's operation was essentially a dental one, performed by a dental surgeon. Thus both Freud and the patient's own father, through his long illness and consequent incapacity, were in a sense castrated. It will be remembered that the servant whom the little boy loved so much (p. 482 of the "Infantile Neurosis") had supposedly had his tongue cut out.

Although the present character-change of the patient was more profound than that of his childhood, it nevertheless resembled the earlier one. At three-and-a-half years he had, as the result of the seduction by his sister and the consequent activation of his passivity, become irritable and aggressive, tormenting people and animals. Behind his tempers lay the masochistic desire for punishment at the hands of the father; but the outward form of his character was at that time sadistic. An element of father-identification was present. In the present character-change, the same regression to the anal-sadistic or masochistic level was present, but the rôle of the patient was passive. He was tormented and abused, instead of being the tormentor. He now lived out his favourite fantasy of Peter the Great and the son whom he killed; and X. played into his hands at his very first visit by discussing with him another Czar and his son! The fantasy of being beaten on the penis was reflected in the delusion of being injured on the nose by X. No element of the father-rôle was present here. Just as the childish tempers were attempts to provoke punishment (in other words, seduction) from the father, so too were the persistent visits to X. and the constant demands for treatment which was obviously castration.

What Freud calls the patient's pendulum-like swing from sadistic to masochistic attitude is, he says, reflected in his ambivalence, present in all his relations. Thus both are the results of his strong bisexuality.

The libidinal significance of gifts runs like a red thread through the entire history of this patient. The wolf-dream which occurred just before the patient's fourth Christmas (and birthday) contained as a leading idea the expectation of sexual satisfaction from the father as the chief Christmas gift. The craving for presents from the father was the prime expression of the son's passivity. The idea of Freud's death was bound up with the (groundless) anticipation of an inheritance from him. This inheritance, especially during Freud's lifetime, had the significance of a gift, and roused just those feelings which Christmas had roused when the patient was a child. A similar rôle was played by the yearly sums of money from Freud: the unconscious passivity which remained unsolved after the first analysis found in these donations a source of satisfaction. Had the patient been as cured of his feminine attitude to the father as he seemed to be, those contributions would have been devoid of emotional significance.

A word as to the patient's attitude to the loss of his fortune. It may seem strange to us that he was able to accommodate himself so easily to the post-war conditions which completely changed his manner of living. But this element of indifference is due rather to nationality than to illness. Those who have come in contact with Russian refugees have been amazed at the rapidity of their adjustment. No one, seeing them in their new life, could guess how different the old had been.

VII. Problems

Certain problems arise from this case, which offers an unusual opportunity for observation by reason of the fact that we have the histories of two illnesses in the same person, both treated with apparent success by analysis. Successful treatment implies that all the unconscious material has been made conscious, and the motivation of the illness become clear.

The second analysis corroborates in every detail the first one, and, moreover, brings to light not one particle of new material. Our entire concern is with a remnant of the transference to Freud. Naturally this remnant implies that the patient has not been wholly freed of his fixation to the father; but apparently the cause of the remaining attachment is not the presence of unconscious material, but insufficient living-through of the transference itself. I say this in the face of the fact that the patient spent four-and-a-half years with Freud and remained well afterward for some twelve years. It is one thing for the analyst to consider a case complete, and another for the patient to do so. As analysts we may be in full possession of the historic facts of the illness, but we cannot know how much living-through (*durcharbeiten*) the patient requires for his cure.

One fact supports our assumption that the patient did not finish his reactions to the father in the course of his first analysis. This was the first case in which a time limit to the analysis was set by the analyst. Freud resorted to this after months and months of complete stagnation, and was rewarded by the decisive material of the case. Until the setting of the time limit the patient had been hardly more than prepared for analysis, little actual work had been accomplished. Now material streamed from the unconscious, and the wolf-dream in all its significance became clear.

When one remembers how glad patients are to retain one last bit of material, and how willing they are to yield everything else in exchange for it, one understands one reason for the effectiveness of a time limit in analysis. Perhaps sometimes the pressure actually brings out all that is there; but I can imagine that an inaccessibility which necessitates a time limit will most often use this limit for its own ends. Such seems to be the case with the Wolf-Man. It would have been useless to continue the analysis longer without the exercise of the one great means of pressure which we have—a time limit: our patient was too comfortable in the analytic situation. There was no way of meeting this resistance other than the removal of the situation itself. This resulted in the patient's bringing sufficient material to produce a cure, but it also enabled him to keep just that nucleus which later resulted in his psychosis. In other words, his attachment to the father was too strong: on the one hand, it would have prevented any analysis whatever, and, on the other, it made the patient inaccessible in his final stronghold.

Why the patient developed paranoia instead of reverting to his original neurosis is hard to say. It may be that the first analysis robbed him of the usual neurotic modes of solution. One asks oneself if the patient was perhaps always latently paranoid. A certain support for this belief is found in the hypochondriacal tendency displayed throughout his childhood, and in his shyness and seclusiveness at adolescence, as well as in his preoccupation with his nose at that time. But the fact remains that he at no time developed delusions or in any way lost his sense of reality. And the chief evidence against this theory is his conduct during his analysis with Freud. Certainly the transference brings to light whatever mechanisms the patient is capable of producing, especially those of a paranoid nature; and, although one part of the childish obsessional neurosis did remind Freud of Schreber, nevertheless in the course of Freud's analysis there was never the slightest manifestation of any paranoid mechanism.

I believe that the paranoid form of the patient's illness can only be accounted for by the profundity and consequent degree of expression of his attachment to the father. For the most part this fixation was represented by the many and varied neurotic illnesses of childhood and later life. These manifestations of his femininity proved curable. We know that the passivity of the man has three possibilities of expression: masochism, passive homosexuality, and paranoia; these represent neurotic, perverse, and psychotic expressions of the one attitude. And in our patient that part of his passivity which was expressed by his neurosis was curable: the deepest portion, which had remained untouched, went to form his paranoia.

The loss of the equilibrium attained after the first analysis was due to Freud's illness. That this should have been the case is not difficult to understand. The threatened death of a beloved person mobilizes all one's love. But the love of this patient for his father—represented by Freud—forms the greatest menace to his masculinity; satisfying it involves castration. To this danger the narcissism of the patient reacts with tremendous force; the love is partly repressed, partly converted into hate. This hate in turn generates the death-wish against the father. Thus Freud's illness, heightening the dangerous passive love of the patient, with consequent increase in the temptation to submit to castration, brings the hostility to a point where some new mechanism is needed to provide an outlet; and this is found in projection. The patient simultaneously rids himself of part of his antagonism by attributing it to another, and provides a situation in which his own hostility finds its justification.

I believe that the insight won during the first analysis was responsible for the patient's final accessibility. Nevertheless, it seems improbable to me that analysis with a male analyst would have been possible. It is one thing to play the persecutor's rôle toward a female paranoiac—already castrated!—and quite another to play it toward a man for whom castration is still a possibility. It must be remembered that in the psychoses the things feared are actually believed in: the psychotic patient is afraid of the actual cutting off of his penis, and not of some symbolic act on the part of the analyst. Fantasy has become reality. Thus the situation is too dangerous for the patient. This is perhaps the one situation where the sex of the analyst is of importance.

By avoiding the homosexual transference the intensity of the transference, which is sometimes a condition of therapeutic success, is of course sacrificed. The entire effect of the treatment is risked.

The case in question offered an ideal compromise on this point, because of the indirect contact with Freud due to the first analysis. For this patient analysis was Freud. It was as though just enough of the father's influence was present to be effective, without the additional degree which would probably have proved fatal to the treatment. It will be seen throughout the present analysis that my own rôle was almost negligible; I acted purely as mediator between the patient and Freud.

Two points seem to me worthy of particular emphasis. The first of these is the mechanism of the cure. I have no explanation for the final turning-point which occurred with the dream (p. 89) about the holy pictures. I can attribute the change only to the fact that at last the patient had sufficiently lived through his reactions to the father, and was therefore able to give them up. The modes of analytic therapy are twofold: the first is the making conscious of hitherto unconscious reaction; the second is the working through (*durcharbeiten*) of these reactions.

The second point involves the primary bisexuality of this patient, obviously the cause of his illness. His masculinity has always found its normal outlet; his femininity on the other hand has necessarily been repressed. But this femininity seems to have been constitutionally strong, so strong, indeed, that the normal œdipus complex has been sacrificed in its development to the negative œdipus complex. The development of a strong positive œdipus complex would have been a sign of greater health than the patient actually possessed. Needless to say, an exaggerated positive œdipus complex often masks its opposite. On the other hand, even this reaction presupposes a greater biological health than that of our patient.

Whether the patient, who has now been well for a year and a half, will remain well, it is impossible to state. I should be inclined to think that his health is in large measure dependent on the degree of sublimation of which he proves capable.

CHARACTEROLOGY

The significance of the three papers on psycho-analytic character-ology to follow—all by Wilhelm Reich—can hardly be over-rated. There are few contributions to be called as unhesitatingly as are these, a "must" for the student, there are in spite of their looseness of style, and perhaps occasionally even of theoretical thought few to be as emphatically recommended for periodic re-reading in the first decade of any analyst's clinical work; and few that will spare the beginner in analysis as much avoidable disappointment—a disappointment which frequently causes him to look to "advanced" analytic schools of Adlerian, or neo-Adlerian, description for assistance.

.Free from theoretical innovations, which at the date of their publica-tion (1928, 1929, and 1931) could only have been premature, these papers attack a fundamental clinical problem concerning the psychology of the ego, by approaching it as a problem of technique. It is this approach, and its single-minded pursuance, that renders them indis-pensable as a supplement to the technical writings and some of the clinical papers of Freud.

From among these the following might be singled out as dealing with or touching upon the subject treated by Reich:

1908: "Character and Anal Erotism" [1]

1913: "The Predisposition to Obsessional Neurosis" [2]

1915: "Some Character Types observed in Analytic Work" [3]

1917: "A Difficulty Encountered by Psychoanalysis" [4]

1919: "Turnings in the Ways of Psychoanalytic Therapy" [5]

1920: "The Psychogenesis of a Case of Female Homosexuality" [6]

The first systematic description of a character-type observed in the transference and encountered there as a "resistance", and the suggestion

[1] Collected Papers, II, London, Hogarth Press, 1924–25.
[2] Ibid.
[3] Collected Papers, IV.
[4] Ibid.
[5] Collected Papers, II.
[6] Ibid.

104

to give preference to its interpretation over that of the rest of the material, the essential premise for Reich's argument we owe to Karl Abraham. His classic observation was published under the unassuming title: "On a Particular Kind of Resistance Against the Psychoanalytic Method" as early as 1919.[7]

[7] *Internationale Zeitschrift für Psychoanalyse*, V, 1919, p. 151. English Translation: *Selected Papers*, London, Hogarth Press, 1927.

ON CHARACTER ANALYSIS* (1928)

By Wilhelm Reich

I

It is seldom that our patients are from the outset accessible to analysis; few indeed are disposed to follow the fundamental rule of analysis and to "open up" fully to the analyst. In addition to the fact that they are not immediately able to feel the necessary degree of confidence in a total stranger, there are their years of illness, their long subjection to the influence of a neurotic *milieu*, their unfortunate experiences with neurologists and psychiatrists—in sum, an entire secondary warping of the personality—all conspiring to create a situation unfavourable to analysis. The overcoming of this obstacle becomes a precondition of analytic work, and might be accomplished fairly easily were it not for the support it receives from the individual make-up of the patient—from, as we may permit ourselves to say, his character, which itself is part and parcel of his neurosis and has been developed on a neurotic basis. There are in the main two methods of meeting these difficulties, particularly that of the evasion of the fundamental rule. One of these, that commonly practised, consists in direct education for analysis by means of instruction, reassurance, persuasion, admonition, and the like. In this case the attempt is made through the establishing of a positive transference to influence the patient in the direction of analytic candour. Extensive experience has shown, however, that this educational or active method is very uncertain in its results, is at the mercy of uncontrollable chance factors, and lacks any sound basis of analytic clarity; the analyst is too greatly handicapped by the fluctuations in the transference situation and finds himself treading uncertain ground in his attempt to render the patient accessible to analysis.

The other method is a more complicated one, and although not

---

* Translated from the original: Über Charakteranalyse: *Internationale Zeitschrift für Psychoanalyse*, XIV, 1928, p. 180. (The author wishes the information to be added that this, and the following two articles, were incorporated "in *Charakteranalyse*, 1933, and in *Character-Analysis*, second (English) edition, New York, Orgone Institute Press, 1945".)

thus far applicable to all patients is much more certain in its operation; it consists in the attempt to *substitute for educational measures
analytic interpretations.* Certainly this is not by any means always
possible; nevertheless it is still the ideal towards which analytic
efforts should strive. Thus, instead of inducting the patient into
analysis by means of advice, admonition, transference manœuvres,
and so forth, the analyst's attention is focused, more passively, on
the *immediate* meaning of the bearing and attitude of the patient:
why he doubts, or is unpunctual, or talks in a haughty or confused
manner, or communicates only one thought in three, or criticizes
the analysis, or produces a super-abundance of too abstruse material.
Hence, for example, the analyst may deal with a narcissistic patient
whose patronizing speech is couched in technical terms by attempting to convince him that this habit of his is prejudicial to the analysis,
that in the interest of its progress he would do better to avoid the
use of technical terminology, to abandon his attitude of haughty
aloofness. Or, on the other hand, the analyst may renounce any such
attempt at persuasion and, instead, wait until he has gained some
inkling of why the patient behaves in just this way and not in some
other. He may then perhaps discover that the patient is compensat-
ing in this way for a feeling of inferiority in relation to the analyst,
and he may be able to influence him through consistent interpretation of the meaning of his behaviour. This second method of procedure, in contrast to the first, is in complete accord with analytic
principles.

From this attempt to replace educational or other active measures,
such as the particular behaviour of the patient seemed to necessitate,
by purely analytic interpretation, there resulted—as unsought as it
was unexpected—an approach to the analysis of *character*.

The foundation of character analysis was laid when Freud spon-
sored the cardinal change in analytic technique which consisted in
denoting as the most important task of analysis the overcoming of
resistances, in place of the direct interpretation of the patient's
symptoms—the technique in use up to the time in question, but now
adhered to only by Stekel and his followers. The technique consisting of the analysis of the resistances fully deserves, as developed
up to the present date, the designation of character analysis. There
would be no justification, however, for superseding with the latter
term the other, more customary one of analysis of the resistances,
if it were not for a particular circumstance which makes the term
"character analysis" the preferable one.

As we review our clinical experience, the necessity becomes clear for distinguishing from among the various resistances which we encounter in the course of treating our patients a particular group of these—a group which may be termed *character resistances*. These acquire their specific imprint, not from their content, but from the patient's individual mode of behaviour. The compulsive character, for example, develops resistances differing specifically in form from those of the hysterical character, as the latter, in turn, from those of the genital-narcissistic, the "impulse-ridden" or the neurasthenic character. The *form* taken by the reactions of the ego—a form which in the face of similarity of experiential content differs according to the character—*is just as much determined by infantile experiences as is the content of symptoms and fantasies.*

II. FROM WHAT DO CHARACTER RESISTANCES DERIVE?

Recently Glover has worked on the problem of differentiating character neuroses and symptom neuroses. Alexander, also, has operated on the basis of this distinction. In my earlier writings I, too, observed it; but a closer examination of case material has made it apparent that this distinction means no more than that there are neuroses with concrete, circumscribed symptoms, and neuroses which are lacking in these; the former were therefore called "symptom neuroses", the latter "character neuroses"; in the former, it goes without saying, symptoms are more conspicuous, in the latter, neurotic character traits. But is there, after all, such a thing as a symptom without a basis in a neurotic reaction pattern—in other words, without a neurotic character? The difference between character neuroses and symptom neuroses is simply that in the latter the neurotic character has produced symptoms as well—that the neurotic symptoms are, so to speak, a concentrate of the neurotic character. That the neurotic character suffers an exacerbation in the form of specific symptoms, on the one hand, and, on the other, is able to find other means for the discharge of damned-up libido, poses a problem for further investigation. But if the fact is recognized that a neurotic character is invariably the underlying basis of a symptom neurosis, then it is clear that in *every* analysis we have to do with "character-neurotic" resistances—with resistances having their roots in the neurotic character; individual analyses will differ only in the varying importance which is attributed to character analysis in the individual case. But to look back upon one's analytic experience is to be warned against underestimating this importance in any case whatsoever.

From the standpoint of character analysis, the distinction between neuroses which are chronic, i.e. which have existed since childhood, and those which are acute, that is of recent development, loses all meaning; for it is not so important whether the symptoms have made their appearance earlier or later as it is that the neurotic character, the soil from which the symptom neurosis springs, was already formed—at least in its essentials—at the time of the passing of the œdipus phase. I will merely remind you of the invariable clinical experience that the boundary line which the patient draws between health and the outbreak of his illness inevitably vanishes in analysis.

Since the onset and occurrence of symptoms leave us in the lurch as regards a valid criterion, we must cast about for others. Let us consider first of all in this respect *insight* and *rationalization*.

Deficient insight is by no means an absolutely reliable characteristic but is nevertheless an important sign in character neurosis. The neurotic symptom is felt as a foreign body and gives rise to a feeling of being ill. The neurotic character trait, on the contrary, such as the exaggerated orderliness of the compulsive character or the anxious timidity of the hysterical character, is something organically built into the character. The subject may perhaps complain of his shyness or timdity, but he does not feel ill on this account. It is only when the characterological shyness rises to the pitch of pathological blushing or the obsessive orderliness to a compulsive ceremonial—i.e. when the neurotic character undergoes exacerbation to the point of the development of symptoms—that its subject feels ill.

There are also symptoms, it is true, into which little or no insight exists and which the patient regards in the light of bad habits or mere idiosyncrasies (such as for example chronic obstipation, mild *ejaculatio præcox*, etc.); yet there are a number of character traits which occasionally are felt to be pathological, such as violent outbursts of rage, gross untidiness, a tendency to lie or drink or squander money, and the like. In spite of exceptions of this sort, insight is an important characteristic of the neurotic symptom, its absence the hallmark of the neurotic character trait.

The second difference of practical importance consists in the fact that the symptom is never so completely and plausibly rationalized as in the neurotic character. Neither hysterical vomiting nor abasia, neither compulsive counting nor obsessive thinking, lend themselves to rationalization. The symptom appears to be meaningless, whereas the neurotic character is sufficiently rationally motivated as not to appear either pathological or meaningless. For neurotic character traits a reason is often put forward which would immediately be rejected as absurd if it were applied to symptoms, such as: "He just is that way"—with its implication that he was born so, that this "happens to be" his character, which cannot be altered. This view is certainly incorrect, for analysis shows that for definite reasons the character had to develop as it did and not otherwise, and that like a symptom it is, in principle, analysable and alterable.

It sometimes happens that in the course of time symptoms become so interwoven into the total personality as to be tantamount to character traits. Thus, for example, a counting compulsion may manifest itself within the compass of a general orderliness or a compulsive system subserve the daily routine; this sort of thing is especially true of the compulsion to work. Such modes of behaviour then pass for peculiarities, for excesses, rather than for anything pathological or of the nature of illness. It can readily be seen, therefore, that the concept of illness is an entirely fluid one—that every possible gradation exists from the symptom as an isolated foreign body, via the neurotic character trait and the "bad habit", to reality-adapted behaviour. Since we cannot use these in-between conditions as a point of departure, however, the distinction between symptom and neurotic character commends itself with regard to rationalization also, despite the artificiality of all such distinctions.

With this reservation in mind, there is nevertheless a distinction to be drawn between the symptom and the neurotic character with regard to their structure. Analytic dissection demonstrates that, as far as its meaning and origin are concerned, the symptom is of far simpler structure than the character trait. Certainly it is true that the symptom is overdetermined; but the more deeply we penetrate into its determinants, the further we get from the field of symptomatology proper and the more does the characterological substratum come to the fore. Thus from any symptom we can—theoretically— arrive at its characterological "reaction basis". The symptom has its immediate source in only a limited number of unconscious constellations; hysterical vomiting, for example, has as its root a repressed fellatio wish and a wish for a child. Both of these are also expressed characterologically—the former in a certain infantilism, the latter in a maternal attitude; but the hysterical character underlying the

hysterical symptom is determined by a multitude of largely antagonistic strivings, and is generally expressed in a specific *attitude* or
mode of behaviour. The latter is less simple to dissect than the
symptom, yet in principle it is, like the symptom, to be derived and
understood from infantile strivings and experiences. While the
symptom corresponds essentially to a definite experience or a
specific wish, the character, the specific mode or pattern of behaviour of a person, represents the expression of his entire past.
Hence it is possible for a symptom to develop with suddenness,
while each individual trait of character requires years for its development. In this connection we must not forget that the symptom could
not have made a sudden appearance if its characterological "reaction
basis" had not been already in existence.

The neurotic character traits in their totality manifest themselves
in analysis as a compact *defence mechanism* against our therapeutic
efforts; analytic exploration of the origin and development of this
characterological "armour" shows that it has also a definite economic
function, namely, it serves on the one hand as a protection against
stimuli from the outer world and on the other as a means for retaining mastery over the libidinal impulses constantly welling from the
id by using up libidinal and sadistic energies in neurotic reaction
formations, compensations, and so on. In the processes which
underlie the forming and maintaining of this "armour", anxiety is
constantly being bound, in the same way for example, according to
Freud's description, anxiety is bound in compulsive symptoms.
But since the means which the neurotic character makes use of to
bind anxiety, as for example reaction formations and pregenital
gratifications, have no permanence, the excessive anxiety, or the
dammed-up libido, sooner or later breaks through, and there then
arise symptoms indicative of the struggle of the ego to maintain
control over this excess. Thus the symptom is explicable from the
economic standpoint also as the expression of an "exacerbation" of
the neurotic character.

Since in its economic function as a protecting armour the neurotic
character has established a certain *equilibrium*, even though a
neurotic one, analysis signifies a danger to this equilibrium. It is
from this narcissistic protective apparatus of the ego, accordingly,
whence proceed the resistances which give to the analysis of the
individual case its particular stamp. But if the attitude, the behaviour and the reaction pattern of the patient represent the analysable and alterable resultant of his total development, there then

exists the possibility of evolving therefrom a technique of character analysis.

III. The Technique of the Analysis of the Character Resistance

In addition to the dreams, associations, slips of the tongue and the rest of the communications of the patient, his attitude and behaviour, that is to say, the manner in which he relates his dreams, commits these slips, produces associations and communicates other material, deserves special attention. The patient who follows the fundamental rule is a rarity; ordinarily it requires months of work of the character-analytic sort to bring him to even a half-way sufficient degree of honesty in his analytic work. The patient's manner of speech, the way in which he looks at the analyst and greets him, the way he lies on the couch, the inflection of his voice, the measure of his conventional politeness, and so on—all these are valuable criteria for estimating the hidden resistances with which the patient opposes the fundamental rule, and their understanding is the most important means of overcoming them through interpretation. The *how* is just as important as the *what* the patient says, as "material" to be interpreted. Often one hears analysts complain that the analysis does not go forward, that the patient does not produce any "material". What is referred to here is usually the content of the patient's associations and communications. But the manner in which the patient keeps silence or indulges in sterile repetition, for example, is equally "material" to be evaluated. Indeed, there is hardly a situation in which the patient brings "no material", and we must realize that it is our own fault if we are unable to utilize the behaviour of the analysand as "material".

That the manner and the form of the patient's communications have analytic significance is certainly nothing new. But that these open up an avenue of approach to the analysis of character in a very definite and relatively complete manner is the subject of the present discussion. Unfavourable analytic experiences with a large number of neurotic characters have taught us that in such cases it is primarily much more the form than the content of the patient's communications which is important. We need only mention in this connection the hidden resistances manifested by the effect-poor, the "good", the over-polite and punctilious, likewise by those patients whose transference is invariably a deceptively positive one, or who are violent in their monotonous and stereotyped demand for love, or who take analysis as a game, and those who are always "armoured", and those with an inward smile for everything and everybody. Such an enumeration could be continued indefinitely, but makes the more obvious the amount of painstaking work necessary to solve the innumerable individual problems of technique involved.

In the interest of a general orientation, and to bring out more fully the contrast between character analysis and symptom analysis, let us take two pairs of patients for comparison. Let us suppose that we have under analytic treatment two patients with *ejaculatio præcox* —one of them a passive-feminine, the other a phallic-aggressive character. We have also two women with a disturbance of eating— one with a compulsive character, the other with a hysteria. Let us further suppose that the *ejaculatio præcox* of both male patients has the same unconscious meaning: fear of the (paternal) penis fantasied as in the woman's vagina. Both patients develop in the analysis a negative father-transference, on the basis of the castration anxiety which underlies their symptom. Both hate the analyst (the father) because they regard him as the enemy who frustrates their pleasure, and both have the unconscious wish to do away with him. In this situation the phallic-sadistic character will ward off the danger of castration by means of insults, depreciation and threats, while the passive-feminine character will become increasingly submissive and friendly. In both patients the character has become a resistance; the former fends off the danger aggressively, the latter avoids it by the sacrifice of his own attitude and a deceptive submission. Obviously, the character resistance of the passive-femine patient is the more dangerous, because he works by secret means; he brings wealth of material, he recollects infantile experiences, he seems in short to co-operate splendidly, but he thereby covers over a fundamental, secret spite and hatred; as long as he maintains this attitude, he lacks entirely the courage to exhibit his true self. If, disregarding this manner of behaviour, the analyst deals only with *what* he brings, no analytic effort or interpretation will bring about any change in his condition. The patient may perhaps even recollect his hatred for his father, but he will not *experience* it unless the analyst interprets in terms of the transference the meaning of his deceptive attitude and behaviour *before* undertaking to interpret the deeper meaning of his father hatred.

In the case of the second two patients, let us suppose that an acute positive transference has developed. The central content of this positive transference is in both patients the same as that of the symptom, namely, an oral fellatio fantasy. But although the positive transference has the same content in either case, there results a transference resistance entirely different in form: the hysteric will perhaps manifest *anxious* silence and shy behaviour, the patient with compulsion neurosis a *spiteful* silence and a cold, haughty demeanour towards the analyst. The defence against the positive transference makes use of various means for the purpose—in one case aggressiveness, in another anxiety. In these two instances the id-wish is the same, but the defence instituted by the ego differs. Further, the form of this defence will always be the same in the same patient; the hysteric will always set up a defence of anxiety, the compulsive one of aggressiveness, whatever the content of the unconscious which is ever on the point of breaking through. That is to say, *in any given patient the character resistance remains always the same, and disappears only with the very roots of the neurosis.*

What follows from these facts, having bearing upon the technique of character analysis? Are there essential differences between it and the customary analysis of resistances? There are such differences, and they have to do with

(*a*) the choice of the order in which the material is to be interpreted;

(*b*) the technique of the interpretation of resistances itself.

With reference to (*a*) : if we speak of "choice of material", we have to expect a serious objection; it will be said that any selection runs counter to basic psychological principles, that the analyst must follow the patient and let himself be guided by him, and that any selection on the analyst's part invites the risk of his falling prey to his own inclinations and tendencies. To this it may be said in the first place that in such a selection it is not a question of passing over analytic material, but simply of preserving a logical sequence in interpretation, corresponding to the structure of the particular neurosis. All material is eventually interpreted; it is only that at a particular moment one detail is more important than another. It should be clear, indeed, that the analyst is always selecting, anyhow, for he has already made a selection when he omits interpreting a dream but instead chooses this or that detail to emphasize. One has also made a kind of selection, obviously, if one pays attention only to the content of the patient's communications and not to their form. Thus the very fact that the patient brings into the analytic situation material of the most varied description compels the analyst to make a selection of the material to be interpreted; what alone is important is that he make in relation to the given analytic situation a *correct* selection. Only during phases free from resistance can the guidance be left to the patient; his compulsion to confess is not to be too much relied upon; in general, patients tend to bring to the fore only the most harmless material—a tendency which when unmasked is revealed, of course, as a resistance.

In patients who because of a particular kind of character development are unable to follow the analytic rule consistently, or in the case of any characterological obstacle to the progress of the analysis, the analyst will be under the ever-present necessity of *isolating the character resistance from the total material and of dealing with it analytically by interpreting its meaning.* This does not mean, of course, that the analyst passes over or pays no attention to all other material; on the contrary, every bit of material is valuable and welcome which throws light on the meaning and origin of the disturbing character trait; the analyst merely postpones the dissection and in particular the interpretation of whatever material is without immediate bearing upon the transference until the character resistance, at any rate in its essential features, is understood and broken down. The dangers attendant upon giving "deep" interpretations in the presence of unresolved character resistances I have already attempted to indicate in my *Zur Technik der Deutung und der Widerstandsanalyse.*[1]

As to (*b*): We will now turn to some special problems of the technique of character analysis. First of all, we must forestall a possible misunderstanding. We said that character analysis begins with the isolating out and consistent analysis of the character resistance. This does not mean that one asks the patient, for instance, not to be aggressive, not to cheat, not to talk in a confused manner, to follow the fundamental rule, and so on. To do so would be not only unanalytic but fruitless. It cannot be sufficiently emphasized that what we are describing has nothing to do with education or the like. In character analysis we put to ourselves the question why the patient cheats, speaks in a confused manner, is emotionally blocked, etc.; we try to arouse his interest in his character traits, in order with his help to clarify analytically their meaning and origin. Thus we simply raise the character trait which constitutes the cardinal resistance above the level of the personality, and show the patient if possible the superficial relationships between the character and the

[1] *Internationale Zeitschrift für Psychoanalyse*, XIII, 1927, p. 141.

symptoms, while it is naturally left to him whether or not he wants to utilize his knowledge to change his character. In principle we proceed no differently than in the analysis of a symptom; what is added in character analysis is merely that we isolate the character trait and confront the patient with it repeatedly, until he has attained objectivity towards it and experiences it like a distressing compulsive symptom. The neurotic character thus takes on the nature of a foreign body, and becomes an object of the patient's insight.

Through gaining such a perspective of the neurotic character a change is quite surprisingly brought about—at first a temporary one —in the personality; and with the further progress of the analysis of character, that instinctual force or personality trait which had given rise to the character resistance in the transference automatically emerges undisguised. To continue with the example of the passive-feminine character: the more thoroughly the patient achieved an objective attitude towards his tendency to passive submission, the more aggressive he became. This was so because his feminine behaviour and attitude of deceit were an energetic reaction against repressed aggressive impulses. But with the aggressiveness we also have a reappearance of the castration anxiety which in infancy had determined the change from active to passive-feminine. Thus the analysis of the character resistance led directly to the centre of the neurosis, the œdipus complex.

One should not be under any illusions, however. The isolation and objectifying of such a character resistance, as well as its analytic working through, usually needs many months and demands unceasing work and above all unflagging patience. Yet once it has been possible to break through, the analytic work usually proceeds rapidly, to the accompaniment of *effectively* charged analytic experiences. If, on the contrary, such character resistances are allowed to go undealt with, while the analyst simply follows the patient in his material, constantly interpreting its content, such resistances form in the course of time a ballast which will be difficult if not impossible to remove. One then increasingly gains the impression that every interpretation of content was wasted, and that the patient never ceases to doubt everything or to pretend acceptance or inwardly to ridicule everything. If the elimination of these resistances was not embarked upon at the very beginning, one finds oneself helpless against them in the later stages of the analysis at a time when the most important interpretations of the œdipus complex have already been given.

In the paper already referred to I have attempted to meet the objection that it is impossible to cope with resistances before knowing what their *infantile* determinants are. The essential thing is first to see through the *present* meaning of the character resistance; for this the infantile material is not always necessary. This latter is needed for the *dissolution* of the resistance. If first one is content to demonstrate the resistance to the patient and to interpret its current or present-day meaning, then very often the infantile material with the aid of which we can then overcome the resistance makes its appearance.

If we emphasize a hitherto neglected fact, we possibly create the unintended impression of depriving everything else of significance. If we here underscore so heavily the analysis of the mode of behaviour, this implies neither a neglect of content nor a modification of the hitherto existing technique; to the latter we only add something that up to now has received too little regard. Our experience shows that the analysis of characterological resistances must be put ahead of everything else; but this does not mean that one analyzes only the character resistance up to a certain date, and then begins with the interpretation of content. The two phases, the analysis of resistances and the analysis of early infantile experiences, overlap for the most part; it is solely a matter of a preponderance of character analysis in the beginning, of "education *for* analysis *by* analysis"—while in the later stages the main emphasis is upon content and the infantile. This is of course no rigid rule but depends on the behaviour of the individual patient. In one, the interpretation of infantile material will be undertaken earlier, in another, later. It is a basic rule which must be emphasized, however, that "deep" analytic interpretations are to be avoided, even though the material itself is perfectly perspicuous, so long as the patient is not advanced enough to assimilate them. This again is nothing new, but it is evident that differences in analytic technique depend considerably on what the analyst understands by "ready for analytic interpretation". In this connection we have certainly to distinguish between content which has an immediate bearing upon character resistance and that which pertains to other spheres. The usual situation is that the analysand is in the beginning ready to take cognizance of the former but not of the latter. In general our attempt at character analysis simply represents an effort to achieve the greatest possible certainty in the matter of preparing the patient for analysis and of the interpretation of infantile material. This leads to the important task of studying and describing systematically the various forms of characterological transference resistances. Their technique then derives self-evidently from their structure.

IV. The Interpretation of the Ego-Defences

It is not difficult to align what we have here described as character analysis with Freud's theory of the forming and resolving of resistances. We know that every resistance consists of an id-impulse which is warded off, and of an ego-impulse which wards it off. Both of these impulses are unconscious. Theoretically, it would seem immaterial whether one interprets the id-striving first, or the ego-striving. Let us take an example. If a homosexual resistance in the form of keeping silent appears at the very outset of analysis, one may approach the id-striving by telling the patient that he is now occupied with affectionate thoughts about the analyst; one has then interpreted his positive transference, but, supposing that he does not take to his heels, it will be a long time before he reconciles himself to this forbidden idea. Hence one must preferably first approach the aspect of the resistance which is more closely related to the conscious ego, the *ego defence*, by only telling the patient at first that he is keeping silent because *for some reason or other*—thus without touching upon the id-striving—he rejects the analysis, presumably because it has become in some way dangerous to him. In the former instance one has attacked interpretatively the id aspect (in this case an erotic impulse) of the resistance, in the latter its ego aspect, the rejection.

By such a proceeding we come to comprehend at the same time both the negative transference in which every defence ultimately ends and likewise the character, the armour of the ego. Elsewhere I have tried to bring out that the superficial and more nearly conscious layer of *every* resistance must necessarily be a negative attitude towards the analyst, regardless of whether the id-impulse that is warded off is one of hate or love. The ego projects its defence against the id-impulse on to the analyst, who has become dangerous, an enemy, because by means of the disagreeable fundamental rule he has provoked id-strivings and disturbed the neurotic equilibrium. In defending itself the ego makes use of very primitive forms of negative behaviour for its protection; it summons hate impulses from the id to its assistance, even when it is a positive erotic impulse which is to be warded off.

If therefore we adhere to the rule of approaching resistances from their ego side, we thereby always resolve as well a certain amount of negative transference, a certain amount of hate, and in so doing avoid the danger of overlooking destructive tendencies, extremely well concealed as they so often are; and at the same time the positive transference is strengthened. Furthermore, the patient grasps ego interpretations more easily, because they are more in accord with conscious experience than are id interpretations, and he is thereby better prepared for the latter upon their advent.

The form of ego defence no matter of what nature the repressed id-striving may be, is always the same, and befitting the patient's personality; and likewise, the same id-striving is warded off or defended against in different patients in different ways. Thus we leave the character untouched if we interpret only the id-striving, but we draw the neurotic character into analysis if we approach the resistance from the standpoint of the defence which they represent, that is, from the ego side. In the former case we say immediately *what* the analysand is warding off; in the latter, we first make it clear to him that he is warding off something, then how he is doing it, what means he employs for this purpose (character analysis), and only finally, when the analysis of the resistance has progressed far enough, is he told, or finds out for himself, against what the defence is directed. On this long detour to the analysis of the id-strivings all the attitudes of the ego connected with these have been analysed, and the great danger of the patient's being told something too early or remaining without effect and without participation is obviated.

Analyses in which so much analytic attention is centred upon the attitudes of the patient take no less long than others; so that we cannot boast of having indicated a means of shortening analytic treatment; but comparison shows that they take a more orderly and purposeful course, while theoretical investigation does not suffer in the least. One merely learns important infantile experiences later than otherwise; but this is more than made up for by the effective freshness with which infantile material comes forth *after* analytic work on the character resistances.

Yet we should not leave unmentioned certain disagreeable aspects of a consistent character analysis. The analysis is a far heavier burden for the patient; he suffers much more than when the character is left out of consideration. This has the advantage, to be sure, of a winnowing process: those who cannot bear it would not have achieved success anyhow, and it is better that this lack of promise should become evident after four or six months than after two years. Experience shows that if the character resistance does not give way, a satisfactory result is not to be expected; that is particularly true of cases with hidden resistances. Overcoming the character resistance does not mean that the character has been altered; naturally that is possible only after the analysis of its infantile sources. It only means that the patient has gained an objective attitude towards his character and an analytic interest in it; once this is the case, favourable progress of the analysis is probable.

V. The Undermining of the Narcissistic Protective Apparatus

As we have said, the essential difference between the analysis of a symptom and of a neurotic character trait consists in the fact that the symptom is from the beginning isolated and objectified, whereas the character trait has continually to be pointed out to the patient in order that he may attain to the same attitude towards it as towards a symptom. It is only rarely that this is easily achieved. Many patients exhibit in only slight degree any aptitude for regarding their character in an objective way; these patients have in exaggerated degree a fear of finding out about themselves. For this, in fact, involves the undermining of the narcissistic protective mechanisms and the unbinding of the anxiety which is bound up with it. If the interpretation of this attitude is unavailing, it is then necessary to present to the analysand the alternative of giving up the analysis, or of expressly agreeing to the analyst's pointing out continually and again and again the character trait in question—a thing which in the course of time will become very disagreeable to the patient.

If, for example, a patient remains affectless and indifferent, regardless of the material he is producing, one has then to do with a dangerous blocking of effect, the analysis of which must be put before everything else if one is not to run the risk of having all the material and all one's interpretations go to waste, while the patient becomes a good analytic theorist but otherwise remains the same. Unless one prefers to give up the analysis of such a case because of "too great narcissism", one may make an agreement with the patient to the effect that one intends to confront him continually with his effectlessness, but that he, of course, may discontinue the analysis at any time he wishes. In the course of time—usually, in my experience, a number of months (in one case it took a year and a half)—the patient begins to find irksome the constant pointing out of his effectlessness and its reasons; for in the meantime one has gradually obtained sufficient clues for the undermining of the protection against anxiety which the blocking of effect represents. Eventually the patient rebels against the danger with which the analysis now threatens him—the danger of losing the protection of his psychic armour and of being confronted with his instinctual impulses, particularly his aggressiveness. But in this rebellion against analytic "chicanery" his aggressiveness is activated, and presently the first emotional outburst, in the sense of a negative transference, in the form of an attack of hatred, occurs. This achieved, the game is won. When aggressive impulses make their appearance, the blocking of effect has been broken through, and the patient becomes analysable. The analysis then proceeds as ordinarily. The difficulty consists in eliciting the aggressiveness.

The same is true when narcissistic patients, in conformity with their characterological make-up, live out their resistance in their manner of speech—when they talk in a haughty or bombastic manner or in technical terms, for example, or when they speak in carefully chosen words or in a confused manner. Modes of speech of this sort form an impenetrable wall, and no genuine experiencing in the analysis is possible until one makes the manner of speech itself the subject of analysis. Here, too, the consistent interpretation of behaviour provokes the patient's narcissism to revolt, for he is loath to hear that his carefully chosen speech, his haughty utterance, his parade of technical terms, are his means of concealing his inferiority feeling from himself and the analyst, or that he talks in a confused manner because he wants to appear particularly intelligent but is unable to express his ideas in simple form. In this manner one breaches the solid ramparts of the neurotic character at a critical point, and creates an avenue of approach to the infantile origins of the character and the neurosis. Naturally it is not sufficient to point out the nature of the resistance now and again; the more stubborn the resistance, the more consistently must it be interpreted. If simultaneously the negative attitudes towards the analyst which are thus provoked are analysed, the danger of the patient's breaking off the analysis is a negligible one.

In other cases the character has been set up as a solid protecting wall against the experiencing of (infantile) anxiety and has served well in this capacity, although at a heavy cost in the enjoyment of life. If such a person then enters analysis on account of some symptom, this protecting wall serves equally well in the analysis as a character resistance, and one very soon realizes that nothing can be accomplished until this characterological armour which covers and absorbs the infantile anxiety is destroyed. This is the case, for example, in "moral insanity" and in manic, narcissistic-sadistic characters. In such cases one is often confronted with the difficult question as to whether the symptom complained of justifies a deep character analysis. For it must be borne in mind, particularly in cases with a relatively good characterological compensation, that if the character analysis destroys this compensation a condition is temporarily created which amounts to a breakdown of the ego. Indeed, in more extreme cases such a breakdown is inevitable before a new ego structure, one adapted to reality, can develop. Even though one must concede that the breakdown would have taken place sooner or later anyway, the symptom in question being merely its first indication, still one will hesitate to undertake the great responsibility involved unless the need is urgent.

In this connection we must not omit to mention that in every case in which it is applied, character analysis gives rise to violent emotional outbursts, often indeed to dangerous situations, so that one must always be technically master of the situation. (Hence beginners should not attempt a consistent character analysis.) A collection of analytic experiences of this description will be published in another place. On this account many analysts will perhaps reject the method of character analysis; in that case they will have to relinquish hope of success in no small proportion of cases. Many neuroses are not accessible to mild measures. The method of character analysis, the consistent emphasis upon the character resistances and the persistent interpretation of its forms, modes of expression and motives, are as potent as they are unpleasant for the patient. This has nothing to do with education; rather, it represents a strict analytic principle. One does well, however, to bring to the patient's attention at the beginning the various foreseeable difficulties and unpleasantnesses involved in analysis.

To what extent is an alteration of the character necessary in analysis? And to what extent can it be brought about?

To the first question there is, in theory, only one answer: The neurotic character must be altered to the extent to which it forms the characterological basis of neurotic symptoms, and to the extent to which it conditions disturbances in the capacity for work and for sexual gratification.

To the second question the answer can only be an empirical one. The degree to which the actual result approximates the desired one depends in each case on a large number of factors. Qualitative changes of character cannot be directly achieved by present-day analytic methods. A compulsive character will never become a hysterical character, a paranoid character will never become a compulsive one; a choleric temperament will never change into a phlegmatic one, nor a sanguine into a melancholy. What can be achieved are quantitative changes which if of sufficient degree are tantamount to qualitative changes. Thus for example, the only slightly feminine attitude and behaviour of our compulsive female patient underwent a steady increase during analysis, while her masculine-aggressive tendencies became less apparent.

In this way the whole being of the patient becomes "different" —a difference which is often more noticeable to outsiders who see the patient only at intervals than it is to the analyst. The inhibited and self-conscious person becomes freer, the anxious and fearful more courageous, the over-conscientious less beset by scruples, the unscrupulous more conscientious; yet a certain indefinable "personal note" never disappears, but continues to gleam through whatever changes in the personality may have taken place. Thus, the formerly over-conscientious compulsive character becomes a realistic and conscientious worker, yet the impulse-ridden character, when cured will nevertheless act with more freedom than the former compulsive; the person cured of "moral insanity" will never take things too seriously and always will be able to get through life easily, while the cured compulsive character, owing to his lack of flexibility, will always have a somewhat difficult time. But after successful character analysis these characteristics remain within limits that do not restrict freedom of function sufficiently to impair the capacity for work or for sexual gratification.

One has every reason to be distrustful of therapeutic endeavours, including one's own. It will require objective criticism and verification to determine whether the assumption is justified that systematic character analysis constitutes a perhaps not insignificant augmentation of our analytic powers.

THE GENITAL CHARACTER AND THE NEUROTIC CHARACTER * (1929)

By Wilhelm Reich

I. The Economic Function of Character Formation

The point of departure in the present inquiry into character formation used to present an everyday therapeutic problem. It has long been known in psycho-analysis that the narcissism of patients, if not making analysis impossible altogether, in many cases sets a limit to the efficiency of analytic efforts. Thus the demands of daily practice having made it necessary to analyse theoretically this "narcissistic barrier" (Freud) and to inquire into its economic significance, its dynamics and origin. Furthermore, one has the experience that in not a small number of cases, while analysis of the unconscious and of repressed infantile experiences apparently proceeds smoothly, therapeutically the patient does not react correspondingly; in such cases one finally gains the impression that all analytic efforts rebound as from an "armour-plate", as though there were a wall between the intellectual ego and the depths of the effective personality, a wall through which no interpretation, no matter how correct its content, could break. Recalling the analytic axiom that successfully influencing a patient presupposes the theoretical knowledge of his psychic dynamics and economics, one will not be satisfied with the explanation that the patient's overly strong narcissism makes him insusceptible to therapeutic influence, but one will rather admit an insufficient understanding of an essential part of the structure of his personality. A study of the difficulties of technique revealed as the most important point of approach that the ego in a number of different patients with the same repressed content adopted highly different attitudes towards analysis in general and towards the fundamental rule in particular. It could furthermore be observed that this attitude adopted by the ego preserved a more or less constant character throughout the whole course of analysis, and that— undoubtedly the most interesting and important aspect of this

* Translated from the original: Der genitale und der neurotische Charakter: Untersuchungen über die libido-ökonomische Funktion des Charakters, *Internationale Zeitschrift für Psychoanalyse*, XV, 1929, p. 435.

phenomenon—the mode of behaviour of the ego was shown in the most marked way during periods of resistance, the nucleus of its attitude preserving a rigid and ever-recurring pattern. It became evident in the course of time that this mode of behaviour was determined by the character of the patient, joining as a constant formal resistive factor the various other resistances mobilized in defence against the content emerging from repression. This constant addition to the specific resistances might be designated by a special term "character resistance"; [1] further experiences have confirmed the earlier presumption that many failures in analysis can be traced back to the oversight of this constant attitude which, at a given moment becomes a resistance.

Starting from the questions, "How is the ego of the patient oriented towards psycho-analysis?—In what typical manner does it react?" it was possible to arrive at a formal definition of "character"; since, in analysis, the ego reacts as it is accustomed, only more markedly and distinctly, character had to be conceived formally as *the typical mode of reaction of the ego towards the id and the outer world*. Thus it was not so much the content of the patient's communications as the way in which they were expressed, not so much the reproach, for example, which the patient expressed against the analyst as his mode of expression which afforded the starting point for the analysis of the patient's character and of the resistance proceeding from it.

We now come to the question why character is formed at all, and what economic function it serves.

The avenue of approach to an answer of the first question is the observation of the dynamic function and the purposeful operation of the characterological reactions: *character is primarily and essentially a narcissistic protection mechanism.* [2] It then seems justified to

---

[1] See Über Charakteranalyse, *Internationale Zeitschrift für Psychoanalyse,* XIV, 1928, p. 180. The concept of "character resistance" is not to be confused with Freud's "ego resistance". It refers to the formal aspect of those phenomena designated by Freud as "ego resistance". The resistance with specific content offered by the ego is called ego resistance. The term "character resistance", however, refers to the typical form adopted in defence against the different contents. This form, by the way, remains the same even if an id resistance or a superego resistance should appear.

[2] It is necessary here to differentiate in principle our conceptions from Alfred Adler's formulations about character formation. Adler began his apostasy from psycho-analysis and the libido theory with the thesis that it was not the analysis of the libido but that of the nervous character ("person-

assume that if the character serves essentially as a protection of the ego, as at present in the analytic situation, it also originated in the first place as a mechanism serving as protection against danger. And the character analysis of each individual case, if traced back to the period of the final formation of the character, that is, the œdipal phase, shows that the character has been formed under the influence of the threatening external world and the pressing claims of the id.

Following up the theory of Lamarck, Freud and in particular Ferenczi distinguished an autoplastic and an alloplastic adaptation in psychic life. The latter denotes the fact that the organism, in order to exist, changes the outer world (technic and civilization); the former denotes that it changes itself. Biologically speaking, character formation is an autoplastic function set into motion by the disturbing and unpleasant stimuli emanating from the external world. In the clash between the id and the outer world which limits or altogether prevents libidinal gratification, and under the influence of the "real anxiety" (*Realangst*) which subsequently develops, the

ality") that was of importance. That he made an antithesis of libido and character and excluded the former from consideration was precisely that which psycho-analysis completely opposed. Starting from the same problem, namely, the purposeful mode of working of what is called the total personality or the characte., we make use of a fundamentally different theory and method. We consider character from a causal point of view when we ask what it is that impels the psychic organism to form a character, and only secondarily do we arrive at its purpose which we derive from this cause (cause: unpleasure; purpose: protection against unpleasure). Adler's point of view, however, was "finalist".

In our attempt to explain character formation on libidinal-economic grounds, we arrive at a wholly different result from that of Adler, who selects the "will to power" as an explanatory principle, and who therewith overlooks the dependence of the "will to power" as a narcissistic partial-striving upon the vicissitudes of the total narcissism and of the object-libido.

Adler's formulation concerning the working inferiority feeling and its compensations is correct, a fact which has never been denied; but he failed to establish their connection with the deeper-lying processes of the libido, particularly of organ libido. We differ from Adler in this very respect: we dissolve the inferiority feeling itself and its effects on the ego in the light of the libido theory.

It has therefore to be considered as a lack of methodological clarity when such inquiries are objected to on the grounds that Adler said this a long time ago. He could not possibly have said it because he used a different method and as far as he arrived at similar results, he still was a psycho-analyst. Such results have received full recognition. In other cases such objections show only that there is a reluctance to investigate again such problems as were Adler's proper field of investigation.

psychic apparatus reacts by erecting a protective mechanism between itself and the external world. In order to grasp this process—
indicated only roughly—we shall have, for the moment, to substitute
the topographical for the dynamic and economic point of view.

The ego, that part of the psychic apparatus which is exposed to
the outer world and which Freud has taught us to look upon as a
protective apparatus against external stimuli, is the locus where
character formation takes place. Freud has described for us in
illuminating and convincing fashion, the struggle which the ego
must wage as a buffer between id and external world (i.e. between
id and superego). The most essential element in this struggle is the
fact that the ego, in its attempt to mediate in the interest of self-
preservation between the two hostile factions, introjects the frustrat-
ing objects of the external world, in particular those which run
counter to the pleasure principle of the id, and retains them as a
moral institution, the super-ego. The morality of the ego, accordingly, does not derive from the id, and is therefore not an outgrowth
of the narcissistic-libidinal organism, but rather a foreign element
taken from the prohibiting and threatening external world. According to the psychoanalytic theory of the instincts, there is at first
nothing in the psychic organism but a mass of most primitive needs
originating in somatic states of excitation. Between these primitive
needs and the outer world the ego is introduced in the course of
development by means of a specific differentiation of part of the
psychic organism, and again on the basis of the primary narcissism
which serves self-preservation. Let us imagine, to illustrate the
point, the case of certain protozoa. Among these certain ones, the
rhizopods and the radiolarians, protect themselves against a rough
environment by means of an armour of inorganic material held
together by a chemical discharge of the protoplasm. Many of these
protozoa form spiral or circular spiniferous shells. The motility of
these armoured protozoa is considerably restricted compared with
that of the simple amœba; the contact with the environment is
limited to the pseudopodia, which, for purposes of locomotion and
nourishment can be protruded through small openings in the armour
and withdrawn again.

We shall have ample opportunity to make use of this comparison,
but even at this point we can define the character of the ego, or
perhaps, in accordance with Freud, the ego itself as the armour that
protects the id against the stimuli of the outer world. The ego, in
Freud's interpretation, is a structural institution. When we speak

of character in this context, we mean not only the external manifestation of this institution, but also the sum total of the modes of reaction which are operated by the ego, and are specific for the particular personality, i.e. an essentially dynamically determined factor which manifests itself in the characteristic appearance (gait, expression, posture, way of speaking, other modes of behaviour). The characteristics of the ego consist of elements of the outer world, of prohibitions, inhibitions of the instincts and identifications of various kinds. The components of the characterological armour are, then, of external, social origin. Before raising the question as to what unites these institutions, and what the dynamic process is that consolidates this armour, we must realize that, although protection against the external world was the main motive for character formation, that is by no means its main function. Against the real dangers of the external world, civilized man has a wealth of protective measures at his disposal: the social institutions in their various forms. As a highly developed organism, he has, in addition, his muscular apparatus with which to flee or to fight, and his intellect enabling him to anticipate and avoid dangers. It is typical for the characterological protection mechanisms that they are set in motion when an element of instinctual danger, i.e. anxiety originating from within and caused by external stimuli irritating the instinctual apparatus is present. It is the task of the character to master the actual anxiety stemming from the damming-up of the energy of repressed instincts, which cannot be discharged.

The relationship between character and repression is to be found in the fact that the necessity of repressing instinctual demands gives origin to character formation, but that on the other hand the character, once formed, makes a great deal of repression needless since the instinctual energies, which are free-floating in ordinary repression, are consumed by the character formation itself. The establishment of a character trait thus indicates the resolution of a repressive conflict achieved either by making repression unnecessary or by transforming an already present repression into a rigid ego-syntonic formation. The processes of character formation thus correspond entirely to the tendency of the ego, as described by Freud, to unify the strivings of the psychic organism. These facts explain also why it is so much more difficult to eliminate repressions which have resulted in well-established character traits, than those that are at the basis of a symptom.

There exists a definite relationship between the starting-point of character formation—i.e. protection against real dangers—and its ultimate function, protection against instinctual danger, anxiety resulting from accumulated libido, and absorption of instinctual energies. Social assimilation, particularly the development from a primitive uncultivated state to civilization, required a considerable restriction of libidinal gratification. The development of mankind, at least so far, has been progressing under the auspices of increasing sexual restriction, and the development of civilization, and of modern society in particular, has been accompanied by growing disintegration and restriction of geniality. With the advancement of civilization, the causes for reality-anxiety decreased at least for the individual; socially, the actual dangers threatening the life of the individual have increased. Imperialistic wars and class struggle undoubtedly make up for the dangers of primordial time. Nevertheless, civilization has brought about the advantage of security as a whole, an advantage that did not fail to produce its opposite. In order to avoid reality-anxiety people had to restrict their impulses; the instinct to destroy can no longer be gratified and the sexual instinct is shackled by social standards and prejudices; any violation of the norm would immediately entail a real danger, such as punishment for infantile masturbation, or imprisonment for incest or homosexuality. *To the extent to which real anxiety is avoided, damming-up of libido and its resultant anxiety increase.* Anxiety resulting from the accumulation of libido and real anxiety accordingly are complementary opposites: *the more real anxiety is avoided, the more intense becomes anxiety resulting from dammed-up libido and vice versa.* The fearless individual gratifies his strong libidinal needs even at the risk of social ostracism. Due to their inferior social organization, animals are more subject to the conditions of real anxiety, but hardly ever suffer from stasis of instinct except under the compulsion of domestication, and even then only under special circumstances. Man, however, though able to diminish real anxiety by means of policemen, laws, and morality, at the same time falls a victim of neurosis, the specific result of anxiety resulting from accumulated libido.

If we have emphasized here *the avoidance of (real) anxiety* and *the absorption of (dammed-up) anxiety* as the two economic principles of character formation, we must not overlook the third principle that character formation, in accordance with the pleasure principle, also strives for the greatest possible pleasure. Although cause and motive of character formation are protection against dangers accompanying instinctual gratification, once the armour is formed, the pleasure principle goes on working, since the character as well as the symptom serves not only the instinctual defence and the binding of anxiety, but also a disguised instinctual gratification. The genital narcissistic character, for example, has not only protected himself against the influences of the external world; he also satisfies a good part of his libido in the narcissistic relation of his ego to his ego-ideal. Instinctual gratifications are of two different kinds. The greater part of the energies of the warded-off instinctual impulses themselves, in particular the pregenital and sadistic ones, are consumed in the establishment and maintenance of the protective mechanism; this does not mean instinctual gratification in the sense of direct, undisguised pleasure, but at least a *lowering of the instinctual tension* similar to that produced by the "disguised" gratification in the symptom; and while, phenomenologically, this decrease of instinctual tension is different from direct gratification, it is of almost equal economic value: both reduce the pressure of the instinctual stimulus. *The instinctual energy is used up in the process of cementing and fusing the contents of the character* (identifications, reaction-formations, etc.). Thus in the dammed-up effects of certain compulsive characters, it is mainly sadism that is consumed in the construction and maintenance of the wall between the id and the external world, while in the exaggerated politeness and passivity of certain passive-feminine characters it is homosexuality.

The instinctual impulses which escape the fate of being consumed in character formation now strive for direct gratification unless they are repressed. The nature of this direct gratification depends on the character formation. Not only the difference between health and illness, but also the difference between the various types of character is determined by what impulses are used in the formation of the character and what impulses are allowed direct gratification.

In addition to the quality of the character, the degree of the characterological armour is of great importance. For if at any given moment the characterological armour against the external world and against the id has reached a degree corresponding to the conditions of libidinal development, "gaps" remain in the armour which provide for the contact with the external world. Through these gaps free libido and other instinctual impulses are brought in contact with the external world, or are withdrawn from it. The formation by the ego of its armour can reach such a degree that the gaps become "too narrow", so that the channels of communication with the external world no longer suffice to warrant a well-regulated libidinal economy and social adjustment. Catatonic stupor impresses us as exemplifying total occlusion, while the character structure of a man with unrestrained impulses illustrates entirely insufficient armouring. It is probable that every permanent conversion of object libido into narcissistic libido is accompanied by an intensification and solidification of the armour of the ego. The compulsive character, whose effects are blocked, has a rigid, unalterable armour which leaves him scarcely any fortuitous possibilities of emotional contacts with the external world; everything ricochets back from its smooth, hard surface. The querulous-aggressive character, on the other hand, has an armour which in spite of his mobility, is always bristling, and his relationships with the external world are on the whole limited to his paranoid-aggressive reactions. As a third example we quote the passive-feminine character; he appears compliant and mild, but analysis proves that his is an armour difficult to dissolve.

The final quality of the character—and this holds true for the typical as well as for the specific—is determined in two ways: first, *qualitatively*, by that stage of libido development in which the process of character formation was most decisively influenced by internal conflicts, i.e. by the specific fixation point of the libido. Accordingly we distinguish depressive (oral), genital-narcissistic (phallic), hysterical (genital-incestuous), as well as compulsive characters (anal-sadistic fixation); second, *quantitatively* by the libido economy which depends on the qualitative definition. One might call the first the historical and the second the present-day conditioning of the character. In the following investigations we shall mainly deal with present-day libido-economic factors.

II. The Difference in the Libido-Economy of the Genital and the Neurotic Character Respectively

The Difference in Libido Economy

If the armour of the character exceeds a certain degree, if it has made use of such instinctual impulses as under normal circumstances would serve the relation with reality, if, subsequently, the ability for sexual gratification, in particular, has been reduced too much, all the prerequisites for the formation of a neurotic character are present. In comparing the character formation and structure of neurotic persons with that of individuals capable of work and love, we find a *qualitative* difference in the means by which dammed-up libido is bound up in the character. It can then be stated that there are adequate and inadequate means of binding anxiety; the prototype of an adequate means being *genital-orgastic* gratification and sublimation; and that of inadequate means all kinds of *pregenital gratification* and *reaction-formation*. This qualitative difference also expresses itself in a quantitative one: the neurotic character suffers from steadily increasing dammed-up libido, for the very reason that his means of gratification are inadequate for the needs of the instinctual apparatus; the other, the genital character, is under the influence of a continuous change between libido tension and adequate libidinal gratification and thus disposes of a well-regulated libido economy. The term "genital character" [3] is justified by the fact that, with the exception of perhaps a few isolated cases, genital primacy and orgastic potency (itself determined by a certain character structure) alone guarantee an orderly libido economy, in contrast with all other libidinal structures.

The historically determined *quality* of the character-forming forces and content thus determines the quantitative regulation of the libido economy and thus also, at a certain point, makes for the difference between health and illness. With regard to the qualitative differences, the genital and the neurotic character, consequently, are to be considered as the paradigmatic types. The real characters are mixed types, and it depends on the deviation from one or the other ideal type whether libido economy is or is not secured. With regard to the quantity of possible gratification, the genital as well as the neurotic character are to be considered average types: either the libidinal gratification is such that it is able to remove the damming-up of unused libido, or it is not; in the latter case, symptoms or neurotic character traits are formed, which impair social and sexual efficacy.

We shall now try to describe the *qualitative* differences of the two ideal types, contrasting in turn the structure of the id, of the superego and, finally, the qualities of the ego which depend on both of the others.

(a) Structure of the Id

The genital character has fully reached the post-ambivalent genital stage (Abraham, *ibid.*), the incestuous desire and the wish to

[3] Cf. the study by Karl Abraham, on which this essay is based: *Psychoanalytische Studien zur Charakterbildung* (Int. Psa. Bibl. No. XXVI, 1925), especially Chapter III: Zur Charakterbildung auf der "genitalen Entwicklungsstufe".

do away with the father (the mother) have been abandoned, genitality has been transferred to a heterosexual object which does not, as in the neurotic character, actually represent the incest object, but has taken over its role entirely or, rather, has replaced it. *The œdipus complex no longer exists* in actuality but has "dissolved"; it is not repressed, but free of cathexis. If the analysis of genital characters is to meet with success, the incest object must first be cathected, a fact that usually involves a transitory damage to the present love relations. The pregenital tendencies (such as anality, oral-erotism, voyeurism, etc.) are not repressed, but have been anchored characterologically in cultural sublimations; partly they participate in direct gratification during fore-pleasure acts and are at any rate subordinated to genitality. The sexual act remains the supreme and most pleasurable sexual aim. Aggression, too, has to a great extent been sublimated in social achievements, while to a smaller extent it contributes directly to genital sexual life, without ever urging exclusive gratification. This distribution of instinctual drives assures corresponding orgastic gratification which, although it can be achieved only by genital means, i.e. in the genital zone, is not limited to the genital system but gratifies also the pregenital and aggressive tendencies. The less pregenital demands are repressed, and the better the systems of pregenitality and genitality communicate with each other, the more complete is the gratification and the fewer are the opportunities for a pathogenic accumulation of libido.

The neurotic character, however—if his native potency is not extremely low and if, as occurs in the majority of cases, he does not live in abstinence—is characterized by an incapability for the adequate orgastic discharge of free, unsublimated libido in orgasm. Orgastically, he is always *relatively* impotent. This fact originates in the following constellation of instincts: either the incestuous objects have an actual cathexis, or the corresponding libidinal cathexis has been used up in reaction-formations. If there is any love relation at all, its infantile nature can be easily seen: the loved woman takes only the place of the mother (sister, etc.) and the love relation is burdened with all the anxieties, inhibitions and neurotic whims of the infantile incestuous relationship (false transference). Genital primacy is either non-existent or not cathected or, as in the hysterical character, its functions are disturbed by the incest fixation of genitality. Sexuality moves—especially in transference neuroses —in the channels of fore-pleasure unless abstinence or aversion to sexuality prevail. Thus a vicious circle is established: the infantile sexual fixation disturbs the orgastic function of genital primacy, which disturbance creates accumulation of libido, the dammed-up libido in turn strengthening the pregenital fixations, etc. As a consequence of this hyper-cathexis and hypertension of the pregenital systems, libidinal impulses insinuate themselves into every cultural and social activity. This of course gives rise to disturbance, because the activity then becomes associated with repressed and prohibited emotions and occasionally even becomes disguised sexual activity (e.g. violinist's cramp). The libidinal contribution to social achievement is not freely available because in repression it is tied up with infantile instinctual aims.

(b) Structure of the Superego

The superego of the genital character is characterized above all by its encouragement of sexuality; therefore there is a high degree of harmony between id and superego. Since the œdipus complex has lost its cathexis, the counter-cathexis of the nuclear elements of the superego has become equally superfluous. It can be said that there are practically no sexual superego prohibitions. The superego is not overburdened with sadistic impulses, not only for the aforementioned reason, but also because there is no accumulation of libido to stimulate sadism and force the superego into cruelty.[4] Since there is direct gratification, genital libido does not conceal itself in ego ideal strivings; its social activities, therefore, are not above all a proof of potency, as in the neurotic character, but provide a natural, narcissistic, but non-compensatory gratification. Since potency is reliable, there are no feelings of inferiority. The ego ideal and the real ego do not differ too greatly, and there is consequently no unsurmountable tension between them.

In the neurotic character, however, the superego is characterized by its rejection of sexuality, which automatically gives rise to the strong conflict and contrast between id and superego. Since the œdipus complex has not been overcome, the nucleus of the superego —the fully retained incest prohibition—disturbs every form of sexual relation. (Details during the sexual act.) The strong sexual repression accomplished by the ego and the resultant accumulation of libido intensify the sadistic impulses which find their expression, among other things, in a brutal morality. (It is well to remember in

[4] Cf. Chapter VII of my book, *Die Funktion des Orgasmus,* on the dependency of sadism on dammed-up libido.

this connection that, according to Freud, it is repression that creates morality, and not vice versa.) Since there is always a more or less conscious feeling of impotence, many social activities become primarily compensatory proofs of potency, which fact, however, does not decrease the feeling of inferiority. On the contrary: since social achievements are frequently evidence of potency, but cannot in any way replace the feeling of genital potency, the neurotic character never rids itself of the feeling of inner emptiness and incapacity, however well he compensates for it. Thus the positive ego ideal demands are steadily raised higher, while the ego, impotent and doubly paralyzed by feelings of inferiority (impotence and exalted ego ideal), becomes more and more inefficient.

(c) Structure of the Ego

Let us now consider the influences exercised on the ego of the genital character. The periodic orgastic relaxations of the libidinal tension of the id result in a considerable reduction of the pressure of instinctual claims of the id on the ego; the id is essentially satisfied and the superego has no reason to be sadistic: it does not exert any particular pressure on the ego. The ego takes over for gratification the genital libido and certain pregenital tendencies of the id *without feelings of guilt* and sublimates the natural aggressiveness as well as parts of the pregenital libido in social achievements. The ego has no negative attitude towards the id with regard to genitality and thus is the more easily able to impose certain inhibitions on the id, since it yields to it in the main respect—libidinal gratification. This would appear to be the only manner in which the id can be held in restraint by the ego without resorting to repression. The manifestations of a strong homosexual tendency will vary according to whether or not the ego gratifies heterosexuality, that is whether or not there is dammed-up libido. This is easier to understand when stated in economic terms, for the reasons that in heterosexual gratification, energy is drained from homosexual tendencies, provided that homosexuality is not repressed, i.e. not excluded from the communication system (*Kommunikationssystem*) of the libido.

Since the ego is under little pressure from the id as well as from the superego—due in the first place to sexual satisfaction—the ego does not have to fight off the id as the ego of the neurotic character has to do; it needs only slight counter-cathexes and thus has sufficient energy for experiences and actions in the outside world; its actions and experiences are intensive and free-flowing; the ego is to a marked degree, accessible to pleasure as well as unpleasure. The ego of the genital character has an armour, but it masters it without being at its mercy. The armour is flexible enough to adapt itself to varying situations of life. The "genital" individual can be very cheerful, or, if necessary, very angry; his reaction to object-loss is adequate grief, but he does not succumb to it; he is capable of intense and devoted love as well as strong hate; he can be childlike at appropriate occasions without ever appearing infantile; his seriousness is natural and not rigid in an effort to compensate, because he does not insist on appearing adult no matter at what cost; his courage is not a proof of potency, but is related to an actual goal; accordingly, under certain circumstances, for instance in a war that he considers unjustified, he will not try to escape the stigma of cowardice but will stand up for his convictions. Since infantile wish-dreams have lost their cathexis, his hatred as well as his love is rational. Both the flexibility and the solidity of his armour are shown by the fact that he is able to open up to the world as intensively, in one case, as he is able to shut himself off from it in another. His ability for devotion is shown above all in his sexual experience: in the sexual act with the loved object the ego almost ceases to exist, except for its function of perception; the armour is temporarily dissolved almost entirely, the whole personality is submerged by the pleasurable experience without any fear of losing itself in it, for his ego has a solid narcissistic foundation which does not compensate but sublimates. His narcissism draws its best energies from the sexual experience. As to his actual conflicts, their rational character and freedom from infantile and irrational elements are revealed in the modes chosen for resolution; and also by the fact that rational libido economy makes a hypercathexis of the infantile experiences and wishes impossible.

In no respect is the individual possessing a genital character stiff or rigid; nor are the forms of his sexuality. Since he is capable of gratification, he is capable of monogamy without compulsion or repression; but he is also capable, if a reasonable motive is given, of changing the object without suffering any injury. He does not adhere to his sexual object out of guilt feelings or out of moral considerations, but is faithful out of a healthy desire for pleasure: because it gratifies him. He can master polygamous desires if they are in conflict with his relations to the loved object without repression; but he is able also to yield to them if they overly disturb him. The resulting actual conflict he will solve in a realistic manner. There are hardly any neurotic feelings of guilt. His sociality is based on not repressed but on sublimated aggression and upon his adjustment to reality. This does not mean, however, that he always bows to reality; on the contrary, more than any other he is capable of criticizing and changing his environment for the reason that his character structure is the opposite of that of the environment, our civilization being entirely obsessional-neurotic (anal and sadistic); his lack of fear of life makes it unnecessary for him to make those concessions to the environment that would be in conflict with his convictions.

If the primacy of the intellect is both a claim of social development and at the same time its goal, it is inconceivable without the primacy of genitality. The supremacy of the intellect not only sets an end to an irrational sex life, but is itself based on a regulated libido economy. Genital and intellectual primacy are interrelated, and determine each other mutually as do dammed-up libido and neurosis, superego (guilt feeling) and religion, hysteria and superstition, pregenital libidinal gratification and present-day sexual morality, sadism and ethics, sexual repression and societies for the rehabilitation of fallen women.

While in the genital character a well-regulated libido economy, borne by the capacity for full sexual experience, is the basis on which the described character traits are built, everything the neurotic character is and does, is ultimately determined by his inadequate libido economy.

The ego of the neurotic character is either ascetic, or susceptible to sexual gratification only with guilt feelings. It is under a twofold pressure: on the one hand, from the continually ungratified id with its dammed-up libido, on the other, from the brutal superego. The ego is hostile towards the id and submissive towards the superego, not, however, without the opposite attitude: flirtation with the id and a clandestine resistance towards the superego. The neurotic's sexuality, unless totally repressed, is predominantly of pregenital character, while his genitality, as a consequence of prevailing sexual morality, has an anal and sadistic tinge—the sexual act being considered dirty and cruel. Since aggression is modified, and anchored partly in the characterological armour, partly in the superego, social achievements are deficient. The ego is either entirely blocked against pleasure and unpleasure (blocking of affect), or open only to unpleasure, since every pleasure rapidly turns into unpleasure. The armour of the ego is rigid, communication with the external world is insufficient with respect to both object-libido and aggression, and is continuously controlled by narcissistic censorship. The functioning of the armour is directed mainly against the inner world: the result of this is a more or less explicit weakness of the reality function. Relations with the outer world are either unnatural, enervated, or contradictory; in no case is the total personality able to participate in harmony. The capacity for full experience is lacking. While the genital character can modify, strengthen or weaken his protective mechanisms, the ego of the neurotic character is completely at the mercy of the mechanisms of his character acting unconsciously in repression; he cannot act differently, even if he wanted to. He would like to be cheerful or angry, but cannot. He can neither love intensely, because, essentially, his sexuality has been repressed, nor can he hate adequately, because his ego cannot cope with a hatred which has become violent through the accumulation of libido and therefore had to be repressed. And whenever he manages to hate or to love, his reaction corresponds only slightly to the rational conditions; unconscious infantile experiences interfere and determine the nature and measure of the reactions. The rigidity of his armour makes it impossible for him to open up to any experience, and at the same time prevents him from completely closing himself up against other experiences when such a course would be rationally justified. Even though he be not averse to sexual experience nor disturbed in the actions preparatory to sexual intercourse, satisfaction either is not achieved at all or it is so much impaired by his lack of drive that the libido economy is not regulated. An exact analysis of the experience during the sexual act allows us to distinguish between various types, such as the narcissistic individual who is not turned towards pleasure but concentrates on appearing especially potent; or the hyper-aesthetic, who is always on guard against touching any part of the body which could hurt his aesthetic feelings; the person with repressed sadism who either cannot get rid of the compulsive thought that he might hurt the woman, or is tortured by guilt feelings for abusing her; the sadistic character to whom the act means torture of the object; the list could be continued indefinitely. Where such disturbances are not altogether manifest, one finds instead the corresponding inhibitions in the total attitude towards sexuality. Since the superego of the neurotic individual has a negative attitude towards sexuality, sexual experiences are rejected.[5] He turns away from sexual experience and thus only a part of the personality participates in the experience.

[5] H. Deutsch, erroneously, postulates this also for the healthy individual.

The feeling of impotency compels the ego to seek narcissistic compensations, whereas the genital character possesses a solid narcissistic foundation. The actual conflicts are permeated by irrational motives which make it impossible for the neurotic character to arrive at rational decisions; the infantile attitude and desire are always present, in a disturbing way.

Sexually unsatisfied and incapable of being satisfied, the neurotic character must, in the end, either become ascetic or live in rigid monogamy, as he believes, for moral reasons or out of consideration for his sexual partner—in reality, because of his fear of sexuality. Since his sadism has not been sublimated, since his superego rages without restraint, since the id continuously urges gratification of its needs, the ego develops both guilt feelings, which it calls social conscience, and a need for punishment by which it schemes to inflict upon itself all that it desires to inflict on others.

III. SUBLIMATION. REACTION-FORMATION AND NEUROTIC REACTION BASIS

Let us now turn to the differences between the social achievements of the genital and the neurotic character.

We have said before that whereas orgastic libidinal gratification and sublimation are the adequate means for mastering the accumulation of libido, as well as of controlling the anxiety stemming from dammed-up libido, pregenital libidinal gratification and reaction-formation are inadequate ones. Sublimation, like orgastic satisfaction, is a specific achievement of the genital character, while reaction-formation is the mode of functioning of the neurotic character. This does not mean, of course, that the neurotic does not ever sublimate nor that the healthy individual has no reaction-formations.

Let us try first to describe theoretically, on the basis of our clinical experiences, the relation between sublimation and sexual gratification. According to Freud, sublimation is the result of the diversion of a libidinal striving from its original aim and its direction towards a "higher", socially valuable one. Thus the drive which is gratified by sublimation must have renounced its original object and aim. This early formulation of Freud has led to the misunderstanding that sublimation and instinctual gratification are antithetic. If, however, we consider the relation between sublimation and the economy of the libido as a whole, everyday experience not only teaches us that the latter is not antithetic but, on the contrary, that a well-regulated libido economy is the very pre-requisite for successful and lasting sublimations. The important factor is that those drives on which our social achievements are based be not admitted to direct gratification—and not that all of the libido remain ungratified. Psycho-analysis of work disturbances shows that the greater the libido accumulation is as a whole, the more sublimation of pregenital libido is disturbed. Sexual fantasies either absorb the psychic attention and divert it from work, or cultural achievements themselves become sexualized and thus move into the sphere of repression.[6] Observations of the sublimation of the genital character show that they are stimulated over and again by orgastic gratification of the libido, that the relaxation of sexual tensions releases energies for greater accomplishment, since temporarily the sexual concepts do not attract any libidinal cathexis. Furthermore, we see in successful analyses that maximum efficiency is reached only when the patient achieves full sexual gratification. The durability of the sublimation, also, is dependent on the regulation of the libidinal economy; patients who lost their neurosis merely by sublimation show a much more labile condition and tend much more towards a relapse than those who not only achieve sublimation but direct sexual gratification as well. Just as complete and, above all, purely pregenital libido gratification interferes with sublimations, orgastic genital gratification promotes them.

[6] "It is indeed said that the struggle with such powerful instincts and the consequent strengthening of all ethical and æsthetic tendencies 'steels' the character; and this, for some specially constituted natures, is true. The view may also be accepted that the differentiation of individual character, now so much in evidence, only becomes possible with sexual restraint. But in the great majority of cases the fight against sexuality absorbs the available energy of the character, and this at the very time when the young man is in need of all his powers to gain his share of worldly goods and his position in the community. The relation between possible sublimation and indispensable sexual activity naturally varies very much in different persons, and indeed with the various kinds of occupation. An abstinent artist is scarcely conceivable; an abstinent young intellectual is by no means a rarity. The young intellectual can by abstinence enhance his powers of concentration, whereas the production of the artist is probably powerfully stimulated by his sexual experience. On the whole I have not gained the impression that sexual abstinence helps to shape energetic, self-reliant men of action, nor original thinkers, bold pioneers and reformers; far more often it produces 'good' weaklings who later become lost in the crowd that tends to follow painfully the initiative of strong characters." Sigmund Freud, Collected Papers, II, pp. 91–92.

Let us now compare, at first in a purely descriptive way, sublimation and reaction-formation. As far as their manifestations are concerned we observe that reaction-formation is cramped and compulsive, sublimation, however, free and flowing. In the latter case the id, in harmony with ego and superego, seems to be in direct contact with reality, while in the former, the impression is created that all achievements are enforced upon a recalcitrant id by a severe superego. In sublimation, the emphasis is on the effect of the action if the action is somewhat libidinally cathected; in reaction-formation, the interest is focussed on the action itself, the effect is rather of secondary importance, and the action is not of a libidinal nature but is negatively determined: it must be omitted. The "sublimating" person can interrupt his work for quite a while; rest is as valuable to him as work; if reactive activity is interrupted, however, restlessness will appear sooner or later which may increase to irritability or even anxiety in case of prolonged work disruption. The sublimating individual may also be occasionally irritated or tense— not because he does not achieve anything—but because he is, so to speak, giving birth to his achievement. The sublimating person *wants* to accomplish things and enjoys his work; the person working "reactively" *must* "robot" according to a patient's persistent formulation, and must begin some new work immediately after having finished the old, because work for him is an escape from rest. Occasionally the result accomplished by reaction-formation may be the same as that of sublimation. Usually, however, reactive achievements are less successful socially than sublimated ones. At any rate, the same individual would achieve far more under the conditions of sublimation than under those of reaction-formation.

While in sublimation there is no change in the direction of the instincts—the instinct is simply taken over by the ego and diverted to a different goal—in the case of reaction-formation, there is a reversal of the direction of the instinct: the instinct is turned against the self and only inasmuch as this reversal is achieved it is adopted by the ego. In the process of the reversal, the cathexis of the instinct turns into a counter-cathexis against the unconscious instinctual aim. The process of disgust, as described by Freud, may serve as an illustration of this. During reaction-formation, the original goal retains its cathexis in the unconscious. The original instinctual object is not abandoned but merely repressed.   Retention and repression of the instinctual goal and object, a reversal of the direction of the instinct, with the formation of a counter-cathexis, are the characteristics of reaction-formation; renunciation (not repression), replacement of the original instinctual object and aim, and continuity of the instinctual trend of the instinct without counter-cathexis, are the characterisitics of sublimation.

Let us further discuss the process of reaction-formation. Its most important economic aspect is the necessity of a counter-cathexis. Since the original instinctual goal is retained, libido is continuously moving towards it, and just as continually the ego must transform this cathexis into a counter-cathexis; it must, for example, derive the energy of disgust-reaction from anal libido, in order to check and control the drive. Reaction-formation is not a process which takes place but once; it is continuous and, as we shall see, a process which expands.

During reaction-formation, the ego is continually occupied with itself; it is its own strict supervisor. In sublimation, the ego has its energies available for the outer world. Simple reaction-formations, such as disgust or shame, are parts of the character formation of each individual. They do not hamper the development of the genital character, and remain within physiological limits because there is no dammed-up libido to strengthen pregenital strivings. But if sexual repression has gone too far, and if, in particular, it includes the genital libido to such an extent that an accumulation of libido results, reaction-formations receiving too much libidinal energy display a quality well known to the practitioner as "phobic spreading" in the case of phobias.

We will illustrate this with the case of a civil servant who, true to his compulsive character, performed his office work in an extremely conscientious way and, in the course of the years, devoted himself more and more to his work, although he did not in the least enjoy it. At the time he came for analysis it was not unusual for him to work until midnight or to three o'clock in the morning. Analysis soon revealed that in the first place sexual fantasies disturbed his work, which in itself made him spend more time on everything ("dawdling"), and in the second place, that he could not allow himself even one minute of rest, particularly in the evening, because hypercathected fantasies then pressed themselves into consciousness. By working at night, he discharged part of the libido, but the considerable remainder, which could not be consumed in this way, accumulated until he could no longer hide his work disturbance from himself.

The spreading of reaction-formation and reactive achievements

correspond, then, to a steadily increasing damming-up of the libido.
When, eventually, reaction-formations no longer suffice to master
the dammed-up libido, when decompensation sets in, when, in other
words, the character of the ego fails to consume the libido, either
undisguised neurotic anxiety emerges or neurotic symptoms are
formed, to consume the excess of free floating anxiety.

Reactive achievements are always being rationalized. Thus our
patient pretended that he was overburdened with work. His exaggerated and mechanical activity not only served the economic
function of relaxing his tension, nor was it used only as a diversion
from sexual fantasies—it also served the purpose of a reaction-
formation against his repressed hatred for his chief (father). Analysis
revealed that the patient's efforts to be of special service to his
superior represented the antithesis of his unconscious intentions.
Such "roboting" cannot be interpreted, in the final analysis, as self-
punishment. Self-punishment is only one of the many meanings of
the symptom. In a deeper sense, the patient wanted not to punish
himself, but, on the contrary, to protect himself against punishment.
The deepest cause of the reaction-formation was the fear of the
consequences of his sexual fantasies.

Neither compulsive toiling nor other reaction-formations are able
to absorb the entire dammed-up anxiety. Let us recall, for instance,
the hyper-motility of the female-hysterical character, or the hyper-
agility and unrest of the neurotic mountain-climber. Both have a
muscular system which is overcharged with unsatisfied libido, both
are continually pushing towards the object, the hysterical girl
openly, the mountain-climber in a symbolic way (mountain—
woman—mother). Their motility, although consuming part of the
libido, simultaneously increases the tension since it does not grant
ultimate gratification; that is why the girl finally develops hysterical
attacks, and the neurotic mountain-climber has to undertake increasingly exhausting and dangerous climbs in order to master the
accumulation of his libido. Since there are natural limits beyond
which the mountaineer cannot go, a symptom neurosis eventually
develops unless, as happens so frequently, he meets with an accident
in climbing.

The sum total of all those mechanisms that serve to absorb the
dammed-up libido and to bind neurotic anxiety in character traits
might be termed the *characterological* "reaction basis" (*Reaktions-
basis*). If the latter fails in its economic function as a result of
exaggerated sexual restriction it becomes the *neurotic* "reaction

basis", the removal of which is the ultimate aim of analytic treat-ment. The expanding reaction-formation is only one of the mechan-isms of the neurotic reaction basis.

The exacerbation of the neurotic character may take place at an early date ; but it can be established in every case that the neurotic character has existed from early childhood, since the period of the œdipus conflict. The neurotic symptom usually shows a qualitative relationship to its neurotic reaction basis. Thus, to cite a few examples, compulsive over-tidiness may increase until one day at an appropriate occasion, it becomes obsessional orderliness; the anal character may develop constipation; characterological bashful-ness produces pathological blushing; hysterical agility and coquetry may grow into hysterical attacks; characterological ambivalence into inability to make decisions, aversion to sex into vaginismus, aggres-siveness or over-conscientiousness into impulses to murder.[7]

A review of the results of this investigation points to the import-ance of making as sharp a distinction as possible between the neurotic and the genital type of character. Since the distinction is based on a quantitative criterion (the extent of direct sexual gratification and accumulation of libido), there must be, between the ideal types, innumerable transitional types or real character forms. Neverthe-less, a typological investigation seems not only justified but impera-tive because of its heuristic value and for the insight it provides in practical work. Since this essay only furnishes a beginning of a genetic typology, it must forego the claim to answer all questions arising from the problem complex of typology. Its immediate task is accomplished if it has succeeded in convincing the reader that the only legitimate basis for psycho-analytic characterology is to be found in Freud's theory of the libido understood completely, and pursued consistently.

[7] Not always, however, is the neurotic symptom in qualitative relation to its reaction. The symptom may represent a defence against surplus anxiety on a higher or lower libidinal level. Thus, a hysterical character may develop a washing compulsion, a compulsive character may produce hysterical anxiety or a conversion symptom. We need not go into any detail to emphasize that the actual cases in our practice represent, for the most part, mixed types in which one or the other character form prevails. It is advis-able, however, to arrive at a diagnosis not on the basis of the symptoms, but on that of the neurotic character underlying the symptoms. Thus, one will diagnose compulsion neurosis in spite of a conversion symptom for which the patient seeks our help, if compulsive neurotic traits predominate in his character.

CHARACTER FORMATION
AND THE PHOBIAS OF CHILDHOOD * (1930)

BY WILHELM REICH

In our clinical experience we are constantly called upon to deal
with the problem of what Freud has named "the narcissistic
barrier". By this we mean in psycho-analysis all those difficulties
which the patient's narcissism opposes to our efforts. Unless we
have a clear theoretical comprehension of this mechanism, to which
we attach the term "narcissistic barrier", we shall have considerable
difficulty in finding the way to overcome it. Protected as we are
against any overweening therapeutic optimism by the bitter experiences of our work and the efforts it demands, we are justified
in the view that it is just these therapeutic difficulties which make it
possible to formulate the most valuable and fruitful problems in
scientific psychology. In fact therapeutic activity presupposes an
understanding of psychical movement and dynamic; and in this
case also we are compelled, owing to the problem in technique
offered by this "narcissistic barrier", to undertake the study of
characterological reactions.

In two papers ("On Character Analysis" and "The Genital and
the Neurotic Character") [1] I have attempted a theoretical discussion
of the problems involved, though thorough substantiation of my
views by clinical case-material had to be omitted owing to lack of
space. In the following paper I hope in part to develop further the
general theoretical formulations of the above-mentioned papers,
while at the same time illustrating them with clinical material.

The main idea of those papers was as follows: that in our practice
we become aware of the narcissistic barrier as a sort of "armour" or
"rampart" of defence, against which our interpretations and therapeutic efforts rebound, unless we are able to break up this narcissistic
defence by means of analysis and interpretation of its purposive
mode of action. Further, that this narcissistic armour represents

* First published in the *International Zeitschrift für Psychoanalyse*, XVI,
1930, p. 353: Über kindliche Phobie und Charakterbildung. Reprinted
from *The International Journal of Psycho-Analysis*, XII, 1931, p. 219.
[1] This volume, pp. 106 and 124.

an expression, which has been definitely formed and permanently crystallized in the psychical structure, of a narcissistic defence. Finally, that this defence finds *formal* expression in a specific mode of reaction on the part of the patient, which is independent of the *matter* of the repressed material to be defended. In addition to the familiar resistances which are assembled against the discovery of every fresh piece of unconscious material, there is further a constant factor of a formal nature, which proceeds from the character of the patient. In view of its origin this constant formal resistance was named "character resistance", and the following is a brief summary of our conclusions concerning it:

(1) The expression of character resistance does not vary with the material which is being produced, but is typical and constant, taking the form of a general attitude, manner of speech, gait, affectations and peculiar ways of behaving. (Smiling, sneering, precise or confused speech, special types of politeness or of aggressiveness, etc.)

(2) In regard to character resistance the significant thing is not *what* the patient says and does, but *how* he speaks and acts, not *what* he reveals in his dreams, but *how* he censors, distorts and disguises this material.

(3) Character resistance remains constant in type for one patient, in spite of varying material. Different characters produce the same material in different ways. For instance, positive father-transference is expressed and resisted in one way by the female hysteric, in quite another by the female obsessional. In the former case we shall probably have anxiety, in the latter aggressiveness.

(4) Character resistance, though it finds a purely formal expression, is, nevertheless, just as susceptible to resolution by analysis as is a neurotic symptom, and can, like the latter, be traced back to infantile experiences and instinctual interests.[2]

(5) At the appropriate moment the character of the patient becomes a resistance; that is to say that, in ordinary life, character plays a part similar to that played by resistance in treatment—it is a protective mechanism in the mind. Accordingly we speak of the characterological defence of the ego against the external world and the id.

(6) If we trace the formation of character back into early child-

---

[2] In realizing this, we are enabled to include the purely *formal* within the sphere of psycho-analysis, which has hitherto been mainly occupied with *matter* or *content*.

hood, we find that it was the product of similar causes, and served similar ends to those which stimulate character resistance in the analytic situation of the moment. The appearance of character as resistance in analysis reflects its infantile origins. And those apparently incidental situations which character resistance brings about in analysis are exact recapitulations of the situations which in childhood instituted the process of character formation.

(7) Thus we have in character resistance a combination of defensive function with the transference of infantile relations to the environment.

(8) From the economic point of view, both character in daily life and character resistance in analysis serve the purpose of avoiding pain, of establishing and maintaining psychical (though possibly neurotic) equilibrium, and finally, the absorption of that quantity of instinctual energy which has undergone or has escaped repression. One of its main functions is the binding of free-floating anxiety, or—the same thing regarded from another angle—the release of dammed-up psychical energy.

(9) In character, as in neurotic symptoms, the past, the infantile, are conserved; they live and are effective in the present.

(10) Thus we see that the consistent resolution of character resistances is bound to give direct access to the central infantile conflict.

These ten propositions on the subject of character are the result of experience gleaned from about twenty specially studied cases. I shall now proceed to demonstrate how in one individual case characterological behaviour was derived from the experiences of childhood, and how this behaviour developed into a resistance. In doing so, I shall follow the path which led from the analysis of character resistance to its origin in certain definite infantile situations.

A man, aged thirty-five years, came for analysis on account of difficulties in his married life and inability to carry out his work satisfactorily. He suffered severely from inability to make decisions, which stood in the way both of a rational solution of his marriage problems, and also of advance and success in his professional life. The patient began his analysis with unusually quick understanding and skill, so that after quite a short time a theoretical explanation of his marriage difficulties could be arrived at by reference to the usual pathogenic conflicts of the œdipus situation. We will pass over the material concerning the relation between his wife and his mother, his superiors and his father, which, though interesting in themselves, contribute nothing new. We will concentrate rather on the delineation of his behaviour, and the relation of this behaviour to his infantile conflict, and to the type of resistance which he showed during treatment.

The external appearance of the patient was prepossessing; he was of medium height, and his bearing was reserved and dignified, serious, and somewhat haughty. Particularly noticeable was his slow, deliberate and dignified gait. It took him quite a considerable time to enter the door and cross the room to the sofa; it was quite obvious that he was avoiding (or concealing) any kind of haste or excitement. His speech was well ordered and deliberate, quiet and dignified; occasionally he would interrupt its course with a sudden emphatic "Yes!", throwing out both his arms as he said it; after which he would pass one hand across his forehead. He used to lie calmly on the sofa, one leg crossed over the other.

There was little or no variation in this calmness and dignity, even when he was speaking of delicate subjects such as are usually likely to be wounding to the patient's narcissism. When, at the end of a few days' analysis, he spoke of his relation to his specially loved mother, it was obvious that he increased the dignity of his manner, in order to control the excitement which was mastering him. In spite of my urging him not to mind, but to give free course to his feelings, he maintained this attitude and his calm manner of speech. In fact one day, when tears came into his eyes and his voice actually faltered, the movement with which he put his handkerchief to his eyes was, nevertheless, as calm and dignified as ever.

So much was already clear: his behaviour, whatever its origin, guarded him against any too violent disturbance in his analysis and protected him against an emotional outburst. His character stood in the way of the free development of analytical experience—*it had already become a resistance.*

When I asked him soon after the occasion when I had perceived his emotion, what his impression was of this particular analytical situation, he replied calmly that it was certainly very interesting, but it had not moved him very deeply—the tears had just escaped from his eyes, and this had caused him considerable embarrassment. My explanation of the necessity for such emotional outbursts and their value was useless. His resistance was visibly strengthened, and his communications became superficial. His manner on the other hand was still further emphasized; he became even more dignified, calm and quiet.

It may have been by the merest chance that one day the term "lordly" came into my mind in connection with his behaviour. I told him that he was acting as if he were an English lord, and that this must surely have its origin in his youth and childhood. I also explained to him the defensive function at the moment of his "lordliness". He thereupon produced the most important item of his private "family romance". As a child he had refused to believe that he could be the son of the small insignificant Jewish shopkeeper that his father was; he must be, he thought, of English origin. He had heard in childhood that his grandmother had had an affair with a real English lord and he imagined his mother to be half English. In his dreams of the future the fantasy that some day he would go as ambassador to England had played a predominant part.

His "lordly" bearing thus expressed:

(1) That he was not related to his despised father (father-hate).

(2) That he was the true son of his mother, who had English blood; and

(3) His ego ideal, that of getting beyond the narrow environment of a lower middle-class family.

This discovery of the constituents of his behaviour caused a considerable modification in his attitude. But it was not yet clear what instinctual trends were being defended by it.

As we pursued the investigation of his "lordly" behaviour, it became clear that this was closely connected with another peculiarity of his character which caused no less difficulty in his analysis; this was his tendency to deride his fellow-men and to take pleasure in their misfortunes. His scorn was the result of his exalted position as a "lord", but at the same time it served to gratify his sadistic impulses, which were particularly strong. As a matter of fact he had already told me that at puberty he had indulged in a wealth of sadistic fantasies. But he had only *told* me this. He began to *experience* them only when we began to track them down in their present-day form—in his tendency to scoff. The "controlled" manner demanded by his position as a "lord" *protected* him from going too far in finding sadistic gratification in scoffing. His sadistic fantasies were not repressed, but were gratified by his scorn, and he was defended against them by his position as "lord". Thus his haughty behaviour had exactly the same structure as a symptom: it served as a defence against an instinctual trend, while at the same time providing gratification for it. There was no doubt that he had, by means of this defence, been able to avoid having to repress all his sadism; that is to say, by means of the characterological elaboration of his sadism into hauteur. Had the circumstances been different, the slight fear of burglars which he had would probably have developed into a regular phobia.

The "lord" fantasy had begun in his fourth year. He had realized the necessity for self-control somewhat later, from fear of his father. To this was added a very important motive for the control of his aggressive impulses, that of a counter-identification with his father. The latter used constantly to quarrel with his mother and make an uproar, and the boy set before himself the ideal of being not like his father, but the exact opposite,[3] corresponding to the fantasy: "If I were my mother's husband, I would treat her quite differently; I would be kind and control my annoyance at her deficiencies." This counter-identification was thus completely under the influence of his œdipus complex—love of his mother and hate of his father.

Dreaminess and self-constraint concealing active sadistic fantasies characterized him as a boy, and represented the "lord" fantasy. At puberty he made an intense homosexual object-choice in the person of a teacher, which ended in an identification. This teacher was, moreover, the very essence of a lord, dignified, calm, self-restrained, faultlessly dressed. This identification began with imitation of his clothes. Other identifications ensued, and at about fourteen years of age his character, as we had it to deal with in analysis, was fully formed. It was no longer a mere "lord fantasy"; he was a "lord" in his actual behaviour.

There was, moreover, a special reason for a realization of his fantasy in his behaviour at this particular age. The patient had never consciously masturbated during puberty. His castration anxiety, which was expressed in a number of hypochondriacal fears, was rationalized as follows: "A dignified person doesn't do such things". His position as a "lord" was thus also a protection against the desire to masturbate.

A a "lord" he felt himself superior to all men, and was in a position to scorn them. In analysis, however, he had soon to yield to the realization that his scorn was superficially a compensation for his feelings of inferiority, just as indeed all his "lordliness" concealed a sense of inferiority due to his lowly origin. The deeper significance of his scorn lay, however, in the fact that it was a

---

[3] Cf. here my investigations concerning identification as regards faults in *Der triebhafte Charakter*, Vienna, Int. Psa. Verlag, 1925.

substitute for homosexual relations. He specially scoffed at men who attracted him; he did not concern himself with others. Scoffing = sadistic activity = homosexual flirtation. In his "lordliness" were united sadism and homosexuality on the one hand, with, on the other hand, their opposite—dignified self-restraint.

During analysis, the patient's "lordly" bearing became intensified with every fresh advance into the unconscious. As time went on, however, these defensive reactions weakened, while his behaviour in everyday life underwent modification, but without ever losing its essential character.

The analysis of his "lordliness" led directly to the revelation of the chief situations of conflict in his childhood and puberty. His pathogenic defences were thus attacked from both sides: through his memories, dreams and other communications—here with little expression of emotion—and through his character, his "lordliness", in which were bound his aggressive affects.

The Characterological Elaboration of the Childish Phobia

A considerable amount of castration anxiety was included in this display of dignified behaviour. The history of the connection between the two things indicated an end-product of a childish phobia, concerning which little has hitherto been known. Between the ages of about three to six years the patient suffered from a very intense phobia of mice. As to the content of this phobia, it suffices to say that it constituted a working-out of his feminine attitude to his father as a regressive reaction to his castration anxiety. Connected with this was a typical masturbation anxiety. Now as the boy's "lord" fantasy developed into "lordly" behaviour, so his phobia decreased. Later there only remained a trace of anxiety just before he went to bed. During analysis, with the resolution of his "lordly" behaviour there arose again, and moreover with emotion, his phobia of mice and his castration anxiety. It was thus evident that a part of the libido involved in his childish *phobia*, or alternatively, the anxiety, had been transferred to and elaborated in his *characterological behaviour*.

We are aware of course of the process by which infantile demands and anxieties are transformed into character-traits; the resolution of a phobia through the institution of a special type of defence against the external world and against anxiety, determined in accordance with the structure of the instinctual trends involved, is a particular instance of this process. In our case it was a dignified attitude which served to bind infantile anxiety. Another typical case is the development of a childish phobia, or indeed of simpler manifestations of castration anxiety, into a passive feminine attitude, expressed perhaps in the form of an exaggerated, stereotyped politeness. Such politeness may become during treatment a character resistance which is frequently very difficult to overcome.

The following case is cited as a further illustration of the transformation of a phobia into a characterological manifestation of personality:

An obsessional neurotic displayed in addition to his symptoms a remarkable and absolute suppression of affect. He was inaccessible to both pleasure and pain, a living machine. During analysis this suppression of affect was revealed as being in the first place a defence against his extreme sadism. He had indeed in adult life entertained sadistic fantasies, but they were subdued and lacked life. One felt that there must be, as motive for this defence, a correspondingly intense castration anxiety, although this was not in the least apparent. Through analysis we were able to trace this suppression of affect to the very day of its origin.

This patient had likewise suffered from the usual childish phobias, in his case, of horses and snakes. Up to his sixth year of age he had had anxiety dreams practically every night accompanied by *pavor nocturnus*. Most frequently he dreamt that a horse bit off one of his fingers (masturbation—anxiety—castration) the dream being associated with intense anxiety. One day he resolved that he would not be afraid again (we will return to this remarkable resolution), and the next horse dream, in which he again had a finger bitten off, was accompanied by no anxiety at all.

At the moment at which the suppression of all affect was achieved, the phobia was resolved. Only in the period after puberty did anxiety dreams occasionally recur.

Now as regards his remarkable decision to feel no more fear: we were not able to explain completely the dynamic processes involved. But we may remark that his life was directed almost exclusively by means of such resolves. Nothing could be done without special resolutions. This capacity to make resolves was the product of his anal obstinacy and of the extraordinarily severe demands of his parents that he should control himself, which he had adopted as his own. His anal obstinacy also formed the dynamic basis for his suppression of affect, which, among much else, represented a general *"Götz von Perlichingen"* attitude to the whole external world. When the patient had been under treatment for six months, it came out for the first time that, every day before he rang my front-door bell, he said three times aloud to himself the *Götz* formula,[4] as a charm to protect him in his analysis. His suppression of affect could not have found better verbal expression.

Thus the chief constituents of this suppression of affect were: his anal obstinacy, and his reaction against sadism. This defensive reaction served to bind not only his sadistic energy, but also his tremendous childish anxiety (the anxiety of dammed-up libido plus castration anxiety). Only when we had worked through this defensive rampart, through a mass of the most various repressions and re-action-formations, did we come up against his intense genital incest wishes.

While the development of a phobia is a sign that the ego has been too weak to obtain control over certain libidinal strivings, the development of a character-trait or of a typical attitude, at the expense of a phobia, indicates a strengthening of the ego in the form of a constant defence against the id and the external world. If the phobia implies a splitting of the personality, then the development of a character-trait involves a unifying of the individuality. It is a synthesizing reaction on the part of the ego to a contradiction in the personality which, as a permanent condition, is unendurable.

In spite of the opposite nature of a phobia and the subsequent character-development, the fundamental motive in the phobia is pursued in the character-trait. The dignity of our "lord", the suppression of affect in our obsessional neurotic, the politeness of the passive feminine character—all these are in fact just as much *attitudes of avoidance* as were the preceding phobias.

The ego, in building up this defence, succeeds in strengthening itself to a certain extent, but at the same time it suffers some impairment of its capacity for action and freedom of movement. And the more this defence injures the capacity for future sexual experience, the greater is this limitation, and the nearer does its structure approach to the neurotic; while at the same time the greater does the probability become that there will be in the future a fresh breakdown of the personality.[5]

When a neurotic illness develops later, the old phobia breaks

[4] [An obscene phrase of refusal to surrender.—Tr.]
[5] Cf. here my discussion of the genital and neurotic character, p. 145 of this volume.

through again, the characterological elaboration proving inadequate to control the dammed-up libidinal excitation and the anxiety caused by the dammed-up libido. We may therefore say that in a typical neurotic illness the following phases may be distinguished:

(1) Infantile conflict between libidinal excitation and frustration.

(2) Relief through repression of the excitation (the ego strengthened).

(3) Partial breach in the repression—phobia (the ego weakened).

(4) Resolution of the phobia by the formation of a neurotic character-trait (the ego strengthened).

(5) The conflict of puberty (or an equivalent): inadequacy of the characterological defence.

(6) Re-establishment of the old phobia or a symptomatic equivalent.

(7) Renewed attempt of the ego to overcome the phobia by means of a characterological elaboration of the associated anxiety.

Among the adult patients who come to us for treatment, two types may be easily distinguished: those in the breakdown phase (phase 6), in whom an old neurosis now caps as a symptom the original neurotic type of reaction (the renewed development of a phobia, etc.); and those who have already reached the reconstructive phase (phase 7), i.e. whose ego has already begun to succeed in incorporating the symptom. A circumscribed compulsion to arrange things, for instance, which has become troublesome, becomes less tormenting when the subject, *with the consent of his whole personality*, succeeds in evolving a ritual of tidiness, which can be so distributed throughout the activities of his daily life as to betray its compulsive character to none but the trained eye. By this means an appearance of self-cure is obtained, but the distribution and levelling of symptoms limits capacity for action no less than did the circumscribed symptom, and the patient now requires treatment, not on account of a troublesome symptom, but on account of a general disturbance in his capacity for work, lack of pleasure in life, and the like. There is thus a constant struggle between the ego and its neurotic symptoms, both of whose end-points consist in *symptom-formation* and *symptom-incorporation*. Every symptom-incorporation is, however, associated with a *characterological change* of greater or lesser significance. These later inclusions of symptoms within the ego are simply recapitulations of those first important processes in childhood by which the transformation of a childish phobia into a character-trait was partly or wholly accomplished.

We have dealt here with the phobia because it is the most interesting and, from the point of view of libidinal economics, the most important expression of a disturbance in the unity of the personality. But the processes which I have described may take place in connection with any anxiety occurring in early childhood; for example, a child's fear of a brutal father, well-founded in reality, may result in permanent character changes, which take the place of the fear such as, let us say, a characterological rigidity, or hardness, etc.

The fact that infantile experiences associated with anxiety, and other situations of conflict connected with the œdipus complex (for the phobia is of course brought forward here only as a special example of these), may result in the production of character-traits, implies that an experience or an intra-psychical situation in childhood is, as it were, recorded twice over: as regards matter, by means of unconscious images, and *as regards form, by means of characterological attitudes of the ego*. Let me demonstrate this by means of a brief clinical example:

Particularly noticeable in a narcissistic, masochistic hypochondriac were his loud, excited and emotional complaints concerning the severe treatment he had received from his father. As regards its *content*, one might summarize all that he brought out during months of treatment in the words: "See what I have suffered through my father; he has ruined me and made me unfit for life." Very thorough work had been done on his infantile conflicts with his father during a year and a half's analysis with a colleague of mine, before he came to me, and in spite of this there had been hardly any alteration in his attitude or his symptom.

Finally a characteristic of his behaviour in analysis struck me. His movements were languid, his mouth drooped as if tired. His speech, scarcely describable in writing, as monotonous and gloomy. When I had guessed the significance of this note in his voice, all was at once clear to me: he speaks as if he were in torment, as if he were dying. I learned moreover that in certain other situations outside analysis he would also sink in this *unconsciously posed* lethargy. *His speaking in this way* also meant: "See what my father has done to me, how he torments me, he has ruined me and made me unfit for life." His attitude was a severe reproach.

The effect of my interpretation of his "dying", reproachful and complaining manner of speaking was astonishing. It seemed as if, with the loosening of this last *formal* foothold of his relation to his father, all the earlier interpretations of analytical material began also to be effective. It was permissible to draw the conclusion that so long as the unconscious significance of his manner of speech was not recognized, a large part of his father-complex remained emotionally bound up in it, and the material relating to it which had been disclosed was, in spite of being made conscious, not sufficiently invested with emotion to be of therapeutic value.

It is thus evident that a single unconscious, infantile process may be recorded and expressed in duplicate: in *what* the individual says and does, and in the *way in which* he speaks and acts. It is sufficiently interesting to be recorded that the analysis of the "what" leaves the "how" untouched, in spite of the unity of matter and form; that this "how" proves to be the hiding-place of similar psychical material as has apparently already been resolved or made conscious in the "what"; and that finally the analysis of the "how" is of particular efficacy in releasing the associated affects. This is owing to the grievous disturbance of narcissistic equilibrium involved in the analysis and interpretation of characterological attitudes.

II
THEORY

FEMALE AND PRECŒDIPAL SEXUALITY

A Historical Survey

The history of the discovery of the psycho-sexual development of the female by Freud and his closest collaborators is long and devious. Occupying the first third of the twentieth century, and a good deal of Freud's analytic reseach, it represents an elaboration upon many disparate observations. Today, when little more than a decade and a half has elapsed since his last paper on femininity appeared, we are, naturally, still occupied in assimilating its contents. A historical survey of the subject is based upon the conviction that the discovery of the "precœdipal phase" constitutes the most important recent advance in psycho-analytic knowledge.

In order to place the contributions collected in this section of the Reader it is best to begin at the beginning, and to follow Freud step by step from the time he worked alone, into the more recent past when he found himself in a situation reminiscent of that of the mythical sculptor, when the female hewn by the chisel of his research came alive and responded with certain discoveries of her own.

The knowledge of female, and along with it, precœdipal, sexuality has slowly evolved through the following stages: the infant and child studied in the Three Contributions to the Theory of Sex[1] *(1905), Freud's first work containing a systematic presentation of psycho-sexual development, is essentially male. The only deviations marked in the female are two: earlier inhibitions of (in late terminology—reaction formations against) sexuality, such as shame, disgust, pity, etc.; and, greater passivity of the instinct components. The development of the two sexes is outlined as moving in parallel fashion, since the guiding erotogenic zones are of an identical nature, either objectively, or, as in the case of the genital (penis, clitoris), subjectively. Only at puberty does the female face the additional task of exchanging the infantile genital for an adult one whose stimulation in coitus will normally cause her to transfer the erotogeneity of the clitoris to the vagina.*

In regard to the choice of the object, the findings of the Three Contributions *of 1905 are no less fragmentary than those concerning*

[1] New York and Washington, D.C., Nervous and Mental Disease Publishing Co., 1910.

159

the difference in the development of the two sexes although the reasons for these defections are different, as will later be seen.

Meanwhile addenda and emendations began to pour in from the "laboratory" of the analytic situation, as well as from the study of mythology, folklore, biography, fiction, and the eagerly pursued analytic interpretation of the dream. In the course of the elaborations upon this material, a focal point in regard to the infantile object-relation, the œdipus complex—discovered as early as 1900—gained steadily in importance. This complex is further developed in the five classic case histories, where also the "primal fantasies" and the "castration complex" become established. In addition, the study of the (pathological) "infantile neurosis" yielded new fundamentals concerning the (normal) development of libido, object, and ego, whereas at the same time a certain complicated change in the employment of partial-libidinal strivings by the ego, is shown to underly "character formation". But, while these (and other) studies of Freud abound in implicit addenda and emendations of the Three Contributions, *the first two explicit supplements appeared only after an interval of eighteen years from the publication of the original paper.*

They are, in a sense, complementary to each other; the first, "The Infantile Genital Organization" [2] *(1923) describes the genital primacy of the child as the "phallic phase", and places in their historical order the appearance of the three separate "antithetic pairs": active-passive, phallic-castrated, and male-female in the mentality of the infant. It thus adds a finishing touch to the description of the castration complex and defines at the same time the sexual aims collateral to the "object-choice", performed by the infant; a performance with which the originally narcissistic child had already been credited in the later editions of the* Three Contributions. *The second paper: "The Passing of the Œdipus Complex"* [3] *(1924), describes the further fate of the "incestuous" object-relations of the child. It explains that the parental object is relinquished under the influence of the "threat of castration", while the relation to it is perpetuated as an internalized one requiring, however, the simultaneous internalization of the object. The result of this narcissistic re-employment of the individual's earliest object-relation is a step in the topographical differentiation of the psychic apparatus: the establishment of the superego, to be distinguished from ego and id.*

With regard to the differences in the development of the male and the

---

[2] *Collected Papers*, II, London Hogarth Press, 1924.
[3] *Collected Papers*, II.

female, the first of these two papers deals with the development of the former alone. "We lack insight", Freud confesses, "into the corresponding processes in the little girl". But *the second paper contrasts the girl nevertheless to a certain degree with the boy, describing her as*

(1) *Accepting castration as an accomplished fact, rather than fearing it as a threat;*

(2) *Lacking, consequently, a powerful motive both for the erection of a superego, and the breaking up of her infantile sexual organization, and*

(3) *Relinquishing, therefore, the œdipus complex much more gradually than the boy, while retaining a strong unconscious wish for a penis and a child from the father.*

Only one year later, however, a totally different paper appeared. It is, in two respects, the reverse of the previous ones: it studies predominantly the female, while employing the male essentially as a foil; and it established, in the case of the girl, a pre-history (Vorgeschichte) of the œdipus complex, while admitting that "the corresponding facts in the boy *are still fairly unknown". So fully does the female, at this late date, come into her own that* Some Consequences of the Anatomical Distinction between Sexes [4] (1925) *cannot be considered merely one more emendation to the* Three Contributions, *but must be called the first of Freud's three papers on Female Sexuality. The central topic of this study is the castration complex of the girl and its effects upon (a) her infantile masturbation and (b) her œdipus complex. With reference to (a): the girl's (second period of) infantile masturbation is disturbed by the "inferiority" of the clitoris: she is forced to rebel against phallic masturbation, which agrees less well with her than with the boy, and to develop a "penis-envy" (with its reaction-formation), in order to accept finally her castration. With reference to (b): this acceptance introduces her to the œdipus complex, with its wish for a penis = child from the father, in supersedance of her previous attachment to the mother who is the original love-object of the infant of either sex.*

A comparison, undertaken at this occasion between the relation of the castration-complex and the œdipus-complex in the two sexes, showed that the castration complex which terminates the œdipus complex of the boy, initiates that of the girl. But, since the œdipus complex is never completely relinquished by the girl, its "heir", the superego, is in

[4] *The International Journal of Psycho-Analysis,* VIII.

*the normal female never as independent, as inexorable, or as impersonal
as in the male.*

*Freud, however, was by that time no longer the sole student of this
difficult subject: the original publications of Abraham's "Äußerungs-
formen des Weiblichen Kastrationskomplexes"* [5]*, Horney's "Zur Genese
des weiblichen Kastrationskomplex"* [5] *and Helene Deutsch's "Phycho-
analyse der weiblichen Sexualfunktionen"* [5] *had preceded his paper.
Of these, Abraham's study presents an abundance of clinical observations, and is even today, to borrow Freud's comment upon it, "still
unsurpassed". Its omission here on the ground that the volume of
Abraham's* Selected Papers [6] *includes it, creates a regrettable gap in
this section, which opens therefore, with Helene Deutsch's paper on
"The Pyschology of Women in Relation to the Functions of Reproduction"* (1925).

Freud's own final papers and articles "On Female Sexuality"
(1931) [7] *and "The Psychology of Women"* [8] *were published six and
eight years later, near the end of his life. They present coherently all
the knowledge that he had either obtained himself or accepted from
those female collaborators, whose work is reprinted in the following
pages. Both these papers of Freud are too well-known to require
review. A mere cross-section of portions of them, that deal with the
normal, reveals the following salient points:*

(1) *There is indeed a long and elaborate period of exclusive mother-
attachment preceding the œdipus complex of the girl.*

(2) *This* precedipal *phase, containing the "pre-history" of the
girl's œdipus complex, extends well into the fourth or even fifth year of
her life, thus encompassing most of her "phallic phase".*

(3) *The sexual* aims *directed towards the mother during this phase
are first* passive, *then* active *(wherever both co-exist or succeed each
other in various strengths), and correspond in their partial-erotic
character to the partial-libidinal stages passed through by the developing infant (oral, anal-sadistic, and phallic).*

(4) *The girl's final* relinquishment *of the mother and the eventual
acknowledgment of her castration—in other words, the change of her*

[5] Cf. bibliography, at end of this section, p. 284.

[6] London, Hogarth Press, 1927.

[7] *The International Journal of Psycho-Analysis*, XIII, 1932, p. 282.

[8] Lecture XXXIII in: *New Introductory Lectures on Psychoanalysis*, New
York, W. W. Norton and Co., 1933.

guiding erotogenic zone and in her object—are in a sense comple-
mentary. For it is the castration, the denial of the male genital by the
mother, which forms the nucleus for the elaborate aggregate of re-
proaches against her who, by this time, has been recognized as being
castrated herself. The mother is thus given up under the impulsion of a
hostility as profound as only the infantile constitution, with its in-
herent ambivalence, is capable of producing.

(5) The final transition from the mother to the father, *i.e. the*
establishment of the girl's œdipus complex, fulfills the biological
necessity of transforming the "masculine" girl into the "feminine"
woman by drawing on her passivity and her remaining positive sexual
strivings. Thus the "child-penis" is ultimately no longer craved from
the mother but from the father. *This outcome testifies to the power of*
"biological factors" which have in the end succeeded in "deflecting
libidinal forces and conducting even active strivings, masculine in every
sense of the word, into the paths of femininity".

This outline shows that the girl, in the course of analytic research has
repaid her debt, as it were, to the boy: whereas the boy lent himself as the
original object for the study of œdipal psychology, the girl eventually
assumes the same rôle for that of the preœdipal *phase. Yet this phase*
obtains, likewise, as does the œdipus complex, for both *sexes; although*
it is less conspicuous, and perhaps less important in the development
of the male.

The discovery of the preœdipal phase occurred late in Freud's life
and came to him as a surprise. Its effect, "comparable", so he writes,
"in another field with the effect of the discovery of the Minoan-
Mycenean civilization behind that of Greece",[9] *is that of a reorienta-*
tion in the ontogenesis of the object-relation of the infant.[10] *Much*
analytic material had to be re-interpreted in the light of this phase
either wholly or partly, that is, as either directly conditioned or at
least over-determined by the individual's earliest relation to his mother.

With regard to the technique *of psycho-analysis, the discovery of*
preœdipal sexuality terminated the period in which the sex of the
analyst might have been of importance. Freud thought it possible "that
women analysts . . . had been able to apprehend the facts with greater
ease and clearness because they had the advantage of being suitable
mother-substitutes in the transference situation with the patients whom
they were studying. . . ." [11] *It may be stated now that this is no longer*

[9] On Female Sexuality.
[10] Cf. the table at the end of the present section.
[11] On Female Sexuality.

true of the present-day analyst. The male analyst of today, beneficiary of Freud's work and that of the authors mentioned by him, becomes the object of this phase of his patient's "transference-neurosis" no less fully than does his female colleague. What may depend on the analyst's sex is merely the sequence in which œdipal and preœdipal constellations become the focus of the transference situation. If his technique is correct, and succeeds in dissolving reaction-formations as well as displacements, the male analyst encounters the same paranoid fear in his female patient of being eaten up by him as a representative of the mother, as would a female analyst. The resolution of this most deep-seated fear is often dramatic and always dependent not only upon the analysis of the passive components of the castration complex, but also upon that of the earliest, and perhaps most regressive, active impulses of biting and devouring.

THE PSYCHOLOGY OF WOMAN IN RELATION TO THE FUNCTIONS OF REPRODUCTION * (1925)

BY HELENE DEUTSCH

This paper, originally presented at the 8th International Psychoanalytic Congress in Salzburg in 1924, is the first important piece of collaboration with Freud on the subject of Female Sexuality and could only have been contributed by a woman pupil. It is complementary to Abraham's Manifestations of the Female Castration Complex (1920), † inasmuch as it studies chiefly the normal functions, not their disturbances, as does Abraham's paper. (It is also, the author informs us, the nucleus of the author's book Motherhood.)

In several of the paragraphs dealing with the rôle of ego ideal played by the child and his relation to the superego the author has been kind enough, upon editorial suggestion, to reformulate and amplify the original text.

Psycho-analytic research discovered at the very outset that the development of the infantile libido to the normal heterosexual object-choice is in women rendered difficult by certain peculiar circumstances.

In males the path of this development is straightforward, and the advance from the "phallic" phase does not take place in consequence of a complicated "wave of repression", but is based upon a ratification of that which already exists and is accomplished through ready and willing utilization of an already urgent force. The essence of the achievement lies in the mastery of the œdipus attitude which it connotes, and in overcoming the feeling of guilt bound up with this.

* First published in the *Internationale Zeitschrift für Psychoanalyse*, XI, 1925, p. 40: Psychologie des Weibes in den Funktionen der Fortpflanzung. Reprinted from *The International Journal of Psycho-Analysis*, VI, 1924, p. 405

† Karl Abraham, Manifestations of the Female Castration Complex, *The International Journal of Psycho-Analysis*, III, 1922, p. 1. *Selected Papers*, London, Hogarth Press, 1927, p. 388.

The girl, on the other hand, has in addition to this a twofold task to perform: (1) she has to renounce the masculinity attaching to the clitoris; (2) in her transition from the "phallic" to the "vaginal" phase she has to discover a new genital organ.

The man attains his final stage of development when he discovers the vagina in the world outside himself and possesses himself of it sadistically. In this his guide is his own genital organ, with which he is already familiar and which impels him to the act of possession.

The woman has to discover this new sexual organ *in her own person*, a discovery which she makes through being masochistically subjugated by the penis, the latter thus becoming the guide to this fresh source of pleasure.

The final phase of attaining to a definitively feminine attitude is not gratification through the sexual act of the infantile desire for a penis, but full realization of the vagina as an organ of pleasure— an exchange of the desire for a penis for the real and equally valuable possession of a vagina. This newly-discovered organ must become for the woman "the whole ego in miniature", a "duplication of the ego", as Ferenczi [1] terms it when speaking of the value of the penis to the man.

In the following paper I shall try to set forth how this change in the valuation of a person's own genital organ takes place and what relation it bears to the function of reproduction in women.

We know how the different organizations of libido succeed one another and how each successive phase carries with it elements of the previous ones, so that no phase seems to have been completely surmounted but merely to have relinquished its central rôle. Along each of these communicating lines of development the libido belonging to the higher stages tends regressively to revert to its original condition, and succeeds in so doing in various ways.

The consequence of this oscillation of libido between the different forms taken by it in development is not only that the higher phases contain elements of the lower ones, but, conversely, that the libido on its path of regression carries with it constituents of the higher phases which it interweaves with the earlier ones, a process which we recognize subsequently in fantasy-formation and symptoms.

Thus the first or oral phase is auto-erotic, that is to say, it has no object either narcissistically, in the ego, or in the outside world. And yet we know that the process of weaning leaves in the unconscious

[1] Ferenczi, A., *Versuch einer Genitaltheorie*, Vienna, Internationale Psycho-analytische Bibliothek, Band XV, 1924.

traces of a narcissistic wound. This is because the mother's breast is regarded as a part of the subject's own body and, like the penis later, is cathected with large quantities of narcissistic libido. Similarly, the oral gratification derived from the act of sucking leads to discovering the mother and to finding the first object in her.

The mysterious, heterosexual part of the little girl's libido finds its first explanation already in the earliest phase of development. To the tender love which she devotes to her father ("the sheltering male") as the nearest love-object side by side with the mother is added a large part of that sexual libido which, originating in the oral zone, in the first instance cathected the maternal breasts. Analysis of patients shows us that in a certain phase of development the unconscious equates the paternal penis with the maternal breast as an organ of suckling. This equation coincides with the conception of coitus (characteristic of this phase) as a relation between the mouth of the mother and the penis of the father and is extended into the theory of oral impregnation. The passive aim of this phase is achieved through the mucous membrane of the mouth zone, while the active organ of pleasure is the breast.

In the sadistic-anal phase the penis loses its significance (for fantasy-life) as an organ of suckling and becomes an organ of mastering. Coitus is conceived of as a sadistic act; in fantasies of beating, as we know, the girl either takes the rôle of the father, or experiences the act masochistically in identification with the mother.

In this phase the passive aim is achieved through the anus, while the column of fæces becomes the active organ of pleasure, which, like the breast in the first phase, belongs at one and the same time to the outside world and to the subject's own body. By a displacement of cathexis the fæces here acquire the same narcissistic value as the breast in the oral phase. The birth-fantasy of this phase is that of the "anal child".

We are familiar with the biogloical analogy between the anus and the mouth; that between the breast and the penis as active organs arises from their analogous functions. One would suppose it an easy task for feminine libido in its further development to pass on and take possession of the third opening of the female body—the vagina. Biologically in the development of the embryo, the common origin of anus and vagina in the cloaca has already fore-shadowed this step. The penis as an organ of stimulation and the active agent for this new erotogenic zone perhaps attains its function by means of the equation: breast = column of fæces = penis.

The difficulty lies in the fact that the bisexual character of development interposes between anus and vagina the masculine clitoris as an erotogenic zone. In the "phallic" phase of development the clitoris attracts to itself a large measure of libido, which it relinquishes in favour of the "feminine" vagina only after strenuous and not always decisive struggles. Obviously, this transition from the "phallic" to the "vaginal" phase (which later coincides with what Abraham [2] terms the "post-ambivalent") must be recognized as the hardest task in the libidinal development of the woman.

The penis is already in the early infantile period discovered auto-erotically. Moreover, its exposed position makes it liable to stimulation in various ways connected with the care of the baby's body, and thus it becomes an erotogenic zone before it is ready to fulfil its reproductive function. All three masturbatory phases are dominated by this organ.

The clitoris (which is in reality so inadequate a substitute for the penis) assumes the importance of the latter throughout the whole period of development. The hidden vagina plays no part. The child is unaware of its existence, possibly has mere vague premonitions of it. Every attempt to pacify the little girl's envy of the penis with the explanation that she also has "something" is rightly doomed to complete failure; for the possession of something which one neither sees nor feels cannot give any satisfaction. Nevertheless, as a zone of active energy the clitoris lacks the abundant energy of the penis; even in the most intense masturbatory activity it cannot arrogate to itself such a measure of libido as does the latter organ. Accordingly the primal distribution of libido over the erotogenic zones is subject to far less modification than in the male, and the female, owing to the lesser tyranny of the clitoris, may all her life remain more polymorph-pervers, more infantile; to her more than to the male "the whole body is a sexual organ". In the wave of development occurring at puberty this erotogeneity of the whole body increases, for the libido which is forced away from the clitoris (presumably by way of the inner secretions) flows back to the body as a whole. This must be of importance in the later destiny of the woman, because in this way she is regressively set back into a state in which, as Ferenczi [3] shows, she "cleaves to intra-uterine existence" in sexual things.

In the "transformations which take place at puberty" (and during

[2] Abraham, K., *Versuch einer Entwicklungsgeschichte der Libido*, Neue Arbeiten zur Ärztlichen Psychoanalyse, 1924.

[3] *Loc. cit.*

the subsequent period of adolescence) libido has therefore to flow towards the vagina from two sources: (1) from the whole body, especially from those erotogenic zones that have the most powerful cathexes; (2) from the clitoris, which has still to some extent retained its libidinal cathexes.

The difficulty lies in the fact that the clitoris is not at all ready to renounce its rôle, that the conflict at puberty is associated with the traumatic occurrence of menstruation; and this not only revives the castration-wound but at the same time represents, both in the biological and the psychological sense, the disappointment of a frustrated pregnancy. The periodic repetition of menstruation every time recalls the conflicts of puberty and reproduces them in a less acute form, at the same time there is no doubt that the whole process of menstruation is calculated to exercise an eroticizing and preparatory influence upon the vagina.

The task of conducting the libido to the vagina from the two sources which I have mentioned devolves upon the activity of the penis, and that in two ways. First, libido must be drawn from the whole body. Here we have a perfect analogy to the woman's breast, which actively takes possession of the infant's mouth and so centres the libido of the whole body in this organ. Just so does the vagina, under the stimulus of the penis and by a process of displacement "from above downwards", take over this passive rôle of the suckling mouth in the equation: penis = breast. This oral, suckling activity of the vagina is indicated by its whole anatomical structure (with their corresponding terms). The second operation accomplished by the penis is the carrying-over of the remaining clitoris-libido to the vagina. This part of the libido still takes a "male" direction, even when absorbed by the vagina; that is to say, the clitoris renounces its male function in favour of the penis that approaches the body from without.

As the clitoris formerly played its "masculine" part by identification with the paternal penis, so the vagina takes over its rôle (that of the clitoris) by allowing one part of its functions to be dominated by an identification with the penis of the partner.

In certain respects the orgastic activity of the vagina is wholly analogous to the activity of the penis. I refer to the process of secretion and contraction. As in the man, we have here an "amphimixis" of urethral and anal tendencies—of course greatly diminished in degree. Both these component-instincts develop their full activity only in that "extension" of the sexual act, pregnancy and parturition.

We see then that one of the vaginal functions arises through identification with the penis, which in this connection is regarded as a possession of the subject's own body. Here the psychic significance of the sexual act lies in the repetition and mastery of the castration-trauma.

The truly passive, feminine attitude of the vagina is based upon the oral, suckling activity discussed above. In this function coitus signifies for the woman a restoring of that first relation of the human being with the outside world, in which the object is orally incorporated, introjected; that is to say, it restores that condition of perfect unity of being and harmony in which the distinction between subject and object was annulled. Thus the attainment of the highest, genital, "post-ambivalent" (Abraham) phase signifies a repetition of the earliest, pre-ambivalent phase.

In relation to the partner the situation of incorporating is a repetition of sucking at the mother's breast; hence incorporation amounts to a repetition and mastery of the trauma of weaning. In the equation penis = breast, and in the suckling activity of the vagina, coitus realizes the fulfilment of the fantasy of sucking at the paternal penis.

The identifications established between the two partners in the preparatory act (Ferenczi) now acquire a manifold significance, identification with the mother taking place in two ways: (1) through equating the penis with the breast; (2) through experiencing the sexual act masochistically, i.e. through repeating that identification with the mother which belongs to the phase of a sadistic conception of coitus. Through this identification, then, the woman plays in coitus the part of mother and child simultaneously—a relation which is continued in pregnancy, when one actually is both mother and child at the same time.

As the object of maternal libido in the act of suckling, the partner therefore becomes the child, but at the same time the libido originally directed towards the father must be transferred to the partner (according to the equation: penis = organ of suckling and to the conception of coitus as a sadistic act of mastery). This shows us that ultimately coitus represents for the woman incorporation (by the mouth) of the father, who is made into the child and then retains this rôle in the pregnancy which occurs actually or in fantasy.

I arrived at this identification-series, which is complicated and may seem far-fetched, as a result of all the experience which I have had of cases of frigidity and sterility.

Ferenczi's "maternal regression" is realized for the woman in equating coitus with the situation of sucking. The last act of this regression (return into the uterus), which the man accomplishes by the act of introjection in coitus, is realized by the woman in pregnancy in the complete identification between mother and child. In my opinion the mastery of "the trauma of birth", which Rank [4] has shown to be so important, is accomplished by the woman above all in the actively repeated act of parturition, for to the unconscious carrying and being carried, giving birth and being born, are as identical as giving suck and sucking.

This conception of coitus reflects the whole psychological difference displayed by men and women in their relation to the object-world. The man actively takes possession of some piece of the world and in this way attains to the bliss of the primal state. And this is the form taken by his tendencies to sublimation. In the act of incorporation passively experienced the woman introjects into herself a piece of the object-world which she then absorbs.

In its rôle of organ of sucking and incorporation the vagina becomes the receptacle not of the penis but of the child. The energy required for this function is derived not from the clitoris, but, as I said before, from the libidinal cathexis of the whole body, this libido being conducted to the vagina by channels familiar to us. The vagina now itself represents the child, and so receives that cathexis of narcissistic libido which flows on to the child in the "extension" of the sexual act. It becomes the "second ego", the ego in miniature, as does the penis for the man. A woman who succeeds in establishing this maternal function of the vagina by giving up the claim of the clitoris to represent the penis has reached the goal of feminine development, *has become a woman.*

In men the function of reproduction terminates with the act of introjection, for with them that function coincides with the relief from sexual tension by ejaculation.

Women have to perform in two phases the function which men accomplish in a single act; nevertheless the first act of incorporation contains elements which indicate the tendency to get rid of the germ-plasm by expulsion, as is done by the male in coitus. Orgasm in the woman appears not only to imply identification with the man but to have yet another motive; it is the expression of the attempt to impart to coitus itself in the interest of the race the character of

[4] Rank, O., *Das Trauma der Geburt,* Internationale Psychoanalytische Bibliothek, Band XIV, 1924.

parturition (we might call it a "missed labour"). In animals the process of expulsion of the products of reproduction very often takes place during the sexual act in the female as well as in the male.

In the human female this process is not carried through, though it is obviously indicated and begun in the orgastic function; it terminates only in the second act, that of parturition. The process therefore is a *single* one, which is merely divided into two phases by an interval of time. As the first act contains (in orgasm) elements of the second, so the second is permeated by the pleasure-mechanisms of the first. I even assume that the act of parturition contains the acme of sexual pleasure owing to the relief from stimulation by the germ-plasm. If this be so, parturition is a process of "autotomy" analogous to ejaculation (Ferenczi), requiring, however, the powerful stimulus of the matured fœtus in order that it may function. This reverses the view which Groddeck first had the courage to put forward, at the Hague Congress, that parturition is associated with pleasure owing to its analogy with coitus. It would rather seem that coitus acquires the character of a pleasure act mainly through the fact that it constitutes an attempt at and beginning of parturition. In support of my view I would cite the following considerations.

Freud [5] has told us that the sadistic instincts of destruction reach their fullest development when the erotic sexual instincts are put out of action. This happens after their tension has been relieved in the act of gratification. The death-instinct has then a free hand and can carry through its claims undisturbed. A classical instance of this is furnished by those lower animals in which the sexual act leads to death.

This applies to the fertilizing male, but repeats itself *mutatis mutandis* in the female also, when the fertilized ovum is expelled after a longer or shorter interval during which it has matured in the maternal body. There are many species of animals, e.g. certain spiders, in which the females perish when they have fulfilled the function of reproduction. If the liberation of the death-instinct is a consequence of gratification of sexual trends, it is only logical to assume that this gratification reaches its highest point in the female only in the act of parturition. In actual fact parturition is for the woman an orgy of masochistic pleasure, and the dread and premonition of death which precede this act are clearly due to a perception of the menace of the destructive instincts about to be liberated.

Conditions of insanity sometimes met with after delivery are

[5] Freud, *The Ego and the Id.*

characterized by a specially strong tendency to suicide and murderous impulses towards the newly-born child.

These facts in my opinion confirm my assumption that parturition constitutes for women the termination of the sexual act, which was only inagurated by coitus, and that the ultimate gratification of the erotic instinct is analogous to that in men and takes place at the moment when soma and germ-plasm are separated.

The interval in time between the two acts is filled by complicated processes in the economy of the libido. The object incorporated in coitus is introjected physically and psychically, finds its extension in the child, and persists in the mother as a part of her ego. Thus we see that the mother's relation to the "child" as a libidinal object is two-fold: on the one hand it is worked out within the ego in the interaction of its different parts; on the other hand it is the extension of all those object-relations which the child embodies in our identification-series. For even while the child is still in the uterus its relation to the mother is partly that of an object belonging to the outside world, such as it ultimately becomes.

The libido which in the act of incorporation has regressed to the earliest stage of development seeks out all the positions which it had abandoned, and the harmonious state of identity between subject and object does not always remain so harmonious in relation to the child as object.

The ambivalent tendencies of later phases of development, which have already manifested themselves in coitus, become stronger during pregnancy. The ambivalent conflict which belongs to the "later oral phasè of development" finds expression in the tendency to expel again (orally) the object which has been incorporated. This manifests itself in vomiting during pregnancy and in the typical eructations and peculiar cravings for food, etc.

The regressive elements of the sadistic-anal phase find expression in the hostile tendencies to expulsion manifested in the pains which appear long before delivery. If these predominate over the tendencies to retain the fœtus, the result is miscarriage. We recognize these elements again in the transitory, typically anal, changes in the character of pregnant women. The old equation, child = fæces, is in this phase revived in the unconscious, owing to the child's position in the body as something belonging to that body and yet destined to be severed from it.

In the oral incorporation a quantity of narcissistic libido has already flowed to the child as a part of the subject's own ego.

Similarly the libidinal relation in the identification, child = fæces, is again a narcissistic one. But as fæces become for children, in reaction against their original narcissistic overestimation of them, the essence of what is disgusting, so in this phase of pregnancy there arise typical feelings of disgust, which become displaced from the child in particular kinds of food, situations, etc.

It is interesting that all these sensations disappear in the fifth month of pregnancy with the quickening of the child. The mother's relation to it is now determined in two directions. In the first place that part of her own body which is moving to and fro and vigorously pulsing within her is equated with the penis; and her relation to the child, which is still rooted in the depths of her narcissism, is now raised to a higher stage of development, namely, the "phallic". At the same time the child gives proof through a certain developing independence that it belongs to the outside world and in this way enters more into an object-relation to the mother.

I have tried thus briefly to reveal in the state of pregnancy deposits of all the phases of development. I shall now return to the mother-child relation that I mentioned before, which begins with the process of incorporation, makes the child a part of the subject's own ego and works itself out within that ego.

In this process the libidinal relations to the child are formed as follows: in the process of introjection the quantities of libido sent out to the partner in the sexual act flow back to the subject's narcissism. This is a very considerable contribution, for, as I have shown, in effecting a cathexis of the partner libido was drawn from the old father-fixation *and* mother-fixation.

The libido thus flowing into the ego constitutes the secondary narcissism of the woman as a mother, for, though it is devoted to the object (the child), that object represents at the same time a part of her ego. The change in the ego of the pregnant woman which follows on the process of introjection is a new edition of a process which has already taken place at a previous time: the child becomes for her the incarnation of the ego ideal modelled after the father which she set up in the past. It is now for the second time built up by introjecting the father.

The narcissistic libido is displaced on to this newly erected ego ideal which becomes the bearer of all those perfections once ascribed to the father. A whole quantity of object-libido is withdrawn from its relations to the outside world and conducted to the child as the ego ideal. In this process the libido becomes desexualized, and the child inaugurates a process of sublimation in the mother, before his existence as a reality in the outer world. This process is later continued in the tenderness of motherhood. It furnishes its contribution to the psychological differences between man and woman. The man measures and controls his ego ideal by his production through sublimation in the outside world. To the woman, on the other hand, the ego ideal is embodied in the child, and all those tendencies to sublimation which the man utilizes in intellectual and social activity she directs to the child, which in the psychological sense represents for the woman her sublimation product. Hence the relation, mother-child, in pregnancy has more than one determinant. Since the child in the uterus becomes a part of the ego and large quantities of libido flow to it, the libidinal cathexis in the ego is heightened, narcissism is increased, and that primal condition is realized in which there was as yet no distinction between ego-libido and object-libido.

This primal condition, however, is disturbed by two factors: (1) the differentiation within the ego does not limit itself to the ideal-formation. The relation to the child contains not only the positive affirming element—"You shall become as my idealized father (or mother) has once been"—but it also repeats the negative, punitive components of the earlier parent relation. In the obscure and complicated transformations occurring in the ego of woman, the child, a psychological neo-plasm, takes the place of the superego as the admonishing, demanding, threatening and punishing institution. Psycho-analytic research has informed us that this differentiation in the ego can lead to a conflict within the ego and to a pathological outcome of this conflict. (2) The second disturbance results from the fact that the child in the uterus is at the same time already an object belonging to the outside world, in relation to which the ambivalence-conflicts of all developmental phases of the maternal libido take place.

Our observations enable us to distinguish two characteristic types of women according to their mental reaction to pregnancy. There are a number of women who endure their pregnancy with visible discomfort and depression. A similar unfavourable change takes place in their bodily appearance: they become ugly and shrunken, so that as the child matures they actually change into a mere appendage to it, a condition highly uncomfortable for themselves. The other type consists of those women who attain during pregnancy their greatest physical and psychic bloom.

In the first case the woman's narcissism has been sacrificed to the child. On the one hand the superego has mastered the ego, and on the other the child as a love-object has attracted to itself such a large measure of ego-libido that the ego is impoverished. Possibly this explains those states of melancholia which occur during pregnancy.

In the other type of woman the distribution of libido during pregnancy is different. That part of the libido which has now been withdrawn from the outside world is directed towards the child as a part of the ego. This can happen only when the formation of the superego is less powerful and the child is regarded less as an object and more as a part of the ego. When this is so, the result is a heightening of the secondary narcissism, which is expressed in an increased self-respect, self-satisfaction, etc.

It seems as though we may conclude from these remarks that that unity, mother—child, is not so completely untroubled as we might suppose. The original harmony of the primal state, inaugurated in the process of introjection during the sexual act, is soon disturbed by manifestations of ambivalence towards the child in the uterus. From this point of view parturition appears as the final result of a struggle which has long been raging. The stimulus which proceeds from the fœtus becomes insupportable and presses for discharge. Every hostile impulse which has already been mobilized during pregnancy reaches its greatest intensity in this decisive battle. Finally the incorporated object is successfully expelled into the outside world.

We have seen that the introjected object takes the place of the ego ideal in the restored unity of the ego. When projected into the outside world it retains this character, for it continues to embody the subject's own unattained ideals. This is the psychological path by which, as Freud [6] recognized, women attain from narcissism to full object-love.

The final and deepest regression takes place in pregnancy through identification with the child: "the trauma of birth" is mastered through the act of parturition.

Having regard to this identity of mother and child, we may perhaps draw certain conclusions from the mother's frame of mind as to the mental condition of the child. This of course undergoes amnesia, and then is only vaguely hinted at in dreams, fantasies, etc.

In actual fact the woman feels as though the world were out of joint and coming to an end; she has a sense of chaotic uneasiness, a straining, bursting sensation displaced from the avenues of birth to her head, and with these feelings is associated an intense dread of

[6] Freud, On Narcissism: An Introduction, *Collected Papers*, IV.

death. Possibly here we have a complete repetition of the anxiety attaching to the trauma of birth and a discharge of it by means of actual reproduction. That which men endeavour to attain in coitus and which impels them to laborious sublimations women attain in the function of reproduction.

It is known that in the dreams of pregnant women there very often appears a swimming child. This child may always be recognized as the dreamer herself, endowed with some quality which makes her, or in childhood made her, particularly estimable in her own eyes—it is as it were an illustration of the formation of the ego ideal in relation to the child. The birth-fantasies of women who are already mothers prove on thorough investigation to represent details of two separate births interwoven into one: the birth of the subject herself (never recalled to memory) and the delivery of a child.

The mental state of the woman after delivery is characterized by a feeling of heavy loss. After a short phase in which the sense of victorious termination of the battle preponderates, there arises a feeling of boundless emptiness and disappointment, certainly analogous to the feeling of a "lost Paradise" in the child which has been expelled. This blank is filled only when the first relation to the child as an object in the outside world is ultimately established. The supposition that this relation is already present during the act of delivery itself is borne out by the observation which Rank [7] has already made in another connection, namely, that mothers who are in a state of narcosis during delivery have a peculiar feeling of estrangement towards their children. These mothers do not go through the phase of emptiness and disappointment, but on the other hand their joy in the child is not so intense as when delivery has taken place naturally. The child which is perceived by their senses is regarded as something alien.

This factor of loss clearly contributes to the joy of finding the child again. Apart from this, it is precisely this last factor of "severance" which completes the analogy with coitus. The vaginal passage constitutes a frontier where the child is for the last time a part of the subject's own body and at the same time is already the object which has been thrust out. Here we have a repetition of the coitus-situation in which the object was still felt to be a piece of the outside world but, being introjected, was on the border-line between the outside world and the ego.

Although the child has been hailed after delivery as an object

[7] *Loc. cit.*

belonging to the outside world, the bliss of the primal state, the unity of subject and object, is nevertheless re-established in lactation. This is a repetition of coitus, rendered with photographic faithfulness, the identification being based on the oral incorporation of the object in the act of sucking. Here again we have the equation: penis = breast. As in the first instance the penis took possession of one of the openings of the woman's body (the vagina), and in the act of mastery created an erotogenic centre, so now the nipple in a state of erection takes possession of the infant's mouth. As in coitus the erotogeneity of the whole body was attracted to the vagina, so here the whole disseminated libido of the newly-born infant is concentrated in the mouth. That which the semen accomplished in the one instance is accomplished in the other by the jet of milk. The identification made in childish fantasy between the mother's breast and the father's penis is realized a second time: in coitus the penis takes on the rôle of the breast, while in lactation the breast becomes the penis. In the identification-situation the dividing line between the partners vanishes, and in this relation, mother—child, the mother once more annuls the trauma of weaning.

The identification, penis = breast, threw light on a remarkable disturbance in lactation which I had the opportunity of observing analytically. A young mother with a very ambivalent attitude towards her child was obliged to give up suckling it, although she wished to continue and her breasts were functioning excellently. But what happened was that in the interval between the child's meals the milk poured out in a stream, so that the breast was empty when she wished to give it to the child. The measures she took to overcome this unfortunate condition recalled the behaviour of men suffering from *ejaculatio præcox*, who convulsively endeavour to hasten the sexual act but are always overtaken by their infirmity. In the same way this woman tried to hasten the feeding of the child, but with the same ill success—it was always too late. The analysis of this disturbance was traced to a urethral source in her, as in *ejaculatio præcox* in the man. In a disturbance of lactation more frequently met with, namely, the drying up of the secretion, the other (anal) components of the process undoubtedly predominate.

The relation between the genital processes and lactation finds very characteristic expression at the moment when the child is put to the breast. Sometimes there is even a convulsion in the uterus, as though it were terminating its activity only now when it resigns it to the breast.

So the act of reproduction, begun in oral incorporation, completes the circle by representing the same situation at the end as at the beginning.

The whole development of the libido is rapidly revived and run through once more, the effect of the primal traumata is diminished by repetitive acts, and the work of sublimation is accomplished in relation to the child. But for the bisexual disposition of the human being, which is so adverse to the woman, but for the clitoris with its masculine strivings, how simple and clear would be her way to an untroubled mastering of existence!

THE EVOLUTION OF THE ŒDIPUS COMPLEX IN WOMEN * (1927)

By J. Lampl-de Groot

In his paper "On Female Sexuality" Freud has expressed agreement with the essentials of this contribution, published first in 1927. "Here," he comments,† "the complete identity of the preœdipal phase in the boy and the girl is recognized, the sexual (phallic) activity in the little girl's attitude towards the mother is stated and proven by observation. The turning-away from the mother is traced back to the influence of the child's acknowledgment of castration, which forces it to abandon the sexual object, and often at the same time the practice of masturbation. The whole development is epitomized in the formula, that the little girl has to pass through a phase of the 'negative' œdipus complex before arriving at the positive one . . ."

One inadequacy is found by Freud in Dr. Lampl's report: the author has failed to describe the hostility which accompanies the girl's turning-away from the mother.

Dr. Lampl, upon editorial request, has put the following note at our disposal:

"In the nineteen years since the appearance of my paper, the observations recorded in it have been fully confirmed by many colleagues as well as by myself. Their full significance, however, was brought out through Freud's magnificent formulation of the preœdipal mother-attachment. The negative œdipal attitude, described by me, is the terminal phase in the female child's early attachment to her mother; it introduces the œdipal father-attachment. The latter is indeed made possible only through the little girl's becoming inimical towards her mother, in other words,

---

* First published in the *Internationale Zeitschrift für Psychoanalyse*, XIII, 1927, p. 269, under the title: Zur Entwicklung des Oedipus Komplexes der Frau.

Reprinted from *The International Journal of Psycho-Analysis*, IX, 1928, p. 332.

† On Female Sexuality: *The International Journal of Psycho-Analysis*, XIII, 1932, p. 295.

through the hostility, referred to by Freud in his criticism of my paper.

"In the meantime reference has also been made occasionally to the significance for the development of the boy of this præœdipal attachment to the mother, in particular to the conditioning of his passive feminine attitude (homosexuality) by it. I hope to describe the influence of this early object-relation upon the ego development of both sexes in the near future." ‡

J. L.-DE G.

Amsterdam,
Holland.

One of the earliest discoveries of psycho-analysis was the existence of the œdipus complex. Freud found the libidinal relations to the parents to be the centre and the acme of the development of childish sexuality and soon recognized in them the nucleus of the neuroses. Many years of psycho-analytical work greatly enriched his knowledge of the developmental processes in this period of childhood; it gradually became clear to him that in both sexes there is both a positive and a negative œdipus complex and that at this time the libido finds physical outlet in the practice of onanism. Hence the œdipus complex makes its appearance only when the phallic phase of libido-development is reached and, when the tide of infantile sexuality recedes, that complex must pass in order to make way for the period of latency during which the instinctual tendencies are inhibited in their aim. Nevertheless, in spite of the many observations and studies by Freud and other authors, it has been remarkable how many obscure problems have remained for many years unsolved.[1]

It seemed that one very important factor was the connection between the œdipus and the castration complexes, and there were many points about this which were obscure. Again, understanding

‡ Cf. R. M. Brunswick: The Præœdipal Phase of the Libido Development, this volume, p. 231.—Ed.

[1] Abraham, Manifestations of the Female Castration Complex, 1920, *The International Journal of Psycho-Analysis*, III, 1922. Alexander, The Castration Complex in the Formation of Character, *ibid.*, IV, 1923. Helene Deutsch: *Psychoanalyse der weiblichen Sexualfunktionen*. Neue Arbeiten zur ärzlitchen Psychoanalyse, No. V. Horney, On the Genesis of the Castration Complex in Women, *ibid.*, V, 1924; The Flight from Womanhood, *ibid.*, VII, 1926. Van Ophuijsen, Contributions to the Masculinity Complex in Women (1917), *ibid.*, V, 1924.

of the processes in male children has been carried much further than with the analogous processes in females. Freud ascribed the difficulties in elucidating the early infantile love-relations to the difficulty of getting at the material relating to them: he thought that this was due to the profound repression to which these impulses are subjected. The greater difficulty of understanding these particular mental processes in little girls may arise on the one hand from the fact that they are in themselves more complicated than the analogous processes in boys and, on the other, from the greater intensity with which the libido is repressed in women. Horney thinks that another reason is that, so far, analytical observations have been made principally by men.

In 1924 and 1925 Freud published two works which threw much light on the origin of the œdipus complex and its connection with the castration complex. The first of these: "The Passing of the Œdipus Complex",[2] shows what happens to that complex in little boys. It is true that several years previously in the "History of an Infantile Neurosis",[2] and again, in 1923, in the paper entitled "A Neurosis of Demoniacal Possession in the Seventeenth Century",[2] its fate in certain individual cases had been described. But in "The Passing of the Œdipus Complex" we have the general application and the theoretical appreciation of this discovery and also the further conclusions to be deduced from it. The result arrived at in this paper is as follows: the œdipus complex in male children receives its death-blow from the castration complex, that is to say, that both in the positive and the negative œdipus attitude the boy has to fear castration by his father, whose strength is superior to his own. In the first castration is the punishment for the inadmissible incest-wish and, in the second, it is the necessary condition of the boy's adopting the feminine rôle in relation to his father. Thus, in order to escape castration and to retain his genital he must renounce his love-relations with both parents. We see the peculiarly important part which this organ plays in boys and the enormous psychic significance it acquires in their mental life. Further, analytic experience has shown how extraordinarily difficult it is for a child to give up the possession of the mother, who has been his love-object since he was capable of object-love at all. This reflection leads us to wonder whether the victory of the castration complex over the œdipus complex, together with the narcissistic interest in the highly-prized bodily organ, may not be due also to yet another factor,

[2] *Collected Papers.*

namely, the tenacity of this first love-relation. Possibly, too, the following train of thought may have some significance: If the boy gives up his ownership of the penis, it means that the possession of the mother (or mother-substitute) becomes for ever impossible to him. If, however, forced by the superior power of that far stronger rival, his father, he renounces the fulfilment of his desire, the way remains open to him at some later period to fight his father with greater success and to return to his first love-object, or, more correctly, to her substitute. It seems not impossible that this know-ledge of a future chance of fulfilling his wish (a knowledge probably phylogenetically acquired and, of course, unconscious) may be a contributing motive in the boy's temporary renunciation of the pro-hibited love-craving. This would also explain why before, or just at the beginning of, the latency-period a little boy longs so intensely to be "big" and "grown-up".

In this work, then, Freud largely explains the connection between the œdipus- and the castration-complex in little boys, but he does not tell us much that is new about the same processes in little girls. Hence his paper, published in 1925, "Some Psychological Con-sequences of the Anatomical Distinction between the Sexes",[3] throws all the more light on the fate of the early infantile love-impulses of the little girl. Freud holds that in girls the œdipus com-plex (he is speaking of the attitude which for the girl is positive: love for the father and rivalry with the mother) is a secondary formation, first introduced by the castration complex; that is to say, that it arises after the little girl has become aware of the difference between the sexes and has accepted the fact of her own castration. This theory throws a new light on many hitherto obscure problems. By this assumption Freud explains many later developmental char-acteristics, various differences in the further vicissitudes of the œdipus complex in girls and in boys, and in the superego formation in the two sexes, and so forth.

Nevertheless, even after this connection has been discovered, there are several problems which remain unsolved. Freud mentions that, when the castration complex has become operative in the girl, that is, when she has accepted her lack of the penis and therewith become a victim of penis-envy, "a loosening of the tender relations with the mother as love-object" begins to take place. He thinks that one possible reason for this may be the fact that the girl ultimately holds her mother responsible for her own lack of the penis and,

[3] *The Internatioral Journal of Psycho-Analysis*, VIII, 1927.

further, quotes a historical factor in the case, namely, that often jealousy is conceived later on against a second child who is more beloved by the mother. But, Freud says, "we do not very clearly understand the connection". According to him another remarkable effect of penis-envy is the girl's struggle against onanism, which is more intense than that of the boy and which, in general, still makes itself felt at a later age. Freud's view is that the reason why the little girl revolts so strongly against phallic onanism is the blow dealt to her narcissism in connection with her penis-envy: she suspects that in this matter it is no use to compete with the boy and therefore it is best not to enter into rivalry with him. This statement gives rise to the involuntary thought: How should the little girl who never possessed a penis and therefore never knew its value from her own experience, regard it as so precious?

Why has the discovery of this lack in herself such far-reaching mental consequences and, above all, why should it begin to produce a mental effect at a certain moment, when it is probable that the bodily difference between herself and little boys has already been perceived countless times without any reaction? Probably the little girl produces pleasurable physical sensations in the clitoris in the same way and presumably with the same degree of intensity as the boy does in the penis, and perhaps she feels them in the vagina too. About this latter fact we received a communication by Josine Müller in the German Psycho-Analytical Society, and I have been told of it by an acquaintance, the mother of two little girls. Why, then, should there be this mental reaction in the girl to the discovery that her own member is smaller than the boy's or is lacking altogether? I should like to try whether the following considerations, which have been suggested to me by experiences in my analytic practice (to be narrated hereafter), may bring us a little nearer to answering these questions.

I think that several points will be clearer to us if we consider the previous history of the castration complex or penis-envy in little girls. But, before doing so, it will be advisable to examine once more the analogous process in boys. As soon as the little boy is capable of an object-relation he takes as his first love-object the mother who feeds and tends him. As he passes through the pregenital phases of libidinal development he retains always the same object. When he reaches the phallic stage he adopts the typical œdipus attitude, i.e. he loves his mother and desires to possess her and to get rid of his rival, the father. Throughout this development the love-object remains the same. An alteration in his love-attitude, an alteration characteristic of his sex, occurs at the moment when he accepts the possibility of castration as a punishment threatened by his powerful father for these libidinal desires of his. It is not impossible, indeed it is very probable, that the boy, even before he reaches the phallic stage and adopts the œdipus attitude which coincides with it, has perceived the difference between the sexes by observing either a sister or a girl play-fellow. But we assume that this perception has no further significance to him. If, however, such a perception occurs when he is already in the œdipus situation and has recognized the possibility of castration as a punishment with which he is threatened, we know how great its significance may be in his mind. The child's first reaction is an endeavour to deny the actuality of castration and to hold very tenaciously to his first love-object. After violent inward struggles, however, the little fellow makes a virtue of necessity; he renounces his love-object in order to retain his penis. Possibly he thus ensures for himself the chance of a renewed and more successful battle with his father at some later date—a possibility which I suggested earlier in this paper. For we know that, when the young man reaches maturity, he succeeds in wresting the victory from his father, normally in relation to a mother-substitute.

Now what happens in the little girl? She, too, takes as her first love-object the mother who feeds and tends her. She too, retains the same object as she passes through the pregenital phases of libidinal evolution. She, too, enters upon the phallic stage of libido-development. Moreover, the little girl has a bodily organ analogous to the little boy's penis, namely, the clitoris, which gives her pleasurable feelings in masturbation. Physically she behaves exactly like the little boy. We may suppose that in the psychic realm also children of either sex develop up to this point in an entirely similar manner; that is to say, that girls as well as boys, when they reach the phallic stage enter into the œdipus situation, i.e. that which for the girl is negative. She wants to conquer the mother for herself and to get rid of the father. Up to this point, too, a chance observation of the difference between the sexes may have been without significance; now, however, a perception of this sort is fraught with serious consequences for the little girl. It strikes her that the boy's genital is larger, stronger and more visible than her own and that he can use it actively in urinating, a process which for the child has a sexual significance. When she makes this comparison, the little girl must feel her own organ to be inferior. She imagines that hers was once like the boy's and that it has been taken from her as a punishment for her prohibited love-cravings in relation to the mother. At first the little girl tries, as does the boy, to deny the fact of castration or to comfort herself with the idea that she will still grow a genital. The acceptance of castration has for her the same consequences as for the boy. Not only does her narcissism suffer a blow on account of her physical inferiority, but she is forced to renounce the fulfilment of her first love-longings. Now at this point the difference in the psychic development of the two sexes sets in, in connection, that is, with the perception of the anatomical difference between male and female. To the boy castration was only a threat, which can be escaped by a suitable modification of behaviour. To the girl it is an accomplished fact, which is irrevocable, but the recognition of which compels her finally to renounce her first love-object and to taste to the full the bitterness of its loss. Normally, the female child is bound at some time to come to this recognition: she is forced thereby completely to abandon her negative œdipus attitude, and with it the onanism which is its accompaniment. The object-libidinal relation to the mother is transformed into an identification with her; the father is chosen as a love-object, the enemy becomes the beloved. Now, too, there arises the desire for the child in the place of the wish for the penis. A child of her own acquires for the girl a similar narcissistic value to that which the penis possesses for the boy; for only a woman, and never a man, can have children.

The little girl, then, has now adopted the positive œdipus attitude with the very far-reaching after-results with which we are so familiar. Freud has explained more than once that there is no motive for the shattering of the positive œdipus complex in the female such as we have in the threat of castration in the case of the boy. Hence, the female œdipus complex vanishes only gradually, is largely incorporated in the normal development of the woman, and explains many of the differences between the mental life of women and of men.

We may now sum up by saying that the little girl's castration complex (or her discovery of the anatomical difference between the sexes) which, according to Freud, ushers in and renders possible her normal, positive œdipus attitude, has its psychic correlative just as that of the boy, and it is only this correlative which lends it its enormous significance for the mental evolution of the female child. In the first years of her development as an individual (leaving out of account the phylogenetic influences which, of course, are undeniable) she behaves exactly like a boy not only in the matter of onanism but in other respects in her mental life: in her love-aim and object-choice she is actually a little man. When she has discovered and fully accepted the fact that castration has taken place, the little girl is forced once and for all to renounce her mother as love-object and therewith to give up the active, conquering tendency of her love-aim as well as the practice of clitoral onanism. Perhaps here, too, we have the explanation of a fact with which we have long been familiar, namely, that the woman who is wholly feminine does not know object-love in the true sense of the word: she can only "let herself be loved". Thus it is to the mental accompaniments of phallic onanism that we must ascribe the fact that the little girl normally represses this practice much more energetically and has to make a far more intense struggle against it than the boy. For she has to forget with it the first love-disappointment, the pain of the first loss of a love-object.

We know how often this repression of the little girl's negative œdipus attitude is wholly or partly unsuccessful. For the female as well as for the male child it is very hard to give up the first love-object: in many cases the little girl clings to it for an abnormally long time. She tries to deny the punishment (castration) which would inevitably convince her of the forbidden nature of her desire. She firmly refuses to give up her masculine position. If later her love-longing is disappointed a second time, this time in relation to the father who does not give way to her passive wooing of his love, she often tries to return to her former situation and to resume a masculine attitude. In extreme cases this leads to the manifest homosexuality of which Freud gives so excellent and clear an account in "A Case of Female Homosexuality".[4] The patient about whom Freud tells us in this work made a faint effort on entering puberty to adopt a feminine love attitude but, later in the period of puberty, she behaved towards an elder woman whom she loved exactly like a young man in love. At the same time she was pronounced feminist, denying the difference between man and woman; thus she had gone right back to the first, negative phase of the œdipus complex.

There is another process which is perhaps commoner. The girl does not entirely deny the fact of castration, but she seeks for overcompensation for her bodily inferiority on some plane other than the sexual (in her work, her profession). But in so doing she re-

[4] *Collected Papers.*

presses sexual desire altogether, that is, remains sexually unmoved. It is as if she wished to say: "I may not and cannot love my mother, and so I must give up any further attempt to love at all." Her belief in her possession of the penis has then been shifted to the intellectual sphere; there the woman can be masculine and compete with the man.

We may observe as a third possible outcome that a woman may form relationships with a man, and yet remain inwardly attached to the first object of her love, her mother. She is obliged to be frigid in coitus because she does not really desire the father or his substitute, but the mother. Now these considerations place in a somewhat different light the fantasies of prostitution so common amongst women. According to this view they would be an act of revenge, not so much against the father as against the mother. The fact that prostitutes are so often manifest or disguised homosexuals might be explained in analogous fashion as follows: the prostitute turns to the man out of revenge against the mother, but her attitude is not that of passive feminine surrender but of masculine activity; she captures the man on the street, castrates him by taking his money and thus makes herself the masculine and him the feminine partner in the sexual act.

I think that in considering these disturbances in the woman's development to complete femininity we must keep two possibilities in view. Either the little girl has never been able wholly to give up her longing to possess her mother and thus has formed only a weak attachment to her father, or she has made an energetic attempt to substitute her father for her mother as love-object but, after suffering a fresh disappointment at his hands, has returned to her first position.

In the paper "Some Psychological Consequences of the Anatomical Distinction between the Sexes", Freud draws attention to the fact that jealousy plays a far greater part in the mental life of woman than in that of men. He thinks that the reason for this is that in the former jealousy is reinforced by deflected penis-envy. Perhaps one might add that a woman's jealousy is stronger than a man's because she can never succeed in securing her first love-object, while the man, when he grows up, has the possibility of doing so.

In another paragraph Freud traces the fantasy "A Child is Being Beaten" ultimately to the masturbation of the little girl when in the phallic phase. The child which is beaten or caressed is at bottom the clitoris (i.e. the penis); the being beaten is on the one hand the punishment for the forbidden genital relation and on the other a regressive substitute for it. But in this phase the punishment for prohibited libidinal relations is precisely castration. Thus the formula "A child is being beaten" means "a child is being castrated". In the fantasies in which the child beaten is a stranger the idea of its being castrated is intelligible at the first glance. It means: "No one else shall have what I have not got." Now we know that in the fantasies of puberty, which are often greatly metamorphosed and condensed, the child beaten by the father always represents as well the girl herself. Thus she is constantly subjecting herself to castration, for this is the necessary condition of being loved by the father; she is making a fresh effort to get clear of her old love-relations and reconcile herself to her womanhood. In spite of the many punishments, pains and tortures which the hero has to undergo, "the fantasies always end happily",[5] i.e. the sacrifice having been made the passive, feminine love is victorious. Sometimes this immolation permits the return to masturbation, the first forbidden love-tendency having been duly expiated. Often, however, onanism remains none the less prohibited, or it becomes unconscious and is practised in some disguised form, sometimes accompanied by a deep sense of guilt. It seems as though the repeated submission to the punishment of castration signifies not only the expiation due to the feelings of guilt but also a form of wooing the father, whereby the subject experiences also masochistic pleasure.

To sum up what I have said above: In little boys, who develop normally, the positive œdipus attitude is by far the more prevalent, for by adopting it the child through his temporary renunciation of the mother-object can retain his genital and perhaps ensure for himself thereby the possibility of winning later in life a mother-substitute; if he adopted the negative attitude, it would mean that he must renounce both from the outset. Little girls, however, normally pass through both situations in the œdipus complex: first the negative, which occurs under precisely the same conditions as in boys, but which they are compelled finally to abandon when they discover and accept the fact of their castration. Now, the girl's attitude changes; she identifies herself with the lost love-object and puts in its place her former rival, the father, thus passing into the positive œdipus situation. Thus, in female children the castration-complex deals a death-blow to the negative œdipus attitude and ushers in the positive œdipus complex.

[5] Cf. Anna Freud: Schlagephantasie und Tagtraum, *Imago*, VIII, 1922.

This view confirms Freud's hypothesis that the (positive) œdipus complex in women is made possible and ushered in by the castration complex. But, in contradistinction to Freud, we are assuming that the castration complex in female children is a secondary formation and that its precursor is the negative œdipus situation. Further, that it is only from the latter that the castration complex derives its greater psychic significance, and it is probably this negative attitude which enables us to explain in greater detail many peculiarities subsequently met with in the mental life of women.

I am afraid it will be objected that all this looks like speculation and is lacking in any empirical basis. I must reply that this objection may be just as regards part of what I have said, but that nevertheless the whole argument is built up on a foundation of practical experience, although unfortunately this is still but meagre. I shall now give a short account of the material which has led me to my conclusions.

Some time ago I was treating a young girl who had been handed over to me by a male colleague. He had analyzed her for some years already, but there were certain difficulties connected with the transference which resisted solution. This girl had suffered from a somewhat severe hysterical neurosis. Her analysis had already been carried a good way. The normal, positive œdipus complex, her rivalry with her sister and her envy of her younger brother's penis had been dealt with thoroughly, and the patient had understood and accepted them. Many of her symptoms had disappeared, but nevertheless she remained to her great regret unfit for work. When she came to me, the unresolved, ambivalent transference to the male analyst was playing a principal part in the situation. It was difficult to determine which was the stronger; her passionate love or her no less passionate hate. I knew this patient personally before she came to me for treatment, and the analysis began with a strong positive transference to me. Her attitude was rather that of a child who goes to its mother for protection. But after a short time a profound change began to take place. The patient's behaviour became first rebellious and hostile and soon, behind this attitude, there was revealed a very deep-seated and wholly active tendency to woo my love. She behaved just like a young man in love, displaying, for instance, a violent jealousy of a young man whom she suspected of being her rival in real life. One day she came to analysis with the idea that she would like to read all Freud's writings and become an analyst herself. The obvious interpretation which we tried first, namely, that she wanted to identify herself with me, proved inadequate. A series of dreams showed an unmistakable desire to get rid of my own analyst, to "castrate" him and take his place, so as to be able to analyze (possess) me. In this connection the patient remembered various situations in her childhood when her parents quarrelled and she assumed a defensive and protective attitude towards her mother, and also times when they displayed mutual affection and she detested her father and wished to have her mother to herself. The analysis had long ago revealed a strong positive attachment to the father and also the experience which put an end to this. As a child the patient slept in a room next to her parents' and was in the habit of calling them at night when she had to urinate; of course, the intention was to disturb them. At first she generally demanded that her mother should come but, later on, her father.

She said that, when she was five years old, this once happened again and her father came to her and quite unexpectedly boxed her ears. From that moment the child resolved to hate him. The patient produced yet another recollection: when she was four years old she dreamt that she was lying in bed with her mother beside her and that she had a sense of supreme bliss. In her dream her mother said: "That is right, that is how it ought to be." The patient awoke and found that she had passed urine in bed; she was greatly disappointed and felt very unhappy.

She had various recollections of the time when she still slept in her parents' room. She said she used often to awake in the night and sit up in bed. These recollections are a fairly certain indication that she observed her parents' coitus. The dream she had as a child may very well have been dreamt after such an observation. It clearly represents coitus with her mother, accompanied by a sense of bliss. Even in later life urethral erotism played a particularly important part in this patient. Her disappointment on awaking showed that she was already conscious of her inability to possess her mother: she had long ago discovered the male genital in her younger brother. The bed-wetting can be construed either as a substitute for or a continuation of masturbation; the dream shows how intense must have been her emotional relation to her mother at that time. Hence it is clear that the patient, after the disappointment with her father (the box on the ears) tried to return to the earlier object, whom she had loved at the time of the dream, i.e. to her mother. When she grew up she made a similar attempt. After an unsuccessful love-affair with a younger brother of her father's she had for a short time a homosexual relation. This situation was repeated in her analysis when she came from the male analyst to me.

This patient stated that she had a special form of the beating fantasy when she was from eight to ten years old. She described it as "the hospital fantasy". The gist of it was as follows: A large number of patients went to a hospital to get well. But they had to endure the most frightful pains and tortures. One of the most frequent practices was that they were flayed alive. The patient had a feeling of shuddering pleasure when she imagined their painful, bleeding wounds. Her associations brought recollections of how her younger brother sometimes pushed back the foreskin of his penis, whereupon she saw something red, which she thought of as a wound. The method of cure in her fantasy was therefore obviously a representation of castration. She identified herself on one occasion with the patients, who at the end always got well and left the hospital with great gratitude. But generally she had a different rôle. She was the protecting, compassionate Christ, who flew over the beds in the ward, in order to bring relief and comfort to the sick people. In this fantasy, which reveals its sexual-symbolic character in the detail of *flying*, the patient is the man who alone possesses his mother (for Christ was born without father), but who finally, in order to atone for the guilt and to be able to reach God the Father, offered the sacrifice of crucifixion (castration). After we broke off the analysis, which the patient gave up in a state of negative transference, a reaction to the disappointment of her love, she tried to translate this fantasy into reality by deciding to become a nurse. After a year, however, she abandoned this new profession for her earlier one, which was more masculine in character and much more suited to her temperament. Gradually, too, her feelings of hate towards me disappeared.

I had a second patient in whom I discovered similar processes with regard to the transference. In the first two months of treatment this patient produced very strong resistances. She acted the part of a naughty, defiant child and would utter nothing but monotonous complaints to the effect that she was forsaken and that her husband treated her badly. After we had succeeded in discovering that her resistance arose from feelings of hate towards me, due to envy and jealousy, the full, positive, feminine œdipus attitude gradually developed in her—there entered into it both love for the father and the wish for a child. Soon, too, penis-envy began to show itself. She produced a recollection from her fifth or sixth year. She said that she had once put on her elder brother's clothes and displayed herself proudly to all and sundry. Besides this she had made repeated efforts to urinate like a boy. At a later period she always felt that she was very stupid and inferior and thought that the other members of her family treated her as if this were the case. During puberty she conceived a remarkably strong aversion to every sort of sexual interest. She would listen to none of the mysterious conversations in which her girl-friends joined. She was interested only in intellectual subjects, literature, etc. When she married she was frigid. During her analysis she experienced a desire to have some profession; this stood to her for being male. But her feelings of inferiority forbade any real attempt to compass this ambition. Up to this point the analysis had made splendid progress. The patient had one peculiarity: she remembered very little, but she enacted all the more in her behaviour. Envy and jealousy and the desire to do away with the mother were repeated in the most diverse guises in the transference. After this position had been worked through, a new resistance presented itself; we discovered behind it deep homosexual desires having reference to myself. The patient now began to woo my love in a thoroughly masculine manner. The times of these declarations of love, during which in her dreams and fantasies she always pictured herself with a male genital, invariably coincided with some active behaviour in real life. They alternated, however, with periods in which her behaviour was wholly passive. At such times the patient was once more incapable of anything; she failed in everything, suffered from her inferiority and was tortured with feelings of guilt. The meaning of this was that every time she conquered the mother, she was impelled to castrate herself in order to get free from her sense of guilt. Her attitude to masturbation also was noteworthy. Before analysis she had never consciously practised this habit; during the period when she was being treated she began clitoral masturbation. At first this onanism was accompanied by a strong sense of guilt; later, at times when her love-wishes in relation to her father were most vehemently manifested, the feelings of guilt abated. They were succeeded by the fear that the onanism might do her some physical harm: "weaken her genitals". At the stage when she was in love with me the sense of guilt reappeared and she gave up masturbating, because this fear became in her mind a certainty. Now this "weakening" of the genital organs signified castration. Thus the patient constantly oscillated between homosexual and heterosexual love. She had a

tendency to regress to her first love-relation—with the mother—
and at this stage tried to deny the fact of castration. To make up
however, she had to refrain from onanism and sexual gratification,
of any kind. She could not derive satisfaction from her husband,
because she hersef really wanted to be a man in order to be able to
possess the mother.

Thus in both the cases which I have quoted it was plain that
behind the woman's positive œdipus attitude there lay a negative
attitude, with the mother as love-object, which revealed itself later
in the analysis and therefore had been experienced at an earlier
stage of development. Whether this evolution is typical cannot, of
course, be asserted with any certainty from the observation of two
cases. I should be inclined to believe that in other female patients
the œdipus complex has had a similar previous history, but I have
not been able to gather enough material from their analyses to
establish this beyond question. The phase of the negative œdipus
attitude, lying, as it does, so far back in the patient's mental history,
cannot be reached until the analysis has made very considerable progress. Perhaps with a male analyst it may be very hard to bring this
period to light at all. For it is difficult for a female patient to enter
rivalry with the father-analyst, so that possibly treatment under
these conditions cannot get beyond the analysis of the positive
œdipus attitude. The homosexual tendency, which can hardly be
missed in any analysis, may then merely give the impression of a
later reaction to the disappointment experienced at the father's
hands. In other cases, however, it was clearly a regression to an
earlier phase—one which may help us to understand better the
enormous psychic significance that the lack of a penis has in the
erotic life of women. I do not know whether in the future it will
turn out that my exposition in this paper explains only the development of these two patients of mine. I think it not impossible that it
may be found to have a more general significance. Only the gather-
ing of further material will enable us to decide this question.

THE SIGNIFICANCE OF MASOCHISM IN THE MENTAL LIFE OF WOMEN * (1930)

By Helene Deutsch

*This paper corrects what Freud felt to be a defect in the preced-
ing study of Lampl-de Groot: her representation of the relinquishment* (Abwendung) *of the mother as a mere "change of object",
and her omission of the fact that such a "turning-away" is accompanied by "most distinct signs of hostility". To this Helen Deutsch
does complete justice: to quote from Freud's summary of her paper:
"She also recognizes the little girl's phallic activity and the
strength of her attachment to her mother", as well as the fact
"that in turning to the father the little girl follows her passive
tendencies (already awakened in her relations with her mother)".†*

*One may add that the paper contains some striking thoughts
beyond its immediate topic, such as general speculations on the
genesis of the feeling of guilt, and reflections upon the exploitation
of various antithetic possibilities of psychological development on
the part of one series of generations as compared with another.*

In the analysis of women we became familiar with the masculinity-
complex before we learned much about the "femininity" which
emerges from the conflicts accompanying development. The reasons
for this later recognition were various. First of all, analysis comes to
know the human mind in its discords rather than in its harmonies,
and, when we turn the microscope of observation upon the woman,
we see with special distinctness that the main source of her conflicts
is the masculinity which she is destined to subdue. It followed that
we were able to recognize the "masculine" element in women earlier
and more clearly than what we may term the nucleus of their

---

* First published in the *Internationale Zeitschrift für Psychoanalyse*, XVI,
1930, p. 172, under the title: "Der Masochismus und seine Beziehung zur
Frigidität."

Reprinted from *The International Journal of Psycho-Analysis*, XI, 1930,
p. 48. The subheading "Part I, Feminine Masochism and its Relation to
Frigidity" has been omitted, since to the author's recollection, no paper
constituting "Part II" was ever written.

† On Female Sexuality, *The International Journal of Psycho-Analysis*
XIII, 1932, p. 295.

195

"femininity". Paradoxical as it may sound, we approached the feminine element with greater interest when it formed part of a pathological structure and, as a foreign body, attracted a closer attention. When we encountered in men that instinctual disposition which we designate feminine and passive-masochistic, we recognized its origin and the weighty consequences it entailed. In the case of women we discovered that, even in the most feminine manifestations of their life—menstruation, conception, pregnancy and parturition—they had a constant struggle with the never wholly effaced evidences of the bisexuality of their nature. Hence, in my earlier writings [1] I showed with what elemental force the masculinity complex flares up in the female reproductive functions, to be once more subdued.

My aim in this paper is different. I want to examine the genesis of "femininity", by which I mean the feminine, passive-masochistic disposition in the mental life of women. In particular I shall try to elucidate the relation of the function of feminine instinct to the function of reproduction, in order that we may first of all clarify our ideas about sexual inhibition in women, that is to say, about frigidity. The discussion will concern itself with theoretical premises rather than with the clinical significance of frigidity.

But first let us return to the masculinity-complex.

No one who has experience of analysis can doubt that female children pass through a phase in their libidinal evolution, in which they, just like boys, having abandoned the passive oral and anal cathexes, develop an erotogeneity which is actively directed to the clitoris as in boys to the penis. The determining factor in the situation is that, in a certain phase, sensation in the organs, which impel the subject to masturbate, tend strongly towards the genital and effect cathexis of that zone which in both sexes we have called the "phallic".

Penis-envy would never acquire its great significance were it not that sensations in the organs, with all their elemental power, direct the child's interest to these regions of the body. It is this which first produces the narcissistic reaction of envy in little girls. It seems that they arrive only very gradually and slowly at the final conclusion of their investigations: the recognition of the anatomical difference between themselves and boys. So long as onanism affords female children an equivalent pleasure they deny that they lack the penis,

[1] Helene Deutsch: *Psychoanalyse der weiblichen Sexualfunktionem.* Neue Arbeiten aur ärztlichen Psychoanalyse, Nr. V.

or console themselves with hopes that in the future the deficiency will be made good. A little girl, whom I had the opportunity of observing, reacted to the exhibitionistic aggression of an elder brother with the obstinate and often repeated assertion: "Susie *has* got one", pointing gaily to her clitoris and labia, at which she tugged with intense enjoyment. The gradual acceptance of the anatomical difference between the sexes is accompanied by conflicts waged round the constellation which we term penis-envy and masculinity-complex.

We know that, when the little girl ceases to deny her lack of the penis and abandons the hope of possessing one in the future, she employs a considerable amount of her mental energy in trying to account for the disadvantage under which she labours. We learn from our analyses what a large part the sense of guilt connected with masturbation commonly plays in these attempts at explanation. The origin of these feelings of guilt is not quite clear, for they already exist in the phase in which the œdipus complex of the little girl does not seem as yet to have laid the burden of guilt upon her.[2]

Direct observation of children shows beyond question that these first onanistic activities are informed with impulses of a primary sadistic nature against the outside world.[3] Possibly a sense of guilt is associated with these obscure aggressive impulses. It is probable that the little girl's illusion that she once had a penis and has lost it is connected with these first, sadistic, active tendencies to clitoral masturbation. Owing to the memory-traces of this active function of the clitoris, it is subsequently deemed to have had in the past

[2] Freud: Some Psychological Consequences of the Anatomical Difference between the Sexes, *The International Journal of Psycho-Analysis*, VIII, 1927. The argument in this paper of Freud's is that the œdipus complex does not develop in girls until after the phase of phallic onanism. Cf. also Deutsch: *Op. cit.*

[3] In his paper on The Economic Problem in Masochism (*Collected Papers*, II), Freud points out that the important task of the libido is to conduct into the outside world the instinct of destruction primarily inherent in living beings, transforming it into the "instinct of mastery". This is effected by means of the organ of motility, the muscular system. It appears to me that part of these destructive tendencies remains attached to the subject's own person in the earliest form of masturbation, which has as yet no libidinal object, and that it is thus intercalated between organic pleasure and motor discharge into the outside world. At any rate I have been able with some degree of certainty to establish the fact that children who are specially aggressive and active have a particularly strong urge to masturbation. (I am speaking here of the earliest masturbation, which is as yet autoerotic). We see too that in little children frustration may provoke an outburst of rage and at the same time attempts at masturbation.

the actual value of an organ equivalent to the penis. The erroneous conclusion is then drawn: "I once did possess a penis."

Another way in which the girl regularly tries to account for the loss is by ascribing the blame for it to her mother. It is interesting to note that, when the father is blamed for the little girl's lack of a penis, castration by him has already acquired the libidinal significance attaching to this idea in the form of the rape-fantasy. Rejection of the wish that the father should have been the aggressor generally betokens, even at this early stage, that rejection of the infantile feminine attitude to which I shall recur.

In his paper "Some Consequences of the Anatomical Difference between the Sexes", Freud sees in the turning of the little girl to her father as a sexual object a direct consequence of this anatomical difference. In Freud's view, development from the castration to the œdipus complex consists in the passing from the narcissistic wound of organ-inferiority to the compensation offered: that is to say, there arises the desire for a child. This is the source of the œdipus complex in girls.

In this paper I shall follow up the line of thought thus mapped out by Freud. After the phallic phase, where the boy renounces the œdipus complex and phallic masturbation, there is intercalated in the girl's development a phase which we may call "post-phallic"; in this the seal is set upon her destiny of womanhood. Vaginal cathexis, however, is as yet lacking.

In spite of my utmost endeavours, I am unable to confirm the communications that have been made with reference to vaginal pleasure-sensations in childhood. I do not doubt the accuracy of these observations, but isolated exceptions in this case prove little. In my own observations I have had striking evidence in two instances of the existence of vaginal excitations and vaginal masturbation before puberty. In both, seduction with defloration had occurred very early in life. [4] If there were in childhood a vaginal phase, with all its biological significance, it surely could not fail to appear as regularly in our analytical material as do all the other infantile phases of development. I think that the most difficult factor in the "anatomical

[4] Even if further observations should prove the occurrence of vaginal sensations in childhood, the subsequent cathexis of the vagina as a sex-organ would still seem to be scarcely affected by the question of whether it had transitorily been a zone of excitation, very soon repressed so as to leave scarcely a trace, or whether it were only in later years of development that it assumed for the first time the rôle of the genital apparatus. The same difficulties arise in either case.

destiny" of the woman is the fact that at a time when the libido is still unstable, immature and incapable of sublimation, it seems condemned to abandon a pleasure-zone (the clitoris as a phallic organ) without discovering the possibility of a new cathexis. The narcissistic estimation of the non-existent organ passes smoothly (to use a phrase of Freud's) "along the symbolic equation: penis = child, which is mapped out for it". But what becomes of the dynamic energy of the libido which is directed towards the object and yearns for possibilities of gratification and for erotogenic cathexes?

We must also reflect that the wish-fantasy of receiving a child from the father—a fantasy of the greatest significance for the future of a woman—is, nevertheless, in comparison with the reality of the penis, for which it is supposed to be exchanged, a very unreal and uncertain substitute. I heard of the little daughter of an analyst mother who, at the time when she was experiencing penis-envy, was consoled with the prospect of having a child. Every morning she woke up to ask in a fury: "Hasn't the child come *yet*?" and no more accepted the consolation of the future than we are consoled by the promise of Paradise.

What, then, does happen to the actively directed cathexis of the clitoris in the phase when that organ ceases to be valued as the penis? In order to answer this question we may fall back on a familiar and typical process. We already know that, when a given activity is denied by the outside world or inhibited from within, it regularly suffers a certain fate—it turns back or is deflected. This seems to be so in the instance before us: the hitherto active-sadistic libido attached to the clitoris rebounds from the barricade of the subject's inner recognition of her lack of the penis and, on the one hand, regressively cathects points in the pregenital development which it had already abandoned, while, on the other hand, and most frequently of all, it is deflected in a regressive direction towards masochism. In place of the active urge of the phallic tendencies, there arises the masochistic fantasy: "I want to be castrated", and this forms the erotogenic masochistic basis of the feminine libido. Analytic experience leaves no room for doubt that the little girl's first libidinal relation to her father is masochistic, and the masochistic wish in its earliest distinctively feminine phase is: "I want to be castrated by my *father*."[5]

[5] That "feminine" masochism has its origin in this regressive deflection of the libido is clear evidence of the identity of "erotogenic" and "feminine" masochism.

In my view this turning in the direction of masochism is part of the woman's "anatomical destiny", marked out for her by biological and constitutional factors, and lays the first foundation of the ultimate development of femininity, independent as yet of masochistic reactions to the sense of guilt. The original significance of the clitoris as an organ of activity, the masculine-narcissistic protest: "I won't be castrated" are converted into the desire: "I want to be castrated." This desire assumes the form of a libidinal, instinctual trend whose object is the father. The woman's whole passive-feminine disposition, the entire genital desire familiar to us as the rape-fantasy, is finally explained if we accept the proposition that it originates in the castration-complex. *My view is that the œdipus complex in girls is inaugurated by the castration-complex.* The factor of pleasure resides in the idea of a sadistic assault by the love-object and the narcissistic loss is compensated by the desire for a child, which is to be fulfilled through this assault. When we designate this masochistic experience by the name of the wish for castration, we are not thinking merely of the bioligical meaning—the surrender of an organ of pleasure (the clitoris)—but we are also taking into account the fact that the whole of this deflection of the libido still centres on that organ. The onanism belonging to this phase and the masochistic fantasy of being castrated (raped) employ the same organ as the former active tendencies. The astonishing persistency of the feminine castration-complex (including all the organic vicissitudes with which is associated a flow of blood) as we encounter it in the analyses of our female patients is thus explained by the fact that this complex contains in itself not only the masculinity-complex, but also the whole infantile set towards femininity.

At that period there is a close connection between the masochistic fantasies and the wish for a child, so that the whole subsequent attitude of the woman towards her child (or towards the reproductive function) is permeated by pleasure-tendencies of a masochistic nature.

We have an illustration of this in the dream of a patient whose subsequent analysis unequivocally confirmed what had been hinted in the manifest content of her dream; this occurred in the first phase of her analysis before much insight had been gained.

"Professor X. and you (the analyst) were sitting together. I wanted him to notice me. He went past my chair and I looked up at him and he smiled at me. He began to ask me about my health, as a doctor asks his patient; I answered with reluctance. All of a sudden he had on a doctor's white coat and a pair of obstetrical forceps in his hand. He said to me: 'Now we'll just have a look at the little angel.' I clearly saw that they were obstetrical forceps, but I had the feeling that the instrument was to be used to force my legs apart and display the clitoris. I was very much frightened and struggled. A number of people, amongst them you and a trained nurse, were standing by and were indignant at my struggling. They thought that Professor X. had specially chosen *me* for a kind of experiment, and that I ought to submit to it. As everyone was against me, I cried out in impotent fury: 'No, I will not be operated on, you shall not operate on me.' "

Without examining the dream more closely here, we can see in its manifest content that castration is identified with rape and parturition, and the dream-wish which excites anxiety is as follows: "I want to be castrated (raped) by my father and to have a child"— a threefold wish of a plainly *masochistic character*.

The first, infantile identification with the mother is always, independently of the complicated processes and reactions belonging to the sense of guilt, *masochistic*, and all the active birth-fantasies, whose roots lie in this identification, are of a bloody, painful character, which they retain throughout the subject's life.[6]

In order to make my views on frigidity intelligible I had to preface them with these theoretical considerations.

I will now pass on to discuss those forms of frigidity which bear the stamp of the masculinity-complex or penis-envy. In these cases the woman persists in the original demand for possession of a penis and refuses to abandon the phallic organization. Conversion to the feminine-passive attitude, the necessary condition of vaginal sensation, does not take place.

Let me mention briefly the danger of the strong attachment of all sexual fantasies to clitoris-masturbation. I think I have made it clear that the clitoris has come to be the executive organ, not only of active but of passive masochistic fantasies. By virtue of its past phase of masculine activity, a kind of organ-memory constitutes it the great enemy of any transference of pleasure-excitation to the vagina. Moreover, the fact that the whole body receives an increased cathexis of libido (since it has failed to find its focus) brings it about that, in spite of an often very vehement manifestation of the sexual instinct, the libido never attains to its centralized form of gratification.

---

[6] In the present argument I am indicating the purely libidinal origin of feminine masochism, as determined by the course of evolution.

In far the largest number of cases, feminine sexual inhibition arises out of the vicissitudes of that infantile-masochistic libidinal development which I have postulated. These vicissitudes are manifold, and every form they assume may lead to frigidity. For instance, as a result of the repression of the masochistic tendencies a strong narcissistic cathexis of the feminine ego may be observed. The ego feels that it is threatened by these tendencies, and takes up a narcissistic position of defence. I believe that, together with penis-envy, this is an important source of so-called feminine narcissism.

Akin to this reaction of repression is another reaction-formation which Karen Horney calls "the flight from femininity", and of which she has given a very illuminating description. This flight from the incest-wish is, in my view, a shunning not only of the incestuous object (Horney), but most of all the masochistic dangers threatening the ego which are associated with the relation to this object. Escape into identification with the father is at the same time a flight from the masochistically determined identification with the mother. Thus there arises the masculinity-complex, which I think will be strong and disturbing in proportion as penis-envy has been intense and the primary phallic active tendencies vigorous.

Repression of the masochistic instinctual tendencies may have another result in determining a particular type of object-choice later in life. The object stands in antithesis to the masochistic instinctual demands and corresponds to the requirements of the ego. In accordance with these the woman chooses a partner whose social standing is high or whose intellectual gifts are above the average, often a man whose disposition is rather of an affectionate and passive type. The marriage then appears to be peaceful and happy, but the woman remains frigid, suffering from an unsatisfied longing—the type of the "misunderstood wife". Her sexual sensibility is bound up with conditions whose fulfilment is highly offensive to her ego. How often do such women become the wretched victims of a passion for men who ill-treat them, thus fulfilling the women's unconscious desires for castration or rape.

I have also observed how frequently—indeed, almost invariably —women whose whole life is modelled on the lines of masculine sublimation-tendencies are markedly masochistic in their sexual experiences. They belong to that reactive masculine type which yet has failed to repress its original masochistic instinctual atttiude. My experience is that the prospect of cure in these cases of relative frigidity, in which sexual sensation depends on the fulfilment of masochistic conditions, is very uncertain. It is peculiarly difficult to detach these patients from the said conditions and, when analysis has given them the necessary insight, they have consciously to choose between finding bliss in suffering or peace in renunciation.

The analyst's most important task is, of course, the abolition of the sexual inhibition in his patients, and the attainment of instinctual gratification. But sometimes, when the patient's instincts are so unfortunately fixed and yet there are good capacities for sublimation, the analyst must have the courage to smooth the path in the so-called "masculine" direction and thus make it easier for the patient to renounce sexual gratification.

There are women who have strong sexual inhibition and intense feelings of inferiority, the origin of which lies in penis-envy. In such cases it is evidently the task of analysis to free these patients from the difficulties of the masculinity-complex and to convert penis-envy into the desire for a child, i.e. to induce them to adopt their feminine rôle. We can observe that during this process the "masculine aims" become depreciated and are given up. Nevertheless we often find that, if we can succeed in making it easier for such women to sublimate their instincts in the direction of "masculine tendencies" and to so counter the sense of inferiority, the capacity for feminine sexual sensibility develops automatically in a striking manner. The theoretical explanation of this empirically determined fact is self-evident.

It is but rarely in analytic practice that we meet with such cases of conditioned frigidity as I have described or indeed with any cases of frigidity unaccompanied by pathological symptoms, i.e. of sexual inhibition without symptoms of suffering. When such a patient comes to us, it is generally at the desire of her husband, whose narcissism is wounded, and who feels uncertain of his masculinity. The woman, actuated by her masochistic tendencies, has renounced the experience of gratification for herself, and, as a rule, her desire to be cured is so feeble that the treatment is quite unsuccessful.

As we know, hysteria which expresses itself in symptom-formation is extraordinarily capricious and varied as regards the nature of the sexual inhibition displayed. One type of hysterical patient is driven by an everlasting hunger for love-objects, which she changes without inhibition: her erotic life appears free, but she is incapable of genital gratification. Another type is monogamous and remains tenderly attached to the love-object, but without sexual sensibility; she exhibits other neurotic reactions which testify to her morbid state. Such women often dissipate the sexual excitation in the fore-pleasure, either owing to the strong original cathexis of the pre-genital zones or because by a secondary and regressive reaction they are endeavouring to withhold the libido from the genital organ which prohibitions and their own anxiety have barricaded off. Here one often receives the impression that all the sense-organs, and indeed the whole female body, are more accessible to sexual excitation than is the vagina, the organ apparently destined for it. But conversion-symptoms turn out to be the seat of false sexual cathexes. Behind the hysterical, pleasure-inhibiting, genital anxiety we discover the masochistic triad: castration, rape and parturition. The fixation of these wish-fantasies to the infantile object here becomes, as we know, the motive factor in the neuroses. If this attachment is re-solved by analysis, sexual sensibility as a rule develops.

In touching briefly on the question of frigidity accompanying phobias and obsessions, mention must be made of the remarkable fact that in these cases the sexual disturbance is emphatically not in direct ratio to the severity of the neurosis. There are patients who remain frigid long after they have overcome their anxiety and even after they have got rid of the most severe obsessional symptoms, and the converse is also true. The uncertainty of obsessional neurosis—in so far as the genital capacity of female patients is concerned—is most plainly manifested in certain cases (several of which have come under my observation) in which the most violent orgasm may result from hostile masculine identifications. The vagina behaves like an active organ, and the particularly brisk secretion is designed to imitate ejaculation.

At the beginning of this paper I endeavoured to show that the masochistic triad constantly encountered in the analyses of women corresponds to a definite phase of feminine libidinal development and represents, so to speak, the last act in the drama of the vicissi-tudes of the "feminine castration-complex". In neurotic diseases, however, we meet above all with the reactions of the sense of guilt, and hence we find this primary-libidinal feminine masochism already so closely interwoven and interlocked with the moral masochism, originating under pressure of the sense of guilt, that we miss the significance of that which is in origin libidinal. Thus many obscure points in connection with the feminine castration-complex become clearer if we recognize that, behind the castration-anxiety, there is further the repressed masochistic wish characteristic of a definite infantile phase of development in the normal feminine libido.

The task of psycho-analysis is to resolve the conflicts of the individual existence. The instinctual life of the individual, which is the object of analytical scrutiny, strives towards the ultimate goal, amidst conflicts and strange vicissitudes, of *attainment of pleasure*. The preservation of the race lies outside these aims, and, if there be a deeper significance in the fact that the same means are employed to achieve the racial aim as to subserve the pleasure-tendency of man's instincts, that significance is outside the scope of our individualistic task.

Here I think we have a fundamental and essential difference between "feminine" and "masculine". In the woman's mental life there is *something* which has nothing at all to do with the mere fact of whether she has or has not actually given birth to a child. I refer to the psychic representatives of motherhood which are here long before the necessary physiological and anatomical conditions have developed in the girl. For the tendency of which I am speaking the attaining of the child is the main goal of existence, and in woman the exchange of the racial aim for the individual one of gratification may take place largely at the expense of the latter. No analytical observer can deny that in the relation of mother to child—begun in pregnancy and continued in parturition and lactation—libidinal forces come into play which are very closely allied to those in the relation between man and woman.

In the deepest experience of the relation of mother to child it is masochism in its strongest form which finds gratification in the bliss of motherhood.

Long before she is a mother, long after the possibility of becoming one has ended, the woman has ready within her the maternal principle, which bids her take to herself and guard the real child or some substitute for it.

In coitus and parturition the masochistic pleasure of the sexual instinct is very closely bound up with the mental experience of conception and giving birth; just so does the little girl see in the father, and the loving woman in her beloved—a child. For years I have traced out in analyses this most intimate blending of the sexual instinct with that of the reproductive function in women, and always the question has hovered before my mind: When does the female child begin to be a woman and when a mother? Analytic experience has yielded the answer: *Simultaneously*, in that phase when she turns towards masochism, as I described at the beginning of this paper. Then, at the same time as she conceives the desire to be castrated and raped, she conceives also the fantasy of receiving a child from her father. From that time on, the fantasy of parturition becomes a member of the masochistic triad and the gulf between instinctual and the reproductive tendencies is bridged by masochism. The interruption of the little girl's infantile sexual development by the frustration of her desire for the child gives to the sublimation-tendencies of the woman a very definite stamp of masochistic maternity. If it is true that men derive the principal forces which make for sublimation from their sadistic tendencies, then it is equally true that women draw on the masochistic tendencies with their imprint of maternity. In spite of this symbiosis, the two opposite poles, the sexual instinct and the reproductive function, may enter into conflict with one another. When this occurs, the danger is the greater in proportion as the two groups of tendencies are in close proximity.

Thus, a woman may commandeer the whole of her masochistic instinctual energy for the purpose of direct gratification and abandon sublimation in the function of reproduction. In the relation of the prostitute to the *souteneur* we have such an unadulterated product of the feminine masochistic instinctual attitude.

At the opposite end of the pole, yet drawing upon the same source, we have the *mater dolorosa*, the whole of whose masochism has come to reside in the relation of mother to child.

From this point I return to my original theme. There is a group of women who constitute the main body figuring in the statistics which give the large percentage of frigidity. The women in question are psychically healthy, and their relation to the world and to their libidinal object is positive and friendly. If questioned about the nature of their experience in coitus, they give answers which show that the conception of orgasm as something to be experienced by themselves is really and truly foreign to them. During intercourse what they feel is a happy and tender sense that they are giving keen pleasure and, if they do not come of a social environment where they have acquired full sexual enlightenment, they are convinced that coitus as a sexual act is of importance only for the man. In it, as in other relations, the woman finds happiness in tender, maternal giving.

This type of woman is dying out and the modern woman seems to be neurotic if she is frigid. Her sublimations are further removed from instinct and therefore, while on the one hand they constitute a lesser menace to its direct aims, they are, on the other, less well adapted for the indirect gratification of its demands. I think that this psychological change is in accordance with social developments and that it is accompanied by an increasing tendency of women towards masculinity. Perhaps the women of the next generation will no longer submit to defloration in the normal way and will give birth to children only on condition of freedom from pain.

And then in after-generations they may resort to infibulation and to refinements in the way of pain—ceremonials in connection with parturition. It is this masochism—the most elementary force in feminine mental life—that I have been endeavouring to analyse.

Possibly I have succeeded in throwing light on its origin and, above all, on its importance and its application in the function of reproduction. This employing of masochistic instinctual forces for the purpose of race-preservation I regard as representing in the mental economy an act of sublimation on the part of the woman. In certain circumstances it results in the withdrawal from the direct gratification of instinct of the energy involved and in the woman's sexual life becoming characterized by frigidity without entailing any such consequences as would upset her mental balance and give rise to neurosis.

Let me now at the close of my paper give its main purport: *Women would never have suffered themselves throughout the epochs of history to have been withheld by social ordinances on the one hand from possibilities of sublimation, and on the other from sexual gratifications, were it not that in the function of reproduction they have found magnificent satisfaction for both urges.*

ON FEMALE HOMOSEXUALITY * (1932)

By Helene Deutsch

This paper, although written at the same time as Freud's "On Female Sexuality", was first published a year later. Today it is still the most important article on the subject, to which it contributes more than the mere demonstration that, to quote Freud, ". . . . the homosexual woman reproduces the mother-child relationship". For, in the first place, it views the love-games between homosexual women as displaying a more or less undistorted reflection of the girl's phallic sexual aims. In doing so it affirms what Freud confessed his experience did not permit him to divine—namely, that the girl does imagine a sexual goal, and it at the same time states the nature of this goal. (Cf. Freud, On Female Sexuality: ". . . probably the child accompanies this clitoral masturbation with images of her mother, but whether she really imagines a sexual goal, and what that goal is, my experience does not make clear.")† In the second place, by treating the problem of guilt feelings it fills another gap left by Freud, who in his paper deliberately avoided discussing this problem. And finally it deals with the child's return to the previously relinquished mother-fixation in consequence of her disappointment in the father and describes the vicissitudes of this return.

This paper is based on the experience gained from the more or less profound analysis of eleven cases of female homosexuality. I should like, first of all, to stress the fact that none of these eleven women presented physical signs which might indicate that there had been a constitutional deviation, physiologically, in the direction of masculinity. The signs of accentuated bisexual disposition mentioned in this paper refer to forerunners of what, in later development, we usually call masculinity. These preliminary stages, however, appear to have no physical correlates, or at any rate none that can be deter-

* First published in the *Internationale Zeitschrift für Psychoanalyse*, XVIII, 1932.

Reprinted from *The Psychoanalytic Quarterly*, I, 1932, p. 484. Authorized translation by Edith B. Jackson.

† *The International Journal of Psycho-Analysis*, XIII, 1932, p. 293.

mined, for the patients showed no physical signs of masculinity. There are, to be sure, certain homosexual types whose personality, mental and physical, including the secondary sexual characteristics, are the type which is appropriate to the other sex; but none of my patients belonged to this type.

The first of the eleven cases of female homosexuality was analysed twelve years ago. Although the patient was aware of her sexual inversion, she did not indulge in homosexual practices; she knew that her erotic potentialities and fantasies were directed towards members of her own sex, and she would unequivocally become sexually excited when she embraced and kissed certain women. Towards these women, she was faithful and monogamous; her relations with them were purely platonic and remained platonic even when she knew that the women had a perverse tendency like her own. There was no particular type of woman which especially attracted her. The women were not in any instance of a masculine type, and she herself was blonde and feminine. She felt no hostility towards men, had a number of male friends, and accepted their favours and courtship without protestation. She had married a man of outspoken masculine appearance, and had several children by him to whom she gave a maternal, even if not excessively warm, response.

She was unable to explain why her homosexuality had not developed in a more active and urgent way; she only knew that her inhibitions against it were too strong—inhibitions which she rationalized on the basis of social shyness, family duty, and fear of psychic subjugation. She could trace her love response to women as far back as puberty, when it began in a typically adolescent way, directed towards teachers and other individuals more or less in authority. I cannot remember whether she characterized these individuals as particularly strict; in any event she was dominated by two feelings: a feeling of being sheltered, and, on the other hand, a feeling of fear of the individual in question. She was never really in love with a man. She had been attracted to her husband originally because she saw in him an exceptionally active and masculine personality. She was disappointed in marriage from the outset because, as she says, in this very relationship her husband failed to come up to her expectations. He lacked passion and was unaggressive particularly in sexual matters, and in other situations as well he failed her when she was most counting on his activity.

The patient came into analysis on account of neurotic difficulties. She had suffered for years from depressions and feelings of anxiety with a particular ideational content: she could not find the courage to assume the fitting authoritative attitude towards women in her employ. As a matter of fact, she expected a great deal of her servants and was upset when they failed to meet her demands, but she was quite unable to give them orders, much less to reprimand them. In situations which required this of her, she was overcome with timidity and anxiety in the presence of the person to be reproved. With every change in the personnel, and the consequent anticipation of a new woman in the household, her anxiety and conflict were greatly intensified. In these situations, moreover, she quite consciously reproached her husband for his lack of zeal in protecting and supporting her.

In recent years, her depressions had become more and more frequent and were intimately associated with the danger of suicide. The patient had already made a number of unsuccessful suicidal attempts; the last one had brought her to the verge of death. It happened that the physician called to her rescue was a close friend of mine, and he assured me that her intention to commit suicide had been genuine.

The patient's analysis for months revolved about the castration complex. At the time of this analysis—twelve years ago—the assumption of a castration complex in women was not such a matter of course as it is today. During the analysis I was so fascinated by the material dealing with this theme, that I was tempted to consider the castration complex the nucleus of her neurosis as well as of her perversion. She was so full of penis-envy that it appeared even in her relation to her little boys whose penis she cut off in dreams and fantasies. Even though the patient was dominated by marked sadistic tendencies, her conscious personality was more reactive in character. That is to say, she was kind and gentle and showed unmistakable obsessional neurotic traits, such as exaggerated decorum and propriety. Her transference to me was very pronouced and was characteristic of that type whose actions as well as conscious response over a long period of time reveal nothing except tenderness, respect and a feeling of safety. The patient was very happy and felt as if she had at last found a kind, understanding mother, who was making up to her all that her own mother had denied her. Her mother had been a stern and distant individual whom the patient had quite consciously hated all her life. After her mother's death (which occurred several years before the analysis began) the patient had a severe depression, during which she made one of her attempts at suicide.

The patient had several attacks of depression during the course of the analysis, following one another at short intervals. They were always accompanied by characteristic dreams and brought to light definite material. I discussed these dreams at the time—twelve years ago—at a meeting of the Vienna Psycho-analytic Society in a brief communication, under the title of *Mutterleibsträume und Selbstmordideen* (Uterus Dreams and Suicidal Ideas). Without presenting these dreams in detail, I may state that they contained practically everything we know about uterine symbolism; they were dreams of dark holes and crevices in which the patient crawled, dreams of comfortable dark places in which the dreamer felt at home and in which she lingered with a feeling of peace and redemption. These dreams appeared at a time when the patient was weighed down by conscious urges to kill herself, and was insisting that if it were not for her relation to me and her confidence in me, no power in the world could restrain her from committing suicide. One special dream-picture kept reappearing in the dreams: the patient saw herself as an infant swaddled with strips of tape or bandages. Her associations to this dream-picture made it clear that two hazy memories were emerging in these dreams. One referred to her last suicidal attempt (with poison): she awoke from a deep loss of consciousness while still strapped to the stretcher; she saw the doctor with a kind smile on his face, leaning over her, realized that he had saved her life (which was quite true) and thought: "This time you saved me, but after all you can't give me any real help."

Another set of associations led to the memory of a dangerous operation which her mother had undergone. The patient remembered seeing her mother, wrapped up as she herself was to be later, transported to the operating-room on a stretcher.

Starting from this memory the analysis led to an aggressive, murderous hate against the mother, which up to this point had been repressed, but which now became the central theme of the analysis. After about eight months' analysis childhood memories began to appear, and these turned out to be the nucleus of her neurosis as well as the nucleus of her perversion. The memories went back to the time between the patient's fourth and sixth years when she was masturbating to an alarming extent—at least from the mother's point of view. It was impossible to decide whether this masturbation really exceeded the normal amount, nor could we determine the content of the fantasies which, presumably, had accompanied the masturbation. But it is a fact, according to the patient's statement, that the mother resorted to the following method of checking the patient's masturbation: she bound the patient's hands and feet, strapped them to the crib, and said, as she stood looking on, "Now play if you can!" This aroused two reactions in the little girl. One was ungovernable rage against her mother, which was prevented by the fetters from discharge in motor activity. The other was intense sexual excitement, which she tried to satisfy by rubbing her buttocks against the bedding, regardless of her mother's presence, or perhaps to vent her spite on her mother.

The most dreadul thing in this scene, for her, was the fact that her father, summoned by the mother, was a passive witness and did not offer to help his little girl despite his tender affection for her.

This memory was recovered in the analysis while the patient was associating to the following dream:

She saw herself behind the bars in a police station, accused of some sort of sexual offence—apparently brought in from the street on suspicion of being a prostitute. The police sergeant, a kindly man, stood on the other side of the railing and did nothing to help her.

This is an almost direct repetition of the childhood situation.

The patient stopped masturbating after this childhood scene, and with this renunciation for a long while repressed her sexuality. At the same time, she repressed her hatred for her mother, to which she had in reality never given full expression.

I do not believe that the scene with her mother, which occurred in the patient's childhood, was traumatic in the sense of causing the patient's later attitude. But concentrated in it were all of the tendencies which had a determining influence on her whole sexual life. Her reproach—that her mother had forbidden her to masturbate— would certainly have been present even without this scene. The hate reaction against her mother, in accordance with the patient's sadistic constitution, was also to be seen in other childhood situations, as well as the reproach that her father did not protect her from her mother. But this scene brought all of these tendencies to the boiling point, as it were, and so became the prototype for later events.

From this time on, all sexual excitement was bound up with the maternal prohibition and with the most intense aggressive impulses towards the mother. Her whole psychic personality resisted these hate impulses, and as a reaction to them there awakened in her an intense sense of guilt towards her mother, which led to a transformation of the hate into a masochistic libidinal attitude. It is, therefore, comprehensible that the patient should reply to the direct question, why she had never yielded to a homosexual attachment, with the answer that she was afraid of becoming subjugated to the sexual partner. She was, indeed, afraid of being masochistically attached to her mother. It will also become clear why she was afraid of the women in her employ and why she chided her husband for not adequately protecting her.

Even though, during her analysis, the patient manifested an exaggerated penis-envy, it did not stand in the centre of her personality, either characterologically or in her behaviour towards men. She was not a woman with a "masculinity complex". However, it seems that this had not always been the case, for in her childhood before the eventful experience and also during puberty, there had been periods in which infallible signs of strongly developed masculine activity could be demonstrated. Especially at puberty many of her interests were quite unusual for a young girl in her social class at the time. This streak of masculinity was splendedly sublimated at the time, and indeed throughout her life. Yet a not inconsiderable part persisted and burdened her psychic economy, as dreams and certain inferiority feelings, etc., clearly showed.

I was very much tempted to assume that the patient was living out her masculinity in her homosexuality. But in this very point she failed to fulfil my analytic expectations, and presented me with a problem at the time which I could understand only years later. In order to adhere to a somewhat chronological order and present the facts as I learned them, I shall, for the time being, discontinue theoretical formulations.

After the above-mentioned part of the analysis had been worked through (after eight months) the father made his first real appearance as a topic of analytic material, and at the same time all of the impulses belonging to the œdipus complex were revived, starting with the chief, unremitting, reproach against the father that he had been too inactive to love his daughter. I should like to emphasize the fact that even at that time it was clear to me that the hate against her mother and the libidinal desire for her were much older than the œdipus complex.

I hoped that the patient's libidinal future would shape up more satisfactorily with a revival of the father relationship, especially when this relationship had been retouched and corrected. I referred her to an analyst of the fatherly type. Unfortunately, the transference did not advance beyond respect and sympathy, and the analysis was

interrupted after a short time. About a year later I met the patient
and saw that she had become a vivid, radiant person. She told me
that her depressions had entirely disappeared. The wish to die which
had been almost continuously present and her nostalgia had
apparently receded completely. At last she had found happiness in
a particularly congenial and uninhibited sexual relationship with
a woman. The patient, who was intelligent and conversant with
analysis, informed me that their homosexual relationship was quite
consciously acted out as if it were a mother-child situation, in which
sometimes one, sometimes the other played the mother—a play with
a double cast, so to speak. Moreover, the satisfactions sought in this
homosexual love play involved chiefly the mouth and the external
genitalia. No "male-female" contrast appeared in this relationship;
the essential contrast was that of activity and passivity. The impression gained was that the feeling of happiness lay in the possibility
of being able to play *both* rôles.

The result of her analysis was evident. Everything that had
come to the surface so clearly in the analytic transference was now
detached from the person of the analyst and transferred to other
women. The gratifications denied her in the analytic situation could
now be found in the relationship with the new objects. It was evident
that the overcoming of her hostility towards the analyst had brought
with it the overcoming of her anxiety and, consequently, a positive
libidinal relationship to women could appear in place of the anxiety
and hostility which had caused the neurotic symptoms—only, of
course, after the mother-substitute object had paid off the infantile
grievances by granting her sexual satisfactions. The analytic treatment had not brought about the further and more favourable solution of the mother attachment, that is, a renunciation of her homosexuality and an inclination towards men. Here I should like to
interrupt my discussion and present some of the other analysed
cases before continuing with the theoretical considerations. For the
sake of completeness, it may be added that after the analysis the
patient made no more suicidal attempts; but I have heard that the
old difficulties with women in her employ have recently begun again.
I suppose that some disturbances in the love relationship occurred,
which probably resulted in a neurotic reaction. But in any case there
has been no suggestion of the depressions as they were before the
analysis.

In the course of the last three years I have analysed several cases
of female homosexuality—cases in which the perversion was more

manifest than in the one just described. Analysis with them began, so to speak, where this patient's analysis left off. All of them were in a more or less consciously recognized mother-child relationship with their love object. Sexual satisfaction was obtained in all those cases from the following practices: close embrace, mutual sucking at the nipples, genital and (more prominently) anal masturbatory stimulation, and intense mutual cunnilingus. Of special interest is the prominence given to the double rôle in these cases also.

One of these patients had divided the double rôle between two types of objects: one type, represented by an insignificant, needy young girl, who would take the part of the child; the other by an older, very active and very authoritative woman with whom the patient herself played the part of the child. The latter type of relationship usually began when the patient, who was very active and professionally ambitious, entered into a sublimated relationship with the woman, remained for a short time in a scarcely noticeable attitude of competition (of which she became conscious only through analysis), and then began to fail in her work in a clearly neurotic way, so that she would be in a subordinate position to the particular woman in question. For example, the end-result of writing a technical article, which had been undertaken jointly, was that the patient —perhaps the more gifted of the two—would play the part of a secretary in editing the work. If sexual approaches were made during work of this kind, the rôle of active seducer was always conceded to the other woman.

From the life history and the analysis, I shall select only the material needed for the theoretical considerations to be presented later.

The patient belonged to a very large family; she had many sisters and two brothers, of whom only one, four years her senior, played a part in her life story. When she was only nine months old, a new sister arrived, a competitor who disputed her right to the mother's breast. She suffered, in early childhood, from all sorts of oral symptoms, from which it was possible to reconstruct a situation which might be described as "oral envy". She remained for a long time in a competitive relation to this sister, to whom, even in childhood, she gave precedence—an evident overcompensation. For instance, she recounted in the analysis that very early in childhood, she had heard that when there is such a slight difference in age and such a striking resemblance between two sisters as there was between her and her sister, only one of them could marry and have children. She thus retired from the feminine rôle in favour of her sister; and in adolescence, when her parents were divorced after the birth of the last child, she waived her claim to the father to the advantage of the other children and remained with her mother.

Very early in childhood, the patient developed reaction-formations to aggressive tendencies which, before the birth of the next sister (when she was six), were suggestive of obsessional neurosis; they did not, however, develop to any great degree. At any rate, during her mother's pregnancy at that time, she reproached herself bitterly because she did not feel as kindly disposed towards her mother and the expected baby as her younger sister Erna did; she was convinced that the latter prayed every morning for the wellbeing of the mother and child.

The analysis uncovered strong aggression against the mother,[1] especially against the *pregnant* mother, and against the newborn child. The life of the patient and her whole character had developed, as it turned out, under the pressure of an attempt to dispel thoughts of killing her mother and the child.

The reaction recurred afresh at the two following pregnancies of her mother—the children again were both girls; and only after the birth of her youngest sister, when the patient was twelve years old, did her psychical situation change. When she was very young, the patient always thought of her father as a mysterious, strange and powerful man, in whose presence one could not help feeling timid and anxious; but her attitude gradually changed, for the father had acquired a heart affection which finally incapacitated him for work. The family was thus involved in material difficulties; and with this stimulus, the patient took over the father's rôle herself, and gave free play to fantasies in which she held good positions and supported the family. As a matter of fact, by dint of hard work she later realized these fantasies.

In spite of the identification with her father, and in spite of the fact that she envied her brother's masculinity, she did not take the competitive attitude toward her youngest sister that she had taken to the other sisters when they were born. She was, on the contrary, highly pleased with the rôle of being a "little mother" and claimed

[1] Melanie Klein's observations shows very clearly how bloodthirsty and aggressive a child's relations to its mother are, especially when an actual event (e.g., the birth of a younger child) mobilizes the aggression. The great value of these observations lies in the fact that they were made directly on children.

the child entirely for herself. In this situation, she was behaving quite normally as far as the œdipus complex was concerned. The analysis showed that this positive œdipus attitude was reached only because she had dethroned her father from his position of supreme and unapproachable power, and that only then could she overcome the intense fear of the masochistic, sexual experience which she desired.

My experience substantiates my assumption that this change of object—the libidinal turning away from the mother to the father—is accomplished with more difficulty, the more aggressive and sadistic are the predominating dispositions in the little girl, not only because the change of object is hindered by the active strivings, but also because the change into the passive attitude must, in cases of this type, assume a marked masochistic character and be repudiated by the ego as dangerous.

Our patient had certainly attained the normal œdipus situation, as her puberty clearly showed, but the ensuing rivalry with her mother provided fresh fuel for the old preœdipal aggression. This intensified her sense of guilt, which could be relieved only by means of a new overcompensation—renunciation of her father and definite persistence in her mother attachment.

To reduce the psychological basis of this relationship to a formula, we might say: "I do not hate you; I love you. It is not true that you have refused me the breast and given it to my youngest (so to speak, pre-œdipal) sister; you gave it to me, and, therefore, I do not need to kill you and the child. It is not true that I have killed the child, for I myself am the child whom you love and suckle." This fundamental attitude towards the mother is reflected not only in the form of the direct oral satisfaction in homosexual intercourse with the young girl (see above), but also in the above-mentioned submissive, passive attitude to the elder love-partner.

It must be noted that homosexuality as stated in the above formula as yet does not involve the œdipus situation, and is a continuation of and a reaction to the pre-œdipal situation.

However, the type of relationship which the patient had with the young girl corresponds not only to the active part of the original mother-child relationship—in which she makes a typical identification with the nourishing mother—but quite clearly makes use of new elements taken from the œdipus situation. The young girl is always a surrogate for her youngest sister—towards whom she actually had assumed a maternal rôle as a lifelong sublimation—but she is unsublimatedly homosexual with her love object, a relatively unknown young girl. In this relationship, she is at times the mother who suckles her child (or the father's child), and at times the suckled child herself. In this sexual experience she is able to transform the hate of her mother into love, for she is given the mother's breast; at the same time, she can be the active, suckling mother and thereby transform the aggression against her mother into activity.

At this point I should like to report some of the dreams which occurred in this patient's analysis, and from abundant material I shall select those which offer confirmation for the above statements even in the *manifest* dream content. One dream ran as follows:

The patient sees herself on the street with her younger sister. She is pregnant. She is in a hurry to reach a house which she sees in front of her. In the middle of the front of this house is a large projecting bay-window with one of the windows open. This is her mother's room; she wants to get there to give birth to her child. She is very much afraid that she will lose the child on the street, that is, that she will miscarry before she reaches the house. She expresses this fear to her sister, and then really does miscarry in the street.

The dream was readily explained by the patient's actual situation at the time. The day before the dream, she had been visited by a young friend, living in another city, whom she had not seen since the beginning of the analysis. This friend was really a homosexual object after the pattern of her youngest sister. They slept together, and the patient held her in her arms, pressed closely against her. But before there was any sexual release, she was upset by an uneasy feeling that the gratification of her homosexual wishes might possibly interfere with the analysis. She therefore made the friend leave the bed—lost her, as it were, out of her arms—in order not to disturb her relationship with me. It is clear that the pregnancy in the dream —the condition in which she has the child with her (within her)— is equated with her experience of the sexual embrace. The longing for her pregnant mother in the dream, which appears as a uterine fantasy in terms of a projecting bay window, and her simultaneous identification with her mother and with the child *in utero* is unusually clear. Furthermore, in the same analytic hour the patient remembered, for the first time, that when she was about three-and-a-half years old, her mother had had a miscarriage. It was in this period of her childhood that she had been deeply attached to her mother and had reacted with such extraordinary aggression to the pregnancy.

The other fragment of the dream: "I am walking with my youngest sister"—likewise expresses the situation before she fell asleep and means: "I have my beloved one beside me." This dream situation betrays the analytically established fact that the sexual relationship with her friend also includes a fulfilment of the œdipal wish, since the new little daughter belongs to her and not to her mother. The dream situation—to reach the mother and bear the child, or, on the contrary, not to reach the mother and to lose the child—portrays with unusual clarity the identity mother-child; that is, "to bear" equals "to be born", and relates to the preœdipal situation at the time of the mother's miscarriage. The fusing of this situation with œdipal wishes and its screening by the wishes of the œdipus attitude also seem to be clear in this case. I shall report only a fragment of a second dream:

The patient lies dreaming on a couch, a figure approaches her and tries to expose her. She tries to shriek and wakes up with the exclamation, "My God, doctor!"

She notices on awakening that she had her hands between her legs.

A series of associations to the dream led to a theme with which her analysis was dealing at this particular time—namely, masturbation. For quite a long time during the analysis the patient had refrained from masturbation because of the embarrassment she might feel in telling me of it. Shortly before, however, she had begun to allow herself to do it—with inhibitions—under the impression that I had nothing against it. Her exclamation, "My God!" referred to me and meant that I should save her from the danger of punishment —that is, protect her or give her my sanction. This interpretation was clear from the asociations, some of which led to the memory of a childhood experience. She had once touched an electric switch with a wet hand, so that the current had run through her, and she could not take her hand away. In response to her outcry ("My God") her mother had hurried to her, and also became a part of the circuit; with this, the current was weakened and the patient was able to release her hand. She had been rescued by her mother's interference. Like her mother, then, in the dream, I was to save her from "touching"—from the consequences of trespassing and doing a forbidden thing, by coming into the circuit of her excitement myself, by embracing her and gratifying her.

This excerpt from the dream serves to illustrate the other important feature of her homosexuality; her conflict over masturbation is brought to this apparently favourable solution by maternal intervention—that is, by the mother's expressed sanction. In another dream:

A tall, heavy-set woman whom she takes to be her mother, although she is taller and heavier than the latter, is in deep mourning because Erna (her next younger sister) has died. The father is standing nearby. She herself is in a cheerful mood because she is about to go away with her father on a spree. A glance at her mother warns her that this will not do, and that she must stay with her grieving mother.

This dream interprets itself. The patient is unable to satisfy her œdipal wishes and cannot be gay and happy with a man, because her feeling of guilt, which refer to the mother whose child she has killed, bind her to her mother and force her into homosexuality. From another long and informative dream, I cite here only a fragment.

She sees herself in analysis with Miss Anna Freud who is wearing men's clothes. This was explained in the dream by the fact that it was necessary for her to change analysts. With me it had been a question of producing free associations, with Miss Anna Freud it was a question of experiences.

On the evening before this dream, the patient was taken by her friends to a lecture held in the rooms of the Vienna Psycho-analytic Society, at which both Miss Freud and I were present. She told me in connection with this dream, that originally Miss Freud and I had been recommended to her as analysts. From the descriptions of us which she had heard, she had made up her mind what we were like; in her imagination Miss Freud represented a maternal ideal a person who was motherly to all children, and ready to give them succour whenever they turned to her for help; my motherliness, she imagined was directed especially towards my own children (that is to say, sexualized). Furthermore, it occurred to her at this point that before making her final decision, she had intended to write to us both, but, as a matter of fact, and as she now remembered for the first time, she had asked only for my address.

The evening before the dream, she had had a chance to compare us. She thought to herself, how true her idea about us had been, and how happy she was to be in analysis with me. This protestation seemed somewhat dubious to me, and I called her attention to the fact that the dream appeared to contradict it. It had struck me that the patient, who had gone to the lecture to see a certain analyst there, had not said a word about him, although he was sitting next to Miss Freud. Furthermore, she had not explained why, in the dream, Miss Freud appeared in men's clothing. A few days later she dreamed:

I am sitting facing her instead of behind her (as I always do) and am holding a cigar in my hand. She thinks, "The ashes are so long on the cigar that they will drop off any second."

She says, as her first association to the cigar: "Only men smoke cigars."

The masculinity, attributed to me, reminded me of the corresponding detail in regard to Miss Freud in the preceding dream. I then remembered that as the patient sat facing Miss Freud at the lecture, she must at the same time have seen on the wall the picture of Professor Freud, in which he holds a cigar in his hand. A similar picture is on my office desk. I showed this to her, and she agreed that the position of the hand holding the cigar was the same as mine in the dream.

Further analysis showed that she had dearly wished to be analysed by Professor Freud, but that this wish, springing as it did from her deep longing for the great man—the father—had been repressed, and that along with it, Miss Freud had been included in the repression. In addition, as already stated, she repressed the fact that she had met the analyst referred to above, and her impression of Professor Freud's picture. The repressed then asserted itself in the masculinity attributed to Miss Freud and me.

The way the father reappears in the dreams testifies to the fact that the patient's turning to the woman corresponds also to a flight from the man. The analysis revealed the source from which this tendency to flight originated: feelings of guilt towards the mother, fear of disappointment and of rejection.

To survey the case again briefly, we see that the first period of the patient's life was passed under somewhat unusual conditions. For a while she was nursed together with a younger sister, and when, finally, she had in her sister's interest to give up suckling, she developed (somewhat justifiably) a marked oral envy. When she was three years old, her mother became pregnant again, and she reacted to the anticipation of the child with great hostility and jealousy. The dream of the miscarriage illustrated the psychic condition of the little girl at the time, and her intense wish that she herself should be the child in the mother's womb.

This dream however was screened by reminiscences from a later period of her life (her twelfth year), and in the identification with her mother she betrayed her wish to have the child herself. This wish already is part of the œdipal attitude, which developed apparently late and slowly, bnt none the less *powerfully*, as we could see in the analysis.

It is hard to say whether her infantile and never relinquished longing to possess her mother for herself alone and be fed and cared for by her, tended to have an inhibitory effect on normal libidinal development, or whether the difficulties of the œdipus complex, as we know them in other cases, were the decisive factors in determining the later fate of the little girl's sexuality. I tried to show, above, in interpreting the dreams, that her return to her mother had not made her relinquish her longing for her father, but that she was constantly and anxiously fleeing from him, and consequently repressing her feminine attitude to men.

From the reported material, I should now like to deduce certain theoretical conclusions, which seem to me to represent important additions to our understanding of female sexuality in general, and of female homosexuality in particular.

It is repeatedly stated that our knowledge of *female* sexuality reaches no further than its correspondence with *male* sexuality in *childhood*. Only in *puberty*, when women really become feminine in the biological sense, are the conditions clearer and more comprehensible. Some of the important processes of the early stages of development were clarified by Freud's paper, "*Some Psychic Consequences of the Anatomical Difference between the Sexes*". In this paper he demonstrates the fact that the œdipus complex is not established in girls until after the phallic phase. I had already discussed [2] the stage in a girl's development which follows the phallic phase, and in which there is a thrust into passivity (*Passivitätsschub*). The central feature of this phase is the wish to be given an anal child by the father. I pointed out, in this discussion, that the thrust into passivity is really a regressive process, and represents a regression to a phase preceding the phallic organization which is identical in boys and girls. We are too readily fascinated, I think, by the events which take place in the phallic phase and by its manifestations and latent potentialities, so that we have emphasized the phallic phase to the neglect of the succeeding stage of passivity, which has been treated

[2] Deutch, Helene: *Psychoanalyse der weiblichen Sexualfunktionen*. Vienna-Leipzig, Int. Psa. Verlag, 1925.

more like a stepchild. We rest content with the fact that the wish to have a penis has been yielded in *exchange* for the wish to have a child, and that then it is up to the normal psychical powers inherent in the child to cope with the next frustration and to solve the new problem without harming itself. There is, I believe, no clinical observation to confute the idea that the intensity with which a child is desired is entirely dependent on the intensity of the preceding wish for a penis; therefore, one may say that the stronger the wish to have a penis, the stronger will be the subsequent wish to have a child; and the more difficult it is to bear being denied a penis, the more aggression will there be in the reaction to the thwarting of the wish for a child. Thus arises a vicious circle which often obscures the state of affairs for analysts; we find repeatedly that the very women whose violent psychic conflict was occasioned by the castration complex (i.e., by penis-envy) are the ones who also have an ardent feminine wish for a child.

A girl may have had a fairly normal sexual development up to the beginning of the œdipus complex and given up all hope of having a penis, so that she is ready for the transition from phallic activity into passivity—that is to say, she is ready to conceive the anal child by her father. This, however, is not sufficient to enable her to withstand the next bitter disappointment, which appears when she is denied a child. Keeping in mind the scheme of libidinal development we must not forget that along with this thrust into passivity a number of active forces are revived and raise their heads again because of the renewed cathexis of pregenital tendencies. They find their place without difficulty in the normal mental economy. For the rôle of the mother with the child, as the little girl playing with her dolls well illustrates, is an active one.

But what happens when the girl recoils in fright from the masochistic danger of the thrust into passivity? And when she cannot bear the actual disappointment of being denied a child, yet is convinced of the futility of her wish to have a penis? Let us get the situation in mind: the child is no longer narcissistically stimulated by the wish for a penis which she recognizes cannot be fulfilled; she feels rejected by her father, because of denial, disappointment or anxiety; she is left with libido which has little opportunity for sublimation. What will she do? She will do what all living creatures do in situations of danger. She will flee for refuge to the shelter where she once enjoyed protection and peace, to her mother. To be sure she had been disappointed by her mother too, but preceding all her denials there had been a time of satisfaction, for the refusing, hated mother had been at one time the source of all gratifications.

There is no doubt that even in the phallic phase the sexual instincts derive some satisfaction from the mother's routine care of the child. But apparently the claims at this time are more intense and they cannot, because of their dependence on the functions which are helping to build the ego, be satisfied to the same far-reaching extent as they were in preceding phases. Let us consider also that the phallic sexual aims were undisguised, that they were voiced easily, and that the mother's horror on her discovery of the wishes betrayed by the child was evident. We know from the analyses of mothers that their horror at the masturbatory actions of the child is the greater, the more their own unconscious memories of their own childhood masturbation are mobilized by direct observation of their children's behaviour. The restrictions to which the child is now subjected will cause a stronger reaction the more the mother herself has excited the child, in her unconscious rôle of seducer. Subsequent *direct* prohibition of masturbation and forcible interference with masturbatory activity rouses the hostility against the disciplinary mother to a high pitch. Moreover, with phallic masturbation comes the *affective* discovery of the anatomical "defect".

We already know that the girl blames her mother for depriving her of a penis. The sadistic impulses of the phallic phase are, accordingly, directed against the mother, and they are probably the impetus for the change of object. The change to a sadistic attitude towards the mother facilitates the passive masochistic attitude towards the father; all of this results from the phase that I have called the "thrust into passivity". It is certain, however, that the aggression is not entirely conducted into the masochistic passive attitude. Much of the aggressive impulse is turned against the disappointing father, and much remains attached to the mother who is now regarded as a rival. The intensity in any case is dependent upon the strength of the phallic activity. Furthermore, the change to masochism will occur with greater intensity, the more it is nurtured from the sources of aggression. Analysis of patients who have a very strong castration complex shows unequivocally how full of danger the passive attitude is as regards the development of masochism, and how blood-thirsty and murderous are the ideas of revenge on the mother, especially on the mother who in fact or fantasy is pregnant, or who already has another child. This attitude supplies the masochism with its moral component in addition, and the strength of the moral component is directly proportionate to the strength of the aggression.

We are thus aware of the dangers with which the little girl is beset in this phase:

(1.) Libidinal masochistic danger because of the expectation that her father may fulfil her wishes.

(2.) The danger of losing the newly chosen object as a result of refusal on her father's part.

(3.) Dangers of narcissistic injury of the ego libido, incident to the realization of the permanent lack of a penis.

In the midst of these great dangers, the libido, as we have said, turns to the earlier object again, and obviously more easily and more ardently the stronger the earlier attachments had been. It is a reversion to previously enjoyed experiences, as it were. I mean by this, that the aggression due to rivalry arising from the œdipus complex and the more highly organized sense of guilt, are now combined with the early infantile ambivalence conflicts.

The economic advantage of this new turning to the mother lies in the release from a feeling of guilt. But it seems to me that its most important accomplishment lies in the protection from the threatened loss of object: "If my father won't have me, and my self-respect is so undermined, who will love me, if not my mother?"

Analytic experience offers abundant evidence of this bi-sexual oscillation between father and mother, which may eventuate in neurosis, heterosexuality or inversion. We see the libido swinging between the poles of two magnets, attracted and repelled. Prospects of wish-fulfilment represent the *attraction* by one pole, frustration, fear, and mobilization of guilt feelings the *repulsion* from the other; and we see the same things happening in the case of other magnets; and as one of the most serious results of this oscillation, an obstinate narcissistic standstill appears somewhere in between. There are cases of blocking of affect, and especially clinical pictures of narcissistic disorders, which do not fit into any of the recognized forms of neurosis, but which do correspond to a standstill in the pendulum swing of libido as just described. If the oscillation is set in motion again in the analytic transference, the obsessional neurosis, whose oscillating ambivalence had been concealed by the emotional block, becomes apparent.

There was in these cases of female homosexuality a longer or shorter phase of indecision, which offers proof that it was not a question of a simple fixation on the mother as the first love object, but rather a complicated process of returning. The decision in favour of the mother as the attracting magnet lies naturally in the old powers of attraction, but also in the repelling forces from other magnets—denial, anxiety, and guilt reactions.

The return to the mother, when once started, needs the completion of still another process before it attains the character of a genuine inversion. First of all, the motives which once really induced the little girl to respond to the biological urge towards the father must be made retroactive. Accordingly, the sexual satisfaction of masturbation, which has been forbidden by the mother, must not only no longer be prohibited, but must be consented to by the mother by an active participation. The denial of the past must be made good by subsequent permissions, and indeed quite as much in reference to the original passive experience as to the subsequent active experience. One might say that the interruption of the phallic activity is made up for by this consent to activity which had been impossible in the past. The form which this active behaviour of the girl towards the maternal object takes, depends on the developmental stage at which the homosexual object relationship is taking place; that is, to speak more correctly, it depends on which is the most predominant stage, for, on closer observation, we see in the reaction *all* phases in which the mother played a rôle, which is equivalent to saying, all the stages of the preceding infantile development. Usually the most urgent tendencies are the phallic ones, and they cause the relationship of one female to another to assume a male character, whereby the absence of a penis is denied. These tendencies can indeed dominate the general picture of homosexuality, and may give rise to a definite, and as a matter of fact, the most outstanding, homosexual type.[3] This type denies the absence of a penis, expects that her feminine object will grant her her masculinity, and accepts phallic

---

[3] The case of female homosexuality published by Freud would also be classified under this "masculine" type, even though the original attitude of the patient was thoroughly feminine, and the masculine wish corresponded only to a subsequent identification with the once loved father. (Freud: On the Psychogenesis of a Case of Female Homosexuality. *Ges. Schr.*, V, trans. in *Collected Papers*, II.)

The two cases of female homosexuality described by Fenichel in *Perversionen, Psychosen, Charakterstörungen*, Int. Psa. Verlag, Wien, 1932 (English translation, by Lewin and Zilboorg, Outline of Clinical Psychoanalysis, *The Psychoanalytic Quarterly*, I and II), illustrate the same mental mechanisms as Freud's case. These cases also represent a "masculine" identification with the father as a reaction to being disappointed by him.

masturbation as a confirmation in the above-mentioned sense. It is then not very important whether the femininity of the object is to be emphasized, or whether both the subject and object are simultaneously affirming possession of a penis, so that the object may also take her turn in playing the masculine rôle. These are two sub-types of the same species. The extent of the old competitive attitude, especially in cases where an early displacement from the mother on to a sister took place, the quantum of masochistic or sadistic component, that is to say, the preponderance of aggressive tendencies or of reactions of guilt, a more passive or a more active casting of the rôle—these are all merely details in the total problem of female homosexuality.

I said that the phallic masculine form of homosexuality was the most outstanding one. But there are always many deeper currents hiding behind it. It is my impression, indeed, that this masculine form is sometimes brought into evidence for the very purpose of hiding the more infantile, but none the less predominating tendencies. The majority of the cases which I have analysed were forced to an honest and extensive relinquishment of their masculine behaviour by the strength of their pregenital urges. The mother-child relationship at pregenital levels, in the deeply entrenched fixation of the pre-phallic phases (whether consciously or unconsciously), dominated the perversion. The wish for activity belonging to the phallic phase is carried along in the regression, and reaches its most satisfactory fulfilment in the homosexual relationship. The frequent expression of the small child, "when you are little and I am big", finds its realization here in this double rôle which is always played in this relationship in which the child does everything with her mother that the mother had at one time done with her. Such freedom of activity, and the giving of free rein to masturbation are motives held in common by all forms of homosexuality. If in the phallic situation the mother compensates for the child's hurt by some sort of assent to the child's belief in the presence of a penis, then, in this new edition of the mother-child relationship, the pre-genital frustrations and denials must also be compensated, and this indeed happens often enough in the satisfaction which homosexual persons derive from their activities. Freud laid special emphasis on the marked preference of the oral mucous membrane in the activities of female inverts in the *Three Contributions to the Theory of Sex* [4]

----

[4] *Ges. Schr.*, V, English trans. by A. A. Brill.

and Jones [5] has found the disposition to female homosexuality in the oral sadistic phase. I feel that all my cases offer thorough confirmation of this dispositional element. I can state, furthermore, with complete security that not one of my cases failed to have a very strong reaction to the castration complex; a complete œdipus complex with exceedingly powerful aggressive reaction could be demonstrated in every case.

The return to the mother-child attitude was always introduced by the wish for the child which had been expected long since in place of a penis, but which had continued to be withheld. One of the sources from which the inversion is nourished is the reaction to the fact: "It is my mother who gets the child, not I." Not until later when the child herself has become a mother does the disposition for cruelty indicated in this reaction find adjustment, and then in a complicated manner in her own mother-child relationship. The above-mentioned patient produced unequivocal evidence for this in her dreams.

Considering the great complexity of the mother-child relationship, it is not surprising that the longing for the mother assumes the character of womb fantasies. We were able to observe this tremendous combination of longing for the mother with a wish to die in our first patient, as a contribution to the subject of mother attachment and fear of death.

I cannot leave this subject without a few remarks on a question which has a bearing in this connection. It is really necessary to explain the little girl's attachment to a maternal object in such a roundabout way? Would it not be much simpler, for instance, to speak of an original fixation and to look for the causes in constitutional factors? I have considered the material without prejudice, and yet in every one of my cases of analysed homosexual women, the light or the shadow cast on the original relationship by the father's presence has played an important and necessary part.

As a matter of fact, in recent years, I think I have occasionally observed a state of affairs in certain cases in which the œdipus complex had apparently played no rôle at all, or almost none, and in which the libido had never known but *one* object—the mother. But these were very special cases, whose whole neurosis had the character of general psychic infantilism with diffuse anxieties and perversions,

[5] Jones, Ernest: The Early Development of Female Sexuality. *The International Journal of Psycho-Analysis*, VIII, 1927.

and whose transference could not be released from an obstinate incorrigible, anxious attachment.

Under the stimulus of Freud's last paper,[6] it would be an undertaking well worth while to collect some of the obscure clinical cases, since they might possibly find their explanation in the primary mother attachment. In this group, in addition to the above-mentioned cases of infantilism, there would surely belong certain forms of hysteria whose "secondary gain" proves so incorrigible because it is a clear repetition of the early infantile situation, when the child was taken care of by the mother.

Returning to my theme, there still remains the question as to when the girl's final decision in favour of homosexuality occurs. It is known that the girl's infantile period of sexual development does not come to such a sudden and radical conclusion as the boy's. The change of object takes place gradually and it would seem that only with puberty comes the final decision both as to the choice of object and the readiness for the passive attitude.

Girls show a much stronger dependence on the mother during the latency period than boys. This may be related to the girl's fear of losing her object, as I have tried to explain above, and also to the type of sublimation, which in girls tends rather to establish affectionate relationships, and in boys is expressed in an active response to the outer world. On the other hand, it appears that during puberty the girl shows a more definite sublimation in the direction of the outer world in the "thrust of activity" (*Aktivitäts-schub*), which I have described.[7] This would indicate that the feminine passive attitude is not completely formed during the infantile phase. The tomboyish period during the girl's puberty is widespread and normal. The girl derives from it the best energies for sublimations and for the formation of her personality, and I think I make no mistake in allowing myself this variation of a statement by Richard Wagner: "The girl who had nothing of the boy in her during her youth will turn out to be a *vacca domestica* in later life." Of course, we are aware of the great dangers which this period of activity conceals with respect to the "masculinity complex" and its neurotic consequences. If it is true that the final change of object takes place in puberty, then this shift to activity must add dangers

---

[6] Freud, Sigm.: Über die weibliche Sexualität, *Internationale Zeitschrift für Psycho-Analyse*, XVII, 1931. (English trans.: Concerning the Sexuality of Woman, *The Psychoanalytic Quarterly*, I, 1932.)

[7] *Op. cit.*

for the heterosexual attitude, and the masculine tendencies of puberty will also contribute their share to homosexuality.

In conclusion, we have still to mention the final struggles in *overcoming* the œdipus complex during puberty. We have a classical example of this in a case of female homosexuality (to which we were introduced in the above-mentioned publication of Freud), which developed in puberty as a result of difficulties with the œdipus complex. However, I must repeat that in all of the cases under my observation the corner stone for later inversion had already been laid in the first infantile period.

THE PREŒDIPAL PHASE OF THE LIBIDO DEVELOPMENT * (1940)

By Ruth Mack Brunswick

This paper contains the only exhaustive discussion of the preœdipal phase of both girl and boy. It is also the only systematic treatment of this subject based—in the author's own words—upon her " . . . collaboration with Freud, begun in 1930, the written record of which consisted of notes typed after discussions with Freud, and of Freud's own marginal comments, ideas and suggestions. . . ." It is the fact of this collaboration that gives the article, which the author most fittingly presented in the Psycho-analytic Quarterly's *issue commemorating the death of the founder of psycho-analysis, the additional value of an indirect, although posthumous, statement of some of Freud's opinions on the subject.*

The editorial omission of the first two pages of the original article, found to be unnecessary at this date, and the insertion of subheadings are intended to facilitate the study of this important contribution.

The present work is a preliminary attempt to correlate our knowledge of the sexes, and to describe that earliest level of the libido development which extends from birth to the formation of the œdipus complex.

Unfortunately, correlation and precision demand the restatement of much that is known or indeed obvious. Sometimes the new formulation differs by only a nuance from the old; but frequently it is exactly this nuance which is significant. For these reasons, I ask the indulgence of the reader throughout a frequently banal and tiresome repetition of many self-evident facts of psycho-analytic theory.

A second apology concerns the apparently schematic character of this work. Only at the end have I ventured to apply the theoretical insight hereby acquired to one or two clinical problems. Yet I need hardly state that clinical observations alone were responsible for what becomes, in such a brief presentation, merely a diagram of early development.

Let us define our terms at once.

*Reprinted from The Psychoanalytic Quarterly, IX, 1940, p. 293.

THE ŒDIPUS COMPLEX AND THE PRECEDIPAL PHASE

Under œdipus complex we understand not only the positive attachment of the child to the parent of the opposite sex, but above all the situation of the *triangle*: the child positively attached to the one parent and in rivalry with the other. The precedipal phase, on the other hand, is for both sexes that earliest period of attachment to the first love object, the mother, before the advent of the father as a rival. It is the period during which an exclusive relation exists between mother and child. Other individuals are of course present in the outside world, especially the father who is an object of affection and admiration, as well as of annoyance when he interferes with the mother's preoccupation with the child. But he is not yet a rival, nor is the strong bond between mother and child split up, as it is destined to be, amongst the various other individuals in the environment. The only person who shares the mother-child relation is the nurse, and she merges ordinarily, though not invariably, into the mother figure.

Examination of the early phase of exclusive mother attachment is beset with difficulties. First of all, this period is the most ancient, the most archaic, and the most foreign to our usual mode of thought. Second, it is overlaid with material from other phases, and is therefore not readily discernible. Third, it is the period of great inarticulateness, so that even direct nursery observations are not easy to make. And finally, the forces of repression have mutilated and indeed often destroyed to the point of making unrecognizable much of this very epoch which contains the roots of all later development.

The complicated chronological relations of the precedipal phase, œdipus complex, and castration complex vary both according to the sex of the child and, individually, according to the time and incidence of traumata, childish observations of the primal scene, the perception of the sexual difference, the birth of another child, etc. In the boy, the precedipal mother attachment is apparently of much shorter duration than in the girl, merging very early into the œdipus complex. This in turn is followed by the castration complex on the basis of which the œdipus complex is destroyed. It is otherwise with the girl. Here, too, the precedipal mother attachment develops into something surprisingly like the œdipus complex of the boy, with the mother as love object and the father as rival.[1] As we shall see,

---

[1] This situation is described by Jeanne Lampl-de Groot in "The Evolution of the Oedipus Complex in Women", this volume, p. 180.

this active œdipus complex of the girl also is destroyed by the discovery of castration although for reasons which differ radically from those of the boy. But out of the castration complex and the ruins of this primitive œdipus complex, there now develops the positive, or passive, œdipus complex of the little girl in which the father is the new love object and the mother the rival.

Thus we see that the little girl traverses a long and complicated route before entering the œdipus complex. Indeed, during the examination of the precedipal phenomena we become uncertain as to the comparative importance of precedipal and œdipal phenomena in feminine development.

At the beginning of her sexual life the little girl is to all intents and purposes a little boy. Her relation to her first love object, the mother, is precisely that of the boy, with similarly conflicting passive and active libidinal strivings. But unlike the boy, the girl must relinquish this love and transfer it to the father, a difficult process which we now know to be at times only partially achieved. Once in the œdipus complex, the normal woman tends to remain there; the œdipus complex of the woman undergoes no such widespread destruction as that of the man. On the contrary, it remains and forms the normal basis of the erotic life of the woman. The resistance of the female œdipus complex to the powers of destruction accounts for the differences in structure of the male and female superego.

It is evident that the sexual development of the woman in contrast to that of the man is complicated by the fact that the woman must give up her first love object, the mother, and transfer her libido to the father, whereas the boy, in passing from the precedipal to the œdipal stage, makes no change of object. But the woman has not only two love objects: she possesses also two sexual organs, the clitoris and the vagina, whereas again the boy has only one. A possible parallel between the love object and the sexual organ will be sought later. We can, however, now make the following statement: that although the woman is obliged to give up one sexual object for another, and one sexual organ likewise for another, the boy is faced with the almost equally arduous task of changing, not love objects or sexual organs, but his own attitude to the original love object, the mother. That is to say, the originally passive male is obliged to develop that full degree of activity towards the woman which is the token of his psychic health.

The phenomena of the precedipal phase should be described in their own terms and not in the terms of the œdipus complex. Inasmuch as the precœdipal phase extends from the beginning of life to the formation of the œdipus complex, it is obvious that the discovery of the sexual difference ordinarily falls within its scope, especially in the case of the girl, in whom the precœdipal phase is so much more extensive than that of the boy. Previous to this discovery the child makes personal but not sexual differentiation between the individuals of its immediate world. It must be remembered that until approximately three years of age, the pregenital zones outweigh the genital in importance. Similarly the boy, judging others by himself, takes for granted the universal possession of the penis, like the mouth, the anus, etc. The girl who has not yet discovered the existence of the penis believes her sexual constitution to be universal.

THE THREE ANTITHETIC PAIRS

Three great pairs of antitheses exist throughout the entire libido development, mingling, overlapping, and combining, never wholly coinciding, and ultimately replacing one another. Infancy and childhood are characterized by the first two, and adolescence by the third. These are (1) *active-passive* (2) *phallic-castrated* (3) *masculine-feminine*. Schematically, but schematically only, these follow upon one another, each characteristic of a given stage of development. We shall attempt to define each stage within its own terms rather than in the terms of a later stage.

The first great pair of antitheses, *active-passive*, governs the beginning of life. That the infant is largely passive is evident; often it must be taught even to breathe and to suckle. One is tempted to state that development consists largely in the supervention of activity over a prior passivity. One is restrained from any such generalization by the fact that not only do we know almost nothing of the essential nature of passivity and of activity, or of their relation to one another, but in addition, it is a matter of speculation whether passivity is converted into activity, or whether certain developmental strivings are specifically active and others passive, and whether in the course of development the active strivings increase in number and intensity and therefore occupy more place. What we do see, and what we are able in some measure to trace at least descriptively and perhaps dynamically, is a constantly growing activity on the part of the child. It learns to sit instead of being held; it reaches out for its own bottle instead of merely receiving it, etc. What we learn is that each bit of activity is based to some extent on an identification with

the active mother, an identification which provides a form for the
activity inherent in the child who does for and to itself what the
mother has done for it, playing the rôles of both mother and child
in the manner typical of childhood. Indeed, the child plays the
rôle of the mother not only towards itself but also towards other
children, animals, and toys, and ultimately and above all towards
the mother herself.

The active-passive phase is prephallic, what Jones calls deutero-
phallic. As I have remarked before, the child takes for granted the
likeness of its own sexual organization to that of others, and the
genital is a matter of no greater concern than the other erogenous
zones, notably, at this early age, the mouth. Thus the sex of the child
is immaterial; and it is to be noted that the rôle of the mother, at
this time prior to sexual differentiation, is not feminine but active.

A new epoch begins with the discovery of castration which
establishes the sway of the second pair of antitheses, *phallic-castrated*. This still does not coincide with masculine and feminine
although by taking cognizance of the presence or absence of the
exclusively phallic genital it more nearly approaches the final pair
than does its predecessor. However, the lack of the phallus is at first
considered individual or accidental, in no sense irremediable. With
the exception of the clitoris, the female genital, including the vagina,
is still essentially unknown. We are all familiar with the reactions of
the child to the discovery of castration. We know that the boy does
not immediately question the sex of the most important person in
his environment, the mother. On the contrary, he takes it for
granted that she at least is phallic. Thus castration as an irretrievable
fact affecting all females is not immediately accepted by the child.
With the final recognition of the mother's castration and the possibility of his own at the hands of the father, the œdipus complex of
the little boy is destroyed.

But whereas the normal male gives up the mother and saves himself from castration, the neurotic faces two possibilities: first, he
represses but fails to give up his love for the mother; and, second,
frequently in combination with the first possibility, he accepts in
fantasy castration by the father, gives it a libidinal significance, and
takes the father as a love object. This we call the negative or passive
œdipus complex.

I should like to offer a suggestion made by Freud in our early
discussions of these problems. The terms "active" and "passive"
œdipus complex are more comprehensive and accurate in their

application to both sexes than the usual positive and negative œdipus complex. According to this new terminology, the precedipal sexuality of the girl becomes her active œdipus complex with the mother as its object. Her passive œdipus complex has the father as its object. For the boy, the active œdipus complex denotes what we ordinarily call the positive œdipus complex with the mother as the object. His passive œdipus complex which we ordinarily term the negative œdipus complex has as its object the father, and is a neurotic phenomenon when occurring to any marked extent. However, I shall retain the older terminology here because of the otherwise inevitable confusion between the terms precedipal and œdipal.

The man in the passive œdipus complex so closely resembles the woman in her œdipal attachment to the father that it seems as if our new understanding of female development should aid us in our examination of the problems of the neurotic man. Freud suggests that on the basis of this new concept of early female sexuality, the precedipal phase of the boy should be thoroughly investigated. [2] The present work is an attempt in this direction. I should like to add that it has been necessary to repeat much of the material contained in Freud's two papers on female sexuality because those findings form the background essential both to the study of the corresponding development of the boy, and to the further examination of these phenomena in the girl.

Let us now return to the first position of the child in which it is passive to the active mother. Normal development demands that activity supervene over passivity. Whether the passivity remains, is given up, or is converted, we do not know. Clinically it appears to give place to activity. The degree to which this occurs is immensely variable. The process is more vigorous in boys than in girls and the actual quantity of activity is undoubtedly greater. The early character of the child depends largely upon the relative proportions of activity and passivity.

It is apparent that the child's earliest activity is, in its outward form at least, a copy of the mother. This is the most fundamental and primitive kind of identification, dependent for its existence solely upon the replacement of passivity by activity and consequently of mother attachment by mother identification, irrespective of any other emotional bond.

One might state that a young child's inability to produce an adequate activity is one of the earliest abnormalities. Passivity then

[2] Freud: *ibid.*, p. 132.

predominates. But what besides constitutional elements interferes with the normal production of activity at this early age? Observations in the nursery have proved useful here. Briefly one may state that every successful act of identification with the mother makes the mother less necessary to the child. As she becomes less necessary, the restrictions and demands which she is obliged to make are increasingly resented. The child which has just succeeded in the difficult task of reliving actively what it has until now passively experienced—and here the repetition compulsion acquires its full significance—is particularly on the defensive in regard to this freshly acquired activity. It is a newly won libidinal position which the child guards zealously. Any activity on the part of the mother is likely to be resented. Therefore, unless the mother accepts a more or less passive rôle, she becomes at best superfluous. The child reacts to her very presence with a kind of primitive, defensive aggression which is a by-product and protection of its activity as well as the defence against its original, barely overcome passivity. The pull of any earlier libidinal position is profound; every step of development is hard-won, and bound therefore to be defended. True aggression inevitably arises when the mother is obliged to hamper this budding activity either by forbidding or compelling certain acts. It is apparent that the resultant aggression derived from the original activity is now directed specifically against the mother who at this time is vested with the authority to restrict, prohibit and command, according to the requirements of the situation and by virtue of the fact that, until her subsequent depreciation because of her castration, she is not only active, phallic, but *omnipotent*.

This is perhaps the simplest of the various ways in which aggression arises. In reality we have to deal with far more ominous situations. Early narcissistic injuries on the part of the mother enormously increase the child's hostility. Conspicuous among these injuries which I shall not attempt to enumerate in detail are weaning, the birth of a brother or sister, the relation between father and mother, the sexual rejection of the child of either sex by the mother; and finally, the depreciation of the mother as the result of her castration. On the basis of these injuries a conflict ensues which demands that the aggression towards the mother be repressed. But inasmuch as every new activity is associated with the repressed hostility, a large amount of normal activity must often be forfeited to insure the success of the repression. An individual hampered in his development ordinarily regresses; when further activity as demanded by development is blocked, a deeper regression to a still earlier, more passive, level takes place. We know that the interest in the genital and the discovery of the sexual difference coincide with a biological "push" which occurs at about the end of the third year of life when the phallic period begins. The organic awakening of the phallic genital leads to the great period of infantile sexual activity. The libidinal desires of the child towards the mother, both passive and more especially active, become intense. They are accompanied by phallic masturbation with the clitoris as the executive organ of the girl. The boy seems to pass with relative ease out of his predominantly passive, precedipal attachment to the mother into the characteristically active, normal œdipus complex. The corresponding phase in the little girl is of course still precedipal. While the genital libido is at its height the castration of the mother is perceived and finally acknowledged with all its implications. Under the threat of castration by the father, the boy abandons the mother as his love object and turns his activity to the formation of his superego and his sublimations, aided undoubtedly by a mildly contemptuous attitude towards the castrated sex, and by the fact that, possessing the phallus himself, he has far less need of it in his love object than the little girl has. Not the mother's castration, but the threat to the boy's own penis results in the destruction of the male œdipus complex.

It is otherwise with the little girl. Here the mother's castration means not only the depreciation of the love object and the possibility of the girl's own castration as in the case of the boy; the mother's castration is above all the doom of the girl's hopes of ever acquiring possession of a penis. The girl abandons the mother as a love object with far more embitterment and finality than the boy. She seeks to transfer her libido to the father, a transference beset by difficulties arising from the tenacity of the active and passive precedipal mother attachment. In the normal girl it is essentially the passive strivings which in the identification with the castrated mother, are successfully transferred to the father in the œdipal phase, and in adult life to the husband. The active strivings are sublimated at this time and only much later find their real scope in the relation of the woman to her own child, in her final and complete identification with the active mother.

Here I should like to call attention to one small clinical observation. Between the girl's attachment to the mother and the attachment to the father there may sometimes be observed a brief interregnum resembling the latency period. One might call it a precedipal latency period. It is a kind of suspension of the libido which has been detached from the mother and has not yet found its connection with the father. It is to be found or at least to be observed especially in girls with a somewhat retarded libido development, in whom the attachment of the mother has persisted beyond the usual length of time. It precedes the fresh wave of sexuality of the passive or positive œdipus complex.

The final pair of antitheses, *masculine-feminine*, comes at puberty. In the boy, the flood of virile libido brings with it for the first time the desire to penetrate the newly discovered vagina. A new relation to the woman is established which, however, has its roots in those remnants of the œdipus complex which have not been destroyed. These vary in quality and quantity. A healthy amount of activity towards the mother in the precedipal and œdipal phases is of immeasurable value to the ultimate relation of the man to the woman.

In the adolescent girl the wave of passive libido, libido, that is to say, the passive aim called forth by the menses and the awakening of the vagina, is directed towards the father in an intensification of the œdipal libido position which we may now call feminine.

THE PRECEDIPAL PERIOD

So much for the investigation of the course of our three pairs of antitheses. We now return to our starting point in an attempt to examine that major phenomenon of the precedipal period, the exclusive mother-child relationship. The relation of the child to the mother is obviously the fundament of its psychic life, the basis and prototype of all later love relationships. We may examine it from two points of view: first, in relation to the zones involved: oral, anal, and genital; and second, from that other angle of the libido development which we have been considering: first and foremost, at this early time, from the active-passive point of view, and, later, from the phallic-castrated.

I should like to say a word here about the concept of the phallic mother, a concept familiar to us from the fantasies of neurotics, psychotics and both normal and abnormal children. Whereas both the active and the castrated mother exist in point of fact, the phallic mother is pure fantasy, a childish hypothesis elaborated after the discovery of the penis and the possibility of its loss or absence in the female. It is a hypothesis made to insure the mother's possession of the penis, and as such probably arises at the moment when the child becomes uncertain that the mother does indeed possess it. Previously, in the active-passive phase, it seems more than probable that the executive organ of the active mother is the breast; the idea of the peniš is then projected back upon the active mother after the importance of the phallus has been recognized. Thus it is a fantasy of regressive, conpensatory nature. We shall continue to use the term "phallic mother", first because of the prevalence of the idea in the neuroses and psychoses, and second because whether the idea is primary or regressive, the term is one which best designates the all-powerful mother, the mother who is capable of everything and who possesses every valuable attribute.

At this early age the only possible contact with the child is a physical one; therefore probably nothing equals in importance the physical care of the infant by the mother or nurse. The entire infantile psychic life runs parallel to this care. The child's rôle is mainly passive, becoming active only in direct response to certain stimuli. The body as a whole, with the erogenous zones in particular, including the skin which plays so important a part at this time, must necessarily be cleansed and handled. We know that well-managed physical care is a source of intense pleasure to the infant and, equally, that rough or unexpected handling has a traumatic effect. It would appear that the first attachment to the mother which is so passive in nature, derives its strength and tenacity in great part from her physical care, and of course above all from her feeding of the child. There is no doubt about the sexual nature of the child's response. Only because at this very early age the genital plays so small a part does the mother-child relationship seem so innocent; then, too, the nature of infantile love is aimless and diffuse, appearing "harmless". Pleasure is obtained from innumerable sources; the child's appetite for it is random and without a particular goal, one reason perhaps, why that appetite remains unsatiated.

We have said that development brings with it increasing activity; so we may expect to find, as is indeed the case, that the child attempts to repeat actively every detail of physical care which it has experienced passively. Here, too, I am obliged to omit concrete examples with one important exception: the mother in the course of bathing and caring for the child is obliged to touch its genitals. A new bit of activity appears when the child, instead of allowing its genitals to be touched by the mother and experiencing pleasurable sensations from this passive experience, touches its own genitals, not to wash them but purely for the sake of those pleasurable sensations with which it has become familiar from the mother's care. Here we have the first basis in fact for infantile masturbation, the first experience of which that masturbation is the voluntary repetition. The child's earliest phallic fantasy is undoubtedly one of playing the rôle of the mother towards itself by touching its genitals and eliciting thereby the same pleasurable sensations originally called forth by the mother. Thus the mother's physical care of the genitals has constituted a true seduction, and is so viewed by the child. The blame incurred by the mother is doubled when later she forbids what she has herself provoked: phallic masturbation. Observations of young children, as well as of a certain primitive type of adult in the course of analysis, make it appear probable that the passive genital aim persists long after the mother's rôle has been largely taken over by the child. Despite a great display of activity, the child at the beginning of the phallic phase still primarily wishes to have its genitals touched by the mother.

When the statement is made that the physical care of the child by the mother constitutes the basis in fact for infantile masturbation, the significance of the primal scene as the sexual stimulus which frequently initiates the masturbation is in no way diminished or disregarded. The point is that the mother's physical care provides the stimulus of the primal scene.

It is easier to discern the phallic phase than the oral and anal phases. The true oral phase is traversed while the infant is still too inarticulate to afford us much material. The anal stage, beginning at approximately two years of age, is more expressive. Here *giving* is initiated in contradistinction to the earlier and more passive *receiving*. The active giving has of course been present in some measure from the very first day of life, as manifested by spontaneous defæcation or urination. In the phallic phase the active attitude takes the lead. In the regression which usually follows the acceptance of castration of the woman at the end of the phallic phase, it is possible to observe both oral and anal phases quite clearly because of our greater similarity to an older child as well as its own increased articulateness.

We have said that the physical care of the child provides the basis for infantile masturbation, with its oral, anal, and phallic fantasies, and its interchanging passive and active rôles. But as has also been stated, there is something else with which we are accustomed to associate infantile masturbation, and that is the primal scene. So long as the exclusive mother-child relation obtains, the relations of the parents are of minor interest to the child. But the moment the active œdipus complex of the boy or girls is formed, the relations between the parents become the object of intense and jealous interest. We know that the child takes every opportunity to observe the sexual life of the parents and that when the opportunity is lacking some substitute is found even if only in fantasy. We have always asked ourselves how the child is able to understand the sexual relations of the parents. The answer may be found in the early physical relation of the child to the mother.

We frequently observe that not only does the child identify itself with the rival father in its love of the mother; it also identifies the father with itself. What does the father do with the mother? The child's answer is that he undoubtedly performs those acts which have been the source of intense pleasure to the child itself: in the oral fantasy, for example, the mother suckles the father. Now while suckling is in part active, every human act being mixed, it is nevertheless originally largely passive, doubtless because it occurs at a time of life when the child is overwhelmingly passive. It must be remembered that there is as yet no sexual difference between the parents. Thus in the fantasy of the oral relation of the parents, the rôle of the father is in part passive. A passive father rôle sounds contradictory to the point of absurdity. But the child's capacity for projecting its own desires upon others should be borne in mind, as well as the fact that active and passive at this time are not associated with the sexual distinction inasmuch as the latter does not yet exist. The counterpart of the passive fantasy of being suckled is the active oral fantasy of suckling. Here the mother is suckled by the child, or by the father.[3] One must never lose sight of the fact that every passive fantasy acquires its active counterpart, and that this play of interchanging rôles is one of the chief characteristics of childhood. I recall one particularly infantile patient whose sole conscious masturbation fantasy was suckling her doll. Just beneath this manifest fantasy in which the mother rôle is dominant was the fantasy of nursing at the mother's breast.

[3] In order to avoid undue confusion on the part of the reader, it should be remembered that suckling is always a transitive verb, although it is frequently used in the opposite sense with a resultant confusion typical of this early phase.

We are aware of the importance of the child's bowel training and how easily it may become traumatic. We speak of the anal-sadistic level of development, and not that the awakening of the anal zone corresponds in point of time to the production of intense aggressive impulses in an individual who has by this time become more capable of expression than he had been during the oral phase. In the nursery one can observe that during the anal period any stimulation of the anal zone (or in the course of an adult analysis, any stimulation of anal mechanisms or material) may cause a violent outburst of rage. There is an etiological connection between anal stimulation and the production of anger. The enemas so frequent in childhood have all the appearance of rape; the child reacts with a tempestuous although helpless outburst of rage which can only be likened to orgasm. Rape appears to be the true motor expression of anal erotism, the anal equivalent of genital orgasm.[4]

In the phallic phase, the original passive desire of the child is to be masturbated by the mother. This passive wish is also ascribed by the child to the father, according to the mechanism described in the suckling fantasy. By the time the active wish to touch the mother's genital is formed, inhibiting influences and prohibitions have usually become sufficiently strong to limit the child in fact though not in fantasy, and not even always in fact to a wish to see the mother's genital. Consequently the most usual coitus concept or equivalent of the phallic phase, in which the vagina is still unknown and the need of penetration not yet formed, is the mutual touching of the genitals. This is indeed what children often do among themselves when attempting to imitate the coitus of the parents.

Thus we see that while the parental coitus is incorporated into the œdipal fantasy life of the child and into its masturbation, nevertheless the understanding and interest which the child brings to the parental coitus are based on the child's own precœdipal physical experiences with the mother and its resultant desires. The biological factor obviously outweighs all others; animals are able to perform the sexual act without any apparent learning process. Undoubtedly at puberty forces come into play which enable the individual to have sexual relations regardless of his prior observations or experiences. But what has always surprised us is not the adolescent's capacity for sexual intercourse, but the amazing understanding which the three- or four-year-old child shows for the sexual relations of its parents. This understanding becomes less mysterious if we consider not only

[4] Freud: *ibid.*, p. 134.

inherited and instinctual knowledge, but also the actual physical experiences of the child at the hands of the mother or nurse.

THE DEVELOPMENT OF A WISH FOR A BABY AND THE WISH FOR A PENIS

I should now like to describe chronologically and in relation to one another the two great wishes of childhood: the wish for a baby, and the wish for a penis. The original, asexual, "harmless" wish for a baby arises very early, is based wholly on the primitive identification of the child of either sex with the active mother, and in the absence of a true object relation to the mother is neither passive nor active. The child wants everything the omnipotent and all-possessing mother has in order to do everything the mother does; and a mother is above all the possessor of a baby. In the anal phase with its new concept of giving and receiving and of increasing object relation to the mother, the wish for a baby acquires a second root: both boy and girl then desire a baby from the mother. This originally passive wish, like every other, acquires an active form: the wish to present the mother with a baby. The boy gives up the passive baby wish when his activity predominates. As his œdipus complex develops, a father identification replaces the earlier identification with the active mother. The girl, on the other hand, gives up her active baby wish when she accepts her own castration and consequent inability to impregnate the mother; the passive wish, however, is retained and is normally transferred from the mother to the father where as we know it assumes the greatest importance. Normality demands that the boy give up his passive wish for a child, and the girl her active wish.

It may be tentatively stated that three types of infantile activity exist. The first, familiar type is the activity of the all-providing mother, seen in the child's earliest identification with the mother. The second, also familiar and much later type arises from the identification with the œdipal father. This type the girl is incapable of achieving in full, try as she may. (These attempts and failures are best known to us from the homosexual relations of women and their rivalry with men.) The little boy with temporary developmental rather than irremediable anatomical inadequacies, and therefore in possession of a full potential father identification, actually achieves an adequate father rôle towards the mother which he relinquishes only under the œdipal threat of castration by the father.

But there exists a third, unfamiliar type of activity in the young child of either sex, apparently inherent in the individual and independent of identification mechanisms. Our ignorance of the nature of activity makes description difficult and we are obliged to resort to analogy. The young page in an opera, a part almost always taken by women, personifies this type of activity and is characteristic of the uncastrated or rather sexually undifferentiated child. Recently a female patient with a strong mother attachment remarked: "It isn't that I want to be a man. I think I really want to be a little boy." The favourite childhood fantasy of this girl was to be a page to royalty.

The activity required for the father identification doubtless utilizes every pre-existing form and then adds the final stamp of masculinity. This ultimate and all-inclusive type of activity is never fully achieved by the girl.

The active wish for a penis of the little girl arises with the observation of the difference between the sexes and the determination to have what the boy has. This original basis is narcissistic. An object root is formed when the little girl realizes that without the penis she is unable to win the mother. Normally the relinquishment of the active penis wish and of the attachment to the mother coincide. Contrary to our earlier ideas, the penis wish is not exchanged for the baby wish which, as we have seen, has indeed long preceded it. In the course of normal development the impossible is given up and the possible retained. The little girl concentrates her energy on the permissible and legitimate desire for a baby. The active penis wish, the wish for the full and permanent possession of a penis, makes way for the passive penis wish, the wish to receive the penis from the man in coitus. Out of this as the little girl knows, she will receive a child. Thus the two wishes finally unite. Originally narcissistic, both wishes next find transient root in the mother relation before finally and permanently attaching themselves to the father.

The Girl's Phallic Masturbation

Let us now examine the phallic masturbation of the little girl, so much less familiar to us than that of the boy. It is a surprising fact that many adult women are unacquainted with both masturbation and orgasm. It is perhaps not correct to call these women frigid; they are responsive in coitus and their pleasure, though difficult to describe, is undeniable. But it is diffuse rather than specific, and it lacks the high, sharp curve typical of true orgasm.

We know that the clitoris is the executive organ of the infantile sexuality of the girl. We know too that the first object of this sexuality is the mother. One of the greatest differences between the sexes is the enormous extent to which infantile sexuality is repressed in the girl. Except in profound neurotic states, no man resorts to any similar repression of his infantile sexuality. The little girl's repression frequently results in a severe limitation of her entire sexuality, with permanent psychic injury. Freud has explained the female distaste for masturbation on the basis of the castration trauma: every act of masturbation reveals anew to the little girl the physical fact of her own castration. Girls seem to give up the use of the hands in masturbation earlier and more frequently than boys, although the same phenomenon is of course to be found in boys. Masturbation is then accomplished by pressure of the thighs. The use of the hands reveals with too much tactile accuracy the actual nature of the girl's genital, and is consequently discarded.

Undoubtedly castration is the narcissistic basis for the repression of masturbation in women. But there is another reason. We have seen that the relinquishment of the first love object of the girl is accompanied by tremendous embitterment. While the little boy acquires what we have come to consider the normal male contempt for women, the little girl, incapable of such contempt because of her own identical nature, frees herself from the mother with a degree of hostility far greater than any comparable hostility in the boy. The mother and the phallic masturbation of the girl are so intimately connected that it seems reasonable to believe that the loss of one is somehow connected with the loss of the other. While the clitoris is undoubtedly used during the positive œdipus complex because the child is obliged to utilize whatever means it possesses, it remains true that the original and, one might say, more appropriate object of the clitoris activity is the mother. Therefore, although the little girl later uses her clitoris in masturbation with passive œdipal fantasies, its original rôle has been lost, in other words, repressed with the original object. We are all familiar with those difficult cases where masturbation has been repressed so vigorously and at such an early age that its recovery in the course of analysis seems almost impossible. These women may nevertheless present strong father fixation, expressed in diverse œdipal fantasies which, however, are unaccompanied by any physical masturbatory activity. I recall one especially instructive case of a woman with a strong father attachment and no ascertainable physical masturbation whatsoever. Her analysis showed that she had been deeply attached to a nurse who had been dismissed when the patient was two years old. The patient had immediately shifted her love of the nurse to her father to whom she became inordinately attached. But masturbation so thoroughly repressed at the age of two years was only recovered at the end of an extensive and successful analysis, in the course of which it became clear that its repression coincided precisely with the repression of the attachment to the mother, or in this case mother-substitute.

The vagina, as we know, derives its sensitivity primarily from the clitoris and secondarily from the anus. It has become a question whether, as heretofore stated, the vagina is always, or even usually, a "silent organ" until adolescence. It now seems probable that an early vaginal sensitivity of anal origin frequently exists. A marked degree of anal sensitivity seems to favour the development of early vaginal sensations, probably because the anus, like the vagina, is a receptive organ and as such transfers its passive sensitivity to the vagina much more readily than does the active clitoris. Needless to say even when such vaginal sensitivity exists, its rôle is decidedly minor and secondary to that of the clitoris as the organ of the infantile sexuality. A correlation of the periods of clitoris and vaginal sensitivity, with the age of the little girl when she gives up the mother and attaches herself to the father should throw valuable light on the relation between the nature of the sexual organ and its love object.

As we know, not every little girl gives up masturbation along with her attachment to the mother. The reasons for the continuance of masturbation are manifold and need not be entered into here. But it is important to note that the repression of masturbation in girls does in reality frequently coincide with the relinquishment of the mother as the love object. When one remembers how difficult it is to penetrate the repressions which surround the little girl's first love object, one arrives at a clue in the equally difficult search for the lost sexuality of some women.

THE RELINQUISHING OF THE MOTHER

We know that the exclusive mother-child relationship is doomed to extinction. Many factors militate against it, the most potent perhaps its primitive, archaic nature. Ambivalence and passivity characterize every primitive relation and ultimately destroy it.

Hostility and rebellion prevail when the passive pull is too strong, or when outside factors hamper the desired activity.

The œdipal attitude of the small boy frequently affords us insight into his preœdipal attitude. An unduly strong, persistent œdipus complex combined with exceptional difficulty in giving it up, even at the risk of castration by the father, almost always signifies the existence of obstacles in the production of the normal œdipal activity. Either there has been too much aggression against the mother for any of the reasons familiar to us, or for reasons unknown the passive bond has been too strong. In these cases the little boy clings stubbornly to his active œdipal relation which he has attained with such difficulty. The clinical picture is that of a profound mother fixation at the œdipal level, but closer study reveals that much of the fixation is passive instead of active, and preœdipal instead of œdipal.

We have already investigated the fate of the girl's relation to the mother, and have seen that the frustrations of the preœdipal period provide the foundation for the jealousy and antagonism manifested by the girl in the normal œdipus complex. In addition to the fact that these earliest levels of development are most threatened with change, repression, and extinction, there are definite grudges which the child bears the mother which are usually the outcome of traumatic external events. In our consideration of the causes of aggression against the mother these grudges have already been mentioned. But in addition to being an early source of aggression against the mother, they play a further rôle in the final dissolution of the mother attachment.

Weaning is doubtless the first major interference in the relationship between mother and child. It is probably true that no matter how early weaning occurs, the infant reacts emotionally not only to the loss of food which can be compensated for in other ways, but to the loss of the breast itself. The disappointment in the mother at this early time constitutes a latent weakness in the relationship, a weakness which later traumata successively reactivate.

We know that an ensuing pregnancy ordinarily so changes the mother's milk that weaning becomes necessary. Later, the birth of a brother or sister further occupies the mother who in fantasy at least has up to now been the exclusive possession of the child. The jealousy and hostility at first directed towards the newborn brother or sister are later referred back to the mother who is of course responsible for the presence of the intruder. The rôle of the father now begins to be perceived and related to the birth of the younger brother or sister. Competition with the father proves futile to the child of either sex; thus its sexual rejection by the mother is inevitable.

It will be recalled that the mother who by means of her physical care of the child has stimulated or indeed initiated its phallic activity, now attempts to forbid the infantile masturbation which she herself has provoked and of which she is the object. We are all familiar with the more or less traumatic reactions of the child to any attempt on the part of the mother to suppress masturbation, whether accompanied by the usual castration threats or not. Almost invariably it is the mother who expresses the threat of castration; but despite this practical fact it is the father who, out of some biological necessity, becomes the castrator of the boy while the mother retains this power over the girl. The castration of the girl by the father seems, like so many things, to be merely a second edition of the original castration by the mother.

The hostile reaction of the child to the threat of castration is well known. But there is another reaction due doubtless to the child's own guilty fear of the dangers of masturbation. The child, fearing masturbation and nevertheless unable to give it up, forms an unspoken pact with the forbidding mother or nurse. These are the children who cannot go to sleep unless the mother is with them, whose life is made miserable by the nurse's day off. They cling to the mother or nurse in the hope that hereby the dreaded consequences of masturbation will be averted. They rebel at being forbidden to masturbate but they are grateful for the aid given in the struggle against masturbation. It is obvious in these cases that the relinquishment of masturbation at the mother's demand has resulted in an undue degree of regressive, passive dependence upon the mother.

But not only does the mother reject and neglect the child and forbid its masturbation. Her culminating crime is her depreciation as a love object due to her castration. To this castration the normal boy reacts with a degree of contempt which, modified, persists throughout his later attitude towards women.

We have already seen that the little girl reacts far more traumatically than the boy to the mother's castration. On the one hand the mother has failed to provide the girl with an adequate genital; on the other hand the girl is obliged to admit that this omission is doubtless due to the mother's own lack of a penis. The mother who is held responsible for the sexual inadequacy, simultaneously ceases to be a love object because of her inferiority. When the girl becomes to a greater or lesser degree reconciled to her own lack of a penis, she determines to take as her love object an individual whose possession of the penis is assured and for whose love it may even be worth while to undergo or, in reality, to accept castration. Castration by the father acquires a libidinal value and a virtue is made out of a necessity. Here the girl identifies herself with the castrated mother; and this indeed is her rôle throughout the passive œdipus complex.

PRECŒDIPAL INFLUENCE UPON LATER FEMININITY

It is impossible to trace the influence of the precœdipal phase on later development without a full and detailed description of the entire infantile sexuality. Let us therefore consider briefly one or two clinical pictures in which precœdipal influences are particularly striking.

The first patient in whom the precœdipal sexuality revealed itself unmistakably was the paranoid woman to whom I have repeatedly referred. The remarkable aspect of this case is the total absence of the normal œdipus complex. The traumatic seduction had so fixed the patient to her first homosexual love object that all further development was blocked. The poverty of psychic growth produced a simple, childlike individual, in whom precœdipal attitudes and mechanisms, normally overshadowed by the complications of the œdipus complex were outstanding. I judged this case to be extremely rare, dependent for its existence on the usual nature and circumstances of the trauma.

But the insight gained in this analysis and applied to other patients demonstrated that the difference was merely one of degree, and further that no particular trauma such as seduction is essential for the production of this clinical picture which instead of being exceptional has proved to be extraordinarily common. The undeveloped, primitive woman with scant heterosexuality and a childish, unquestioning attachment to the mother, presents herself almost regularly to a woman analyst. This type of individual does not consult the male analyst because of a total lack of contact with the man. The degree to which a woman is successful in giving up her first love object and concentrating her libido upon the father determines her entire later life. Between the exclusive attachment to the mother on the one hand and the complete transfer of the libido to the father on the other hand, the innumerable gradations of normal and abnormal development are to be found. It might almost be said that partial success is the rule rather than the exception, so great is the proportion of women whose libido has remained fixed to the mother.

THE PRECEDIPAL PHASE OF THE MALE

The præœdipal phase of the male, despite its comparative brevity, is perhaps less dramatic than the woman's, but equally far-reaching. It results in what we have come to consider the typical neurosis of the man: his passive attachment to the father in the so called negative œdipus complex. In this presentation I am obliged to confine myself to those observations which have led me to believe that the submissive attitude of the man to the father has its origin in the præœdipal phase. The consideration of other important etiological factors such as masochism, is necessarily omitted.

We have seen how closely the little girl in her active præœdipal attachment to the mother resembles the little boy in his active œdipus complex. We now see that the boy in the negative or passive œdipus complex closely resembles the little girl in her passive, positive œdipal relation to the father. Unable to achieve the full activity of the male in the father identification, the girl falls back upon her identification with the active mother. Under the influence of castration, she shifts her passivity from the mother to the father. But the boy too may come upon obstacles in his œdipal father identification. The first of these is the presence of what I should like to call the "nuclear passivity" of the child, that original passivity of wide constitutional variation with which it is born into the world. Somehow, either as the result of a strong tendency to regress, or because of the presence of an unknown point of fixation at the præœdipal level, or because of some constitutional inability to overcome the primary inertia, the development of activity is impaired. An additional hindrance is undue aggression towards the mother. The external causes of hostility are manifold, but in addition certain human beings probably possess, actually or potentially, a greater number of aggressive impulses than the normal. When activity is thus impaired at its origin it seems highly probable that traces of this impairment, like those somatic evidences of injury to the germ plasm itself, become evident somewhere in the course of later development.

During the active œdipus complex of the boy, aggression towards the mother may manifest itself as sadistic love. But a fundamental hostility seriously interferes with the full formation of normal œdipal love, and persisting ambivalence further undermines the relation. These individuals are sensitized to traumata, and the œdipal rejection and disappointment frequently result in a regression to the earlier mother attachment which as we know belongs to the active-passive rather than the phallic-castrated level. This regression makes it possible for the neurotic boy to avoid the entire topic of castration. Inability to accept the castration of the mother is in itself a usual cause of regression. Under these circumstances only phallic individuals are acceptable as love objects. In this clinical picture of manifest male homosexuality, the influence of the precedipal phase is unmistakable.

But the main neurotic type which results from precedipal fixation is that of the man with a passive œdipus complex. Under the stress of the maternal castration, the little boy has identified himself with the mother and has taken the father as his love object. We have described the manner in which the girl shifts her passivity from the mother to the father, and have seen that the neurotic boy pursues a similar course. But the boy who because of the mother's castration has shifted his passivity from the mother to the father has not gained by the transaction. His possession of the phallus is further threatened by his love of the father. The various methods of solving this dilemma are reflected in the innumerable clinical manifestations of the neuroses. A paranoid psychosis may result when the love of the father is so strong as to become intolerable. Sometimes, on the other hand, the individual succeeds in shifting his passivity from the father back to its original object, the mother, thus avoiding the paranoid sphere of the father. In these cases a neurosis results which is characterized throughout life by a pendulum-like swing from one parent to the other. Where these individuals have succeeded in more or less permanently attaching themselves to the mother, a so called "mother-fixation" results. It has always been assumed that these individuals could not relinquish their œdipal object. But closer examination reveals that the mother who cannot be given up is the phallic mother, and that the relationship is dominated not by the usual active œdipal love but by an attachment which is to a large extent precedipal and passive. Because of the primitive nature of this passive, tenacious attachment to the mother, an intensely ambivalent relationship between the man and his mother-substitute results. His passivity and his dependence upon the phallic mother are resented and rebelled against by his entire masculinity. Here it is evident that the persistence of the precedipal passivity has led to a malformation of the œdipus complex itself, and has played a major rôle perhaps in the genesis and certainly in the maintenance of the passive love of the man for his father.

While I am inclined to believe that unresolved, unassimilated passivity is in large measure responsible for these abnormalities of development, there exists also a primitive activity whose nature and possible pathogenic rôle has not yet been studied.

It is axiomatic that the difficulties of investigation and the tentativeness of our findings vary inversely with the age of the child under examination. This axiom is my excuse for the fragmentary nature of this work.

FURTHER PAPERS ON FEMALE SEXUALITY:

ABRAHAM, KARL: Manifestations of the Female Castration Complex. *The International Journal of Psycho-Analysis*, III, 1922, p. 1, *Selected Papers*, London, Hogarth Press, 1927, p. 338.

FENICHEL, OTTO: The Pregenital Antecendents of the Œdipus Complex, *The International Journal of Psycho-Analysis*, XII, 1931, p. 141.

HORNEY, KAREN: On the Genesis of the Castration Complex in Women, *Ibid.*, V, 1924, p. 50.

—— The Flight from Womanhood: *Ibid.*, VII, 1926, p. 324.

—— The Denial of the Vagina: *Ibid.*, XIV, 1933, p. 57.

JONES, EARNEST: The Early Development of Female Sexuality, *Papers on Psycho-Analysis*, Baltimore, William Wood, 1938, 4th edition, p. 556.

KLEIN, MELANIE: Early Stages of the Œdipus Conflict, *The International Journal of Psycho-Analysis*, IX, 1928, p. 167.

LAMPL-DE GROOT, JEANNE: Problems of Femininity, *The Psychoanalytic Quarterly*, II, 1933, p. 489.

For FREUD'S comment on some of these contributions, see Section IV of his paper "On Female Sexuality" in *The International Journal of Psycho-Analysis*, XIII, 1932, p. 294–297.

AN ONTOGENETIC TABLE

A CHRONOLOGICAL CHART OF THE PRINCIPAL STAGES IN THE
DEVELOPMENT OF THE PSYCHIC APPARATUS

*The following tabulation of some of the basic data concerning the
ontogenesis of the psychic apparatus, was originally drawn up as a
teaching device. Its purpose was to recall, as distinctly as possible, to the
participants in an introductory course in psycho-analysis not the data
as such, but their* correlation. *It appeared desirable to present the
students with at least a* scheme *for the coordination of the single steps
in the development of the psyche, and to do so in spite of the extreme
individual variability in the chronology of these steps. The three aspects,
libido-, object-, and ego-development, as applied to the altogether
fictitious case of the "normal", were therefore, after a condensation of
their salient points to key-words and key-phrases, juxtaposed so as to
correspond to a mean in the age-levels of the child. The tabulation,
extremely schematic though it must necessarily be, has been found to
assist materially in a "three-dimensional" understanding of the subject.*

*The papers of Freud employed as source material are too well-known
to require enumeration. The nucleus of the table, as will easily be
recognized, is that drawn up by Abraham in his "History of the
Development of the Libido".[1] Added to this were: Abraham's account,
contained in the text of his book, of the appearance of different inhibitory functions accompanying the development of the libido, (aug-
mented by some abstractions from later remarks made by Freud); and
Abraham's references to psychopathology.[2] The corresponding data
concerning "Latency Period" and "Phallic Phase" were inserted. An
indication of the periods, dominated successively by the three antithetic
pairs, "active-passive", "phallic-castrated", and "musculine-feminine",
completed the tabulation of the development of the libido; a chronology
of topographical differentiation, and the accompanying development of
the sense of reality (according to Ferenczi's classic description [3]) con-*

[1] *Selected Papers,* London, Hogarth Press, 1927, p. 496.
[2] Cf. Fenichel's quotation of Abraham's table in his *Perversionen,
Psychosen, Charakterstörungen,* Vienna, Int. Psa. Verlag, 1931, p. 120.
[3] *Contributions to Psychoanalysis,* Stages in the Development of the Sense
of Reality, Boston, Richard Badger, 1916, p. 181.

cluded the tabulation of the development of the ego proper. The inclusion, finally, of the ontogensis of the object (-relation), i.e. the precœdipal and œdipal constellations (as described perhaps most fully by Ruth Mack Brunswick in the report on her collaboration with Freud [4]*) required the setting-up of a double column which makes it possible to distinguish between the male and the female, wherever the development of their object-relations diverges.*

To counteract, to a certain extent at least, the rigidity of coordination —unwarranted by the facts, yet unavoidable in a diagrammatic presentation—the age-levels contained in the first column of the table were represented by markers to be imagined as unfixed, and to be moved upwards or downwards (as indicated by the arrows stemming from them) for an adjustment of the years of life to the individual variants in the chronology of the development stages. [5] *The chronological inter-relations between the various columns require a similar adaptation by the reader of the schematic "mean" indicated by their juxaposition, to the variety of results to be reckoned with if the data in question are coordinated on the basis of individual clinical observations.*

The presentation of the chart in this section is intended to facilitate the integration of the late discovery of the pre-œdipal phase with the earlier body of knowledge concerning the psycho-sexual development of the human.

R. F.

[4] Cf. this volume, p. 261.

[5] Cf. e.g., Freud's reminder that the "effects of seduction", as well as the "dates of the appearance of siblings, of the discovery of sexual intercourse, the soliciting or rejecting behaviour of the parents, etc., can effect an acceleration and maturation of the infantile sexual development" (On Female Sexuality: *The International Journal of Psycho-Analysis*, XIII, 1932), as well as the indubitable rôle played by constitutional factors.

III
MISCELLANEOUS

THE "DOCTOR GAME", ILLNESS, AND THE PROFESSION OF MEDICINE * (1926)

By Ernst Simmel

The exemplary combination of vivid clinical observation and penetrating theoretical interest shown in this paper characterizes all the major contributions of Ernst Simmel. For all its brevity, inhomogeneity, and perhaps certain limitations inherent in the period in which it was written, the present article is as instructive today as it was almost twenty-five years ago at the time of its first appearance. The late author himself felt that it should be reprinted in its original form; its emendation, therefore, is left to the reader.

We often see a child playing at being a doctor and we remember games of this sort in our own childhood. Indeed, this game is frequently one of the few memory-traces which survive the infantile amnesia. Freud has stated that this game is "the repository of the child's ideas about marriage", and this gives it, together with "playing at father and mother", "a peculiar importance in the symptomatology of later neuroses".[1] The forbidden coitus- and pregnancy-fantasies of very early childhood appear in a new guise in the features of the game of "doctor and patient" and in the morally unobjectionable wish to cure or be cured. The sadistic conception of the sexual act is clearly betrayed in the instruments of the little physician: penis-equivalents in the form of make-believe stethoscopes, thermometers, enema-syringes and surgical knives. The illness itself often signifies in more or less disguised form pregnancy in the mother. The "doctor-game" is frequently combined with the game of "father and mother", the rôle of sufferer being allotted to a doll which represents children in general. The doll's behaviour is usually a kind of "negative therapeutic reaction" to the treatment it undergoes; it begins by losing its limbs and finally perishes. It is sacrificed to the castration-complex of its guardians, whom it enables to give

---

* First published in the *Internationale Zeitschrift für Psychoanalyse*, XII, 1926, p. 528, under the title: Doktorspiel, Kranksein und Arztberuf.

Reprinted from *The International Journal of Psycho-Analysis*, VII, 1926, p. 470.

[1] Freud, On the Sexual Theories of Children, *Collected Papers*, Vol. II.

play to aggressive tendencies really aimed at their brothers and sisters, the rivals for their parents' love.

Hence, in the "doctor-game", which is a symbolic form of activity, *all* the tendencies which enter into the œdipus conflict find expression. It is a repetition of the primal scene, the child who impersonates the physician identifying himself with the father and the child who acts the patient with the mother.

At first sight it seems curious that children should repeat over and over again (and derive pleasure from the repetition) so painful an experience as that of medical treatment. We know that Freud has taken this circumstance as one of the starting-points of his theory of the compulsion to repetition.[2] According to him, one of the things which pleases the child in the game is that he is able to pass from the disagreeable rôle of infantile passivity to the active rôle of the adult, the physician. The question remains what interest the other child who takes part in the game has in repeating the painful experience of the patient; but the answer to this is obvious if we extend the concept of "activity" to cover what I have just described. The "doctor-game" gives to *all* the children engaged in it the possibility of actively staging and enjoying the whole primal scene, which was originally unpleasant just because the child was obliged to play the part of the inactive third party who had no share in the proceedings.

Of play in general Freud says that in it "the compulsion to repetition is closely blended with direct instinctual gratification".[3] After what I have already said the pleasurable and very considerable element of instinctual gratification in the "doctor-game" is quite clear. Here play answers the same purpose as that of dreams and neurotic symptom-formation: the fulfilment, by means of symbolic distortion, of desires which are incapable of entering consciousness. In dreams and neurosis, however, they are incestuous wishes *returning* from under a state of repression, whereas the "doctor-game", which occurs at a time when the œdipus experience is still an *actual* conflict, is designed to help the subject in his endeavour to master the original experience. As we know, the œdipus complex is finally resolved into the different possible identifications through the influence of the castration-complex [4]; but during the whole transitional period the child finds himself constantly obliged to ward off the ever-recurring, traumatic effect of the primal scenes or to conceal

[2] Freud, *Beyond the Pleasure-Principle.*
[3] *Loc. cit.*
[4] Freud, The Passing of the Œdipus Complex, *Collected Papers*, Vol. II.

from himself the fact that the parents still *continue* to be unattainable sexual objects. It is by "repression" that the child finds an escape from the intolerable truth about the sex-relations between the parents, or evades comprehension of it, and the success of this repression depends upon the possibility of withdrawing from the painful idea a quantitatively and qualitatively adequate amount of libido.[5] The libido which flows back from the object to the ego and is there regulated by the dynamometer of infantile anxiety forces its way out again to the object-world in the motor activity of play.[6] In the *form* given to the symbolic content of the play we see the pleasure-principle at work, whilst the *tendency* to play, the "play instinct", represents the compulsion to repetition, the necessity to give expression to a thing in order to be able to repress it.

In my opinion, the more or less successful achievement of *complete* repression is as closely bound up with the process of introjection as is identification itself. The more complete the incorporation of the object which causes disappointment, the more thoroughly is it repressed and removed from external perception, and the more complete is the identification. But the greater in that case becomes the volume of ego-libido pressing for discharge. We may say that the less a child still retains of knowledge or understanding of its parents' marital relations, the more clearly and the more whole-heartedly will it play the game of father and mother, i.e., stage and enact the conception. It might be said (though for reasons of space we cannot discuss the question further here) that introjection is the regressive form available for full understanding, while expression in action is the regressive form available for acquiring understanding. Let us recall here Freud's example of the little boy who mourned the death of a beloved cat by crawling on all fours and miaowing.[7] At this stage it is impossible for the child, because he lacks verbal images, to use the activity of thought as a means of surmounting a foregoing of pleasure, that is to say, a loss. He is able to reproduce it in words only by introjecting the object and withdrawing the libido attaching to it. An accumulation of ego-libido thus takes place and leads to the game of "being the cat". We know, too, that at the earliest period of his life the child's mental apparatus works only

[5] Freud, Repression, *Collected Papers*, Vol. IV.

[6] This view is in agreement with the experience of Melanie Klein, who has emphasized the fact that children "endeavour to abreact in play the impressions of the primal scene".

[7] Freud, *Group Psychology and the Analysis of the Ego.*

according to the primary process and that he gradually acquires his serious capacities through a piecemeal introjection of those personalities in his environment whom he loves. Upon this depends not only his powers of communication with them but also his increasing independence of them whereby he first takes his separate place as subject in the object-world represented by the œdipus conflict. In this "the first period of puberty" his libido receives a reinforcement from genital sources which the primary process is no longer capable of mastering. The mental processes of "binding" are set in motion and build up the ego. Thereupon the object-ideas of the parents introjected *afresh*, come back from their state of repression, that is from the id into the ego, and (following the analogy of the dream-censorship) are tolerated by the ego in so far as they conform to an ego-ideal of reality, i.e. in so far as they are disguised by means of this ideal.

We can understand that at a time when the process of building-up the infantile ego is still going on, the "doctor" is a peculiarly suitable ego ideal, besides representing very many of the interests of the id. From the child's point of view a doctor is permitted actively to employ all the mechanisms of pleasure which are forbidden to the child himself. The physician pays no heed to clothing and does not feel shame. He is allowed to hear and see everything and to busy himself unpunished with urine and fæces. He knows all the mysteries of the difference between the sexes and how children come, and he exercises a kind of omnipotence over the body of the patient, as the father does over the mother. The child will give preference in his play to this or that feature of "being a doctor", according to the special urgency of his own erotogenic zones and instinct-components. Or he may indulge his aggressive, sadistic tendencies in a special way in the rôle of operator ("the love of the knife"), in order by giving active expression to castration-*pleasure* to spare himself castration-*anxiety*. It seems that the "doctor-game" is peculiarly calculated to reveal very clearly the psychobiological function of play, namely, the exercise of those mental mechanisms which are necessary for the successful solution of the œdipus conflict. Moreover, in that the super-ego attracts to itself to some extent the superfluous ego-libido in the form of object-libido made subjective, and, by way of the real ego ideal, accomplishes something in the outside world, the active behaviour of play does modify that world in part and prevents introversion of the conflict, i.e. neurosis.

Thus we see that the activity of play is a preliminary to the practising of a profession, only in the latter case the model of the resolved œdipus complex is followed, whilst play reflects the actual process of resolution.

It may be interesting in this connection to consider the "doctor-game" at a point where we can see it as it were in *statu nascendi*, namely, as it may be observed in psycho-analytic treatment. The expression through action and behaviour which takes place during treatment and which is at the bottom of the "transference-game" is often hardly a new edition, at any rate it is but a kind of first edition. The patient is confronted with the result of the re-emergence of repressed material. The excess of ego-libido, which is "bound" in the symptom, and which originally attached to incestuous objects in the form of object-libido, flows towards the analyst. Thus a basis is formed for an understanding of the psycho-analytic situation, i.e. the patient's recognition of the emotion of love for the physician and the anticipation of its frustration. And just as formerly the œdipus conflict was thrust out of consciousness by this means, so now, when it is being brought back into consciousness, it follows the same route.

The first signs of anxiety shown by the patient indicate the failure of the attempt at transference and the setting in motion of the repetition-mechanism as a result of the process of introjection—that is to say, the patient is taking refuge in active behaviour in order to defend himself from conscious understanding. Instead of the passive rôle of the analysand he endeavours to assume the active rôle of analyst and to begin by analysing the analyst himself, trying to discover all the secrets of his personal and family life. Disappointed in this attempt, the patient tries to equalize the unbearable tension between ego and superego to avoid any sense of guilt or anxiety of conscience by making his parental superego conform more and more completely to the ego ideal which he attains through the analyst. And he tries to imitate the latter by drawing more and more people directly and indirectly into the sphere of psycho-analytical observation and treatment. He wants to play at being the "doctor" in order to escape the rôle of patient. He wants to save others by means of psycho-analysis in order to save himself from being analysed. One begins to see how it is that anxiety of conscience, the last of the protections against stimulus, drives some analysands themselves to become ("wild") analysts, to express in action the part of the physician, to "play the doctor" in order to escape the realization of what their own analysis reveals.

We can imagine how the child who was formerly in the position of the patient is impelled to take the rôle of the physician in the "doctor-game".

Perhaps a practical example taken from a case analysed may make this still clearer and may help us to understand how the same person who plays at being a physician may be inclined, or even obliged, to reassume the rôle of patient.

A woman who suffered from heart disease (clinical diagnosis: essential extrasystole) had a great and apparently hopeless longing for a child. She prevented conception (from which she was also protected by vaginismus) owing to her dread lest her heart trouble might cause her to die in giving birth. After a certain phase of the treatment, in which she showed herself without any understanding ("emotional stupidity") of such explanations as had to do with the *psychic* genesis of her symptom, she constantly begged me instead to examine her physically, addressing me in a roguish, infantile manner as "Uncle Doctor". Disappointed in her therapeutic scoptophilia and exhibitionism, she tried to divert my interest from herself to her mother, who also suffered from heart disease and who, the patient informed me, was much more ill than herself, having suffered since the birth of a sister some years younger than the patient. She desired me, therefore, to treat her mother and at any rate to examine her. When I had repeatedly refused, she produced in a dream the hallucinatory fulfilment of the wish embodied in her "doctor-game". The dream was as follows: she gave up to her mother one of her own treatment-hours with me. Her mother was lying on the sofa with the upper part of her body exposed for examination. The dreamer watched anxiously, "fearing" that the diagnosis would be unfavourable. The analyst placed his stethoscope on the mother's breast and it turned out that this instrument, intended for penetrating examination, had a point like a sharp dagger, which penetrated the mother deeply in the neighbourhood of the heart. The dreamer awoke in terror.

The dream betrays clearly the patient's unconscious intention. The analyst was to play at "doctor" with her in order that she, in the rôle of the patient, might enjoy expressing in her behaviour her passive surrender to him in the part of father-imago; that is, might carry this attitude into action without intellectual insight into it. When, however, the physician refused her, as the father had formerly done in the game of "father and mother", she identified herself with him and tried to play the doctor with her mother through the agency of the analyst. By actively dramatizing the primal scene in the interest of her scoptophilia, she resigned herself to playing the part of the spectator, on condition that the analyst by his treatment should commit the crime of matricide in her stead and thus absolve her.

The mother as the hated object in the œdipus conflict is completely introjected—repressed; she is wholly merged in the ego. The father, as the loved object, is only incompletely repressed, i.e. he becomes part of the subject in the superego. In passive feminine masochism the ego submits to the superego [8] as the mother does to the father. We see that this patient acquired the same illness as her mother because her superego, being completely devoted to the interests of the id, had not applied the superfluous ego-libido to the modification of the outside world (in play or in the practice of a profession) but had returned.it to the ego, "which is essentially a body-ego", to be transformed in the inner world, as motility within. In analysis she endeavoured to give it active expression outwardly, to play the doctor, in order not to have to be ill; that is to say, she tried as far as possible to replace the superego belonging to her id by the reality-ideal of the physician, who represented real conscience and was to deliver her from introversion of the conflict. She desired to regain health by practising healing. The active physical expression achieved in her illness was designed as an escape from anxiety and an equalizing of the tension between ego and id. It was transformed into a mental activity through her attempt to escape from anxiety of conscience and the tension between ego and superego. By converting the sense of guilt [9] into sympathy [10] she tried to rise from suffering *in company with* another [11] to *pity* [12] for her, from the function of patient to that of physician.

This somewhat cursory glance at the distribution of parts, both in the "doctor-game" of children and in the adults' game of transference to the doctor during psycho-analytic treatment, shows us that we are justified in concluding that the same instinctual impulse may make a given individual into a physician or a patient. This shows that the psychogenesis of the profession of medicine in an individual is a repetition of its phylogenesis now familiar to us through the researches of Róheim.

Róheim demonstrated that the medicine-man of primitive races represents a cultural advance, by way of transformation of instinct, upon the practitioner of black magic. "In the magician we find

---

[8] Freud, The Economic Problem in Masochism, *Collected Papers* Vol. II.

[9] *Schuldgefühl.*   [10] *Mitgefühl.*   [11] *Mit-leiden.*   [12] *Mit-leid.*

sadistic instincts unsublimated, while in the medicine-man the same instincts appear inhibited through identification with the victim, i.e. in a sublimated form." [13] Like our patient in her fantasy the man who practised black magic had perpetrated the primal crime—the incorporation and introjection of the parent-substitute. In order to be absolved the magician had to free himself from this substitute, now transformed into an excremental symbol, and to do this he had to project his crime, incorporating the symbol in others, in order subsequently to rid them of it again. The introjected parent-substitute became the substance which caused disease and which must be ejected in order that the patient might recover. The possibility of reincorporating it in another as a substance which may promote recovery arises only when an advance has been made from the oral-anal-sadistic level to the genital libidinal impulse. It is only then that the excremental symbol becomes the symbol of sperma, penis and child. Our patient came to grief in the œdipus conflict over the synthesis (confluence) of her pregenital and genital libidinal tendencies, and endeavoured to make up for this by the "doctor-game" in the psycho-analytical treatment, by releasing from repression the morbid substance introjected into the ego (the mother-substitute) and absorbing it into the superego. Hence she became not only father but mother, and even the mother of her mother, to whom she could restore health—life—the life which she had received from her. The patient endeavoured to free herself from the compulsion of the feminine-masochistic attitude in the ego by establishing a kind of bisexuality in the superego. This shows us that there is a deeper and more unconscious meaning underlying the superstitious mistrust felt by the laity for treatment by physicians who are themselves ill and of whom one hears it said that "they cannot even cure themselves". There is to some extent always the suspicion that, in order to relieve their masochistic ego from suffering, such persons will change the current of the sadistic impulses of their superego from inner to outer motility and direct them towards their patients.

But there is also a danger that in the attempt to prevent this happening the physician may himself regress to the rôle of patient. This is the more likely to happen if, as I have already said, his choice of profession was not originally based on the final identification following the resolution of the œdipus conflict, but if his professional activity can still be regarded as a mode of acting, a "doctor-game", designed to defray the cost of repression. Such a physician

[13] Rôheim, Nach dem Tode des Urvaters, *Imago*, IX, pp. 83 ff.

rediscovers in the patient the incestuous object which has taken on the rôle of patient by the very processes of identification which have made him himself a physician.

In a course of lectures which I gave at the Berlin Analytical Institute, and to which I gave the title *The Art of Medicine and Psycho-Analysis*, I suggested an explanation of the by no means uncommon circumstance that specialists fall a victim to the particular disease which they treat. At that time I had not seen the results of Róheim's ethnological researches and I based my view on analyses conducted by myself and on what Freud teaches us in *Totem und Taboo*. I called physicians of this type *"partial"* physicians, and suggested that, from the psycho-analytical point of view, their practice of their profession was similar to a perversion. For their own unconscious, incestuous libidinal impulses, bound to a particular erotogenic zone, cause them to hyper-cathect the particular organ of the patient (or some specialized branch of medicine) with so great an amount of libido that all the rest of the human being eludes the consciousness or at least the understanding of these physicians owing to the relative displacement of libido on to a single organ. It is really a kind of organ-fetishism, which acts as an anti-cathexis and defrays the cost of repression. That is to say, the specialist does not effect a transference to the patient but identifies himself with him. Instead of restoring the diseased organ to health he endeavours to lay hold of it by introjection, to "repress" it (an attitude precisely like that of our patient towards her mother's heart-trouble), and the consequent damming-up of his ego- or organ-libido makes him ill himself. Once more he introverts the relations with his patients and once more regresses from understanding to introjection, from verbal expression to action—from suffering in sympathy with [14] the patient (pity) to suffering in company with him. [15]

Thus I have seen specialists in gastric diseases succumb to gastric disease, psychiatrists to psychoses, and psycho-analysts (owing to a "counter-identification" taking the place of counter-transference) to neuroses and depression. I have heard, too, that a certain lung specialist developed asthma after having been frequently called out at night to an old man who suffered from that disease, at a time when the physician himself was going through a neurotic conflict. This observation applies not only to the physician, but also in particular to the scientist engaged in specialized research. His epistemephilic impulse, nurtured by his incestuous scoptophilia, falls under a

[14] *Mit-Leid.*   [15] *Mit-Leiden.*

taboo and compels him, in accordance with the law of talion, once
more to introject and to give active expression to processes relating
to a given "erotogenic zone" when he is inhibited from understanding or from seeking to understand them. This means that the organ
which disease attacks in himself is that in connection with which he
wished to pursue his investigations, or in other words "to sin".

Various defensive measures often make their appearance as reactions. These are designed to defend the subject in the choice of his
profession from his destructive impulses. Let me quote just two
examples to show how the physician may on the one hand safeguard
his patients against himself and on the other protect himself against
himself. For instance, I know a very busy physician who, in order
to treat his patients successfully, feels himself obliged to hate them
consciously. But to prevent this affective attitude from interfering
with his practice he isolates it in time from his day's work. In the
morning, before his consultation hours, his custom is to walk rapidly
up and down his empty consulting room and vehemently to execrate
the patients who are awaiting his help and call them every kind of
filthy name. On the other hand, there are many physicians who in
their professional attitude regress unconsciously to the "excremental
symbol" regarded as the introjected morbid substance, i.e. the
parent-substitute. To these men the excremental symbol is replaced
by money (= fæces) upon which they displace the whole incestuous
significance of their patients. This has the effect of a taboo upon the
patient's money, so that the physician may not handle it or receive
(introject) it if he desires himself to remain well or free from a sense
of guilt. He avoids an inhibition in his work at the cost of an inhibition in making money.

Thus in the most modern relations between doctor and patient
—the bartering of health for money—we see that the most remote
archaisms intrude themselves in their prehistoric interdependence.
For every physican repeats in himself not only the psychic ontogenesis of his calling but also its psychic phylogenesis. The proof of
this statement is to be found by observing the "doctor-game" of
children, in which we have already recognized the outlines of the
profession in later life.

So I was not at all surprised when I once had the opportunity
of observing a game of this sort in its primitive form. It might be
called the "primal doctor-game", because it was quite undisguisedly
based on the significance of the patient as at once enemy and father.
I will now describe the game.

A twelve-year-old patient, who suffered from compulsive onanism with sadistic fantasies, told me that he used to play this game with other boys of his own age when he was six years old. For our discussion it does not matter whether the game was really played in every detail as he told it or whether he had supplemented it with later fantasies.

The boys played at surgical operations. The parts were allotted as follows: one boy, who had somehow made himself unpopular, was the patient, while the others were surgeons and assistants; two of them had special rôles: one acted the nurse who "gave the anæsthetic", and the other was the "spirit" of the patient.

The operation was always acted as follows: the surgeons and the boy who was later to act the "spirit" fell upon the patient and beat him with sticks, trying if possible to hit his penis. They then pretended to eat him up, and each physician tried to snatch from his colleagues the largest possible part of him, preferably "part of his bottom." The remains were burnt in an imaginary bonfire and all that was left of the patient (the body of the boy who had been operated upon) was buried in the ground, a proceeding which was indicated by covering him with a tablecloth. The physicians, drunk with the blood of their victim, then danced a wild dance, treading on him as he lay on the ground; the "spirit", meanwhile, had hidden in a corner and had to dart in and out among the dancers and pinch one or the other without being seen. The "colleagues", always supposing that one of their number had played this trick finally started a general fight, till at last they all made it up and finished by sucking sweets together.

In this primal "doctor-game" in a modern nursery, in which a primal compulsion to repetition was working itself out, we see in every detail processes appearing in the form of play which Freud, reasoning from the agreement of the compulsive phenomena exhibited by neurotics, with the ceremonial of savages, supposes to have taken place in the primal horde.[16] I cannot at this point touch on many interesting features of the game as we have it here—for instance, the light it throws on the conception of professional etiquette and on projected feelings of guilt. I would only select certain points which are germane to our subject.

When I suggested to this boy that surgeons really do not kill their

---

[16] Freud, *Totem und Taboo*. Cf. also Rôheim, Nach dem Tode des Urvaters. *Loc. cit.*

patients but make them well, he replied that at the time when he played the game he did not "as yet" know that. He thought at that time that surgeons were people who hated everyone else and therefore wanted to kill them. He had twice had some experience of them in their professional capacity. On the first occasion his mother had an operation for the removal of an internal growth and this episode terrified him greatly. On the other occasion the same surgeon removed a growth from the boy's nose. In his terror the child defended himself so violently that the surgeon "by mistake" knocked out one of his teeth. It is perfectly clear that the child identified the surgeon with his own extremely stern and tyrannical father, from whom he tried to escape because of castration-anxiety. In the nose-operation actual form was given to his identification with his mother, who also had been operated on by the father-surgeon (i.e. had submitted to coitus with him). At the same time there was realized the danger of passive feminine surrender to the father—namely, castration—being made into a woman. Through the symbolic interpretation of the surgeon's assault the son felt himself castrated by, and thus prevented from identifying himself with, the father. In the "surgeon-game" he recovered the active father-rôle. In the game, as in dreams, the wish-fulfilment was represented in reverse form, for actually it was only through the operation (castration) that he became the surgeon. It is by piecemeal cannibalistic incorporation in general and by the castration of the patient in particular (surgeon-imago) that the passive subject (the patient) first acquired the powers which in the infantile fantasy are employed by the active subject in his victorious struggle during the primal scene. By introjection of the father he becomes the father, just as the father himself first becomes a man by making the mother a woman, i.e. by ravishing (introjecting) her penis. This also is incorporated, in the form of an excremental symbol, as the parent-substitute ("bottom"), the nates naturally standing simultaneously for the breasts. The latter are then permitted to remain as a perpetual source of gratification in the outer world [17] (compare the sucking of sweets as a token of reconciliation) and make it possible for the subject to resign himself to the rôle of child. The fact that this patient in his "doctor-game" often acted the gentle nurse, who alleviates pain by anæsthetics, betrays his regressive instinctual tendency towards the function of the primal

[17] Cf. Karl Abraham, Zwei Stufen der oralen Entwicklungsphase der Libido, *Entwicklungsgeschichte der Libido auf Grund der Psychoanalyse seelischer Störungen*, 1924.

mother, who by suckling her infant sends it to sleep and frees it from pain.

Thus in this most primitive of all "doctor-games" we see the child's ego, in the struggle between the different identifications, already striving to build up his superego out of them. It endeavours to free itself from the rôle of *feminine* passivity and to revert to that of *infantile* passivity, in which it has no longer passively to submit to its superego (as the mother submits to the father) but can take pleasure in the demands of the superego by looking upon it as its child, its own production. I have come to see that the medical practitioner must in a very special way have accomplished in his superego a synthesis of the conception of a "primal mother", differentiated into father and mother. Otherwise he will transfer to his patient, who is the projection of his ego, the unbearable tension between his superego and his ego (i.e. his sense of guilt disguised as sympathy).

The views of a psycho-analyst on the profession of medicine would, however, be incomplete if we did not in conclusion recall that the physician, in the social economy of distribution of labour, represents in his person a biological, psycho-physical function discovered by Freud in the "pleasure-principle" and designated by him "the guardian of life". The destructive tendency of the compulsion to repetition—the death-instinct—which presses for the equalization of all tensions, and especially for the abolition of all objective sources of tension, is modified by the claim of the narcissistic libido. This represents the desire for life through love—a desire which is primordial and which subsequently is regressively repeated again and again by way of introjective incorporation (introjective repression). When the level of the ego-libido (the self-preservative instinct) [18] is raised, *anxiety* becomes mobilized as a psychic defence while physical pain, the equivalent of anxiety, forms a physical defence against stimulus. The instinct of destruction menaces the subject in both simultaneously. For every morbid process is, when the demand of the ego-libido is strengthened, a heightened vital process, which of itself evolves the tendency to accelerate relief from tension. The "circuitous route to death",[19] which is what life represents, is travelled more rapidly by means of disease, and every diseased organ is thereby threatened with the deleterious consequences of the abrupt subsidence of libido—i.e. with orgasm. Mental anxiety and physical pain are in general the alarm-signals

[18] Freud, On Narcissism: an Introduction, *Collected Papers*, Vol. IV.
[19] Freud, *Beyond the Pleasure-Principle*.

which summon the physician to the sufferer's assistance. In the light which psycho-analysis has thrown on the problem of disease we see fresh avenues opening out for our curative methods. It is not necessary for me here to dwell on the liberation of mankind from anxiety and from the symptoms which are its equivalents. But liberation from organic pain, such, for instance, as announces the presence of a morbid inflammation or the susceptibility to bacterial infection, requires of the physician of the body not primarily operative interference but courage to adopt a new technique, comparable to that achieved by analysts through the methods formulated by Freud. In every case the physician must take into account the libidinal constitution of his patients. He must inform himself of the causes of the peculiar erotogenic demand of the organ which is attacked by disease (i.e. which is pressing to live at a more rapid pace), and he must try to assist the adjustment of the economy of the narcissistic libido. The physician who, out of pity (that is in order to avoid his own sense of guilt), feels it to be his duty *only* to annihilate or alleviate by means of narcotics is in danger of destroying the "guardian of life" and so becoming himself the agent of the instinct of death.

AN EXAMINATION OF METAPHOR

PSYCHO-PHYSICAL PROBLEMS REVEALED IN LANGUAGE *
(1940)

BY ELLA FREEMAN SHARPE

The employment of metaphor by the patient in the course of his verbalization presents itself to the author as indicative of the regressive revival of the same typical experiences, whose common occurrence in the life of the infant seems to have conditioned the metaphor in human language. These experiences are of an affective nature; control and discharge of affect, at first a sphincter-function, becomes later linguistic; and while the word, with regard to its roots is considered by Sharpe an expression of ideation, it is, as far as its onomato-poetic qualities are concerned, looked upon as an expression of affect. Metaphor, finally, is understood by the writer as reflecting in its literal meaning the infantile situation in which the earlier pre-linguistic discharge of affect had originally occurred.

In prefacing the reprint with the summary appended to the original, it is hoped to assist in the understanding of a paper, whose author deliberately chose a somewhat loose literary fabric in order to weave into it many notes, written while listening to her patients.

ABSTRACT

(1) Metaphor evolves alongside the control of the bodily orifices. Emotions which originally accompanied bodily discharge find substitute channels and materials.

(2) Spontaneous metaphor used by a patient proves upon examination to be an epitome of a forgotten experience. It can reveal a present-day psychical condition which is based upon an original psycho-physical experience.

(3) In metaphor that is the expression of vital emotion the repressed psycho-physical experiences have found the verbal images in the pre-conscious that express them. The earliest of all verbal timages are the sounds of words and hence the importance of phonet-

* Reprinted from *The International Journal of Psycho-Analysis*, XXI, 1940, p. 201. Original title: Psycho-physical Problems Revealed in Language: An Examination of Metaphor.

ics and the value of listening to a patient's *phonetic* associations. The person who speaks vitally in metaphor *knows*, but does not know in consciousness what he knows unconsciously.

(4) An examination of metaphors used by patients reveals as one would expect a preponderance of images based upon experiences of the pregenital stages and the repressed œdipus wishes.

(5) They reveal also something of the early incorporated environment.

(6) Metaphor gives information concerning instinctual tension. The metaphors of depression denote the zero hour, exhaustion and immobility, giving us the physical setting which first accompanied the psychical feelings; prolonged crying, bed-wetting, loneliness and exhaustion. Other metaphors give pictures of futile activity, achievement of no goal; continual thwarting and obstructing of the self. Others again reveal pent-up energy, a straining at the leash, desire and fear of "letting go", as in the bow and arrow image.

(7) Information is to be gained by noting the type of image that comes most frequently from any given patient. I have found that a wealth of auditory imagery is often accompanied by a marked absence of visual, and, when visual imagery prevails, auditory images are lacking, thus giving one an indication of the connection of conflicts with a particular sense.

I propose to deal in this paper with one aspect of psycho-analytical treatment, namely, the value of understanding the metaphorical language used by articulate patients. Words both reveal and conceal thought and emotion. In psycho-analytical treatment our task is often that of getting through barrages of words to the sense experience and the associated thoughts. But words too can reveal the union of these and we are greatly helped if we believe this and can recognize the revealing phrase. Metaphor fuses sense experience and thought in language. The artist fuses them in a material medium or in sounds with or without words. The principle is metaphor.

Metaphor has been a subject of debate and investigation from Aristotle to our own time. One of the latest exponents expresses himself thus: "The investigation of metaphor is curiously like the investigation of any of the primary data of consciousness; it cannot be pursued very far without our being led to the borderline of sanity. Metaphor is as ultimate as speech itself, and speech as ultimate as thought." [1]

[1] John Middleton Murry, *Countries of the Mind.*

One explanation of metaphor has been that it reveals the divine in man and that his spiritual qualities and aspirations find expression in language that has a concrete significance. For example, "My spirit flew in feathers then" is according to this view witness to the soaring aspiration of the soul which is forced in language to the mundane illustration of a feathered bird in order to illustrate a quality of the spirit.

Psycho-analytical research, however, endorses the views of those who from the definition of metaphor as "a transference of a word to a sense different from its signification"[2] maintain that the displacement is from physical to psychical and not *vice versa*. "No word", says Grindon, "is metaphysical without its having first been physical." [3] Locke said: "We have no ideas at all, but what originally came either from sensible objects without, or what we feel within ourselves."

The intellectual life of man is only possible through the development of metaphor. No student of language I have read gives any theory as to how the process of metaphor, which is the accompaniment of civilization, evolves. Neither have I found the fact explicitly pointed out that though we inherit the vast language deposits of our predecessors yet every child in so far as it comes to use and evolve metaphor repeats in itself those same processes that led to civilization. Implied or crystallized metaphors that we use like the coin of the realm reveal past ages of history. Individual metaphors used in analysis reveal also the experiences of forgotten years. Just as in the study of language we find no word is metaphysical without its first having been physical, so our search when we listen to patients must be for the physical basis and experience from which metaphorical speech springs.

My purpose in this communication is simple and elementary, namely, to give the general condition upon which the evolution of metaphor depends, and then to illustrate by clinical material. I have made broad classifications of this material, giving references to actual analyses to illustrate the fact that a live metaphor reveals a past forgotten experience and that this was originally a psychophysical one. Space does not permit of detailed classification.

My theory is that metaphor can only evolve in language or in the arts when the bodily orifices become controlled. Then only can the angers, pleasures, desires of the infantile life find metaphorical ex-

[2] Aristotle, *Poetics*.
[3] L. H. Grindon, *Figurative Language: its. Origin and Constitution*.

pression and the immaterial express itself in terms of the material. A subterranean passage between mind and body underlies all analogy. The simplest example I can give to show this, which I believe to be the pattern on which all metaphor evolves is the following.

I was told by a young husband that his wife had been confiding to him how angry she felt about their young son's frequent "accidents". He had replied to her: "Of course you feel angry, that's natural, but don't let John see your anger. Think to yourself you must keep your anger in and hold it in till you get to another room and then you can let it out." This is metaphor. The father is speaking in words that refer to sense-perceptible object but they are used to denote a different order or category, namely—emotion. In time the young son will go through this same process of thinking with regard to his actual urine and fæces: "I must hold it, and hold it in until I get to another room." When the ego stabilizes this achievement of body control and it becomes automatic, the emotion of anger and pleasure which heretofore accompanied bodily discharges must be dealt with in other ways.

At the same time as sphincter control over anus and urethra is being established, the child is acquiring the power of speech, and so an avenue of "outer-ance" present from birth becomes of immense importance. First of all the discharge of feeling tension, when this is no longer relieved by physical discharge, can take place through speech. The activity of speaking is substituted for the physical activity now restricted at other openings of the body, while words themselves become the very substitutes for the bodily substances. Speech secondly becomes a way of expressing, discharging ideas. So that we may say speech in itself is a metaphor, that metaphor is as ultimate as speech.

The words that exist in our language today are themselves derived from two sources, namely, onomatopœia and roots, which represent respectively the affective and ideational aspects of language. Under the term onomatopœia are grouped all words based upon imitation of natural sounds, such as hiss, scream, chuckle, blast, suck, cuckoo. These words imply sense-perception, not thought. The second classification is "roots". These are about five hundred in number and from them all the derivations are made which comprise the tens of thousands of words in a civilized tongue. "Roots" are the organized crystallized sounds that emerged in primitive civilization and include in them all the essential names needed for expressing relationships between man and man, man and his environment, his self-preservative and procreative powers. Ideational language evolves from "roots".

The words that exist in our language today are themselves feeling without thought (i.e. onomatopœia), (2) thought without feeling (i.e. ideational), (3) metaphor, which like a symptom, is a compromise between ego, superego, and id.

I will speak first of "affective" language and then of metaphor. The affective type of utterance which corresponds to the anematopœic source of language is easily distinguishable in simple words and phrases expressing emotion such as, "damn", "blast", "oh God!", "good heavens!", etc. These are a direct expression of feeling and in an analytic session the analyst's job is to correlate the emotion with the appropriate thought, the appropriate person and the cause of the inner tension. The words and phrases of this type are a psychical discharge which in infancy and early childhood would have been accompanied by a bodily one. Words have been substituted for the physical product. But isolated words and phrases are not the only form of onomatopœia. A patient occupied half an hour of one session relating to me the actual hardships a dear relative was suffering. She closed the recital by remarking: "I feel I have been bleating about my own *lamentable* condition, but they are not my woes but hers." That is, the whole half hour's recital was the bleating of the lamb, the language, whatever its content, was affective, and on the patient's psychical condition thus betrayed must the attention of the analyst be concentrated. The choice of the word "lamentable" is an illustration of phonetics, the method by which the mother tongue is acquired. Another patient remarked: "I have talked a long time, I have never hesitated or paused for a word." Another said triumphantly: "Make sense out of all that if you can!" Another paused after a few minutes' talk and said: "This is all vaporing."

When such comments are made by the patient upon what he himself has said, the functioning in words and its purpose become fairly obvious. The content matters little. The first patient's words are in principle "affective". He had been maintaining a long flow of urine. The second had thrown up a smoke screen, the third had been passing flatus. When the patient makes no comment of this revealing nature, the affective nature of language may not be so obvious. Many a skilled exposition on science, art, politics, philosophy occurring during an analytic session serves the same unconscious purpose as the foregoing more obvious defences. Only when the analyst can find that these discourses serve the same purpose as a stream of urine, a smoke screen, flatus, bleating, is he able to get behind words to the unrecognized, unfelt anxiety.

Metaphor. When dynamic thought and emotional experiences of the forgotten past find the appropriate verbal image in the pre-conscious, language is as pre-determined as a slip of the tongue or trick of behaviour. Metaphor, then, is personal and individual even though the words and phrases used are not of the speaker's coinage. The verbal imagery corresponding to the repressed ideas and emotions sometimes found even in a single word will yield to the investigator a wealth of knowledge.

The clinical material I present to you with the deductions made from it has been gathered from individual analyses. The words and phrases embodying imagery of different types were noted down at the time of usage and correlated with the general problem being dealt with at the time. Space does not permit of detailed analyses of the illustrations. Every metaphor I recount here has been tested in analytical experience. Not one of them is to be dismissed as a *façon de parler*, which is so often the very objection the patient will make if attention is drawn to the way he has expressed himself.

The first selection consists of phrases which in the analytical setting proved to have within them an ultimate reference to specific suckling experiences.

The patients were talking of *psychical* difficulties. The metaphors revealed an original psycho-physical basis. For example:

"I've wandered off the point and can't find it again."
"I've lost sight of what I came for."
"It's the way I set about things that's wrong."
"When I wander off the point bring me back to it."
"Don't pounce if I go off the point."
"I see your point of view, but I don't take it in."
"If I could only get started I could go on again."
"This psycho-analytical technique is too vague, it should be a definite application to a particular point of focus."

Here are further more detailed revelations:

"When I do anything I seem to have my eye on something else all the time."
"I am distracted because the tail of my eye is on something else."
"I can't finish one thing properly, I'm wanting to go on with the next thing."
"I can't get the whole day squeezed in, it's too much."

There is no need to analyse these examples. Their meaning is self-evident if one accepts and believes the pre-determination of language when it expresses emotion.

The inert baby of infancy is revealed when an adult says wearily to the analyst:

"I'm sleepy, leave me alone, don't worry me!"
"I'm glad you don't ram psycho-analytical theory down my throat."
"Why don't you rouse me and make me do something?"
"Take me by the scruff of the neck and push me to the analysis."

The analyst has no doubt of the oral experiences when a patient says: "You know when I have a drinking bout I drink as if I may be a long time reaching an oasis again, as a camel might feel after crossing a thirsty desert." Or again: "To me life's a desert without a woman." "Last night", said another patient of this type, "I went from room to room, back and fro, trying to get a meal ready and I was tired out at last and yet only managed a meagre meal."

An indication of different types of psychical reactions to weaning are revealed in the following:

"Life is a closed book to me. I have asked too much of life."
"She laces herself up, no loving emotion ever comes from her, but she is ready enough to criticize all the time."
"She's always giving me the cold shoulder."
"My interest flashes *up* whenever a point of that kind is raised."
"When I get what I want it turns to dust and ashes in my mouth."

The mechanisms of melancholia are implicit in this last metaphor. "Dust to dust, ashes to ashes"—the object is dead, within the mouth.

One reason why reversion to visual thinking has its advantages is made clear in these words:

"Oh I'm only thinking of a mountain peak in Skye, just looking at it. I can't describe it, besides it's my private thing and I don't want to share it with you."

An oral problem reveals itself as the core of an inhibition in adult sublimation in this rumination:

"Such countless images come to my mind, I'd like to recount my experiences and let others enjoy them too, but one must have a *fixed point or points* on which to build up and evolve the whole and I find it difficult to settle down to one and to start."

This man is a bachelor. He cannot settle down and marry the woman he loves, nor will he until the oral conflict is solved.

A patient of mine as an infant was on one occasion flung down from the mother's breast on to a bed by the mother herself who was an anxious hysterical woman worried by her own scanty milk supply. At intervals this patient when the appropriate stimulus occurs will make this type of remark:

"Well, he's got unhorsed and I'm glad."

"Now she's fallen by the wayside, I'm glad it's not me."

"I'm glad I've got to know he's the kind of person who picks a person up one day and drops her the next. I know what to expect and I shan't blame myself if it happens to me which I generally do."

The prevailing metaphor this patient chooses for rifts and changes in personal relationships is always a sudden and violent one: unhorsing, dropping, flinging aside. I have no doubt of the reference in these to the basic reality experience with its many psychical results, although she was not six months old at the time of the occurrence.

From the group of metaphors I have given the following conclusions can be drawn.

(1) Actual experiences at the breast were registered by the infantile ego. These found the appropriate verbal imagery.

(2) Difficulties in physical and mental manipulation in adult life, such as awkwardness, "doing things the wrong way" and an inability to keep to the point (physical or mental) have their origins in sucking experiences.

(3) Adult characteristic psychical traits can begin in suckling experience such as an easily distracted mind, an inability to concentrate.

(4) Where suckling experience has been accompanied by traumatic occurrences the patient unconsciously expects a repetition of these.

(5) The actual responses between mother and infant in suckling having been incorporated become part of the psychical make-up of the individual.

The second classification is that of metaphor in which the transferred reference from body to mind is anal and urethral. The first examples are the spontaneous remarks of patients concerning depression:

"I am sodden with despair."

"I have struck another patch of depression."

"I am in a trough of depression, a rut of depression."

"If I could be pulled out of this depression."

"What took me out of the depression was——"

"I'm depressed, I suppose I'm making heavy weather of my troubles."

"I'm depressed, there's a deadly feeling of being in a rut."

I could multiply examples of this nature. From the analysis at any given time when such phrases were used I have no doubt that the psychical state of depression first accompanied bodily states when the child lay cold, wet and miserable in bed waiting in hopelessness or fearfulness of being lifted up and rescued from the rut. (I would point out here that I am dealing with depressed patients who were articulate in a special way, that is they had found the metaphor which bridged a present-day emotional state with a past psycho-physical experience.)

A patient on one occasion said to me: "I dreamt about a depressed state but feel all right this morning, which is a change for me." I responded with a metaphor, as I was then testing out my conclusion about the psycho-physical situations giving rise to the later depressed cycles of feeling. I said: "Well, that's better than having the whole day *swamped* by affect." He replied: "What I dreamt of was a burn ⁴ in Scotland. I know I was on the wrong side of it, it gradually grew bigger and I was anxious to get on the right side of it, but I couldn't, it got bigger and bigger and I couldn't manage to get on the right side, but all the same this morning I know I deal with difficult situations in my life better, they seem more manageable, I've more sense of proportion."

Another equally illuminating remark was made by a patient who started a session by referring to many present-day actual worries and saying: "I'm making heavy weather of them all." I inquired, "What kind of weather comes to your mind?" "Oh!" he replied, "heavy snowstorms, like my dream last night. I was in a room, a snowstorm was raging outside. I was crying, something had gone wrong but some woman was comforting me as if I were a child. I remember her saying: 'Yes, but you are managing things much better, you are improving'." That is, amelioration of the superego was being accomplished in the analysis. As a child he was under the dominance of a strict Scotch nurse who made the normal problems of childhood into abnormal ones.

I will summarize the inferences to be drawn from the foregoing.

⁴ Scottish for "brook" (stream).

From an exhaustive examination of metaphor concerning depression I am of the opinion that the original psycho-physical situation that may for some children become of cardinal importance is that of lying helpless, wet and cold in bed. The fantasies Mrs. Klein has made familiar to us are very appropriate to this state. The infant is literally empty and in a cold mess. It cannot help itself and must wait for external help. The word "depressed" itself means literally "squeezed out of, pressed out from."

Here is another group of metaphors that arose out of childhood experiences before automatic sphincter control over anus and urethra was attained:

"Rain and sun on the landscape, it's not the same place, not beautiful any more, just what I feel when I'm in a panic state of mind, can this be the same place as when I feel quiet?"

"I had such a rude awakening."

"She passes such sweeping judgments, and I do the same."

"I'm terrified, I can't control my thoughts."

"This couch reeks with verbosity."

"I'm terrified of making a mess of things."

"I think I've now the capacity not to lose my temper."

"I feel I've landed myself in a mess."

"I let them have a few home-truths about their behaviour. I used to have them myself."

"I'm not so fussed today. I've not nagged at myself so mercilessly."

"I'm sorry I made that fuss yesterday. Can we go on and tidy up yesterday's analysis?"

"I woke up feeling something awful was going to happen. I was confused in my brain. Would something snap? I know what patients mean now when they say they are going 'potty'."

The analysis during the hour when these last words were uttered revealed a visit the day before to a nursery where napkins were being washed. The mother was irritable, the father attentive to the baby. It was possible during the session to infer the setting of the patient's own infantile sexual desires towards her father, in a sudden messing which was followed by a mother's scolding. She remarked concerning a tentative present-day love situation: "Rather than be disappointed I atrophy my desires and always have." She suffers from constipation.

These images bear witness to the fact of the stressful time during which bodily control was acquired. "Judgments are sweeping, awakening rude, the little boy's trousers are let down before other people." The environment has been incorporated. "I keep nagging at myself." Terror of consequences fantastic and real prevail in connection with bodily "accidents".

More detailed pictures of the vicissitudes of this time in a child's life are given in the following examples. A patient said: "I couldn't get to the analysis yesterday, I sat and drank and looked at the clock, I've only just managed to get here today." I asked: "How do you feel you have *just managed*, what made the difference?" He replied: "By not thinking I was walking. While I could forget I was walking and just walked, I could get here."

The analysis from this point brought to the patient's mind memories of having wetted himself, of having messed in his trousers, the difficulty of walking in this condition and the fear of the nurse's anger when she discovered what he had done. "I feel in a state of tension," another patient remarked; "it reminds me of myself as a child with a bow and arrow, all ready to let the arrow fly and then not daring to do it. One never knew where it might fly, whom it might hit. It's a right image too for the body as well as the mind— fear of 'relieving' yourself when you really need to do so."

The following example is illuminating because it gives evidence of two phases in a child's life. The patient remarked: "I felt furious, but not a hot and angry fury, but deadly cold rage. I said hardly anything, but my voice was icy and controlled. To my mind a more dangerous anger than a hot one. Like an iceberg, it gores a ship and the ship is lost, it might have survived in the most angry seas." This metaphor gives in pictorial form what can happen within the psyche when bodily control has become automatic. Aggression formerly discharged through the lax sphincter becomes the main characteristic of control itself. Unconscious control of the bodily openings and the unconscious superego are then inseparable. The superego takes on the quality of a physical sphincter, rigid, implacable and merciless in judgment. Adaptations made through the ego, a willingness to co-operate in the gradual development of the power of self-control are inseparable both from a tolerant, unhurried external environment and manageable internal anxiety. In the "iceberg" metaphor one realizes that the establishment of urethral control was made from fear. Little psychical adjustment was made, no loving adaptation. "Control" is, if anything, representative of more anger than less.

The next set of examples is miscellaneous in type. Some need only to be repeated to reveal the repressed thought, others are worthy of detailed examination. The simpler ones are:

"Whenever I get an erection I feel guilty, God only knows why."

"I can't think, *for the life of me*, what I'm afraid of."

"I went upstairs twice the girl I was, after she said: 'Of course you will marry and have children'."

"I am afraid to swank at someone else's expense."

"She has her little sillinesses and I have mine." (Said by a male patient.)

"My conception about analysis is this."

"I feel obtuse today." That is, the patient had no point, the allusion being to the holiday which meant there would be no analysis the next day and Sharpe (the point) would not be available.

"I wouldn't touch her with a branched pole." This remark occurred in one day's analysis. The next day the patient had dreamt of losing his riding "crop". "Crop" by derivation signifies a branching thing, a swelling, an enlargement. "Crop" has a secondary meaning of "to cut off". An ultimate bodily reference I have found in such phrases as "an argument soon cropped up between us", "a difference soon cropped up".

The disappointed child who has become clean in her habits to please her father for unconscious œdipus wishes speaks in this way: "I bring my dreams to you intact and nothing is developed from them, nothing comes of them."

In the next illustration a man speaks whose whole efforts are directed to reparation. He leads an active, busy life attending to other people's property, a noted successful estate manager, adapted to certain aspects of external reality, but his own creative possibilities, physical and psychical, are not used. He said very tensely: "Analysis is such a strain, life is a strain." I said: "What is the kind of image you get when you think of *strain*?" He replied at once: "Oh, those girls who spend their lives invisibly mending the holes in other people's clothes."

The following phrase proved to have in it an implicit sight of the parents together in intercourse. "My wife and I were together last night. To a casual observer *contemplating* the intercourse it would have looked all right I know, but it wasn't really."

Said another patient: "I'm so disappointed, I had hoped to shape my ideas on these children's problems and get them out on paper, but I haven't, I've just got a bursting feeling in my body instead." The hysterical conversion symptom persists, the metaphorical expression has not yet been accepted.

A forgotten experience is implicit in the following metaphor. The patient was speaking of a neurotic young man. She said of him:

"His desperation grows; as it grows, he grows more and more pompous. I have a desire then to prick the balloon, but I don't see him becoming less."

A patient had great difficulty in deciding whether or not to accept a post involving both added prestige and great responsibility. It was unconsciously a choice of accepting femininity, as the analysis revealed during the time of her indecision. The fantasies underlying her indecision were revealed in her repeated metaphor: "Am I *cut out* for this job? I don't think I'm *cut out* for it."

I finish with an example of a single word which revealed the core of a profound psychological illness. I noticed a patient used the word "really" very often. I gave it for a time no significance, thinking, if I thought at all, that it was a habit he had acquired, just as others say "I mean", "Do you see?" unnecessarily. Gradually however his "really" forced itself on my attention and I became curious, the more so as I reflected that this patient had the gift of words. He was a poet and a translator of foreign works. He was the last person *really* to use meaningless words, since they were the stuff of imagination for him. So I studied the setting of the analysis when he ejaculated the word "really".

I found the following. Whenever he was surprised into saying something critical about me, my belongings, or the analysis, he put up his hand in a beseeching way and said in an apologetic deprecating voice: "*Really*, Miss Sharpe . . . ." I correlated these transference affects with the underlying infantile and childhood emotional situations that were being represented and they included: the appearance of a new baby, the awareness of parental intercourse when he slept in the parents' room, the sight of the female genital, the sight of menstrual blood. That is, the patient used the word "really" when he was expressing thoughts (in the transference) that indicated criticism, anger and fear, and since the transference situation gathered within itself the infantile ones already referred to I can now put the word "really" where it belongs and indicate its significance.

"Another baby, really?—Really!"
"Made by father and mother, really?—Really!"
"A person without a penis, really?—Really!"
"Is that blood on her nightdress, really?—Really!"
"I think she's dirty, is she, really? Really!"
"I feel like killing, really?—Really!"

In nine cases out of ten a patient will use "really" as a *façon de parler*.

Here in the tenth, in the one word "really?" "Really!", the core of
the neurosis was implicit, for it meant: "I see these things, know
these things, but they are not real; I feel like this, but I mustn't feel
like this, not really."

IV
UNCOLLECTED PAPERS OF KARL ABRAHAM

UNCOLLECTED PAPERS OF KARL ABRAHAM

The works of Karl Abraham, with whom in December, 1925, as Freud has expressed it, "a perhaps irretrievable piece of the future of our young science had to be buried" [1] are today regarded as classics. And indeed almost every one of his communications, even those merely illustrative and apparently obsolete, possesses permanent value. Practice and theory are, to Abraham's mind, but complementary aspects of the same subject: his clinical observations contain always, at least implicitly, a theoretical "moral", and his theoretical contributions are abstracted from clinical pictures of an unsurpassed accuracy of outline. Only a few writers have been able to display, at times, the ingenuity that marks all of Abraham's work. And no one has taken his place.

Karl Abraham's prominence in the "psycho-analytic movement" of his day is on record. Beside his work, a substantial part of which seems to have eluded the printer, we have left but one photograph of his likeness. Its features grow more transparent over years devoted to the absorption of Abraham's thinking, until one believes one sees in them all the attributes of the author: the unerring eye, the sharp nose with its "flair" for the essential and a mouth cut to brevity of expression. Yet the bearing is reticent. The contemplative attitude betrays the skeptic; the image is that of a man who tempers intransigeance of conviction with the humility of the scientist; and the portrait appears illuminated by the imperceptible humour that delights the reader.

Since the editor was denied the good fortune of a personal contact with Dr. Abraham, he may be permitted to complete the picture, after the fashion of a mosaic, by excerpting a few memorial remarks, made by Abraham's friends. [2]

". . . Abraham was as exemplary a disciple as he was a teacher . . . His faithful and unconditional loyalty towards the person of Freud and the psycho-analytic movement were balanced by a preservation of his independence which had him express doubt and disagreement whenever these appeared justified to him by objective reasons. Even when personal matters were linked with scientific questions, as inevitably

[1] Memorial on Abraham: *Internationale Zeitschrift für Psychoanalyse*, XII, 1926, p. 1.

[2] Doctors Ernest Jones, Sandor Rádo, and Hanns Sachs, from: Memorial, *Internationale Zeitschrift für Psychoanalyse*, XII, 1926, pp. 189 ff.

happens during the organizing phase of a movement. Abraham's attitude remained consistent. More often than one might assume he undertook the task of cautioning Freud, and without hurting or provoking him, firmly carried through the fight for his opinion. Whenever later events justified his opinions it never occurred to him to make any claims because of it. It was always he, who, to quote Goethe, 'knew how to subordinate himself with dignity'. . . ." (Sachs).

" . . . Abraham was not a voluminous writer, and the actual amount of what he wrote is less than one might expect from one's sense of their significance. His printed publications, excluding merely verbal communications, consist of four small books, containing altogether less than three hundred pages, and forty-nine other papers amounting to about four hundred pages. . . . Very many of these were only a page or two long, and only five exceeded twenty pages. The fact just mentioned is doubtless to be correlated with what was perhaps the most salient feature of all Abraham's writings, namely, a remarkable conciseness. . . ." (Jones).

". . . His oldest love concerned language, and he remained faithful to it, in spite of his exhausting life-work. Thus it was that he was able to analyse patients of various countries in their native tongues; and so also could the busy physician and scholar relax in his leisure hours by reading Aristophanes in the original. . . ." (Sachs).

". . . He described psychic phenomena as graphically as if they were somatic—visible and palpable preparations. He has created lasting models of analytic description, and furnished the perfect type of case history to be found in psycho-analytic literature: concise, completely objective, and yet vivid. It is significant that Abraham, in spite of the unusual abundance of his findings has scarcely coined a single abstract term. His thinking never followed the track of abstract notions. His theorems always take facts as their starting point, and return to them by way of genetic connections. It is as if the former embryologist went on with his studies, only now working on psychic material. . . ." (Rádo).

The present section, devoted to several of his papers, hitherto untranslated, or not collected in book form, is intended to supplement the English collection of his work.[3]

[3] *Selected Papers*, London, Hogarth Press, 1927.

SHALL WE HAVE THE PATIENTS WRITE DOWN THEIR DREAMS * (1913)

A classical example of the "Kleine Mitteilung" ("Brief Clinical Communication"), adding new determinants to a much over-determined, typical piece of "acting-out".

In a short paper on "The Employment of Dream Interpretation in Psycho-analysis" (1912), Sigmund Freud briefly considered the question of whether or not it was of advantage to let patients put down their dreams in writing, immediately after awakening. He came to the conclusion that such a procedure was superfluous. "Even if the substance of a dream is in this way laboriously rescued from oblivion, it is easy enough to convince oneself that nothing has thereby been achieved for the patient. The associations will not come to the text, and the result is the same as if the dream had not been preserved."

My own experience causes me fully to share this view. The question, however, seems to me to be of considerable interest to the psycho-analyst who in his everyday practice makes use of the interpretation of dreams. Therefore, I should like to bring forward certain experiences met with in my own practice. These occurred in connection with precisely those patients whom I had already told that it was useless to write down their dreams.

Observation 1. A patient had a very elaborate and eventful dream associated with strong affects. Upon awakening he drowsily reached for his writing material which he had put at his bedside in spite of the analyst's instructions to the contrary. The next morning, he brought me two quarto pages full of notes. But what he had written proved to be nearly illegible. The striving to rescue the dream from oblivion obviously was countered in this case by the opposite striving (repression). The result was a compromise in that the dream actually was written down, but in illegible writing, preventing it from giving any information.

Observation 2. A patient whom in answer to his question I had

---

* Translated from the original text: Sollen wir die Patienten ihre Träume aufschreiben lassen? *Internationale Zeitschrift für Psychoanalyse*, I, 1913, p. 194.

warned against writing down his dreams, produced a whole series of dreams in one of the succeeding nights. Awakening in the midst of the night, he tried ingeniously to rescue from repression the dreams he considered very important. Owning a dictaphone he spoke into the machine a description of his dreams, significantly disregarding the fact that it had recently not been working properly. The record was not clear therefore. The patient had to supplement a good deal from memory. The analysis of the dream was accomplished without very much resistance. This leads me to suppose that the dream would have been preserved just as well without being recorded.

But, failing to learn from this experience, the patient tried again. The dictaphone was repaired, and gave on the morning after the dream night a rather understandable production. But, as the patient himself acknowledged, the content was so confused that he had to organize it. He succeeded in doing so, but not without difficulty. The following nights produced an abundant dream material covering the same complexes. As this could be sufficiently reproduced without any mechanical help, this case too proved the uselessness of an immediate recording of dreams.

Observation 3 proves most strikingly how useless it is to oppose by such means a powerful tendency to repression.

The patient complained for several weeks of being unable to re-member a certain dream. She related that the same dream had recently recurred every night. Awakening in fright, it was her inten-tion to tell me the dream the next morning, but each time she forgot its content. One day she told me she would keep writing material ready that night in order to be able to take notes on the dream im-mediately upon awakening. I advised her against this, observing that a striving which created dreams night after night would find its way into consciousness without such help; for the time being, the resistance opposing this was still too strong. She saw the point and abandoned her intention. But when she went to bed the wish to recall that night's dream returned. The patient prepared pencil and paper. She actually awoke in a state of fright from her usual dream, turned on the light, and wrote down some notes. She fell asleep again, her mind at ease in the feeling that she could no longer lose the dream. Next morning she overslept and came late to the analytic hour (resistance). She handed me a sheet of paper, saying that in her hurry she had not re-examined it that morning.

It was somewhat difficult to decipher the few words she had scribbled down, owing to the indistinct writing (see Observation 1).

The words were these: "Write down the dream against agreement."
Her resistance had won out. The patient had written down, not the
dream, but only her intent of doing so. Then, satisfied with herself,
she had fallen asleep.

About a week after this futile attempt she was able to relate the
following dream which had occurred several times since. Its content
had its source in a strong transference. The patient dreamed that I
was approaching her, and each time her dream ended with her
awakening in fright. The reason for keeping the dream secret ceased
to exist after other symptoms of transference had made a detailed
analysis of the above-mentioned incident necessary.

I should like to indicate briefly the motives which lead patients
to attribute such importance to an immediate writing-down of their
dreams. Frequently it is a matter of transference. A patient who
brings notes of a dream to the analytic hour wants (unconsciously)
to prove to the analyst by means of these notes that the dream has
particular reference to the latter. Sometimes a dream handed to the
analyst in writing has the character of a gift presented to him, as
though the patient wanted to say: "I am offering you the most
precious thing I have." Obviously neurotic vanity is here involved.
Many patients with pronounced narcissism are positively in love
with the beauty of their dreams. They rescue them from oblivion
because they consider them precious.

Just as the auto-erotic neurotic likes to retain products of his
body, just as he is anxious not to lose more than absolutely necessary
of his bodily substance, so in the same way he is on guard that none
of his intellectual products should be lost.

ON PARAPRAXES WITH AN OVERCOMPENSATING TENDENCY * (1922)

A category of slips of the tongue, not described by Freud in his Psychopathology of Everyday Life.

Here the repressed unconscious hampers the word-formation not directly, but indirectly, through a reaction-formation. The distortion is, therefore, to be understood as the interference, not of a fragment of another word-image, but of an unconscious effect to prevent the appearance of such a fragment.

The publication date of this contribution is interesting, inasmuch as Abraham's observation is of the same kind, and was made at the same time as those that led Freud, a year later, to the establishment of his second topographical hypothesis in The Ego and the Id.

It can be said of all the numerous phenomena described by Freud in his *Psychopathology of Everyday Life* that they are antagonistic to the conscious intentions of the person concerned. The tendency running counter to conscious interest takes, however, a different course in various forms of blunders. For instance, it can fall a victim to repression; this happens when we forget words, proper names, etc. In the example "aliquis" quoted by Freud, forgetting this word prevented certain "painful" associations from becoming conscious. On the other hand, the effect of mistakes in speaking or writing is different; here the tendency that is disagreeable to consciousness has forced its way in a disturbing manner into the performance that consciousness had in view. Blunders can be divided into two groups according to their effects; namely, those blunders in which the tendency that is diverted from consciousness is neutralized, and those in which it can express itself at least by hints.

For some time now I have occasionally come across blunders during my psycho-analyses which seem to belong to a third variety, not mentioned in the *Psychopathology of Everyday Life*. I recently met with a frequently recurring example of this kind in a patient, which is the occasion of this short communication.

* First published in the *Internationale Zeitschrift für Psychoanalyse*, XIII, 1922, p. 345: Über Fehlleistungen mit übercompensierender Tendenz.

Reprinted from *The International Journal of Psycho-Analysis*, V, 1924, p. 197.

The patient, whose articulation is usually quite normal, tends to duplicate the first syllable of proper names by making a slight stutter. This condition troubles her very much and keeps her in a state of anxiety during the time she is teaching in class. She is afraid of being asked to read aloud for fear of coming across a proper name which would stimulate the trouble.

One day she told me of a name she had mispronounced on one of these occasions. The blunder was certainly a mistake in pronouncing a word, but not of the duplicating kind just mentioned. She had altered the Greek name Protagoras into Protragoras.

Her associations very soon led to another mistake in speaking which actually was a duplication of the first syllable, and which had occurred a few moments before the blunder "Protragoras". She had said "A-alexandros" instead of "Alexandros". This blunder she voluntarily brought into connection with an infantile tendency she had indulged in to an unusual degree, namely, that of playing with names or words by distorting them so they came to sound like the "indecent" words in childish language. It is hardly necessary to remind readers that children's words almost always consist of two similar syllables. These words are used for persons, animals, and objects in common use by the child, but more especially for the names of various parts of the body and bodily functions. These latter words often remain in use long after the child has adopted the language of adults and no longer says "bow-wow" but "dog". My patient tended for a long period to make all possible names imitate the forbidden words, and this applied especially to those names in which the syllables "a" or "po" occurred.

Freud has already estimated the significance of these kind of tendencies. He finds that this playing with words is also occasionally carried out against the person's will.[1]

The first syllable of the name Protagoras has been changed into the word "popo" ("buttocks"), which was hovering in the patient's unconscious, in a simple manner by leaving out the "r" and duplicating by a stutter the first syllable of the word. The patient had actually done this kind of thing many times. The variation in the present instance is explained by the affect of anxiety which united with the mistake that had immediately preceded this one. The tendency to express further forbidden words becomes repressed. Instead of the risky leaving out of the "r" in the first syllable of "Protagoras", an "r" is inserted in the second syllable where there should not be one.

[1] Cf. *Psychopathology of Everyday Life.*

This blunder thereupon prevents an infantile-sexual tendency from entering the conscious stream of thought. The mechanism made use of, however, is the exact opposite of that which had given rise to the forbidden tendency. The blunder bears the character of over-compensation.

During treatment a few days later the patient in speaking of a death omitted the first "n" in the word "Kondolenzbrief" (letter of condolence), saying "Kodolenzbrief" instead of "Kondolenz-brief". This mistake also proved to be one of over-compensation, i.e. for the purpose of avoidance.

The disturbing influence in this instance did not proceed from a word used by children, but from the foreign word "Kondom" (condom), which we usually pronounce as though the second syllable ended with a nasal (French) "n". After overcoming some resistances the patient brought to light a peculiar association between the words of Kondom and Kondolenzbrief. Some time ago a death had occurred in the patient's family, and the relatives had assembled in a room belonging to the patient's brother. The young man had neglected to put away a couple of condoms (Kondoms) which were lying on the table packed up in the form of a *letter*. This created a painful impression on the condoling (kondolierenden) relatives! If I mention that the patient for years had envied her brother's masculinity and more recently his sexual freedom, it is not difficult to recognize that an element of infantile sexuality (castration complex) is concealed also in this example. I am unable to give further details for reason of discretion.

The effect of the blunder is obvious. The disturbing idea "Kondom" could have acted quite easily by substituting an "n" for the "l" in "Kondolenzbrief", especially as the first syllable also contained the letters "on". The opposite happened, however; the "n" is eliminated from the first syllable. The blunder has, therefore, the same effect of over-compensation as we saw in the first example, but the mechanism is different. In the first example a consonant belonging to the first syllable is inserted in the second syllable, whereas in the second example a consonant is removed from the first syllable in virtue of which the two syllables become assimilated (Ko-do).

A few days later the patient told me a dream in which she was in a compromising situation with a man and was discovered by her mother. She added that "the scene took place in the *partrerre* of a house".

The mechanism of this blunder is the same as in the example

"Protragoras". I should imagine that the superfluous "r" in the second syllable acts against the tendency to remove the same letter from the first syllable. "Paterre" sounds like the Latin "pater". The latter word occurred not long ago in another blunder and clearly alluded to her father. The man in the dream with whom the patient was surprised by her mother very soon turned out to be a representative of her father. It is to be noticed that a duplicating pronunciation of the commencing letters of "parterre" would produce the treacherous word "papa", and this had been avoided in a manner exactly similar to that of the forbidden word "Popo" [2] in the first example.

It seems to me justifiable on the basis of these examples to speak of over-compensating blunders. I can express no opinion about the relationship of frequency in which they stand to the recognized forms. In order to show that the above examples originating in the same person are not unique, I will mention a blunder of a similar character which occurred in a man. I can only recount it as he gave it to me, for I was not able to analyse it with him. I feel, however, that my explanation of it contains a great measure of probability.

What my friend told me is as follows: "Whenever tonsillitis is mentioned I am always embarrassed because of the Latin name of the disease. I am always on the point of saying 'angora' instead of 'angina'." I expect that the word "vagina", which has a similar sound, was endeavouring to appear in the place of the word "angina". The error then concerned the first half of the word. Such a mistake in speaking would be exceedingly painful in company, so the tendency for the error was displaced to the second half of the word. to designate tonsillitis as "angora" was at all events a comical mistake, but had in itself nothing of the painfulness of the one avoided. However, as my friend mentioned, the mistake had never actually happened. There only existed an habitual readiness for its perpetration. It is also clear here that the defensive tendency maintains the upper hand.

These kinds of blunders should not by any means be placed in essential contrast to the remainder. It is certainly worth noting that a defensive, over-compensating tendency succeeds in place of an impelling one. In the psychological sphere we know of similar precesses in various forms. In an anxiety-dream, after its analysis it is not the affect of anxiety, defence or flight that seems to be the essential thing, but that impulse of the dreamer whose fulfilment

[2] German nursery term for "behind".

the dream serves; it is all the same whether the wish-fulfilment succeeds or is inhibited.

It seems fitting to draw a comparison of the phenomena described here with some symptoms of the obsessional neurosis. One thinks, for instance, of the repeated testing to see whether the gas tap is turned off. An escape of gas could kill the relatives of the neurotic. His hand would like to obey the unconscious command to leave the gas tap on. The typical outcome of the conflict in obsessional neurotics is the victory of caution. Although this is the outcome, psycho-analysis quite rightly lays the chief weight on the repressed impulse and on the unconscious. It is just the same with the cases described here, which express an external victory of the censorship similar to that in anxiety-dreams and many obsessional symptoms.

FATHER-MURDER AND FATHER-RESCUE IN THE FANTASIES OF NEUROTICS * (1922)

A supplement to Freud's analysis of the Œdipus legend, and its application to clinical psycho-analysis.

"Rescue fantasies" are among those wish-creations of neurotics that are familiar and quite comprehensible to us since the time when, in 1910, Freud explained their unconscious meaning and traced their origin to the parental complex.[1] In these fantasies a neurotic sometimes rescues his father, at other times his mother, from danger of death. Fantasies of saving the mother's life arise chiefly from the son's tender feelings, and according to Freud's analysis also contain, in addition to the rescue tendency, the wish to present the mother with a child. Rank[2] later made a more elaborate study of these fantasies; he[3] and Harnik[4] have enabled us to understand the fantasies of rescuing the mother which are found in the works of poets.

Freud pointed out that the tendency to rescue the father is chiefly the expression of an impulse of defiance on the son's part. He also refers to the usual form in which these fantasies commonly appear. The son generally rescues some representative of the father, for instance, a king, or any other highly placed person, from an impending danger to life. In another place[5] he gives an example of a typical fantasy of father-rescue but without giving a detailed analysis of it. I have often come across the same fantasy in my

* First published in the *Internationale Zeitschrift für Psychoanalyse*, VIII, 1922, p. 71. Vaterrettung und Vatermord in den neurotischen Phantasiegebilden.

Reprinted from *The International Journal of Psycho-Analysis*, III, 192, p. 467. Original title: Rescue and Murder of the Father in Neurotic Fantasies.

[1] *Jahrbuch der Psychoanalyse*, II, 1910, p. 396; also in *Kleine Schriften zur Neurosenlehre*, Vierte Folge, p. 210.

[2] Belge zur Rettungsphantasie, *Zentralblatt für Psychoanalyse*, 1910–11, I, p. 331.

[3] Das Inzestmotiv in Dichtung und Sage, 1912, and *Internationale Zeitschrift für Psychoanalyse*, II, 1914, p. 43 ff.

[4] *Imago*, 1912, I, p. 507.

[5] In the *Traumdeutung* in the discussion of day-dreams and also in the discussion of an example in the *Psychopathology of Everyday Life*.

patients, and I may presume other analysts to be familiar with it. I should like therefore to submit its unconscious content, particularly its symbolism, to a closer examination, and I hope to show that we ought not to be satisfied with recognizing a neurotic product of this kind as the effect of the infantile defiance that Freud has already perceived in it. Deeper analysis seems to me necessary; as will be shown, it yields important information about the patient's unconscious, and it also gives us an insight into the deeper layers of other closely-related fantasies which we shall draw on for comparison.

In the fantasy I have in mind the patient imagines he is walking along a street. He unexpectedly sees coming towards him at a terrific pace a carriage in which is sitting the king (or another highly placed personage). He instantly seizes the horses by the reins and brings the carriage to a standstill, thus saving the king from the risk of death.

If we first of all consider only the manifest content of the rescue fantasy we easily recognize it as the opposite of the œdipus myth. The person saves the king's life, instead of taking it—as Œdipus does. In the manifest content the son has nothing to do with the risk of death the king runs; in fact, the son runs this risk himself for his father's sake.

On the other hand, it is worth noting those parts of the manifest content of the two fantasies that are in agreement. In both fantasies the meeting with the kind is represented as due to chance; and it is particularly striking that in both of them the king is advancing in a carriage.[6]

If we now use our definite knowledge that in the unconscious "king" is synonymous with father, and "rescue" with killing, then the far-reaching agreement of the rescue fantasy with the œdipus myth becomes quite evident. In the œdipus myth, it is true, the killing of the king occurs undisguisedly; but this variation is explicable from the fact that the upper layer of the myth represents a crime in the remote past, from which every member of the people who fabricated the myth consciously thinks himself far removed. The neurotic, on the other hand, is himself the central point of the manifest content of the rescue fantasy; the transformation of an onslaught into a rescue is due to the stricter application of the censorship.

[6] Dr. Carl Müller drew my attention to this parallel in a discussion at the Berlin Psycho-Analytical Society.

The rescue fantasy contains a whole series of details the determination of which is in no way explained by our having recognized the king as the father, and the rescue as containing an ambivalent meaning which includes his destruction. Those elements in the fantasy which are predominantly symbolic are: driving, the carriage, the horses, their bolting, the street, the chance meeting, pulling up the horses.

Beginning with the first-mentioned element, driving, the sexual-symbolic significance of which is quite familiar to us, we arrive at a layer of latent fantasies with the meaning: the son becomes—unexpectedly—a spectator of the father performing coitus.

The symbolic significance of the horses now becomes evident, and the over-determination of each element is here shown in a particular instructive manner. In the cases where I have analysed this fantasy the carriage was constantly pictured as a carriage and pair; the two animals in movement together are comprehensible as symbols of the parents. The meaning of the bolting now becomes clear. In many dreams, and in those fantasies of neurotics which are accompanied by anxiety, coitus (and also onanism) is represented by a movement that becomes quicker and quicker, and cannot be moderated or stopped.[7] This reminds us, for example, of the anxiety of certain neurotic persons on going downhill or downstairs; their anxiety refers to the danger they run of losing control of their speed. The same patients also commonly feel anxiety while being conveyed in any vehicle which they cannot stop at will at any moment (railway-trains, etc.). These patients protect themselves against the danger to which they would be exposed were they, if only for a moment, to surrender control over their libido; they displace their anxiety, however, on to the situations mentioned, which are well-suited to act as symbolic substitutes for the repressed ideas.

If the bolting of the the animals represents the sexual act, then the intervention of the son who stops the horses can only correspond to the tendency to prevent the parents' intercourse. The intention to "separate the parents" is among those impulses which we find particularly often originating in the œdipus complex. The censorship conceals this intention; in its place appears the *chance* which causes the son to arrive on the scene just at the moment when the furious onrush begins.

Although in the manifest content the well-meaning motive of

[7] The relations of these phobias to repressed urethral erotism cannot be gone into here.

the rescue fantasy comes to expression, the motive of defiance predominates at its deeper level—the defiant meaning which Freud has already recognized as the essential motive in rescuing the father. A contrast to the fantasy of rescuing the mother at once becomes clear; in this later wish-formation the son procreates a child with the mother, while in the father-saving fantasy he prevents the father from doing the same thing. The close relation of the two ideas is now evident. To this may be added the tendency, which Freud has already appreciated, of being "quits" with the father by saving his life; the father now "owes" his life to his son, just as the latter "owes" his to the father.

This analysis does not so far do justice to the manifold determination of the horse as a sexual symbol. Associations lead further to the horse as a symbol of male power, and also as a symbol of the male sexual organ, just as in the analysis of dreams with a similar content. Locomotives, automobiles, steamers, etc. are known as dream-symbols with the same meaning; common to them all is the idea of an urgent forward advance with a force that cannot be checked. If, therefore, the son successfully holds up the bolting horses, he thereby proves his superiority over the male power of the father whom in his childish idealizing admiration he had raised to the rank of king, i.e. to the most powerful of men. But in preventing the father (at a deeper level of the fantasy) from carrying out the act which is indicated symbolically, he robs him of the masculinity which had been the object of such admiration. The rescue fantasy is now seen to contain the impulse to castrate the father besides that of killing him and separating the parents; everyday psycho-analytic experience shows, moreover, that fantasies of killing and castration are always most intimately associated with each other. Before discussing the castration symbolism, and particularly the idea of the son's genital superiority which is represented in the fantasy, we must consider a further determination of the horse, and also the significance of the carriage in rescue fantasies.

The king, who embodied originally all the ideals of masculinity, travels proudly in a carriage as befits his importance. The carriage serves him as a vehicle, the horse as a draught-animal; both are symbols of a woman, i.e. the mother. We can now recognize the expression of a further wish in the bolting of the horses: the mother is in league with the son, she "runs away" from the father; she even brings him (the father) into danger of death and delivers him up, so to speak, to his son. But if it is the mother who threatens the father's life, and the son who endeavours to save it, then the son's neurotic sense of guilt is effectually relieved. A dream quoted below will support this interpretation.

One other symbol has still to be considered—namely, the street in which the event takes place. In the Œdipus myth also the murder of the father occurs in the street, and not in the royal palace or elsewhere. This detail must signify something as do all the others. Now we know that the street is a common symbol of the female genitals; and by applying logically our knowledge of symbolism on this point we are able to discover both in rescue fantasy and in the Œdipus myth an element which has not so far been noted in them.

The street in which the son and father join issue needs no further comment. The idea of a contest about the maternal genitals, however, covers two different kinds of unconscious fantasies. The first is easily recognizable. A duel between father and son is a frequently recurring motive in myths and dreams. In virtue of its particular symbolism, however, the Œdipus myth gives to this combat the further significance of a competitive struggle for genital superiority.

King Laios is not the only occupant of the carriage. He is accompanied by a driver, a herald, and two servants. The King and the driver endeavour to force Œdipus out of the way as he advances towards them. Œdipus resists and gives the driver a blow. The King now aims a blow at Œdipus and hits him on the head with his thorny stick. This causes Œdipus to attack the King with his staff; he kills him, so that the King falls backwards from the carriage. Then the King's attendants engage Œdipus in a hand-to-hand conflict, in which Œdipus wins.

The metaphorical language is very clear here.[8] The blow on the head is a typical castration symbol. Œdipus does not defend himself with a proper weapon, but with a stick—again a usual sexual symbol —against his father's especially dangerous stick, and thus clears his path to his mother. The killing of a number of men serves to emphasize the hero's superiority. They are all merely minor representatives of the father's figure. Moreover, it is significant that the father first of all opposes the son, on which the latter deals the first blow, not at the father himself, but at the driver, i.e. a representative of the father. The father then attacks the son, and only at the end does the latter kill him in self-defence. Here is repeated the theme with which the myth opened: the father endeavours to destroy

[8] It is not my present intention to give an exhaustive analysis of the myth, I only mention a few points regarding the content of the symbolism.

the life of his new-born son; therefore Œdipus' later deed bears the character of retaliation, and thereby gains some extenuation.

Now we are familiar with a typical neurotic fantasy in which the son's conflict with the father is transplanted into the earliest past, i.e. into the period before the son's birth. These peculiar fantasies are well-known to every psycho-analyst, e.g. the fantasy of the son witnessing parental sexual intercourse while in his mother's body. Certain dreams, in which the dreamer wishes to pass along the birth passage, but finds his way barred by his father (i.e. his genital organ), occupy a special position among these products.

One of my patients dreamed he was on a ship coming from the sea into a canal; the ship got into a kind of morass and collided with a carman who was coming from the opposite direction with his cart. Ship and cart are quite comprehensible in this connection as male sexual symbols. The boggy canal represents the mother's bowel (earth). According to infantile theories procreation and birth take place by way of this passage. The dreamer coming from the sea on a ship reminds us of the representation of the birth of the hero in many sagas; [9] water is one of the most frequent birth symbols. I cannot here go into the individual determinants of this dream, but will return to the birth symbolism concealed in the Œdipus saga.

When the fatal meeting with Laios occurs, Œdipus is on his way to his yet unknown parents. In a narrow part of the road he meets his father who is driving towards him, just like the carman in my patient's dream. There can be no doubt that a birth fantasy is contained in the myth at this point; the son must, as it were, first remove his father out of the way in order to be born. Once more we are reminded of the beginning of the myth, namely, of that oracle which prophesied to Laios that his son would kill him and then marry his own mother. On hearing this Laios arranges that the new-born son should be exposed on the mountains with his feet pierced (castration symbol). The father therefore prevents the son's entry into life by exposure on the mountains, and the way to the mother by castration. Œdipus' later journey to Thebes is a second representation of his birth. Again his father appears in his path, and this time the son kills the father without recognizing him —the new-born child has always to learn to recognize its parents. In the rescue fantasy these tendencies are made unrecognizable by a higher degree of repression and distortion (conversion into the

[9] Cf. Rank, *Der Mythus von der Geburt des Helden.* Schriften zur angewandten Seelenkunde, No. 5, 2. Auflage, 1921.

opposite) than exists in the myth which we are comparing with it. As the analysis of the rescue fantasy gave us hints of the symbolic content of the Œdipus myth, so from this myth a new light is thrown on those deeper layers of the rescue fantasy which are subjected to extensive distortion.

Our knowledge of the rescue fantasy and œdipus complex can be supplemented from yet another side. Neurotics who produce father-saving fantasies occasionally furnish dreams which supplement these fantasies in a peculiar way. I will quote an example. The dream is as follows:

"I am sitting on the left of my mother in a little dog-cart to which one horse is harnessed. My father is standing by the off-wheel. His position signifies that he is speaking or has spoken to my mother, yet no words were heard; at all events my mother apparently took no notice. He looked very tired and pale. He turned away silently from the dog-cart and went off in an opposite direction to the one in which we were going. When I saw him disappear I expected he would soon come back, and turned to my mother, saying, 'We can drive to and fro in the meantime'. My mother made a slight movement with the reins which she held in her hands, and the horse began to move slowly. After a few moments I took the reins out of her hands, whipped up the horse, and we drove off quickly."

Psycho-analysts will easily recognize that this dream originated in the œdipus complex. The son takes the seat on his mother's left in the dog-cart, which is only built for two persons, and this seat is the husband's. The father is set aside, he looks pale and tired, keeps silence, and disappears. We must consider the expectation of his return as a product of dream distortion which was necessary to circumvent the censorship. While the removal of the father is represented in a relatively simple manner, the second chief constituent part of the œdipus fantasy, the union of the son with the mother, is concealed in a complicated symbolism which merits our particular consideration. The incest is represented by the journey of mother and son together. It begins significantly enough at the moment when the father has disappeared. Our dream therefore commences where the rescue fantasy ends; for this latter is concluded by the death of the father. Up to this moment the mother has curbed her libido and that of her son (libido = horse). When the son proposes "to drive to and fro" (symbol of coitus movement) it is the mother who gives the signal, and the horse starts (symbol of erection). The movement proceeds with increasing speed, which we understand in the sense discussed above.

In this dream we find the horse again representing male activity, but at the same time also the female libido, and besides this it is also a penis symbol, just as in the rescue fantasy. It is of interest, however, that in both instances the son takes possession of the reins, whereby he assumes the rôle of the father. One particularly striking agreement between the two fantasies is the "running away"; in the dream the mother runs away with the son, and this is accompanied by the increasing pace of the horse, just as in the fantasy of the bolting horses.

The foregoing analysis leaves no doubt that even the day-dreamings which are apparently most simple owe their origin to the co-operation of the most varied kinds of impulses. Hence they need a most careful analytic investigation into all their details. In the present case this analysis makes possible instructive comparisons with other fantasies which make use of very similar symbolisms. The symbolism of the carriage, horses, driving and the increasing speed is suited to bring to expression in a high degree of condensaion quite a number of repressed sexual tendencies. Along such paths we obtain an insight into the alternating phases of the struggle between impulse and repression, both in the individual and in the masses who create the myths.

TWO CONTRIBUTIONS TO THE STUDY OF SYMBOLS * (1925)

The importance of these two discoveries is in no way diminished by the doubt which one might entertain as to whether they actually concern "symbols" in the strictest sense of the word.

1. OBSERVATIONS ON THE SYMBOLIC MEANING OF THE NUMBER THREE

The frequent occurrence of the number three in the various products of the human imagination has long been a familiar fact. It is equally familiar that its symbolic meanings vary. As a symbol of the male genital the number three is especially well-known. In addition the number three is known to the triad—father, mother, and child. In the dreams of my patients I have several times met with the number three in another, less familiar meaning. In this connection it is not my intention to consider one of the numerous possibilities in the individual interpretation of the symbolism of numbers; rather, what I have in mind is a typical determination based on general human considerations.

There are three openings of the human body—oral, anal and urogenital, which attract the child's attention to a maximum degree because they serve at the same time to take in food and to evacuate, and besides possess the most important erotogenic functions. They seem to be represented in dreams by the number three, specially competing with one another. A neurotic patient of mine, whose dreams revealed to me the significance of the number three in a particularly forceful way, harboured in her unconscious an abundance of wish fantasies, partly of an oral-cannibalistic, partly of an anal character.

I have thought it worthwhile to point out a similar significance attaching to the number three in fairy tales and in myths. Psychoanalysis has disclosed to us how far-reachingly they coincide with individual fantasies. A very impressive parallel to the meaning of

* Translated from the original: *Zwei Beiträge zur Symbolforschung.* (*a*) Zur symbolischen Bedeutung der Dreizahl. (*b*) "Dreiweg" in der Oedipus-Sage. *Imago*, IX, 1925, p. 122.

the number three above referred to is contained in Grimm's fairy tale of the "Wishing-Table".

A father sends his three sons abroad. Each of them learns a craft, and his apprenticeship finished, he receives a gift from his master. The oldest is given a small table that, on order, carries everything one might care to eat. The second son receives a donkey who on the order: "Donkey, stretch out", spews forth gold pieces for its owners from his bowels. The third son receives a sack that contains a cudgel; when told to do so, the cudgel comes out of the sack, thrashes any adversary of its owner, and returns to the sack at the latter's command.

The first gift means a wish-fulfilment in the field of the oral zone. Every child probably wishes to obtain by the "omnipotence of his thoughts" any food at any time.

The second gift has a similar meaning. The appreciation of feces and their identification with gold are well-known to child psychology. The second gift means the fulfilment of the wish to procure oneself any sum of money by way of anal production.

What the third gift means is not quite so obvious, but we easily understand it if we remember the typical symbolic meaning of the cudgel. The sack with the stick cannot be misinterpreted. The orders given to the cudgel by its owner: "Out of the sack, cudgel", and "Into the sack, cudgel" make it clear that they mean erection followed by its opposite. Thus the third son is equipped with the gift of an unlimited potency which can be evoked at will.

Thus the fairy tale contains three wish-fulfilments which correspond to the three erotogenic zones. Their sequence coincides strikingly with the three phases of the libido discovered by Freud. In the first phase the erotogenic significance of the mouth prevails, in the second that of the anus, and in the third, the definite phase, that of the genitals.

Furthermore, it is noteworthy that at the beginning of the story the two older brothers laugh at the youngest. The oldest brother, however, soon loses his magic table to a fraudulent inn-keeper who, lodging him on his journey home, replaces it with an ordinary table. At home, the father derides him when he tries in vain to obtain delicious dishes by means of the table. The second brother does not fare any better with his donkey. He, too, is cheated by the inn-keeper, and laughed at by his father. On the basis of the psycho-analytic interpretation of fairy tales it may be presumed that both, inn-keeper and father, represent the jealous father. Only the youngest son defeats the inn-keeper through his virility, the symbol of which is the cudgel. It is he alone who obtains his father's recognition.

Thus this fairy tale confirms the actual experience that not through infantile fantasies of an oral or anal character does a boy become a man, but only through successfully establishing genital primacy. Our fairy tale is especially instructive, however, with regard to the symbolism of the number three.

2. "The Trifurcation of the Road" in the Legend of Œdipus

In a short paper on the symbolism of a neurotic rescue fantasy [1] I have attempted to prove that the fantasy of rescuing one's father corresponds in marked degree to the legend of Œdipus, and that this is true not merely with regard to the latent content of that legend. I tried to show that both fantasy structures make use of a similar symbolism in their presentation of a similar content. This similarity of symbols has not so far attracted our attention sufficiently. In the latent content of both fantasy structures, the son witnesses the sexual intercourse of his parents; he seeks to prevent this by killing his father, thus rescuing his mother.

In the Œdipus myth, the son's encounter with his father's fast-careering chariot (symbolism of coitus!) occurs at a particular spot. In the different versions of the myth a "narrow pass" or "cross-roads" are mentioned. The narrow pass as a symbol to the female genital would harmonize with the rest of the symbolism. The interpretation is more difficult in the other case. ὁδὸς σχιστή means, strictly speaking, not "cross-roads", but, literally, "divided-road"— which might be rendered by something like "parting of the ways". We find the expression "trifurcation" (Dreiweg) in a German translation of the tragedy of Sophocles. The symbol of the "narrow pass" easily fits into our theory. However, the "trifurcation" appears at first sight not very comprehensible.

Professor Freud called my attention to the difficulty of fitting in this detail when I submitted to him the above-mentioned paper for his opinion. There was apparently one obvious possibility of interpretation. The parting of the ways might, as in the myth of Hercules, symbolize a doubt on the part of the wanderer. Or Œdipus, at the moment of his encounter with King Laios, is in the gravest doubt

[1] Vaterrettung und Vatermord in den neurotischen Phantasiegebilden. (Father-Murder and Father-Rescue in the Fantasies of Neurotics, this volume, p. 299.)

about his lineage. But such an explanation would be much too rationalistic. Certainly it would not cover the latent content of this passage in the myth. Moreover, it would not answer the following objection. The narrow place is described as offering space for either Œdipus or the chariot of Laois. If it were a "divided road", it should be particularly easy for either one to make way for the other. Therefore, only such an interpretation of ὁδὸς σχιστή can be considered satisfactory as also explains the peculiarity of the story.

Considering these difficulties I completely left out of consideration in the referred to article, this particular question. Shortly afterwards a dream brought by a patient of mine gave to the trifurcation an explanation which in my opinion meets all requirements. This is the dream content:

"My mother has died, and I am attending the funeral. The scene then becomes indistinct. I go away and then return to the tomb. I am under the impression of being in Russia, and that Bolsheviks have profaned the grave. A hole has been dug in the ground. I see something white down below; it may be the shroud. Then the scene again changes. Now my mother's tomb is at a place where two roads meet, merging into a wide highway. The tomb rises only a little above the surrounding ground, cars run over it. The cars disappear, and now I myself am driving over it, to and fro."

Analysis reveals the incestuous character of the dream. In the unconscious of the patient there exist definite necrophilic fantasies. Not until his mother had died was he able to possess her. The violation of his mother (the digging of the hole in the mound) is ascribed to the Bolsheviks for reasons of "censorship". Frequently in the dreams of our patients the Bolsheviks represent those wishful impulses which defy conventional morals. According to the free associations of the dreamer, the shroud which is visible down below signifies the fact that the body is naked. The patient associates dark with white (hairiness). Thus in the dream, instead of the dreamer's own unconscious urge to violate his mother, we find this act already perpetrated by other persons. It should be noted that we speak of "violating" a tomb as well as "violating" a woman.

The indeterminate number of the malefactors (Bolsheviks) occurs in the dream in the form of the many cars which drive over the tomb. Prior to this, the tomb symbolized the mother who has been dishonoured by many men. The identification of mother with prostitutes thereby becomes more than obvious.

The place where several roads meet is of course characterized by particularly heavy traffic. We remember that places of heavy traffic, such as railway stations, department stores, etc. are frequently used as symbols of prostitution. At the same time we remember that the road symbolizes the female, the car the male genital organs. We can no longer misinterpret the meaning of the driving to and fro over that spot.

Another statement of the manifest content of the dream is of importance, namely the fact that the tomb rises a little above the ground. This is explained by the repressed fantasies of my patient who imagines finding a protuberance (penis) on the female body. In many of his dreams his mother appears with masculine functions, he himself with feminine functions. In the dream in question he plays the active part, under the peculiar assumption, however, that his mother is no longer alive.

His mother's tomb represents her body, and especially her genital. The two dream scenes contain such allusions. We have come to understand first the significance of the hole in the ground, and secondly that of the inconspicuous elevation. The spot where this flat tomb is found gives us a special indication which can scarcely be misunderstood. The two roads which merge into a wide highway are the two thighs which join with the trunk. Where they join is the site of the genitals!

As the dreamer approaches the scene where a number of men profane his mother, they vanish and he takes possession of her. *That is exactly what happens in the legend of Œdipus. Œdipus* encounters Laios, who is in the company of other men, at the *trifurcation.* Œdipus slays Laios and the others. Then he sets out on his way to find his mother. If we understand the symbolism of the ancient legend in this way, Œdipus' fight with Laios is a *fight for the genital of the mother.* So we understand why neither father nor son can yield to the other.

Thus we come to the unexpected result that the *trifurcation* has the same meaning as the *narrow pass.* The former symbolizes the site of the female genital; the latter its shape. The two versions nevertheless have different bearings. The version of the trifurcation (place of heavy traffic) definitely represents the mother as a prostitute. The encounter in the narrow pass gives expression to another concept, namely the fantasy of meeting one's father before birth inside one's mother's body (the fantasy of intra-uterine coitus observation). Further details regarding this problem are to be found in the paper referred to above.

OBSERVATIONS ON FERENCZI'S PAPER ON "SUNDAY NEUROSES" * (1918)

The following excerpts from Ferenczi's article in Further Contributions to the Theory and Technique of Psychoanalysis[1] *may serve as points of reference for Abraham's "Observations":*

". . . Sunday is the holiday of present-day civilized humanity. But one is mistaken if one thinks that a holiday is only significant as a day of physical and psychic rest; for the recuperation that it usually affords us, the factor of mood is of great importance. It is not only that on this day we are our own masters and feel ourselves free from all the fetters that the duties and compulsions of circumstances impose upon us; there occurs in us—paralleling this—a kind of inner liberation also. . . .

"But it is not given to everyone to vent their holiday wantonness so freely and naturally. The neurotically disposed will be inclined on precisely such occasions to a reversal of affect, either because he has much too dangerous impulses to control which he must mount guard over closely particularly when tempted by the bad example of others; or because his hypersensitive conscience will not overlook even little omissions. Beyond the untimely depression of these 'spoil-sports', however, their repressed impulses as well as the self-punishment fantasies mobilized against them, which have been activated by the holiday, may be manifested in little hysterical symptoms (headaches, depression, gastro-intestinal symptoms, oversleeping.) . . .

"An indication of the correctness of this conception is afforded by the fact that in addition to the periodic but quite transitory 'Sunday Neurosis' there also occurs a more protracted 'vacation neurosis'. Over and above the minor hysterical symptoms already mentioned, we find here quite frequently a peculiar and characteristic alteration of mood. I refer to a certain tense boredom which those afflicted with it are unable to dispel by any means of diversion,

---

* Translated from the original: Bemerkungen zu Ferenczi's Mitteilung über "Sonntagsneurosen", *Internationale Zeitschrift für Psychoanalyse*, V, 1918, p. 208, p. 203.

[1] The International Psychoanalytic Library # 11, edited by Ernest Jones, London, The Hogarth Press, 1926, pp. 174 ff.

accompanied at the same time with an incapacity for work which is painful to them 'Laziness with qualms of conscience'—'A laziness which you can't enjoy'—these are expressions with which one patient attempted to characterize this state of feeling. Another spoke of a longing for something undefined, and recalled having as a child pestered his mother by the hour with the vague demand: 'Mother, give me something!' Whatever his mother gave him on such occasions left him unsatisfied; he kept on whining until he got a good scolding or spanking; only then was he satisfied. May not such ungratified wishes also lie concealed behind Sunday Neuroses. . . .?

"The longing of mankind for holidays is as great as that for bread. Panem et circenses! Freud demonstrated in Totem and Taboo *why it was that the totem clan felt the impulse on certain occasions to tear to pieces the otherwise worshipped totem animal. And the Bacchanalia and the Saturnalia have their analogues among all peoples, including contemporary ones; even church holidays, and the Purim of the Jews, have affiliations therewith. We may suppose that certain slight residentuals of this atavistic striving for liberation are also involved in the weekly recurring holiday mood which Sunday represents, and in those emotionally sensitized, play a causative rôle in 'Sunday Neuroses'. . . ."* [2]

I, too, have not infrequently met with the temporary worsening of nervous conditions in relation to Sundays, holidays, vacation periods, etc. The following observations on the etiology of these vacillations are by no means intended to contravene Ferenczi's statements, but merely to supplement them to a certain extent.

A considerable number of persons are able to protect themselves against the outbreak of serious neurotic phenomena only through intense work. Owing to the exaggerated repression of their impulses, they are in constant danger of having their excess excitation transformed into neurotic symptoms. They make violent efforts to find escape from the demands of their libido by overstraining themselves in their vocational activities, in their studies, or in the discharge of other duties. They get into the habit of doing an amount of work far beyond normal requirements. Work becomes indis-

[2] The last two paragraphs of the above quotation, occurring in the original German text *Bausteine zur Psychoanalyse*, Int. Psa. Verlag, 1927, pp. 183–184 do not appear in the reprinting in *Further Contributions*, but were translated especially for *The Reader*.

pensable to them, just as morphine does to the morphinomaniac; and the urgency of this need steadily increases. When a neuropath of this kind suffers an outbreak of a real neurosis, physicians and laymen alike are prone to give a specious etiology, namely "overwork". In some cases work is unable to keep permanently in suppression the urge of libido. There comes a moment when the libido forces its way to expression, in however disguised form. In other cases, and these are the cases we are considering here, more or less serious and acute neurotic symptoms appear *if and when the work is interrupted by influences from without.* In this way the mental balance which has been maintained with difficulty through working is overturned for the duration of a Sunday, a holiday, or, possibly even for a longer period. When work begins again, the patient *immediately* feels better.

But there is another circumstance to be considered in addition. Most persons make use of a Sunday to enjoy themselves. They go to dances, for example; they keep company with persons of the opposite sex. Thus a Sunday reminds our patients unpleasantly of their inhibitions, and in particular of their being unable to approach the opposite sex. One of my patients avoided going on the street on Sundays, so as not to see pairs of lovers. He stayed at home, in a sad mood, restless and uneasy. This suffering from a feeling of insufficiency disappears when Sunday at last ends. On Mondays our patients are inclined to develop a certain feeling of superiority, because their co-workers are not as efficient as they are on "blue Monday".

During the war 1914–18, I watched many soldiers perform their military duties with exaggerated scrupulousness. By so doing they kept themselves comparatively free of symptoms. But every furlough had an unfavourable influence upon them in intensifying neurotic phenomena. There was, for example, an officer who suffered from serious neurotic difficulties during the involuntary inactivity of trench-warfare. He asked to be transferred to some other section of the front, preferably to one where much fighting was going on, in order to get rid of his neurotic difficulties.

When such a person is forced into inactivity by illness or accident, the outbreak of a neurosis, or the getting worse of an existing one is not infrequently the consequence. In such cases the popular tendency is to connect the neurosis etiologically with the illness, the accident, or whatever else may have occurred previously. But in many cases it can be ascertained at once that the repressed libido has overpowered the patient during the period of his forced inactivity.

With regard to the regular recurrence of "Sunday neurosis", I should like to call attention to the fact that there is another regular rhythm in the waxing and waning of neurosis that has not been dealt with in psycho-analytic literature. I am referring to the everyday vacillations in the condition of neurotics. Doctors are particularly familiar with the neurotic type which manifests a depressive mood in the morning and euphoria in the evening. It would be worthwhile to investigate separately and individually these peculiarities which characterize many neuroses. I know from a single case how an anxiety hysteria became worse every year in wintertime when the days were shortest and just as regularly disappeared with the lengthening of daylight hours.

THE HISTORY OF AN IMPOSTOR IN THE LIGHT OF PSYCHO-ANALYTIC KNOWLEDGE *
(1925)

An application of psycho-analysis to problems of biography, criminology and education.

The "Impostor" (note the deliberately descriptive diagnosis) is a study of an individual representative of a group of psychopaths who are known to psychiatrist, victim, and judge as "swindlers" or "confidence men". Their defect is a characterological *one; and Abraham shows that the essential prerequisite for a normal char- acter-formation appears actually to have been lacking in the infancy of his "patient". It is the* œdipus complex *that has never been developed and, consequently, could never be overcome by the im- poster, who therefore remained essentially narcissistic.*[1]

This "formula", although described from a single subject, who was not analysed but merely interviewed and observed, appears entirely valid. The child achieves the transition from narcissism to object-libido by first cathecting his œdipal objects and by exchang- ing them later for the members of the group in which he is destined to live. The lack of an œdipal constellation is therefore likely to prevent a satisfactory social adaptation. Deficient in object-libido, the "impostor" invites acceptance and rejection from his objects by displaying what might be termed but an "object-libidinal mode" of narcissistic behaviour. The unmitigated ambivalence, indigenous to the early stage from which his make-up derives, compels the monotonous repetition of a pattern which reflects—as perhaps we surmise at this date —a disturbed pre-œdipal phase, never brought to an end through an entry into the œdipus complex.

The clinical material upon which the following essay in criminal psychology is based was not obtained from psycho-analytical treat- ment in the strict sense of the word. The subject matter is the story

* First published in *Imago*, XI, 1925, p. 355, under the title: Die Geschichte eines Hochstaplers im Lichte psychoanalytischer Erkenntnis.
Reprinted from *The Psychoanalytic Quarterly*, IV, 1935, p. 570. Trans- lated by Alix Strachey.

[1] It is difficult to imagine the author's reasons for the omission of detail in regard to the adult *vitasexualis* of his subject.

of a man about whom I had to make a report from a psychiatric point of view, as an army doctor, in the year 1918, and whom I came across again five years later in unusual circumstances. The limited time allowed for making an official report of this kind and the conditions in which work had to be carried on at the medical station did not permit of a regular psycho-analysis.

Nevertheless the life of this man presents some quite extra-ordinary features from a psychological point of view; for in recent years his social behaviour underwent a reversal which was completely contrary to all psychiatric experience. But this element of the extra-ordinary—this contradiction of experience—can be satisfactorily explained if we take into consideration the familiar and well-grounded empiric findings of psycho-analysis. Again, the facts of this case seem specially well suited to prepare the ground for one of the future fields of application of psycho-analysis, i.e., criminology. I therefore hope that the unusual nature of the case will be held to justify its appearance in this psycho-analytical publication.

This man, whom I will call N., was twenty-two years old when he began his military service. He had already been convicted and imprisoned a number of times by civil courts in various parts of the country. He was sent into the army directly after his last term of imprisonment and there he received his military training. His superiors knew all about his former way of life; and yet the same thing happened there as had so often happened before. In a very short time N. had enlisted universal sympathy, had gained the confidence of his comrades and was looked upon with special favour by his company commander. At the same time he began to abuse the trust that was placed in him. But just as his frauds seemed about to come to light he and a number of his comrades received their marching orders and went to the Balkan front.

As nothing was known in his field regiment about his previous life it was still easier for N. to win the confidence of the authorities by his astute behaviour. As a professional draughtsman he soon found employment; but his demeanour also made him seem especially suited to carry out business transactions. And so he was entrusted with money and allowed to make purchases for his company in the towns near where they were halted. In the town of "X" he got to know two or three soldiers who were living there in great style, and he was at once seized with his old propensity (about which I will speak later). He, too, set up to be an important person and in four days he spent one hundred and sixty marks of the money which had

been given into his keeping. During a second expedition of this kind
he found out that his defalcations had been discovered. So instead
of returning to his regiment he moved on to a larger town. Here he
put stripes on his uniform and passed as a corporal. He had also got
hold of some railway passes and had them stamped while he was
with his company, so that he would now travel anywhere he pleased.
He returned to Germany. But here, and in Berlin especially, the
military supervision was too strict and he met too many old acquaintances to be able to stay any length of time; so he set off for
Budapest, having first donned the insignia of a colour sergeant. From
there he travelled to Bucharest, falsifying his passes all the time. Here
the military police were so watchful that he returned to Budapest,
where he succeeded in gaining the *entrée* into highly respected
families. He was delightfully ready to help them to obtain food, and
in this way he received considerable advances in money from them,
which he used for his own purpose instead of procuring the food he
had promised. When things became too hot for him in Budapest he
went to Vienna. There he was soon caught and sent back to his own
garrison town. It may already be noted that N. could win over with
the greatest ease persons of every age and class, men and women
alike, and then cheat them, but that he never showed any great aptitude for evading the arm of the law. It was only after he had been
captured that his ability showed itself once more. What happened
was that he very soon lulled the suspicions of his captors and so
made his escape without having to resort to any kind of force.

When N. had been in custody for two and a half months he had
gained such an influence over his jailers, who were in all other
respects conscientious and experienced men, that the gates, as it
were, opened before him of their own accord. One of his jailers was
called away while he was talking to N. in his cell and, being now
quite unsuspicious, left his keys behind him. N. took them, unlocked
the doors and was a free man. He wandered on till he came to a small
railway station, boarded a train and got off at the nearest large town.
Everywhere he managed to take the responsible officials in. He
worked for three weeks as a painter in a warehouse. Then, being in
danger of discovery, he had to leave the town. Armed with forged
papers he travelled through the length and breadth of Germany.
He once more masqueraded as a fine gentleman in one city and,
setting up to be an art critic, got money on false pretences from
his new patrons and spent it right and left. After a period of this
"civilian life" our hero was obliged to quit the scene of his activities.

He spent a short time in Berlin and then returned to Budapest.
There for the first time he put on the uniform of an officer. He went
back to Germany as a "lieutenant" and lived for months on a grand
scale in a number of watering places, all of the best kind. As a young
officer he had access to the best company in all of them. His assured
and amiable manner always made him the centre of a wide circle of
acquaintances in a very short time. As soon as the danger of being
found out in his countless frauds became too great in any of those
places he would vanish to a large health resort in Upper Bavaria and
then reappear after a time in another watering place. In the meanwhile he promoted himself to first lieutenant, which was the highest
rank he could attain at his age. No one guessed the real facts about
this young officer who was decorated with war medals and who
related his experiences in such an interesting and modest fashion.
Finally, however, he was arrested and once more taken to his garrison
town.

The charges against him had assumed vast proportions. He had
been guilty of desertion, had pretended to have a commission in the
army, and had committed an extraordinarily large number of em-
bezzlements, forgeries and frauds.

The military court which was enquiring into N.'s case showed
a complete understanding of and interest in his psychological peculiarities, and as the presence of some kind of pathological compulsion
in his behaviour was suspected, a psychiatric examination of his
condition was ordered to be made.

I saw N. on the first occasion in his detention cell. It was at once
evident that his case was so complicated as to necessitate his being
kept for a fairly long period at my observation station. But the latter
possessed no adequate arrangements for preventing a prisoner—
and such a clever prisoner—from escaping. At my suggestion the
court ordered that he should be put in an attic in my hospital and
kept under supervision there. Three especially reliable and intelligent volunteers were to mount guard over him. In order to prevent
his gaining any influence over them they had strict orders not to go
into his room and not to talk to him.

N. was accordingly taken to the hospital by his three guards. No
difficulty was experienced in doing this. But ten minutes later,
wishing to make certain that he was being properly looked after and
guarded, I went up to his room and found to my astonishment
that there was no guard outside his door—only two empty chairs.
Entering his room I came upon an unexpected scene. N. was sitting

at a table, drawing. One of his guards was posing as a model and the other two were looking on. It appeared that N. had already made friends with them on the way to the hospital by telling them about his talents as a draughtsman and had promised to draw their portraits. During his stay at my station, which lasted for several weeks, N. made no attempts at flight and behaved perfectly well.

In order to be able to make a judgment about N.'s mental condition I had, first of all, to get to know his early history. Since he seemed to have a special talent for telling fantastic stories I had to be very cautious about accepting his statements about himself and to verify them from authoritative sources. But I may say at once that all that he told me about his past was in agreement with the official information on the subject. I could never discover that he had suppressed any facts or made false additions to them or altered them in his favour. On the contrary, he spoke of his delinquencies with the greatest frankness, as he did later on before the court. But he was unwilling to talk about his intimate feelings and thoughts.

I soon learned from N. that his transgression dated from very early years. And his record at the reformatory where he had been sent for several years confirmed his statement.

N. was the youngest of a large number of brothers and sisters. His father was a minor official and the family was poor. There was no particular indication of any hereditary mental taint. But even as a small boy N. had, in contrast to his older brothers and sisters, shown an uncontrollable desire to be grand. When, at the age of five, he was taken to spend the mornings at a kindergarten he turned away from the less well-dressed children and would play only with the children of well-to-do families. As soon as he went to school he noticed with envy that many boys had nicer things than he, that they had decorated and varnished pencil-cases or coloured pens. So one day—he was six at the time—he went to a stationer's near the school and pretended that he was the son of a general who lived in the neighbourhood. He at once got the things he wanted on credit; and now he could proudly hold his own with the sons of the rich. This first fraud of his was of course soon discovered and he was punished. But his desire to be able to vie with his more fortunate fellows was unconquerable and found expression in further misdeeds. One of his schoolmates possessed a large army of toy soldiers, whilst he had only a few. His longing not to be outdone left him no peace. He finally stole six or seven marks from his mother, bought some toy soldiers and showed his schoolfellows that he had as many and as fine soldiers as the other boy.

At school, N. was seen to be a talented boy from the very beginning. But it seemed as if his work did justice to his capacities only so long as he felt he was being noticed or favoured in some way by his teacher. He was constantly occupied with wild ideas of running away. On one occasion he got money from his teacher on false pretences. On other occasions he used to borrow books from his comrades and sell them. An attempt was made to get him to go through a higher school; but this failed because he had not the necessary perseverance. The fantastic streak in him was continually cropping up. One of his teachers remarked that he seemed to be suffering from megalomania. His school career was therefore put an end to and he went into a commercial house as an apprentice.

Up till now N.'s wrongdoings had been almost entirely confined to school and family life. As an apprentice he soon proceeded to steal the postage money and was dismissed after a few months. He found another position, but he did not like it and left it on his own account after a few days. Next he was sent into a gardener's business; but he soon ran away from it, got into bad company and drifted about until he was finally put into a reformatory.

What was so often to happen to him later on happened in the reformatory. The director, recognizing N.'s artistic talents and his desire to rise in the social scale, tried to satisfy both these things along proper channels. N., as a favourite pupil, felt fairly comfortable here, and for some time there seem to have been no complaints about him. Through the director's good offices he was allowed, although still a reformatory boy, to go to a polytechnic in another town. But here he was without the steadying influence of his patron and after a little while he became involved in a criminal charge and had to leave the school. When he came back to the reformatory he behaved as so many youths do in such circumstances. Having received some real or supposed slight he ran away, and during the short time in which he was at large, he was guilty of all sorts of misdemeanors.

At nineteen he turned up in Berlin and got a job there. But he did hardly any work, set up to be a gentleman and made bad debts. He managed to make his way into good society, as he had always wanted to do. The reformatory boy became a welcome guest in very exclusive student circles. In dress, mode of life and behaviour he had become a member of the upper class. But the sources from which he obtained the means of doing this were distinctly shady, and in the end he had to take to his heels to avoid arrest. Now began a regular Odyssey through South Germany, the Tyrol and Switzerland. Everywhere he went he committed punishable actions by leaving debts unpaid and swindling in all sorts of ways; and everywhere he was prosecuted by the law. In Switzerland he spent a month in prison and then had to leave the country. Back again in Germany, he served a number of sentences for his previous derelictions. He wandered from court to court and from prison to prison. During his last period in prison he quickly gained the good will of the governor and was entrusted with the care of the prison library. After he had served all his sentences he was sent to the army, as we already know. This was in 1915.

I shall for the present give only the general drift of my report on N., and leave what I have to say about him from a psychological point of view to a later point. I could not discover that N. was suffering from any mental disorder in the usual sense of the word; nor was there the slightest sign of mental deficiency. On the contrary, he was a man whose intelligence was above the average and who had considerable artistic gifts. His deviation from the normal consisted solely in his social behaviour. I assumed that there was a deep-seated disturbance of his emotional life which was responsible for his antisocial impulses. Even under the most favourable circumstances such impulses had been absent in him only for very short periods of time. They would very soon break out again with what was clearly an irresistible force.

The clinical description of cases like these uses the expression "moral insanity". But the law does not recognize the fact that an abnormal state of emotional life can render a man unaccountable for his actions. The military court, whose attitude to the prisoner was extremely humane and understanding, could not question N.'s responsibility and was obliged to pass a longish sentence on him in accordance with the letter of the law.

I may say that in my report on N. I stated that, according to general psychiatric experience, his condition was permanent and unalterable.

I heard nothing more on N. between the date of his conviction in August, 1918, just before the end of the war, and four or five years later, when I was asked by a civil court to make a fresh report on him. The circumstances were remarkable. It appeared that up till the spring of 1919 N. had been guilty of a series of offences along

the old lines. In the course of his examination before a magistrate—
an examination which, for one reason or another dragged on for
years—N. had stated that he had committed those offences under
the influence of his old pathological compulsion, but that shortly
afterwards his criminal impulses, which had existed since childhood,
had completely left him. Since the last four years he had settled
down and had stuck to his work and never transgressed the law.

If N.'s statements were true I had made a great mistake in my
judgment of his case, especially in my prognosis of it. The first thing
to do was to ascertain what his behaviour really had been since his
conviction five years ago. From what he now told me himself and
from what I learned from official sources I was able to reconstruct
the following story:

When the war was over, N. was set free under the terms of a
very extensive amnesty. He at once proceeded to commit a series
of offences of the old kind. In the general upheaval which took place
after the war a clever person like himself found plenty of profitable
opportunities. In spite of his long record of detentions and convictions, he was able everywhere to gain the confidence of persons
in authority, only to abuse it sooner or later. At that time so-called
"volunteer corps" and other military organizations were being
formed. N. belonged to a number of these within the space of a few
months. In each of them he was received with open arms, and
his popularity was shown by the fact that he was invariably made
treasurer. He would then embezzle the money, be obliged to quit
the force, and begin his game somewhere else. On one occasion
his assertion that he had been an officer in the war was believed and
he was given a commission in the force and did in fact discharge the
duties of an officer in it.

But the opportunities in this direction soon came to an end and N.
had to return to civilian life. Between March and June of 1919 he
behaved in the old way, stealing money, bilking his creditors and so
on, and was wanted by the police in various places.

Then came the great change. There was no doubt, from the
evidence before me, that since June, 1919, N. had not committed
a single illegal action and had never been prosecuted or wanted by
the police or any other authority. Reliable witnesses deposed that
he had a fixed abode and worked hard. His professional work was
highly thought of. Two commercial men of good repute in whose
business N. had had a position stated that they had found him absolutely loyal and dependable especially in financial matters, and this

for several years. Both witnesses knew all about N.'s former life and had kept a sharp eye on him, but they had never discovered any cause for complaint. N. was married and led the life of a respectable middle-class family man. He was well liked and respected in the society of the town in which he lived although he now no longer sought, as of old, to impress his fellow men.

The evidence left no doubt whatever that N. had completely changed his mode of life. But such a change ran counter to all accepted psychiatric experience. If an individual exhibits an asocial attitude at such an early age and has not adapted himself to social life by the time he is twenty-six, but has lived all along a life of fraud and imposture, as was the case with N., all that we know about such behaviour obliges us to deny the possibility of a spontaneous cure. Nor did we know of any forces which could exert this unwonted effect. Very unusual circumstances must have come into play here— circumstances which we do not in practice expect to come across.

The solution of the problem was a psychological one. We will therefore first turn our attention to N.'s life and consider certain facts and esperiences in it and his reactions to them. I may mention that while I was examining him in 1918 he was less inclined to talk to me on this subject. I was his military superior, and at that time his attitude to every representative of paternal authority was still too rebellious and defiant (why this was so we shall presently see), but when I saw him again in 1923 the impression he gave was that he quite accepted our relative positions. He felt that he was my equal in civil life and could tell me about himself without any of his old distrust. Thus our second meeting, although much shorter, furnished me for the first time with many important and even fundamental explanations of his social behaviour in former days and gave the clue to his recent transformation.

As has been said, N. was the youngest of a large family in straitened circumstances. There was a long interval of time between him and his brothers and sisters who were half or quite grown up when he was born. As a small child and later he used again and again to hear his mother say how unwelcome he had been as her late-born offspring. While the elder children were already able to earn a little, he was merely another mouth to feed and he used to hear unkind remarks about himself which showed that he was simply looked on as a burden on the family budget. Quite contrary to what is so often the case with late or last-born children, he felt that his parents and his brothers and sisters not only did not love him but were hostile to him. And, in the last resort, his social behaviour was a reaction to this impression of his early childhood.

We need only call to mind the well-substantiated psycho-analytical observation that children gather their first experiences of love and, indeed, learn how to love in relation to their earliest *entourage*. Under circumstances such as I have just described a child cannot develop a satisfactory object-love. His first attempts to direct his libido on to the human beings around him must necessarily fail; and he will then be involved in a backward-flowing narcissistic cathexis of the ego, while at the same time he will produce a strong attitude of hatred towards his objects.

Seen from this angle, N.'s conduct in the kindergarten and at school becomes perfectly comprehensible. He scorned his parents as they had scorned him. He wanted to have rich parents who would not regard him as an economic liability. From very early on he showed his most attractive side to every person who could stand for his father or his mother or his brothers and sisters. Every teacher and every schoolfellow must be fond of him—must provide a perpetual source of gratification for his narcissism. But his identification of the people around him with his family went still further. He had to disappoint those who loved him so as to be revenged on them. That everybody without exception should be taken in by him afforded his narcissism additional gratification of an intense sort. We may call to mind a word that has entered into many languages and say that N., who felt unloved in early childhood, was under an inner necessity to be "amiable", that is, "able to be loved", to all people, only to show that he was "unable" to deserve such a feeling. This method of behaviour is reminiscent of the dichronous actions—i.e., actions consisting of two phases—of obsessional neurotics.

N.'s craving to be the centre of a large circle of people deserves special attention. He told me himself that his greatest pleasure was to feel that "everything was revolving round him". Such a situation was in fact the direct opposite of his position as a child. It is true that N. invariably managed to put a sudden end to this glorious position. Obeying an irresistible compulsion to repeat, no sooner had he won everybody's favour than he had once more to become an outcast. And then, one day, there came the still unexplained transformation.

In June, 1919, N. was wandering from one town to another and living from hand to mouth by obtaining false credit and by other fraudulent means. Then a piece of good fortune befell him, the importance of which for a man like him cannot fail to strike the psycho-analyst.

N. got to know a woman who began to feel an interest in him at their very first meeting. She was considerably older than he and was a partner in an industrial concern. As soon as she heard about his having no work and being destitute she undertook to help him. In her firm he found a field for his artistic talents which was well paid and brought him into contact with people of good standing. He entered into a more intimate relation with his benefactress, who was a widow with several half-grown-up children. Later on he married her, and rose to a place of responsibility in the business, which incidentally ensured him a very good social position. In this ideal situation of security and contentment he had only one worry—the various prosecutions which were still hanging over his head.

When I saw N. again in 1923 this situation of external happiness and, I think I may say, of internal peace had become stabilized in the course of a few years. Before that he had been obliged to give up every good position he had had from some pressing, unconscious need. Why had this not happened in this instance, and why had he been able to enjoy the fruits of his change of fortune and live on good terms with his fellow men?

A simple psycho-analytic proposition will provide the answer. All his former states of passing prosperity had only represented a momentary gratification of his narcissism. But a state of that sort carried within it the seeds of its own destruction. N.'s ambivalent impulses were far too strong to allow him to attain any kind of mental equilibrium. It may be, too, that a strong unconscious sense of guilt was attached to his temporary "successes", which quickly put an end to his happiness, as an act of self-punishment.

I have already tried to show that in N.'s case his libido became fixed in a state of narcissism as a result of a regressive process, brought on by the severe disillusionment he had suffered in early childhood. In other words, N. had not, as a small boy, been able to extract as much pleasure of his œdipus attitude as other children do (though in very varying degrees). He had not had enough love from his mother; and he had not the possibility of elevating his father into an ideal figure. On the contrary, we see that he had very early been dominated by the wish to have a different father. Furthermore, he had not been able to identify himself with his brothers and sisters in his œdipus struggle against his father; for they and his parents had formed a world of enemies around him. Thus his œdipus complex underwent no proper development, and as a natural consequence none of those processes of sublimation could take place which testify to a successful mastery of the œdipus complex and without which the individual cannot find his proper place in the organism of society.[1]

The transformation which took place in N.'s life in 1919 signified nothing less than a complete reversal of his situation at home when he was a small child: A woman, older than himself, takes a liking to him at first sight and showers proofs of her maternal solicitude upon him; and presently she shows that she loves him. No one stands in the way of this love between mother and son, for her husband is long since dead. There are two sons who have a prior right to her love; but she prefers him, although he has appeared so late in her life, and marries him and thus puts him and not her own sons in the place of her dead husband.

Thus, apart from suddenly finding himself in comfortable circumstances both from a social and a financial point of view, N. obtained through this woman a complete fulfilment of all the childhood wishes that arose from his œdipus complex. When I alluded to the obvious significance of a mother that his wife had for him he answered, "You are certainly right. Very soon after I got to know her I used to call her 'little mother', and I still can't call her anything else." And as he spoke he showed strong feelings of affection and gratitude. These feelings showed that he was experiencing something more than the mere gratification of a narcissistic craving for love. I got the impression that he had achieved, later in life and in relation to a substitute person, something which he had not been able to achieve in his childhood—that is, a libidinal transference on to his mother. I do not, of course, mean to say that he had evolved a fully formed object-love, had completely overcome his narcissism; but simply that he had managed to effect some degree of progression

---

[1] We must not forget that the œdipal attitude, which we rightly regard as the source of serious and lasting conflicts in the mental life of the child and growing youth, is at first a source of real and imaginary pleasure. The child, however, learns gradually to give up the major and most important part of its wishes in this connection (that is, those wishes which are socially unacceptable) if it is granted a certain restricted amount of pleasure. Such a sum of pleasure seems to be essential in helping the child successfully to overcome its ambivalence towards its parents. If it receives no pleasure at all, it will not manage to modify its œdipus complex properly and all its libido will flow back to its ego once more.

of libido from its narcissistic fixation towards object-love—how much I do not know. Only a proper psycho-analysis of his case could tell us any more than this.

It may furthermore be pointed out that none of these fulfilments of N.'s wishes involved a sense of guilt. There was no father for him to put aside, since he was already long since dead. There was no need for him to make an attack upon the mother, since she came forward of her own will both as a tender mother and as a loving mistress. There were no brothers and sisters for him to combat, for they completely accepted his special position in the new family. Thus, for the first time in his life, N. was in a position to enjoy exclusive and, it may be added, irreproachable pleasures.

This attitude on the part of a mother-representative who lavished on him not only her maternal solicitude but her erotic feelings had brought him a late fulfilment of those œdipus wishes which had remained ungratified in his childhood; but it had also drawn his libido away from its narcissistic adherence. And so for the first time he succeeded in transferring a certain amount of libido on to an object.

Such a complete psychological fulfilment of an infantile wish-situation as this must be regarded as an exceptional event. One can in no way reckon upon the advent of what did in fact happen, as if by a miracle, to N. Therefore I think that the pessimistic prognosis of my report was in general justified, although in this one instance it turned out to be wrong.

It was justified in another respect, too. When N. came to see me for the last time he himself laid stress on the fact that things were going well with him. But at the same time, being an intelligent man, he had certain fears. He said that he must admit to himself and to me that it all depended upon his relations to his wife whether the present situation would last. If that relationship should ever be undermined he was certain that his old proclivities would break out again; for, at bottom, his old, instinctual unrest was still there.[2]

We might be tempted to call N.'s case an instance of "cure

[2] I may refer the reader to the second report on N., in 1923, which showed that his last offences were committed just before the great change occurred, so that they were on a par with all his earlier ones, that is, they were manifestations of an irresistible impulse coming from unconscious sources.

through love", if we were certain that he really had been cured in the sense that his improvement was a permanent one. But be that as it may, so great a transformation in the social behaviour of a man with such a history as N.'s is a remarkable phenomenon which can be understood only from the point of view of the psycho-analytical theory of the libido.

But from a practical point of view, too, this change deserves our fullest attention. The present case shows very impressively that we should not overestimate the part played by hereditary taint—by "degeneration"—in the origins of dissocial and criminal impulses. What the prejudiced eye of academic psychology still persists in regarding as innate and therefore unalterable in the individual we must consider as to a great extent acquired during the early years of life and must trace back to the operation of very early impressions of a psycho-sexual nature. This not only implies a revision of erroneous views; it gives us new possibilities, new points of departure and new angles of approach for the treatment of dissocial persons, especially adolescents.

I am glad to say that on this subject I find myself in complete agreement with Dr. Aichhorn, whose knowledge of this class of individuals is so comprehensive. Aichhorn's [3] writings have shown how important is the pupil's positive transference to the teacher in reformatory schools; and he had rightly made the establishment of such a transference the keystone of reformatory education.

If we bear in mind the magical effect that N.'s first successful transference had on him when he was already a grown man we can form some idea of the results that might follow from a properly established and well-directed transference in youthful individuals. As a reformatory boy N. had, it is true, been lucky in finding a humane and understanding teacher. But what this teacher did not succeed in doing, in spite of his sympathetic attitude, was to set up a lasting transference. This lack of a firm emotional tie allowed N. to relapse into his old ways and did not enable permanent instinctual sublimations to be formed. These sublimations were not achieved until his libido had been, for the first time, lastingly transferred to someone.

We practising psycho-analysts in particular have often complained that our therapeutic work covers only a relatively small class

[3] Verwahrloste Jugend. *Die Psychoanalyse in der Fürsorgeerziehung.* Int. Psa. Bibliothek, Bd. XIX, 1925. Translated into English: *Wayward Youth.* New York: Viking Press, 1935.

of persons and that, although it penetrates deeply into each individual case, it does not extend over a wide class of cases. If we agree with Aichhorn's view that, generally speaking, the establishment of a transference is a sufficient basis for enabling dissocial youths to be influenced, whereas it is only those cases which are complicated by neurotic disturbances which require a regular psycho-analytic treatment, we should find opened to us a new field of activity in which the knowledge obtained by the analytic observation and treatment of neurotics would find ample scope. Aichhorns' thesis is a very promising educational advance which has been made possible by Freud's psychological discoveries. We cannot but admire the generous eagerness with which Aichhorn is endeavouring to push forward his educative work.

Let us take a last look at the life story of our impostor. In the psycho-analysis of neurotics we often come across the consequences of too much spoiling in early years, with the result that the child's demand for love has been unnecessarily encouraged. Among "dissocials" we shall, I think, more often find that the libido has undergone a different fate in early life. In them, it is the lack of love which being, as it were, a lack of spiritual nourishment, is the first predisposing cause of the appearance of dissocial characteristics. It creates too great an amount of hatred and rage, which are first directed against a small circle of persons but later grow to include the whole social environment. Where there is a predisposing cause of this kind, the child will not naturally develop a character which can make good social adaptations. The existence of a narcissistic regression of the libido, such as was to be inferred in N.'s case would also point to an inhibition in the formation of character, an arrestation on a lower level.

In time, too, these findings of psycho-analysis will have to receive the recognition that is their due in criminological quarters. Quite recently Reik has made a comprehensive study of the sense of guilt [4] and has established an important line of connection between analytical research into the neuroses and criminology. There are two respects in which the theories of psycho-analysis can be of service to the knowledge of crime and the criminal. In the first place, analysis provides new psychological points of approach for an understanding of the person concerned. In the second place, the treatment of young dissocial persons on psycho-analytic lines, or in harmony with those

[4] Reik, Theodor: *Geständniszwang und Strafbedürfnis*. Int. Psa. Bibliothek, Bd. XVIII, 1925.

lines seems to hold out hope of preventing them from committing criminal offences.

I hope that the present contribution will have added a little towards the establishment of a connection of this sort between psycho-analysis and the science of crime.

V

REFERENCES BY FREUD

REFERENCES BY FREUD

Distinguished by their brevity from all other articles in The
Reader, *and by Freud's having made references to them, each
item collected herein treats a narrowly circumscribed subject.
Whether confirming or illustrating, applying or supplementing a
tenet of Freud, all of these communications have, in time, become
addenda to his writings. Passages contained in articles of length
are excerpted; short articles are reprinted in full. Each piece of work
is preceded by Freud's reference to it, in lieu of an introduction.*

DREAMS IN PAIRS

FREUD: "Franz Alexander, in his essay on pairs of dreams, shows that not infrequently two dreams which occur on the same night play separate parts in the fulfilment of the dream function, so that taken together they provide a wish-fulfilment in two steps, a thing which each alone does not do. If a dream-wish has as its content some piece of forbidden behaviour towards a certain individual, then that person may appear in the first dream undisguised, while the behaviour is only faintly indicated. In the second dream it will be the other way around. The behaviour will be openly shown, but the person will be made unrecognizable, or else some indifferent person will be substituted for him. . . . A second and similar relation between two members of a pair of dreams is that in which the one represents the punishment and the other the sinful wish-fulfilment. It is as if one said, 'If I take the punishment on myself, then I can do the forbidden thing.' " [1]

ALEXANDER: It very often happens that two or more dreams in the same night stand in some sort of relation to one another. In the *Traumdeutung* Freud speaks of the way in which successive dreams which all contain the same latent content grow progressively clearer. Often, however, the relation between pairs of dreams is still closer: not only is the content connected but there is also a dynamic or, more correctly, an economic connection. A certain dynamic relation between pairs or series of dreams which express the same wish is nearly always present. The following is the simplest type of a relation of this sort. The first dream may, for instance, express the incest-wish, the sexual act being disguised symbolically. For example: "I am driving a carriage with my mother." In the second dream the act is disguised less, or not at all, but the incestuous object is replaced by a harmless one. The two dreams are then complementary to one another and permit, as it were, a complete gratification of the wish in two stages, by which it escapes the notice of the censor. The obvious economic gain for the repressed tendency is that through dividing the gratification into two stages a fuller satisfaction is

[1] *New Introductory Lectures on Psychoanalysis*, New York, W. W. Norton & Co., Inc., 1933; Lecture I: Revision of the Theory of Dreams, p. 42.

rendered possible, though the economic work of the censor remains the same. Both the symbolically disguised sexual intercourse with an incestuous object and the manifest sexual act with an indifferent person are, if taken alone, capable of entering consciousness; they express the real wish, however, only incompletely. But taken in connection with each other, the second dream having reference to the first, they constitute a complete representation of the repressed tendency. If we look out for it we come across this mode of representation so frequently that it is superfluous to give examples.

There is another, more interesting and more complicated mechanism, very like the one I have just mentioned. Here the economic connection is still closer: the second dream only arises out of the first and is conditioned by it. We see this mechanism plainly in the following pairs of dreams:

Dream I: "A wedding-feast is in preparation. My brother is going to marry my *fiancée*, but the clergyman fails to appear and so the wedding cannot take place. I say to my brother that probably we could find another clergyman. However, nothing happens and the wedding cannot take place."

Dream II (the same night): "We and a girl whom we know are looking at photographs together. Amongst them we see the photograph of my brother-in-law's mistress. We both begin to laugh because she is so plain, and I say that my brother-in-law would certainly maintain that she looked very interesting."

The patient had the day before brought to the analysis a dream which, as we shall soon see, had a similar latent content, but which we did not discuss during the analytic hour. "A Chinaman and an Englishwoman who live in the same boarding-house as myself wish to have intercourse. I should have to be present because there is no other room available, but it would be extremely embarrassing to me to be forced to witness the act. Fortunately, however, nothing happens."

Different as their manifest content is, all three dreams have the same meaning. In the first the brother's wedding is frustrated (there is no clergyman there) but, in order to shift the blame from himself and to hide his malicious joy over the disaster to the marriage, it is the dreamer who is the person to say, with a gesture of hypocrisy, that they could probably find another clergyman, as though he himself were very anxious for the wedding to take place. In discussing the dream the patient soon remembered a scene in which his elder brother had a quarrel with his wife and said that he would get a divorce. On that occasion the patient detected in himself a secret joy and was ashamed of his own malice.

The meaning of the second dream is expressed more directly and is almost undisguised. In this dream the patient is laughing at a girl whom his brother-in-law had already thrown over and who was very plain, and, moreover, he was doing this together with another girl who also disliked the one at whom they were laughing. The question is: why does the second of the two girls appear in the dream and why does he need a companion in giving way to his malicious satisfaction? The answer to this question reveals the real meaning of the dream. The girl in whose company he laughs at his brother-in-law's former mistress shares his antipathy to her. And it is the reason for the dislike displayed by the girl who appears in the dream which is the essential *tertium comparationis*: the two girls are rivals. So that the dreamer chooses this girl to share in his derisive laughter because he hates the brother-in-law's mistress from a similar motive, namely, from jealousy. This reveals his passive homosexual fixation to his brother-in-law, which gives rise to the wish to separate him from his mistress. Or, to put it more accurately, it shows his malicious satisfaction in the separation which has already taken place and in the fact of the girl's ugliness. Similarly, the desire to frustrate his brother's wedding arises out of a passive fixation to him.

The difference between the two dreams is this: in the second, the dream about the brother-in-law, the malice is openly expressed and its homosexual motives are clearly indicated in the part played by the girl who shares his feelings, while in the dream about his brother the only thing manifest is the interest, ego-syntonic but none the less hypocritical, in his brother's wedding taking place. To put it quite shortly: in the first dream the latent wish is more strongly repressed. Or to express it in another way: the dream about the brother corresponds more closely to the demands of the superego, even though this is really deceived by the dreamer's hypocrisy, for after all the wedding cannot take place. Now the economic reason for this difference is obvious: feelings against the illicit relations of his brother-in-law are less strongly condemned by the censor (super-ego) than similar feelings against his brother's legal marriage. And in the main the homosexual fixation to the brother-in-law is not so strongly repressed, as being less incestuous, than that to his brother. But there is another dynamic factor which I wish to empha-size, and it is just this which interests us now. In the first dream the patient behaves in a most lofty manner; only in the second dream does he reap the benefit of this hypocritical self-mastery. For, having done his best to promote his brother's marriage in the first dream, he is able in the second to indulge with a quiet conscience in malicious feelings against his brother-in-law's mistress. In the first dream he satisfies the moral demands of the superego; in the second he is free to transgress again. The moral credit which he acquires in the earlier dream is used to pay for his guilt in the later, and release an uninhibited gratification of the repressed tendency. His untroubled enjoyment of his malicious feelings in the second dream is made possible by his moral behaviour of the first.

I would now recall that the patient had brought to the previous sitting a dream the latent content of which was similar to that of the pair of dreams. It is only from this first dream that we can understand the deepest unconscious basis of the other two. Here sexual intercourse between the Englishwoman who lived in his boarding-house and the Chinaman is frustrated. The meaning is clear. The boarding-house corresponds to his home. The circumstance in the dream that he was obliged to be present during coitus, because there was no other room available, is an allusion to his parents' bedroom, where he slept as a little child; and the alien inhabitants, the Chinaman and the Englishwoman, are contrast-figures for his nearest relations, his father and mother. The most deeply repressed wish in all three dreams is that of hindering his parents' coitus and separating them from one another.. The wish to separate which recurs in all three dreams—the brother-in-law from his mistress, the brother from his wife, the Chinaman from the Englishwoman, refers ultimately to the parents. Here we observe a certain sequence. The more the persons are disguised the less does the action need to be masked. Thus, in the dream of the foreigners the sexual act is clearly retained, while the incestuous objects are not only disguised but actually transformed into contrast-figures. In the dream about the brother-in-law the wish to separate appears in a modified form as malicious delight in the ugliness of the woman. In the dream about the brother, where an incestuous object (the brother) makes his appearance, the wish to separate is directly denied. This is an example of the mechanism I described at the beginning.

The mechanism by which the allaying of the feeling of guilt in the first dream makes it possible for an otherwise repressed wish to be gratified without inhibition in the second is plainest in pairs of dreams of which the first is a punishment-dream and the second a wish-fulfilment, sometimes actually ending in a pollution. I will give an instance of two such dreams.

Dream I: "I am on the sea-shore. My brother comes up in a rowing-boat. He gets out but immediately jumps back into the water by the boat. The boatman is very angry with him for jumping back into the water and begins to abuse him, but my brother pays no attention to him. Now my brother is out of the water again and we go off together. The boatman behind us continues to shout and I say to him that he has no right to abuse me, for I have done nothing. We run towards the town and the boatman pelts us with stones from behind. Curiously enough, it is only I who am in danger and not my brother, for he has suddenly vanished."

Dream II: "I am with a little girl of about eleven or twelve years old. She says that I may kiss her arm on a certain place at her elbow (as if it were difficult to do). But I am able to do it and kiss her all over the upper part of her body."

The details of the analysis of these dreams are of no importance at the moment. The first is a punishment-dream, in which the punishment affords at the same time gratification of a passive homosexual wish (being pelted with stones from behind by the boatman). The essential feature, however, which was emphasized in the telling of the dream, is that the dreamer was punished though quite innocent, for it was his brother and not he who jumped into the water. He is punished for his brother's act. The brother's sinful act is incest (to spring back into the water = back into the maternal uterus). The boatman who punishes is the father, who has placed him on the sea-shore (brought him into life) and separated him from the mother (the water). The compensation for the injustice suffered in this dream is enjoyed in the second dream, which ends in a pollution. An experience from the day before suggested the little girl whom he kissed. He had met on the previous day at the analyst's house a little girl of five or six, accompanied by her mother. He had been struck by the precocious, boastful manner and speech of the little girl. His association to kissing the arm at the elbow was that it was there that he and his brother loved to kiss their mother when they were little children. He even thinks that he copied his brother in kissing his mother in this way. Thus the pollution-dream is clearly a mother-incest dream. Having been unjustly punished in the first dream for his brother's offence, he thereby justifies himself for committing incest with full gratification in the second, and this in the same way as his brother, for he kissed the little girl in the way in which his brother kissed his mother.

The connection between the two dreams is obvious, and we see that the punishment-dream serves as a sop to conscience, so that it may not disturb the gratification in the second dream. We can see at once that this mechanism corresponds to that of the obsessional neurosis, in which activities displaying a masochistic tendency to self-punishment serve to liberate other, sadistic, tendencies. The account must balance. And the same principle is at the bottom of the manic-depressive mode of reaction, in which the torturing period of depression and self-condemnation is followed by the period of mania with its freedom from inhibitions. Punishment and licence are here divided into two successive phases; in the obsessional neurosis they exist simultaneously side by side. In the manic period conscience is quite powerless; it has exhausted its over-severe control in the melancholic phase.

I will quote another short but very characteristic example of a pair of dreams.

Dream I: "I ask some one to give me a newspaper. He is an unknown man, who scolds me and will not give me the paper."

Dream II: "Some one is giving me change. He gives me the right change but I do not give him the equivalent in return."

Both dreams are clear allusions to the analysis. The day before, the patient saw a newspaper in my room and asked me to let him look at it. I refused his request with some non-committal remark. The relation of the second dream to the analysis is also clear. When he was last paying his fee he remained in my debt for a small sum which was left over in changing a larger note. In the first dream I insult him unjustly—the unknown man is a familiar allusion to the analyst. In the second dream he is able to do me a material injury without incurring any guilt. The unconscious train of thought which underlies these two dreams is: "As the analyst was so disobliging as not to let me look at his paper I will not pay what I owe him." In this pair of dreams we see most clearly and simply the mechanism which I have described. The patient makes me guilty, in order to be free from a feeling of guilt towards me. Thus the analyst takes on the rôle of the superego in the pairs of dreams that I quoted earlier. In the first of those the superego has its account paid: it even receives more than is owing. It can give undue play to its punishment-tendencies and inflicts unjust punishment, in order that it may be disregarded in the second dream. We have an exactly similar procedure in politics where each party waits for the opposing party to compromise itself by going too far.

The last pair of dreams, in comparison with the earlier ones, shows us the genesis of the superego as postulated by Freud. Here the patient's unconscious behaves in relation to an actual person in authority (the analyst) as it did towards the superego in the other pairs of dreams. This is the reversal of the original process of introjection which led to the setting-up of the superego.[2]

[2] Franz Alexander, Dreams in Pairs and Series: *The International Journal of Psycho-Analysis*, VI, 1925, p. 446.

DREAMS AND MYTHS

FREUD: "Very often pictures and situations appear in the manifest content of the dream which remind one of well-known themes from fairy tales, legends and myths. The interpretation of such dreams throws light on the original motives which created these themes, though naturally we must not forget the change of meaning which this material has undergone during the passage of time. Our work of interpretation uncovers what one might call the raw material, which often enough may be regarded as sexual in the broadest sense of the word, but which has found the most varied application in later elaborations. When we trace things back like this, we often arouse the rage of all investigators who do not share the analytical point of view, as though we were seeking to deny or underestimate all the later developments which the raw material has undergone. Nonetheless, such ways of looking at things are instructive and interesting. The same is true of the tracing back of various motifs of plastic art —as for example when J. Eisler (1919), guided by the dreams of his patients, interprets analytically the young man playing with a little boy, portrayed in the Hermes of Praxiteles. Finally, I cannot help mentioning how often mythological themes find their explanation through dream interpretation. The story of the Labyrinth is found to be a representation of anal birth; the tortuous paths are the bowels, and the thread of Adriadne is the umbilical cord." [1]

I. THE HERMES MOTIF IN DREAMS

EISLER: Through the work of a number of writers—as for example Freud, Abraham and Rank—it has become a recognized fact that mythological allusions are to be found in many dreams. In the following paragraphs I should like to report two dreams which at the same time supply an indication of the conception held by antiquity of the figure of the god Hermes.

A male patient with a mild neurosis, who at the time was struggling against strong masturbation impulses, dreamed that he was

[1] Sigmund Freud, *New Introductory Lectures on Psychoanalysis*, New York, W. W. Norton & Co., 1933; Chapter I: Revision of the Theory of Dreams, pp. 39–40.

climbing a steep staircase, at the same time carrying a child in his arms. He awoke from this dream with an erection.

According to Freud, climbing stairs is a symbol of sexual intercourse. In this instance, however, it could signify the erection of which the dreamer was increasingly aware. "The little thing", "the little fellow", *das Kleine, der Kleine* is the genital, says Freud in *The Interpretation of Dreams*. So the dreamer would seem to experience the desire to grasp his erected organ in his hand. The symbol of the child held in his arms remains a little puzzling, since the idea is here, rather, of something feminine—that is, of mother and child. Behind this lies the secret wish to give birth to a child: possibly the feminine character of the dreamer is expressed herein; or the dream may have an historical basis in reality. The dreamer's awakening might be regarded as the consequence of this "dream which awakens the dreamer" (*Wecktraum*), or, on the other hand, it may express his resistance against the temptation to masturbate. The really remarkable thing in this otherwise quite transparent dream is the symbol of the child carried in the arms of the dreamer. In this he unconsciously reproduces an idea familiar to Greek sculpture—an idea traceable to its source in the statue of the *Hermes of Olympia* of the famous Praxiteles, the Hermes who carries the little Dionysos in his left arm, while with his right hand (which is missing) he offers him a bunch of grapes. Now for the Greeks, both the little Dionysos and the bunch of grapes were the mythological (or the artistic) projection of a state of intoxication. To the cult deity Dionysos (death and resurrection), moreover, is attributed a phallic significance, just as to the child in the arms of the dreamer. The beauty in the creation of Praxiteles lies in its perfect actualization (sublimation) of the narcissistic feeling underlying it. This is characteristic of most antique sculpture and is the essence of their peculiar charm. The great calm that manifests itself in these works even in the very climax of action and that stands in such contrast to the sculpture of the Renaissance, filled as it is with so much inner movement (as for example in the work of Michelangelo), is based precisely on this narcissistic concept of form. This finding is not without interest in its bearing upon the genesis of the feeling for and appreciation of the arts.

The second dream, that of a severely ill neurotic—of which I report merely a fragment—is as follows: "I do not know whether it was at the beginning or towards the end of the dream that I was floating in air. I felt like a beautifully proportioned Greek youth (καλὸς καὶ ἀγαθός), and was shrouded in a beautiful, flowing silken robe—which at the same time reminded me of a kimono. This floating seemed to go on for many days—possibly with interruptions, since I repeatedly changed the garment I was wearing. This latter also took part to a certain extent in this motion, and I remember vaguely that it was wholly without seams. In this floating I changed position like a bird; often I seemed to be face downwards; and I made peculiar movements with my feet, as if treading water."

We have here the beginning of a so-called "biographical dream" —the patient called it a "destiny dream"—having its source in fantasies of intra-uterine existence [*Mutterleibsphantasien*]. All this is clear enough to the analyst, as also its relation to the neurosis, which is manifested in this case in severe insomnia and morphinism. The opening sentence of the dream is an extremely felicitous phrasing of the feeling of "eternity", the source of which is to be found in the unconscious perception of intra-uterine existence. The garment "wholly without seams" is a cowl; that is, it represents the mother's body. The patient—who, preoccupied with religious ideas, considered himself the victim of family relationships—gave as his initial association the scene from the New Testament in which the Roman legionaries divide the garments of the crucified Christ: "But his coat was not sewn together, but woven from the top down, in one piece".[2] Here again is an instance of the feeling of eternity. The second association to the dream was the recollection of a condom which he had found at the age of thirteen, after his father's death, and which he had used as a plaything. This resulted in a most embarrassing scene, after which he became preoccupied with the intimate life of his mother. The criticism which had its inception at this time, and the change in his feelings associated with it, were coincident with the onset of his insomnia. Owing to unsuccessful medical treatment, the patient is crippled in both feet; but in his dream, in contradiction to this, he sees himself as beautifully proportioned. The expression he himself uses, καλὸς καὶ ἀγαθός, reminds him of the statute of Hermes which was in his parents' home and which he was said to

---

[2] Strikingly enough, such a statement cannot be found in the Synoptic Gospels, but only in St. John, the visionary, XIX, 23: "Then the soldiers, when they had crucified Jesus, took his garments, and made four parts, to every soldier a part; and also his coat: now the coat was without seam, woven from the top throughout."—The Turkish fez, too, has to be made of one piece—and likewise the Jewish prayer garment, the "talis", beneath which one symbolically isolates oneself from the world; this latter may not be seamed with any other thread. That it is also used to pull over the shroud further supports its symbolic meaning of the mother's body.

have resembled in his earlier years. Since the floating, in the dream, represents the movement of the embryo or fœtus, the treading water again points to the state of Hermes. We know that Hermes is distinguished among the principal Greek gods by his ability to fly, that wings in his heels were his attribute. The "narcissistic" Hermes which we deduced from the first dream is fittingly supplemented by this messenger of heaven concealed within the mother's body—who, because of his "secrecy", was also the god of thieves.[3]

II. THE LABYRINTH

EISLER: The following dream is a birth-rescue fantasy of which the structure is as obvious as the symbolism which it uses is transparent. It is given as a memory from the period of puberty.

"I have somehow been captured and taken to a cylindrical tower. It is half dark in the room; the light seems to be coming from above. Presently I notice that I am swinging in space from a rope, and below me I can hear water flowing. The rope, which is wound around my chest, is loose enough to permit me to make thrusting movements in all directions. At last I again felt solid ground under my feet, while at the same time the tower, or tube became narrower and narrower, closing in around me. I squeezed myself through, so that I felt the pressure of the walls against both shoulders. Through remarkably tortuous passages I succeeded after long wandering in getting out into the open."

The dream was evoked by the reading of a romantic tale of prison and escape, the events of which the dreamer sought to relive in fantasy. At the same time he ascribes a lively sexual curiosity to the same period. Noteworthy in the dream are the symbolic representation of the umbilical cord and the "hallucination of feeling" accompanying the act of birth (the pressure on the head is displaced to the shoulders). The winding passages through which rescue into freedom takes place are a reference to the infantile sexual theory made use of in the construction of the dream. According to Freud, birth per anum is undoubtedly here symbolized (the winding subterranean passages signify the intestine).

Perhaps this dream will throw light upon the meaning attaching to the Labyrinth of Greek mythology. The Labyrinth is an integral

[3] Joseph Eisler, translated from the original: Beiträge zur Traumdeutung. I. Das Hermesmotiv im Traume. *Internationale Zeitschrift für Psychoanalyse*, V, 1919, p. 295.

part of the legend of Theseus, mythical King of Athens. In his fundamental study on *The Myth of the Birth of the Hero*, Otto Rank has shown how the mythopoeic faculty of every people is fond of putting special emphasis upon the manner of origin of its heroes (unusual manner of birth), and equally of confronting the hero, upon his entrance into the world, with hostile forces, which however he is eventually able to overcome (the *Familienroman* of Freud). It is true that the story of the Labyrinth does not occur at the beginning of the Theseus legend, but it nevertheless constitutes its dominant theme and supplies the basis of the true kingship of the hero, so that one may well regard it as the nucleus of the legend. It now contains the "myth of the birth" of Theseus. The labyrinth from which he saves himself with the aid of the "thread of Ariadne", after slaying the Minotaur, represents that mysterious and secret place from which all life emerges. It tends to corroborate such a supposition that Theseus, after his "rescue", faithlessly abandons Ariadne (the mother). It is possible that the author (or authors) of this legend were actuated by the same infantile sexual fantasy [4] as finds expression in the dream reported above.[5]

[4] There are a number of children's games which make use of the labyrinth motif. These consist in general in a more or less complicated assembling of balls into a central space.

[5] Joseph Eisler, translated from the original: Beiträge zur Traumdeutung. II. Das Labyrinth. *Internationale Zeitschrift für Psychoanalyse*, V, 1919, p. 297.

ON THE TAMING OF FIRE

FREUD: ". . . In one of the notes to my book on *Civilization and its Discontents* I mentioned—although incidentally—the conjecture which might be drawn from psycho-analytic material on the subject of primitive man's acquisition of power over fire. I am led to resume this theme by Albrecht Schaeffer's opposition,[1] and by Erlenmeyer's striking citation of the Mongolian law which prohibits urinating upon ashes. . . ."[2]

ERLENMEYER: In *Civilization and its Discontents*[3] Sigmund Freud puts forward the following hypothesis with reference to the cultural significance of man's acquiring the use of fire:

"Psycho-analytic material, as yet incomplete and not capable of unequivocal interpretation, nevertheless admits of a surmise—which sounds fantastic enough—about the origin of this human feat. It is as if primitive man had had the impulse, when he came in contact with fire, to gratify an infantile pleasure in respect of it and put it out with a stream of urine. The legends that we possess leave no doubt that flames shooting upwards like tongues were originally felt to have a phallic sense. Putting out fire by urinating—which is also introduced in the later fables of Gulliver in Lilliput and Rabelais's Gargantua—therefore represented a sexual act with a man, an enjoyment of masculine potency in homosexual rivalry. Whoever was the first to deny himself this pleasure and spare the fire was able to take it with him and break it in to his own service. By curbing the fire of his own sexual passion he was able to tame fire as a force of nature. This great cultural victory was thus a reward for refraining from gratification of an instinct." Further, it

---

[1] Schaeffer's paper, entitled *Der Mensch und das Feuer* (Man and Fire), does not qualify for reprinting. It is speculative, incoherent, and devoid of factual data to such an extent that even the eventual, though apparently inadvertent, confirmation of Freud's interpretation contained in it, is of no particular value. It appeared in 1930, in the *Psychoanalytische Bewegung*, II, p. 201.

[2] Sigmund Freud, Acquisition of Power over Fire. *International Journal of Psycho-Analysis*, XIII, 1932, p. 405.

[3] *Civilization and its Discontents*, Jonathan Cape and Harrison Smith, New York, 1930; footnote, pp. 50, 51.

is as if man had placed woman by the hearth as the guardian of the fire he had taken captive, because her anatomy makes it impossible for her to yield to such a temptation. It is remarkable how regularly analytic findings testify to the close connection between the ideas of ambition, fire and urethral erotism.[4]

These notions have not remained undisputed. The most vigorous criticism of them appears in a paper by Albrecht Schaeffer entitled *Der Mensch und das Feuer*, as follows:

" ' Fantastic sounding,' says Freud apologetically, in describing his hypothesis, and at the very start I must take exception to the word 'fantastic'. I may, I think, be allowed to do so, since the word selected by the man of science is one that comes within my own province. To my mind this conjecture about the circumstances which led to man's mastery of fire cannot possibly be called fantastic; on the contrary, it is simply devoid of fantasy. A notion, indeed, as entirely lacking in fantasy (i.e. the power to imagine any sort of real conditions or occurrences), turned to such pure theory, as anyone could demand from a man of science."

No doubt Schaeffer's objection is intended to apply not to this particular hypothesis only, but also to the method by which it was arrived at. The construction or fiction of a primal man strikes him as a hazardous one. "For", he says, "what sort of human conditions are we to envisage, what kind of primal epoch must we imagine, what manner of man, and what was the fire which he encountered and succeeded in extinguishing? "

The fiction of a primal man and a primal horde has, however, a far greater measure of reality than that, say, of the primal plant (*Urpflanze*) conceived of by Goethe. At the same time, of course, it will not always be possible to substantiate by means of historical examples our conjectures about what took place in that primal epoch.

Yet just in this particular instance of primitive man's attitude towards fire we can adduce special historical evidence which to my thinking directly illustrates Freud's thesis.

In the *Jasa*, the code of laws given to the Mongols by Genghis

[4] The last two sentences of this paragraph, from the original Freud text, do not occur in Erlenmeyer's quotation.

The connection: playing with fire, dreaming of fire and enuresis had, as Storfer has pointed out (*Psychoanalytische Bewegung*, II, 1930, p. 210), suggested itself to Freud as early as 1905 (*A Fragment of the Analysis of an Hysteria Patient.*)—ED.

Khan, we find in a catalogue of various crimes the following: that he who urinates into water or upon ashes shall be punished with death. In a book by Hammer-Purgstall,[5] entitled *Geschichte de Goldenen Horde in Kiptschak*, this part of the *Jasa* is reproduced as follows:

"There are fourteen offences which shall be punishable with death. They are, first, adultery, sodomy, theft, murder and, further, lying and witchcraft. Likewise, he shall suffer death who does not return the runaway slave to his master; he who in a fight or a raid does not gather up and return to his chief the weapon or booty he has let fall; he who a third time squanders any property entrusted to him; he who, in a single combat, helps one of the two combatants; the deserter and the rebel; he who *pisses in water or upon ashes*; he who slays beasts after the manner of the Moslems and not of the Mongols." [6]

In another passage in this book, Hammer-Purgstall points out that this enactment shows an affinity with the prohibitions of the Pythagoreans.[7] "As the Pythagoreans were forbidden to pass urine facing the sun,[8] so the Mongols were forbidden, under penalty of death, to do so into water or upon ashes."

The peculiarity of these ordinances is also reflected in the manners and customs of this race. "They cleansed themselves with fire and not with water, for they never washed and even believed that to bathe in the river was to call down lightning from heaven." And, speaking of lightning, the same writer declares: "All Mongols feared it excessively: only those of the tribe of Uriangkut would conjure it it with magical incantations. In the midst of the most terrific thunderstorms they would revile the thunder and lightning with loud howls."

These quotations surely indicate that primitive man's relation to fire, to ashes that harbour fire, and to the sun was, in fact, subject to those tensions which Freud postulates in his hypothesis. When Genghis Khan led a small horde of nomads to conquest and to the foundation of the greatest empire the world has ever known, he reckoned amongst the dangerous instincts which must be threatened

---

[5] Hartlebens Verlag, Pesth, 1840, p. 187.

[6] Hammer-Purgstall, p. 50.

[7] p. 191.

[8] *Converso ad solem vultu non mingendum.* Diogenes Laertius: *Pythagoras* XVII.

with the death penalty the passion for extinguishing fire. This shows what importance he attributed to the renunciation of this instinct in the service of progress.

These historical facts furnish a remarkable confirmation of Freud's views on the cultural significance of this renunciation.[9]

[9] E. H. Erlenmeyer, Note on Freud's Hypothesis Regarding the Taming of Fire: *International Journal of Psycho-Analysis*, XIII, 1932, p. 411.

ON DREAMS OF FLYING

FREUD: "But why do so many people dream that they are able to fly? Psycho-analysis answers this question by stating that to fly or to be a bird in a dream is only the disguise for another wish, at the recognition of which one can arrive via more than one linguistic or objective bridge. When the inquisitive child is told that a big bird, such as the stork, brings little babies, when the ancients have equipped the phallus with wings, when the vernacular designation of the sexual activity of man is in German the expression 'to bird' (*vögeln*), when the male member is directly called *l'uccello* (bird) by the Italians—all these facts are but a small fragment of the large mass of material which teaches us that the wish to be able to fly signifies in the dream neither more nor less than the longing to be capable of sexual accomplishment.[1] This is an early infantile wish."[2]

FEDERN: No type of dream presents such a challenge to the inquiry of the psychologist, or gives him such cause to ponder, as does the dream of flying. Even the dreamer marvels at the wonderful art, sometimes to the accompaniment of the feeling of having redis-covered a long lost ability, of a wish to preserve it now forever and to teach it to others, and of the feeling, often, that onlookers marvel at this wonderful performance of which they themselves are incap-able. Even after waking, there frequently remains a feeling of pride which only gradually gives way to the realization that this goal attained through the dream, this fulfilment—which seemed so certainly achieved—of a universal wish of mankind, has faded into nothingness. But in many persons who often and throughout their lives have dreams of flying there persists a memory of a blissful inflating of the ego which carries over with a mood of happiness into the waking state, and which despite the voice of criticism repeatedly

[1] According to the investigations of Paul Federn (1914), and of Mourly Vold (1912), a Norwegian investigator whose work lies outside the field of psycho-analysis. (This footnote, occurring in the original text, is missing in the English translation of *Leonardo*.—ED.)

[2] Sigmund Freud, *Leonardo da Vinci: A Psychosexual Study of An Infantile Reminiscence;* after the English translation of A. A. Brill, Moffat, Yard & Co., New York, n.d., pp. 107–108.

makes us believe in wonder in the field of the psychological.[3] This
subject of the dream of flying is a theme of affective interest, and all
the resistance encountered by the findings of Freud with regard to
unconscious sexual wishes comes to the fore if one brings forward
the sexual causation of dreams of flying. It is on this account that it
seems to me desirable to discuss briefly the manifold sources and the
mechanism of dreams of flying, and to speak in this connection of
the conversion symptoms belonging to this typical dream sensation.

We wish to examine separately the question of sources and of
mechanism, and we shall not be surprised to discover many and
varied sources of the sensation of flying. The mechanism by which
these manifold dream thoughts eventually result in the same sensation must be fundamentally the same, in so far as the sensations of
flying are the same. We know, however, that the quality of the sensation of flying itself may vary considerably in the same dreamer;
usually each variant is known to the dreamer. Still more varied is
the method of flight in the dreams of different people. For full
clarification we should therefore establish the type of regression in
each variety of flying. This is possible up to a certain point. In
investigating the sensation of flying we come to the gratifying conclusion that nearly all the explanations so far discovered by science
are based on correct observations and are useful in so far as they
reveal dream-sources of the sensation or its variations or individual
mechanisms of regression. A contradiction between the customary
explanations and the theory of Freud based on analysis is due to
faulty formulation of the problem. In addition to Freud's discovery
that the latent dream content of dreams of flying is usually a sexual one,
there is room for other dream-sources, and particularly for elucidation of the psychic structure by means of which a dream-thought
appearing to the conscious mind so very disparate can achieve such
enigmatic regressive representation. In *The Interpretation of Dreams*
Freud has rightly attacked the notion that observations of sensations, persisting on waking, which yield a clue to the material
represented in the dream could make superfluous the question of
the unconscious source of the dream and of its meaning. The fact for
example that the movement of the chest can be apprehended by
self-observation as a remnant of the sensation of flying will appear a

[3] In the appendix to his translation of Havelock Ellis's *The World of
Dreams*, Kurella has very creditably collected and discussed the historical
and mythological material bearing upon the significance of flying dreams
for the belief in the soul and in transmigration.

sufficient explanation only to those who see in dreams nothing more than an expression of fortuitous and dissociated waking psychic elements. But those who have learned to accept Freud's psychic determinism of all psychic processes as a scientific principle will recognize in the question of unconscious dream-sources the problem of the specific determination of this particular dream. The various processes which are registered in the dream as the sensation of flying are of etiological significance, then, only if they are pathologically exaggerated. In such case the affected organ may somatically facilitate the inception of the dream sensation. The sensation of flying can occur, however, without demonstrable somatic stimulus and on a purely psychogenic basis. . . .

To discuss first the sexual root of dreams of flying: this has been communicated by Freud in his *Interpretation of Dreams*, and has since been confirmed by other analysts. His formulation received another, and literary, confirmation at the hands of Mourly Vold [4] of whose work its editor, O. Klemm, promises in the preface that "with its plain setting forth of empirical material and its carefully considered ventures in interpretation, it will retain a permanent place. . . ." Vold states that if (a) tactile sensibility is inoperative, (b) a light and pleasant breath is exhaled, and, at times, (c) muscular contractions are present, then "a slight sexual vibration of the muscles of the torso—or perhaps of the whole body—releases sentimental sensations of motion and ideas which . . . assume the form of dreams of floating. . . . *The force acting from the torso itself is clearly of a sexual nature*". In Latin he adds that this type of dream occurs in connection with a complete or beginning erection, or in very rare cases with an actual nocturnal emission.

These statements are in complete accord with the psycho-analytic experiences I am going to report, if we disregard the "vibration of the torso". It is almost amusing to see how bitter a resistance opposes the discoveries of Freud, in that an author, at the very moment when with many apologies he reports the sexual etiology of certain dreams—the very thing for which Freud was always reproached— can completely forget that Freud explicity pointed this out. Mourly Vold says, namely, that "it is rather a matter for surprise that this motive has not been emphasized by the dream psychologists".

I myself communicated this specific etiology to the Psycho-

[4] *Über den Traum. Experimental-psychologische Untersuchungen von D. J. Mourly Vold*; Leipzig, 1912.

analytic Association four years ago—this on the basis of statements with regard to waking from dreams of flying. Professor Freud has included this communication in the latest edition of *The Interpretation of Dreams*: [5] "Dr. Paul Federn (Vienna) has propounded the fascinating suggestion that a great many dreams of flying are dreams of erection, since the remarkable phenomenon of erection, which constantly occupies the human fantasy, cannot fail to be impressive as an apparent suspension of the laws of gravity (cf. the winged phalli of the ancients)." I suspect therefore that it is the physical process in the penis which finds its representation in the dream in flying. We are well acquainted with the fact that sexual processes achieve symbolic representation in most manifold forms, so that characteristically only a single feature or a single detail of the sexual activity or of the sexual organs is represented. Generally, in these representations, an object symbol corresponds to a given object, a symbolic process to an event or occurrence; one must distinguish, for example, between the erected penis and the process of erection as a dream source. . . .

Every analysis of a dream of flying discloses also motives other than sexual ones, although usually closely connected with the latter. Thus one cannot fundamentally separate exhibitionism, vanity and ambition. One can find as the dream-source, in particular, the wish to surpass (*ein Überflügeln wollen*) (Artemidorus), a wish-to-disregard-certain-persons, the wish to look down upon them (Freud, Stekel, Adler). The significance of the wish to travel, as emphasized by Ernest Jones, is on the one hand closely related to the sexual significance of travelling, to the erotic *Wanderlust* of adolescence especially, and on the other to death wishes, as already stated by Freud, confirmed a number of times by Stekel, and considered of importance by Jones himself. All these dream-sources which I mention only in summary combine to constitute a multiple determinant of the dream of flying. The most important and the most frequent source, however, is erection. This is perceived by the infantile psyche—also biogenetically—as flying. The corresponding normal sensory perception, not as magnified dream-wise, belongs in the category of vertigo. Thus can be demonstrated the beginning of the psychic alteration, namely the conception of erection as the desire to fly, and the end, the regression to the sense organ. The mechanisms which in the individual case can make this potential representation into an actual one are clear only in so far as an acute

[5] George Allen & Co. Ltd., London, 1913. Translated by A. A. Brill.

increase in masculine libido may give rise to a dream of flying. It remains a question, however, how far we have to do with a historical and how far with a purely psychological regression. With the answer to this question are connected important problems relating to the psychology of the neuroses. . . . [After the discussion of a case, the author concludes:]

We may assume with certainty that sexual sources gave rise to the sensation of flying, in opposition to the resistance of the censorship, that regression persisted for a brief time into the period of waking, and that the conscious psyche became aware of it in the form of vertigo as the corresponding process in the equilibratory apparatus. Since this sensation of dizziness was the same as during the neurosis, the indication is that the regression, otherwise present only in the dream, occurred during the neurosis in the waking state also. While therefore in the healthy psyche flying exists only as a potentiality, an idea capable of entering consciousness and without sexual accentuation—in the neurosis this idea is enormously intensified, constantly stimulating the sensory sphere and bringing about regression. If we remember that motives of ambition may also be the basis for the sensation of flying, we shall not be surprised to find that neurotic vertigo is so often associated with the anxiety of ambition. The relationship between sexuality and ambition, on the one hand, and neurotic vertigo on the other does not require demonstration solely through ideas of flying. We know that various bodily movements which cause vertigo through regression occur as sexual symbols. I hope I have been able to show by means of this specific example the significance of typical dream sensations for the understanding of conversion symptoms.[6]

On the Dream Symbolism of the Cloak

FREUD: "Let us consider symbols a little longer. There were some which we thought we had grasped, but about which we were nevertheless troubled because we could give no account of how that particular symbol got its particular meaning. In such cases any confirmation we could get from other sources, from philology, folklore, mythology or ritual, was particularly welcome. An example of this kind was the symbol of a cloak. We held that in a woman's dream a

---

[6] Paul Federn, translated from the original: Über zwei typische Traumsensationen. 3. Über den Flugtraum. *Jahrbuch für Psychoanalyse*, VI, 1914, pp. 111–113, 125–126, 131–132, 133–134.

cloak stood for a man. I hope now you will be impressed when you hear that Reik (1920) tells us: 'In the ancient marriage ceremony of the Bedouins the bridegroom covers the bride with a special cloak which is called an *aba*, and at the same time utters the ritual words: "Let no man in the future cover thee but me".' [1]

REIK: The most striking confirmation of sexual dream symbolism, the significance of which has been recognized by psycho-analysis, has so far been supplied by comparative philology, mythology and folklore. It is in precisely those instances where it is difficult to recognize the *tertium comparationis* between two objects which are likened to each other or symbolically equated that a surprising amount of light has sometimes been thrown by material from mythology and ethnology. It is therefore of value to collect parallels to dream symbols from folk psychology—symbols of which the sexual significance is remote from conscious thinking. Such a dream symbol, of which the origin is obscure, would seem to be the cloak, which is cited by Freud as among the examples of typical sexual symbols, and which can very often be interpreted with certainty as representing the male genital.

Several very pretty parallels to this dream symbol are to be found in Joseph Eisler's *Weltenmantel und Himmelszelt* (1910). The author writes: "Even today, among the Jews of Spanish extraction in the Levant, the bridal canopy (*huppah*) is formed out of the spread-out prayer-coat (*talith*) of the husband. In the extremely ancient bridal ritual of the Bedouins, the bridegroom covers the bride with a special cloak called an *aba*, accompanying this act with the ritual words: 'From now on, nobody but myself shall cover thee.' Ezekiel knows of this ritual covering of the bride: 'Now when I passed by thee, and looked upon thee, behold, thy time was the time of love; and I spread my skirt over thee, and covered thy nakedness: yea, I sware unto thee, and entered into a covenant with thee, saith the Lord God, and thou becamest mine' (*Ezekiel*, XVI, 8)." The same custom is recorded as Eisler seems to have overlooked, in the Book of Ruth (ch. III). According to Eisler, Zeus also covered Hera with a cloak in the ceremony of the ἱερὸς γάμος. The ingenious author interprets this cloak as a cosmic symbol. It is certain, in fact, that in later stages of religious evolution it actually developed into the

---

[1] Sigmund Freud, *New Introductory Lectures on Psychoanalysis*, New York, W. W. Norton & Co., Inc., 1933; Chapter I; Revision of the Theory of Dreams, p. 38.

V. REFERENCES BY FREUD

Weltenmantel of his title—as becomes clear from the wealth of material which he presents. But its original grossly sexual meaning is not thereby altered.[2]

[2] Theodor Reik, translated from the original; Völkerpsychologische Parallelen zum Traumsymbol des Mantels ; *Internationale für Psychoanlyse*, VI, 1920, p. 350.